Challenges to peacebuilding

Challenges to peacebuilding: Managing spoilers during conflict resolution

Edited by Edward Newman and Oliver Richmond

United Nations University Press
TOKYO · NEW YORK · PARIS

© United Nations University, 2006

The views expressed in this publication are those of the authors and do not necessarily reflect the views of the United Nations University.

United Nations University Press
United Nations University, 53-70, Jingumae 5-chome,
Shibuya-ku, Tokyo, 150-8925, Japan
Tel: +81-3-3499-2811 Fax: +81-3-3406-7345
E-mail: sales@hq.unu.edu general enquiries: press@hq.unu.edu
www.unu.edu

United Nations University Office at the United Nations, New York
2 United Nations Plaza, Room DC2-2062, New York, NY 10017, USA
Tel: +1-212-963-6387 Fax: +1-212-371-9454
E-mail: unuona@ony.unu.edu

United Nations University Press is the publishing division of the United Nations University.

Cover design by Mea Rhee

Printed in India

ISBN 92-808-1126-6

Library of Congress Cataloging-in-Publication Data

Challenges to peacebuilding : managing spoilers during conflict resolution / edited by Edward Newman and Oliver Richmond.
   p. cm.
 Includes bibliographical references and index.
 ISBN 9280811266 (pbk.)
 1. Peace-building. 2. Conflict management. I. Newman, Edward, 1970–
II. Richmond, Oliver P.
JZ5538.C483 2006
327.1'72—dc22   2006003771

Contents

List of contributors vii

List of acronyms ix

Introduction. Obstacles to peace processes: Understanding spoiling... 1
  Edward Newman and Oliver Richmond

Part I: Spoiling, violence, and mediation............................ 21

1 Internal and external dynamics of spoiling: A negotiation approach 23
  Karin Aggestam

2 Understanding the violence of insiders: Loyalty, custodians of peace, and the sustainability of conflict settlement............... 40
  Marie-Joëlle Zahar

3 The linkage between devious objectives and spoiling behaviour in peace processes...................................... 59
  Oliver Richmond

4 Terrorism as a tactic of spoilers in peace processes............... 78
  Ekaterina Stepanova

5 Spoilers or catalysts? The role of diasporas in peace
   processes 105
   Yossi Shain and Ravinatha P. Aryasinha

6 "New wars" and spoilers 134
   Edward Newman

Part II: Cases 151

7 Northern Ireland: A peace process thwarted by accidental
   spoiling 153
   Roger Mac Ginty

8 Why do peace processes collapse? The Basque conflict and
   the three-spoilers perspective 173
   Daniele Conversi

9 Peace on whose terms? War veterans' associations in Bosnia
   and Herzegovina 200
   Vesna Bojicic-Dzelilovic

10 Spoilers in Colombia: Actors and strategies 219
   Carlo Nasi

11 The Israeli-Palestinian peace process: The strategic art of
   deception 242
   Magnus Ranstorp

12 Spoiling peace in Cyprus 262
   Nathalie Tocci

13 The Abkhazia and South Ossetia cases: Spoilers in a nearly
   collapsed peace process 282
   George Khutsishvili

14 Spoilers and devious objectives in Kashmir 301
   Jaideep Saikia

Index 320

Contributors

Karin Aggestam is lecturer and director of peace and conflict research at the Department of Political Science, Lund University.

Ravinatha P. Aryasinha is a PhD candidate in international relations at the School of International Service, American University, Washington, DC; and minister (political) in the Sri Lanka Embassy in Washington, DC.

Vesna Bojicic-Dzelilovic is a research fellow in the Centre for the Study of Global Governance, London School of Economics and Political Science.

Daniele Conversi is a visiting academic at the Department of Government, London School of Economics, and senior lecturer at the University of Lincoln.

George Khutsishvili is chairman and founding director of the International Center on Conflict and Negotiation, Tbilisi, Georgia.

Roger Mac Ginty is a lecturer in the Post-war Reconstruction and Development Unit, Department of Politics, University of York.

Carlo Nasi is assistant professor at the Political Science Department of the University of Los Andes, Colombia.

Edward Newman is director of studies on Conflict and Security, Peace and Governance Programme, United Nations University.

Magnus Ranstorp is research director of the Centre for Asymmetric Threat Studies at the Swedish National Defense College.

Oliver Richmond is Reader at the School of International Relations, and Director of the Centre for Peace and Conflict Studies, University of St. Andrews, UK.

Jaideep Saikia is a security analyst from Assam, India.

Yossi Shain is professor of comparative government and diaspora politics in the Department of Government, Georgetown University.

Ekaterina Stepanova is senior researcher at the Center for International Security, Institute of World Economy & International Relations, Moscow, where she heads a research group on non-traditional security threats.

Nathalie Tocci is Marie Curie Fellow at the Mediterranean Programme, Robert Schuman Centre for Advanced Studies, European University Institute, Florence.

Marie-Joëlle Zahar is an assistant professor in the Department of Political Science at the University of Montreal.

List of acronyms

AKEL	Progressive Party of the Working People (Cyprus)
AKP	Justice and Development Party (Turkey)
ANIA	Americans for a New Irish Agenda
ASALA	Armenian Secret Army for the Liberation of Armenia
AUC	Autodefensas Unidas de Colombia
BiH	Bosnia and Herzegovina
CHP	Republican People's Party (Turkey)
CIRA	Continuity IRA (Northern Ireland)
CIS	Commonwealth of Independent States
CRS	Socialist Renovation Movement (Colombia)
CSO	civil society organization
CTP	Republican Turkish Party (Cyprus)
DA	demilitarized area
DIKO	Democratic Party (Cyprus)
DISY	Democratic Rally (Cyprus)
DP	Democratic Party (Cyprus)
DPA	Dayton Peace Agreement
DRC	Democratic Republic of the Congo
DUP	Democratic Unionist Party (Northern Ireland)
ECHR	European Court of Human Rights
EDEK/KISOS	Social Democrats Movement/United Democratic Union of Cyprus
EDI	United Democrats Movement (Cyprus)
EE	Euskadiko Ezkerra – Basque Left (Spain)
ELN	National Liberation Army (Colombia)
EOKA	National Organization of Cypriot Fighters

LIST OF ACRONYMS

EPL	Popular Liberation Army (Colombia)
ERC	Esquerra Republicana de Catalunya (Spain)
ETA	Euskadi Ta Askatasuna – Basque Homeland and Freedom (Spain)
EU	European Union
FARC	Revolutionary Armed Forces of Colombia
FSB	Federal Security Service (Russia)
GO	governmental organization
HB	Herri Batasuna – Popular Unity (Spain)
HDZ BiH	Democratic Union of Bosnia-Herzegovina
HRHB	Croatian Republic of Herzeg Bosna
HVIDRA	Association of Croatian Military Invalids of the Homeland War (Bosnia and Herzegovina)
HVO	Croatian Defence Council (Bosnia and Herzegovina)
HZHB	Croatian Community of Herzeg-Bosna
ICTY	International Criminal Tribunal for Former Yugoslavia
IDF	Israeli Defence Forces
IDP	internally displaced people
IGO	intergovernmental organization
INGO	international non-governmental organization
IO	international organization
IP	Initiative for the Peace (Colombia)
IR	international relations
IRA	Irish Republican Army
ISI	Inter Services Intelligence (Pakistan)
IU	Izquireda Unida (Spain)
JCAG	Justice Commando for the Armenian Genocide
JKLF	Jammu and Kashmir Liberation Front
KAS	Koordinadora Abertzale Sozialista – Patriotic Socialist Coordinating Council (Spain)
LoC	line-of-control
LTTE	Liberation Tigers of Tamil Eelam (Sri Lanka)
LVF	Loyalist Volunteer Force (Northern Ireland)
M-19	Movimiento 19 de Abril (Colombia)
MAQL	Armed Movement Quintín Lame (Colombia)
MPLA	Popular Movement for the Liberation of Angola
NATO	North Atlantic Treaty Organization
NCA	National Constituent Assembly (Colombia)
NF	National Front (Colombia)
NGO	non-governmental organization
NIS	newly independent state
OECD	Organization for Economic Cooperation and Development
OHR	Office of the High Representative (Bosnia and Herzegovina)
OSCE	Organization for Security and Cooperation in Europe
PA	Palestinian Authority
PA	People's Alliance (Sri Lanka)

LIST OF ACRONYMS

PASOK	Panhellenic Socialist Movement
PC	Plan Colombia
PFLP	Popular Front for the Liberation of Palestine
PLO	Palestine Liberation Organization
PNV	Partido Nacionalista Vasco – Basque Nationalist Party (Spain)
PP	Partido Popular – Popular Party (Spain)
PRT	Workers' Revolutionary Party (Colombia)
PSOE	Socialist Party (Spain)
RCD-Goma	Rassemblement Congolais pour la Démocratie-Goma
RIRA	Real IRA (Northern Ireland)
RoC	Republic of Cyprus
RS	Republika Srpska
RUC	Royal Ulster Constabulary
RUF	Revolutionary United Front (Sierra Leone)
SDA	Party of Democratic Action (Bosnia and Herzegovina)
SDS	Serb Democratic Party (Bosnia and Herzegovina)
SFOR	Stabilization Force (Bosnia and Herzegovina)
SFRY	Socialist Federal Republic of Yugoslavia
TKP	Communal Liberation Party (Cyprus)
TRNC	Turkish Republic of Northern Cyprus
UBP	National Unity Party (Cyprus)
UÇK	Kosovo Liberation Front
UDA	Ulster Defence Association
UDI	unilateral declaration of independence
UDIVIDRA	Association of Volunteers and Veterans of Homeland War (Bosnia and Herzegovina)
UDR	Ulster Defence Regiment
UNHCHR	UN High Commissioner on Human Rights
UNHCR	UN High Commissioner for Refugees
UNITA	National Union for Total Independence of Angola
UNMIK	UN Mission in Kosovo
UNOMIG	UN Observer Mission in Georgia
UNP	United National Party (Sri Lanka)
UNPROFOR	UN Protection Force (Bosnia and Herzegovina)
UP	Unión Patriótica (Colombia)
UUP	Ulster Unionist Party
UVF	Ulster Volunteer Force

Introduction
Obstacles to peace processes: Understanding spoiling

Edward Newman and Oliver Richmond

Our record of success in mediating and implementing peace agreements is sadly blemished by some devastating failures. Indeed, several of the most violent and tragic episodes of the 1990s occurred after the negotiation of peace agreements ... Roughly half of all countries that emerge from war lapse back into violence within five years. These two points drive home the message: if we are going to prevent conflict we must ensure that peace agreements are implemented in a sustained and sustainable manner.[1]

Many cease-fires and peace agreements in civil wars are initially unsuccessful and give way to renewed, and often escalated, violence. Progress is often incremental, in some cases spanning decades. Many peace processes become interminably protracted: lengthy and circular negotiations in which concessions are rare, and even if fragile agreements are reached they stumble at the implementation phase. Given the huge material and human costs of a failed peace process, the consolidation of peace processes and dealing with threats to implementation are crucial areas of scholarship and policy analysis. This volume explores the factors that obstruct conflict settlement by focusing on the phenomena of "spoilers" and "spoiling": groups and tactics that actively seek to hinder, delay, or undermine conflict settlement through a variety of means and for a variety of motives. The context within which such groups are examined in this volume is one of "civil armed conflict" where some form of peace process is under way and where at least one of the parties to the conflict is either engaged in or committed to a peace process.

Notions of the success and failure of conflict management and resolution have shifted in recent years in order to account for lengthy peace processes in which there emerges a negotiating culture but little indication of the final disembarkation point of an overall solution. Though there have been some remarkable successes in peacemaking since the end of the Cold War, it has become apparent that traditional thinking about the conduct and outcomes of peace processes may be in question. Indeed, there have been some notable failures, and even where peace processes seem to have come to fruition – in the Middle East and Northern Ireland, for example – it soon becomes evident that reaching an agreement is far from enough if implementation proves to be problematic. At the same time, we increasingly understand the complex underlying causes of conflict and its perpetuation, and this has brought with it a pervasive understanding – at least in the West – about what a peace process should "look like". Indeed, a liberal peace and its different incarnations are now generally agreed to be the objective of peace processes.[2] This means that any outcome should ostensibly be democratic, incorporate free and globalized markets, and aspire to human rights protection and the rule of law, justice, and economic development. It is in this context that the normative judgement contained in the terms "spoilers" and "spoiling" is often constructed. If disputants attempt to prevent a peace process attaining these objectives then they are, according to the prevailing mindset of the liberal peace, spoilers.

This volume examines this phenomenon both from a theoretical perspective and via a series of topical case studies. It builds upon important work which has been carried out on spoiling in peace processes and on so-called "devious objectives" on the part of disputants. The idea of devious objectives suggests that, contrary to standard analyses, an examination from the vantage point of the disputants provides significant insights into why peace processes may become protracted. From this perspective, we cannot assume that a compromise solution is the objective of the disputants involved in a conflict settlement process. Indeed, disputants may become involved in a settlement process in order to improve upon their prospects, but not necessarily by means of a compromise with their adversary. A settlement process carries with it a series of assets that the disputants may value. The disputants may therefore harbour devious objectives, unrelated to the attainment of a compromise solution, which might include motives such as achieving time to regroup and reorganize; internationalizing the conflict; profiting materially from ongoing conflict; legitimization of their negotiation positions and current status; face-saving; and avoiding costly concessions by prolonging the process itself. A starting point is therefore to identify what views, perceptions, or misperceptions the disputants have formed from their understanding of the conflict and all the actors involved.

This study builds upon the notable work which has already been carried out on spoilers in peace processes by looking at the spoiling of peace processes from a broader perspective; this includes actors not only within the conflict zone, and actions which are not necessarily expressed only as violence. Perhaps most importantly, it considers the normative context in which spoiling behaviour is identified and then conceptualized as the liberal peace, in which a mixture of coercion and persuasion is used to create "democratic" entities in which the rule of law, human rights, free markets, and development are evident. As we will see, the ideal of peace processes as a function of the liberal peace does not always converge with the reality on the ground. Moreover, the different components of the liberal peace are not necessarily co-terminal.

This is a relatively unexplored area. In the light of protracted and sometimes flawed peace processes which sometimes regress into renewed violence in a variety of cases spanning many years, and the ability of (often relatively small) groups to disrupt conflict settlement, it demands greater attention. This volume endeavours to achieve this through theoretical analysis and contributions from regional experts on specific peace processes.

The phenomenon of spoiling and its implications for peace processes

The definitions of spoilers and spoiling in this volume, and the types of groups and tactics considered in this context, are notably broader than those employed in most existing literature. Indeed, it is an express intention herein to problematize the concept of spoiling and relate spoiling to specific conflicts and environments, rather than view it as an abstract concept that can be applied in a generalized manner. This is not to suggest that it is impossible to generate propositions regarding spoiling which have general explanatory value. Indeed, this volume attempts to deepen understanding of the types and impact of spoiling, and strategies for addressing actors who obstruct peace processes. But the volume has an open mind in terms of which actors might be considered "spoilers" and what activities might be considered "spoiling". As such, the volume argues that our approach to spoiling and spoilers cannot be delinked from normative considerations of conflicts or peace processes. In particular, we cannot necessarily assume that all peace processes are equitable or fair to all parties. Thus, the act of labelling a particular group as a "spoiler" may reflect a political agenda which is an extension of the conflict itself, or the interests of third parties. In addition, the volume acknowledges that contemporary conflicts are complex, diverse in nature, and involve an array of actors, motives, and processes both within the conflict area and from outside. From such a perspective, traditional conceptualizations of peacebuilding, conflict settlement processes, and the role of disputants and third parties can seem rather limited.

This volume adopts a broad definition of spoiling behaviour. At the core of this are the activities of any actors who are opposed to peaceful settlement for whatever reason, from within or (usually) outside the peace process, and who use violence or other means to disrupt the process in pursuit of their aims. Parties that join a peace process but then withdraw and obstruct, or threaten to obstruct, the process may also be termed spoilers. Similarly, there are parties that are a part of the peace process but which are not seriously interested in making compromises or committing to a peaceful endgame. They may be using the peace process as a means of gaining recognition and legitimacy, gaining time, gaining material benefit, or avoiding sanctions, and thus can be described as having "devious objectives". Finally, spoiling includes actors who are geographically external to the conflict but who support internal spoilers and spoiling tactics: ethnic or national diaspora groups, states, political allies, multinational corporations, or any others who might benefit from violent conflict or holding out. So-called civil or domestic conflicts are, in reality, often influenced or characterized by international processes, causes, and consequences. There is therefore no reason to confine this analysis of spoiling to a zone of armed conflict.

Starting propositions

The very notion of "spoilers" suggests a binary between those "for" and "against" conflict settlement, but most evidence shows that peace processes are not so simple. There is a capacity for spoiling in most actors at different phases of the process. Indeed, in some ways spoiling is part of peace processes, as much as conflict is a function of social and political change. What became very apparent during this research project, and in particular during a number of workshops held by the participants, was that there exists a major disagreement on the normative implications of the terms "spoilers" and "spoiling", in particular when used as a noun rather than a verb. Some argued that spoilers are easily identifiable by their stance against a peace process, subtle or not. Others argued that the terms are subjective, depending to a large degree on the bias of third parties in particular, and therefore indicative of hegemony and power. This relates to the context of contemporary peace processes. Internationally sponsored peace settlements in the contemporary international system generally tend to follow similar lines. They are all envisaged within the so-called liberal peace framework noted above, where settlements include constitutional agreements, demobilization, demilitarization, resettlement and return of refuges, democratization processes, human rights safeguards, the rule of law, and the free market. The emphasis on these different components may vary from settlement to settlement, but the overall liberal peace package underpins all international perspectives on settlement in conflict zones in which international organizations, regional organizations, donors, NGOs, and diplomats become involved. Many observers would argue that if we take this as a starting point it becomes relatively easy to identify spoiling behaviour when it is in opposition to the components of the liberal peace. Thus, any actor who obstructs this is seen as a "spoiler".

However, the liberal peace is sometimes problematic. Democracy (at least polyarchy), human rights (especially in terms of civil and political rights), market values, globalization, self-determination, and the idea of the state are not necessarily universal values, nor appropriate in conflicted or divided societies. Moreover, the manner in which they are being promoted is, arguably, not even-handed and certainly loaded in favour of the market and the *status quo* rather than social justice. Therefore, peace processes themselves are not always equitable or "fair". By labelling as spoilers every group which does not conform to such a peace process, we may be making a value judgement about the nature of that society and trying to apply "universal" values. Thus the concept of "spoiling" can be subjective, and alludes to broader normative debates about the "best" way to organize (post-conflict) societies.

What is clear is that all parties have the potential to be spoilers; the phenomenon is more an issue of tactics, not actors. The labelling of actors and activities as "spoilers" and "spoiling" may reflect subjective criteria of evaluation and "external" rationality and power. The concept of "spoilers" has negative connotations, but in asymmetrical disputes the basis of negotiations may sometimes be perceived as inequitable or unfair. In such situations, actions which may be construed as "spoiling" may appear legitimate (at least the objective, if not the tactics) according to an alternative rationality.

It is essential to approach the subject from an "inside-out" perspective. This requires a significant change in the analysis of peace processes and spoilers, which tends to assume that there is a commitment to a compromise, based on a rational calculation that a compromise peace is attainable and desirable. However, taking an inside-out view – trying to understand the dynamics of the conflict from the point of view of disputants

– might suggest that what an outsider sees as spoiling may be viewed by insiders as a legitimate attempt to shape a peace process or end it if it does not offer the potential for a satisfactory outcome in their eyes.

An important proviso is that it is wrong to assume that all – or even most – conflict situations can be resolved by accommodation or that a peace process is about finding consensus amongst parties that basically all seek peace. Some groups have clear incentives for the continuation of violent conflict, or for prolonging a negotiation process while they continue to manoeuvre to gain more military resources and more support, allies, and recognition.

This volume has as a core element the idea that "spoiling" is in many ways a subjective and potentially broad concept. This introduction gives a clear starting point for the definition of spoilers, but we still observe that the concept is inherently political and perhaps in certain circumstances even problematic. The authors have been given some freedom to interpret "spoiling" in this broad, subjective, and "critical" manner. Indeed, there was no desire to impose a uniform definition of "spoiling" or "spoilers", because a component of the volume is to problematize the concepts. Inevitably, therefore, the use of the concept is not uniform in all cases. Some of the authors have taken a narrow and more conventional approach: for example, a recalcitrant militant group splits away from a political movement because the latter has signed on to a peace process which the splinter group does not support; the splinter group then uses violence in an attempt to undermine the peace process. Others have taken a broader and more controversial approach to the concept, including non-violent "spoiling" and "spoiling" by external actors. This, it is hoped, is part of the added value of the volume.

Key research questions

This volume aims to deepen understanding of the difficulties faced in establishing and consolidating peace processes by focusing upon those groups that seek to "spoil" efforts to resolve conflict. The early chapters in this volume take a thematic or theoretical approach in trying to extend the ideas of this introduction, whilst later chapters apply the framework to various case studies. All of the chapters share an interest in approaching contemporary conflict and conflict resolution from a "critical" perspective.

There are a number of research questions and themes that provide overarching guidance to the chapters in this volume. These include the following.

It is important to gain a clear understanding of the tactics, motivations, and funding of "spoilers" in order to understand what causes, motivates, and escalates spoiling. Considering spoiling across a variety of cases provides the possibility of demonstrating patterns in the dynamics of spoiling, which is important for furthering our understanding of impediments to peace processes, but also in providing policy-makers with a clearer understanding of how to respond to these impediments.

It is also important to have an operational understanding of what the difference is between "politics" in a peace process – such as, for example, the rational objection to terms and conditions that are perceived to be unduly detrimental to one's cause or unfair – and "spoiling". What is acceptable within a peace process, and what is unacceptable? How much "spoiling" (including violence) can a peace process absorb? The thematic and case study chapters offer several perspectives on this. Some analysts would argue that from within the broadly accepted liberal peace framework it becomes fairly easy to identify spoiling behaviour, while others would challenge the very nature of the liberal peace concept.

The recent events in Cyprus and in other cases indicate that spoiling may actually work in certain circumstances, and produce tangible gains. This raises the question as to whether spoiling is a normal part of a peace process. It is also necessary to ask whether it is it possible to identify patterns in environmental variables (such as the nature of peace settlements, the role of external actors, the political economy of the conflict, disputes over natural resources, or the influence of significant diaspora groups) that give rise to the ability of spoilers to exert leverage. For example, in the context of diaspora support for the Tamil Tigers or for the IRA, or US support for Israel, it is obvious that this not only empowered actors to resist a peace settlement but also allowed them to adopt more ambitious goals than might otherwise be expected.

Clearly, there is a relationship between the nature of the conflict and the spoiler phenomenon. How far-reaching this is, and how the intensity of the conflict may affect the tendency towards spoiling, needs to be further examined. How do the nature and dynamics of the war have a bearing on the impact/nature of spoilers and spoiling? For example, if the conflict is characterized by a struggle over natural resources or illegal commercial activities, or a conflict over territorial secession or recognition, does this have a bearing upon the nature/dynamics of spoiling? In turn, if the motives of the protagonists are basically "greed" or basically "grievance", does this have major implications for the nature and impact of spoiling, and the chances of defeating spoilers or bringing them into the process? This raises the question of which actors may have an interest in the continuation of violent conflict – warlords and criminals, international commercial actors, private military services, or military bureaucracies, for example.

What is the relationship between the nature of third-party mediation in a peace process and the nature of spoiling? For example, what impact might the presence of multiple external parties and donors have in a peace process? Furthermore, do the tactics of spoiling demonstrate the exercise of asymmetry and asymmetrical power? This has at least two dimensions. Firstly, when a group with relatively weak power can exert a disproportionate amount of leverage or disruption (e.g. through the use of atrocities and terror), can peace processes "absorb" such tactics without failing? If so, how, and to what extent? How much violence can a peace process tolerate whilst still remaining viable? Secondly, asymmetry can be applied in terms of sovereignty, representation, and resources. Control of legal and political representation and resources – and reluctance to relinquish them – may be a key variable.

This also raises the question of how the presence of external "third-party" peace facilitators may condition the tactics and motives of spoiling. In what circumstances can third-party involvement both encourage and discourage spoiling? Does the number of external initiatives (i.e. multiple as opposed to one single initiative), and the level of coordination amongst external initiatives, have a bearing on the dynamics of spoilers and spoiling? Local actors/protagonists may have relationships with external actors, which can result in attempts to gain leverage. The momentum of major peace processes can play into the hands of "spoilers" or even encourage spoiling, as external third-party facilitators do not want their efforts to result in "failure". Can this encourage concessions (and thus encouragement) to spoilers? Connected with this, does the internationalization of conflicts through the involvement of the United Nations and international tribunals condition the dynamics of "spoiling"?

Much of the above locates the spoiler phenomena in the context of conflicts with specific characteristics. Spoilers and spoiling tactics may be symptomatic of "contemporary conflict" and so-called "new wars". The new wars thesis argues that contemporary civil wars are generally characterized by state failure and competition over resources and illegal gains, criminal warlords, and ethnic (but not necessarily ideological) rivalry; that civilian casualties and displacement have been dramatically increasing as a proportion of all casualties in conflict, and especially since the end of the Cold War; that civilians are increasingly targeted as an object of new wars; and that atrocities and ethnic homogenization are key hallmarks of contemporary conflict. Within these "new wars" it is quite possible that some actors have a vested interest in the continuation of armed conflict. Added to these dynamics, it is also germane to consider what impact the terrorist attacks of 11 September 2001 and the "war on terror" have had upon the dynamics and functioning of "spoiling", especially on the part of insurgents and other non-government protagonists. For example, we have seen many states clamping down upon funding and external support for "spoilers", often through the coordination of multilateral agreements. External countries may now place greater pressure upon "spoilers" to fall into line, and governments may be tempted to label "spoilers" as "terrorists", with all the implications which would follow from this.

Outline of the volume

The first part of this volume explores a range of issues relating to spoiling from a thematic perspective. Karin Aggestam's chapter, "Internal and external dynamics of spoiling: A negotiation approach", addresses the dynamics of spoiling as well as the wider notion of devious objects in peace negotiations. Her analysis, from a negotiation theory approach, confirms the ambiguous and sometimes problematic use of the concept of spoiling in peace processes. She suggests that spoiling should be viewed as "situated action" – that is, actors behaving according to situational rationality – and that it should be considered not only in relation to violent action, but also from an inside perspective of negotiation. "Spoiling" depends on the specific context of conflict as well as on the interplay between inside and outside actors of the peace process. It is also a value-laden concept. Actors tend to be diagnosed as either for or against a peace process. However, it is difficult to distinguish spoiling strategies from competitive negotiation strategies, and it is hard to draw a decisive line between intentional and consequential spoiling. Finally, the notion of spoiling tends to be viewed as a rather static phenomenon, whereas in practice it is highly dynamic as the actors' goals may alter during a peace process. Aggestam suggests in closing that leadership and mobilization for a peace process, and the perception by the public that this process is just and inclusive, are critical prerequisites to limit the power of spoiling and extremist violence.

Marie-Joëlle Zahar's contribution, "Understanding the violence of insiders: Loyalty, custodians of peace, and the sustainability of conflict settlement", focuses on actors who are "inside" peace processes. It considers when and under what conditions insiders resort to violence, and how foreign custodians of peace can respond to this. She argues that insiders will only resort to violence if and when the reasons that drove them to accept peace are no more. While some of these reasons are context-specific (availability of resources to restart the war, such as a regional war economy and external patrons), others are process-specific. In other words, the course of peace implementation can generate dissatisfaction among insiders. In order to secure the sustainability of peace, custodians must not only "neutralize" the environment in such a way as to prevent actors from accessing resources that could reignite war, they must also steer peace in such a way as to consolidate insider loyalty to the process. Thus, Zahar suggests that, contrary to common wisdom, peace implementation is not a technical matter. It is a highly political act that may, under some conditions, contribute to the promotion of devious objectives that jeopardize the sustainability of peace.

Traditional approaches to peace processes have tended towards an omniscient, impartial, external perspective of a specific conflict, and have tended to assume that a compromise solution is the objective of all parties concerned. They assume that the introduction of a peace process and a third party into a conflict automatically modifies the negotiating positions of the disputants. No longer are they aiming for victory on the battlefield or through various other forms of violence, but for a compromise around a negotiating table. Oliver Richmond challenges this thinking in his chapter, "The linkage between devious objectives and spoiling behaviour in peace processes". His starting point is that compromise solutions to conflicts and wars are not necessarily viewed by disputants as the optimum rational outcome of a peace process. Consequently, spoiling behaviour towards a peace process represents a form of rejection of some aspect of that process by some groups and their constituencies. Yet paradoxically, disputants often realize that a peace process is still valuable to them, even if they do not agree with the sort of compromise agreement being suggested by third parties. Disputants therefore hold "devious objectives" not necessarily related to a liberal peace compromise, which is assumed to be the most desirable outcome of a peace process. Richmond's chapter argues that spoiling behaviour and devious objectives indicate that disputants may not have accepted aspects of the liberal peace as the basis for their desired solution. Devious objectives may indicate that they value a peace process for certain resources it may provide, but do not envisage the sort of outcome the international community or third parties desire. Richmond's conclusions describe how understanding the phenomenon of devious objectives indicates the likelihood of spoiling behaviour of all types emerging in a peace process.

When spoiling involves the use of violence against civilians for political purposes – for example to influence or disrupt a peace process – the debate turns to terrorism. Ekaterina Stepanova's chapter explores "Terrorism as a tactic of spoilers in peace processes". She notes that one of the objectives of the peace process is to end fighting, but violence almost never comes to a halt with the initiation of negotiations and often continues during peace implementation. In practice, declaring a cease-fire may help negotiations to get started, but cease-fires are neither necessary prerequisites for negotiations nor are they easily sustainable, particularly during the earlier stages of negotiations. Violence is not antithetical or alien to peace processes – it accompanies peace processes. Indeed, violence tends to increase either before or immediately following the key events in negotiations, such as the signing of a peace agreement. A period immediately after the signing of a peace agreement is one of the most risky stages of the peace process, when the scale and intensity of violent incidents can temporarily increase.

The effects of this on negotiations and peace implementation are multiple and diverse. The most obvious impact of violence is that of destabilizing (spoiling) negotiations or peace implementation that may threaten a relapse into war or at least stall the peace process. While this is certainly the most common scenario, it is not the only one. At times violence, on the contrary, seems to push the parties into negotiation, bringing the peace process forward and serving as a catalyst for it. Also, while in some cases acts of violence can discourage external actors and mediators from getting involved, in other cases violence may actually raise the profile of a conflict and the conflict management effort, raise the level of external interest in the conflict, and encourage external actors to intervene more actively in the process. Sustained or high-profile acts of terrorism should not be allowed to impede the peace process. At the same time, according to Stepanova, rigid counterterrorist measures, if undertaken separately from the peace process, are almost as likely to obstruct the peace process as terrorist acts by spoilers. Ironically, counterterrorist campaigns, while not particularly successful as specific antiterrorist tools, can be very efficient in undermining whatever confidence-building efforts had been in place (as most vividly demonstrated in the course of the Israeli-Palestinian conflict). Thus, counterterrorism in the context of peace processes must be approached in terms of its wider implications and effects.

Yossi Shain and Ravinatha P. Aryasinha's chapter, "Spoilers or catalysts? The role of diasporas in peace processes", examines the role and significance of diaspora groups as potential and actual spoilers. Their chapter considers which types of conflicts/peace processes are vulnerable to spoiling due to diaspora influence; what is at stake for diasporas in such conflicts/peace processes; what determines a diaspora's capacity to influence conflicts/peace processes; what modalities are used by diasporas in influencing conflicts/peace processes; and what is the nature of the relationship between diasporas and conflict.

The relationship between the nature and sources of armed conflict and spoiling is a challenging topic. Do the nature and dynamics of a particular conflict have a bearing upon the impact and nature of spoiling? Edward Newman's chapter, "'New wars' and spoilers", considers if certain types of contemporary conflict – especially types of civil wars – give rise to spoiling by actors who have little interest in peace because they find incentives in the continuation of violence, public disorder, and the political economy of war. The protagonists in such conflicts – sometimes described as "new wars" – exploit the political economy of conflict for material gain, and only a peace process which holds significant material gains would be acceptable. The chapter thus considers the relevance of "new wars" literature for the spoiling phenomenon in contemporary civil wars, and whether prevailing types of conflict may defy conventional conflict resolution approaches.

The second part of this volume explores these issues and propositions with reference to a number of case studies. To give authenticity to these accounts the case studies are mostly presented by analysts from the regions in question, providing insights which can only come from local perspectives. Roger Mac Ginty begins with "Northern Ireland: A peace process thwarted by accidental spoiling". He argues that the Northern Ireland peace process was constructed with spoilers in mind after political peace initiatives ended in failure between 1972 and 1993. Various factors accounted for these failures, but the initiatives all shared the common trait of excluding powerful veto holders. Rather than excluding groups and constituencies prepared to make and capable of making any new political solution unworkable, the peace process of the 1990s deliberately sought to include veto holders. As a result, opportunities for spoilers were drastically reduced. Mac Ginty suggests that this makes the case particularly interesting, as Northern Ireland may be in a position to offer lessons to other peacemaking processes on structural and procedural factors that limited spoiling. In addition, spoiling behaviour in Northern Ireland often adopted subtle forms, thus raising questions on the conceptual boundaries of spoilers and spoiling behaviour.

Mac Ginty argues that spoilers, in the sense of violent actors deliberately seeking to thwart a peacemaking process, have had a limited impact on the Northern Ireland peace process. Spoilers failed to mount and sustain large-scale violent campaigns, failed to attract widespread community support, and ultimately failed to prevent the reaching of a major peace accord. Post-accord problems owed little to the deliberate strategies of violent spoilers. Three spoiler-limiting factors were at work to account for this. First, the inclusive peace process strategy adopted by the British and Irish governments meant that the main actors capable of using political violence were involved in the peace process, at least in the crucial phase of negotiations. Second was the development of penalties for the use of violence. The third factor limiting spoiling in the Northern Ireland peace process was environmental. Many of the elements present in other conflict societies that facilitated spoiling – such as natural resources – were absent in Northern Ireland. Crucial here was the absence of external spoilers (or sponsors of spoilers), and the absence of portable marketable goods such as diamonds. Finally, Mac Ginty elaborates on a number of conclusions: spoiling can be both violent and nonviolent; spoiling can be intentional and unintentional; spoiling will vary in nature at different stages of a peace process; intentional spoiling is often sophisticated in its choice of targets; attention given to violent veto holders can have a negative impact on the quality of any peace resulting from a peace process; and finally, the greed thesis is unlikely to offer a stand-alone explanation of spoiling.

The second case is also from Europe. Daniele Conversi's chapter is on "Why do peace processes collapse? The Basque conflict and the three-spoilers perspective". He considers the rise and fall of peace initiatives in the Basque country, identifying a "culture of violence" that has materialized over years of conflict. He also explores the effects (which he argues are overwhelmingly negative) of the external context. The US-led "war on terror" since 2001 has disrupted the Basque peace process and radicalized nationalist politics throughout Spain. Conversi develops a "three-spoilers perspective" with reference to the Basque conflict. In this he argues that the emergence of potential spoilers should be identified at three interconnected levels: at the local level, with the persistence of a "culture of violence"; at the state level, with the central government officially adopting a non-negotiating, no-compromising posture; and, since 9/11, at the international level, with the intrusion of US foreign policy. At the local level, Conversi emphasizes a culture of violence from which grassroots spoilers tend naturally to emerge. However, he argues that the international context inspired by the war on terror is fundamentally important to understanding spoiling.

This volume expressly takes a broad view of spoiling in terms of actors and activities. Vesna Bojicic-Dzelilovic's chapter, "Peace on whose terms? War veterans' associations in Bosnia and Herzegovina", takes such a view. Her chapter focuses on war veterans' associations as one particular type of non-state actor engaged in undermining a peace settlement in the specific context of Bosnia. For a number of reasons this case provides different insights into the issue of spoiling in contemporary conflicts, and the complex strategies needed to pacify them. Her chapter starts with a brief analysis of the political and economic goals behind the 1992–1995 war, focusing on Bosnian Croat self-rule as a political project and goal of the spoiling pursued by Bosnian Croat war veterans' associations. She then reflects on the terms of the peace agreement, indicating some of the main areas in which implementation was obstructed by this group. The analysis of the war veterans' associations deals with their origins and position in the Bosnian Croat post-war power structures, the sources of their funding, and their official and hidden agendas. The probe into spoiling tactics focuses on three important aspects of the peace agreement: refugee return, war crimes' prosecution, and institution-building. This is followed by a brief analysis of the impact of various strategies that the international community, as a custodian of peace, has used to sustain its implementation.

Carlo Nasi's chapter on "Spoilers in Colombia: Actors and strategies" describes how spoilers threatened to derail every single peace process in that country, and how the identity of spoilers changed throughout the various peace negotiations. Depending on the peace process in question, spoiling activities were carried out by rebel groups (or their splinter factions), the armed forces, the Colombian Congress, drug-traffickers, entrepreneurs, right-wing paramilitary groups, and even the US government. This chapter introduces the nature and evolution of the Colombian armed conflict and then explores the specific peace negotiations of a number of the governments since the early 1980s, analysing the role, tactics, and relative success of spoiling in each case.

Nasi's chapter suggests that a wide variety of actors have attempted to spoil the various peace negotiations in the past two decades, and they have increasingly resorted to violence in order to achieve their goals. Like other chapters in this volume he concludes that spoiling actions neglect the context in which a peace process takes place. In the case of Colombia, there were clearly problems with the framework of the peace processes at important junctures.

In his chapter, "The Israeli-Palestinian peace process: The strategic art of deception", Magnus Ranstorp examines the mistrust and lack of understanding on both sides which characterize this difficult case. He argues that the role of culture and competing narrative "myths" drive the underlying conflict dynamics between the parties. These images of the other are widely reflected within respective communities across the divide, and fundamentally shape and drive the Machiavellian strategic behaviour of both the Israelis and the Palestinians. In this sense, understanding the cultural aspects and dynamics of conflict and negotiation dynamics becomes imperative and raises the question as to the viability of Western-oriented peace processes, especially as competing cultural traits are deeply embedded within social interactions on both sides. Moreover, it questions the effectiveness of third-party intervention that does not take into account these cultural factors.

Ranstorp suggests that spoiling exists across the Israeli-Palestinian conflict spectrum, with varying degrees of ability to shape, redirect, and sabotage the peace processes. The asymmetry of power is a driving force behind the adoption of "devious objectives" by disputants in relation to how far to impose and resist the peace process itself. Both sides believe inherently in the justness of their cause and that time is on their side.

In her chapter on "Spoiling peace in Cyprus", Nathalie Tocci similarly argues that "spoiling characterizes the very nature of the persisting conflict in Cyprus" and the failure of numerous peace processes on the island. She suggests that spoiling has taken the form of actions undertaken by parties normally involved in the long-lasting peace process under the aegis of the United Nations, and aimed at bolstering specific (spoiling) bargaining positions. This has taken place both within the context of negotiations and outside it through unilateral measures. As a result, it has been difficult to distinguish spoiling from "legitimate" political actions aimed at bolstering an actor's bargaining position. Indeed, what has constituted spoiling to one party has represented legally and morally legitimate action to another. In line with other cases in this volume, Tocci suggests that the distinction between spoiling and "normal politics" has thus been a question of degree rather than one of clear-cut categories.

George Khutsishvili's chapter on "The Abkhazia and South Ossetia cases: Spoilers in a nearly collapsed peace process" considers the situation in the newly independent states of the former Soviet Union. The conflicts in Abkhazia and South Ossetia have passed through armed hostilities and large-scale humanitarian crisis, and are now in a protracted, frozen, "no peace – no war" stage. Yet the corresponding peacebuilding process has never moved beyond an inadequate and undeveloped stage. The final case by Jaideep Saikia, "Spoilers and devious objectives in Kashmir", similarly applies the concept of spoiling to a conflict which seems to defy resolution. Saikia considers how a range of actors could be considered in the context of spoiling: Indian intelligence, the Indian army, Indian bureaucracy, the Pakistani army, Pakistani intelligence, and the *jihadi*. Both of these final chapters demonstrate that spoiling can be applied to a range of actors both inside and outside a peace process, and indeed when there is not even a solid process.

Conclusions

Some propositions relating to the findings now follow. The nature of the peace process – and the nature of the peace to be implemented – is critically important to its chances of success. It is important that the terms of reference of the peace process itself do not sow the seeds of spoiling. To the highest extent possible, it should be non-zero-sum, consensual, locally owned, and internationally and regionally supported. The peace process should not be imposed upon an unwilling or disengaged public; it must as far as possible be able to accommodate the legitimate concerns of all parties; it must seek to secure not only immediate goals such as peace and stability but also human rights and the rule of law. Peace processes and agreements which reflect asymmetrical relationships are especially vulnerable to spoiling when they are not sensitive to the concerns of weaker groups who feel the peace process is "rigged" against them. In peace processes it is essential that the leaders of the protagonists are credible and legitimate representatives, and thus can "deliver" their constituents.

Spoiling and the obstruction of peace processes tend to be associated only with the attitudes and intentions of actors who are direct participants in the conflict. However, it is essential to consider a broader range of actors and factors.

- Third parties themselves may bring incentives for spoiling in terms of resources, recognition, and favouritism to one or the other party. At other times third parties may play into the hands of spoiling by projecting the idea that any form of settlement is a priority, and thus raising opportunities for getting aid from international donors – which spoilers may come to see as an end in itself.
- Similarly, when multiple international actors are involved in promoting or funding a peace process a lack of coordination can complicate the picture and result in behaviour that effectively constitutes spoiling. Parallel mediation provides opportunities for manipulation by spoilers.
- Do not underestimate the influence – both positive and negative – of actors far removed from the conflict zone. Diaspora groups can wield significant influence (in terms of creating or hindering international pressure, and in terms of support and funding) for consolidating or opposing a peace process.

Spoiling in peacebuilding (not only during conflict settlement) is also crucially important. Extremism in post-conflict societies has often been overlooked as donors and international actors have concentrated on achieving "peace" and stability (and their own exit). When extremism of violence is transferred into extremism in politics – even "democratic politics" – spoiling can continue by other means.

Democracy – together with justice, human rights, and free-market economics – is something that should be introduced carefully and sensitively in "post"-conflict societies.

It is wrong to assume that all – or even most – conflict situations can be resolved by an accommodation of conflicting interests, or that a peace process is a process of finding consensus amongst parties that basically all seek peace. Some groups have clear incentives for the continuation of violent conflict or contesting the nature of peace. There is evidence that certain environmental variables (such as the nature of peace settlements, the role of external actors, the political economy of conflict, disputes over natural resources, and the influence of significant diaspora groups) give rise to certain types of spoiling activity. Amongst these factors, powerful groups whose primary intent is economic gain may not respond positively to conventional conflict resolution methods based upon the concept of compromise.

It is clear that the terms "spoilers" and "spoiling" can represent normative judgements that prescribe a great deal of agency for third-party custodians of a peace process. The former term indicates incorrigible actors unable to support a peace process. The second, perhaps more realistically, implies a tendency for any actor to consider spoiling at certain stages of a process for political reasons, as a strategy rather than as a behavioural pattern.

This provides us with an operational understanding of what the difference is between "politics" in a peace process and "spoiling", and therefore what type of behaviour is unacceptable. What are acceptable are strategies that do not call into question the integrity of the peace framework as a final outcome. How much "spoiling" (including violence) a peace process can absorb is related to this question. Obviously, as disputants and third parties require as a bare minimum the survival of the process, even if the end is not in sight, one should not expect high and sustained levels of violence. Where this does occur, it is clear that we are dealing with actors who cannot be reconciled to a liberal peace compromise.

Opposition and recalcitrance should always be anticipated during a peace process – even one which appears to enjoy broad support from the principal protagonists and communities. There will often be factions which are marginalized, which seek objectives outside the peace process, and which have the capacity to inflict violence in an attempt to undermine a process they do not support. This should not necessarily be taken as a sign that the peace process is under fundamental threat or in crisis. Indeed, sometimes it is a sign that the process has potential and is progressing, and that marginalized groups are desperate as they see a process taking root which will undermine their position and further their marginalization. Therefore, spoiler violence must be taken in context. It must not be allowed to derail the peace processes, and the public and the media must be encouraged to put this into perspective in order to maintain public confidence.

In cease-fire situations or peace processes in which UN peacekeepers are deployed, UN peacekeepers must be robustly equipped and mandated in order to be able to resist militant spoilers, with force when necessary, within their capacity.

Groups which seek to "spoil" efforts to resolve conflict often do so because they see the peace process as undermining their rights, privileges, or access to resources – physical, strategic, or political. They may also have rejected the liberal peace model, and often are open to the use or threat of violence. While they need not necessarily be non-state groups, they often are. This does not mean that states and officials do not spoil, as in the recent example of Greek Cypriot policy towards the Annan Plan of 2004. This means that third parties need to have a very clear idea about what aspect of their proposals, or desired outcome, is likely to conflict with that of the disputants, and of the interlinkages between moderates, hard-liners, and radicals, between disputants and their constituencies. It is in such interlinkages that the dynamics of spoiling lie, and they are used both to disguise and to propagate spoiling behaviour. It is important to note the difference between the use of spoiling, violent or non-violent, to *shape* a negotiating process and its use to destroy it. Spoiling behaviour – at least from those within a peace process – is normally designed to shape a process rather than to end it, because disputants recognize the potential assets the process may offer. This is one of the key patterns of spoiling, and one which theorists and policy-makers need to consider.

It is clear from the assessments made in the cases presented in this volume that spoiling activities do often work, in a number ways. They may raise new questions within a peace process, attract or divert attention to or from certain issues or actors, provide marginalized actors with a voice, delay or postpone progress in a process or future rounds of talks, prevent implementation of agreements, elevate the interests of one particular party, or illustrate the need to include other actors in discussions. Spoiling behaviour, at its most successful, seems to lead not to the end of a peace process, but to the inclusion of new sets of interests, the recognition of proto-political actors, and sometimes further concessions and the commitment of more international resources. By not ending the process, everything remains on the table, and disputants still have access to all of the indirect resources a peace process provides, including recognition, legitimacy, and resources, both financial and political. Thus spoiling behaviour balances the threat of the end of the process and a reversion to violence with the desire of most parties to retain the inherent assets of any such process. In this sense, spoiling is a normal part of a peace process.

The above seem to represent the key dynamics of spoiling as an inherent part of contemporary peacemaking, where recognition, legitimacy, resources, territory, and sovereignty constitute key sites of contestation.

Within this complex realm, disputants operate in a transnational context, are capable of multiple alliances, and often harbour ambiguous or devious objectives based upon conflicting norms and interests. In the interstices of such norms, spoilers find fertile ground upon which to manipulate peace processes.

Notes

1. UN Secretary-General. 2005. *In Larger Freedom: Towards Development, Security and Human Rights for All*, 21 March. New York: United Nations, para. 114.
2. See, among others, Richmond, Oliver P. 2005. *The Transformation of Peace*. London: Palgrave; Paris, Roland. 2004. *At War's End*. Cambridge: Cambridge University Press; Rasmussen, Mikkel Vedby. 2003. *The West, Civil Society, and the Construction of Peace*. London: Palgrave; Duffield, Mark. 2001. *Global Governance and the New Wars*. London: Zed Books.

Part I
Spoiling, violence, and mediation

1

Internal and external dynamics of spoiling: A negotiation approach

Karin Aggestam

Introduction

Peace processes are often rife with strategic and tactical deception and even those who sign peace agreements may cultivate violence in order to undermine their new "partners" in peace. Multiple actors in civil wars rarely simultaneously choose peace; those who seek to end a violent conflict will often face opposition from parties who are excluded or who exclude themselves from peacemaking. Such spoilers – leaders and factions who view a particular peace as opposed to their interests and who are willing to use violence to undermine it – pose a grave threat to those who risk making peace.[1]

Peacemaking is highly complex, divisive, and uncertain in its outcome. Yet the spoiler problem paradoxically tends to be a predictable phenomenon in most contemporary peace processes. The implications of spoiling – that is, actions taken to undermine a peace process in general and negotiation in particular – have gained increasing attention in the last decade as several peace processes have collapsed. However, in academia it is a relatively unexplored area of research. Stephen Stedman introduced the notion of spoilers and spoiling and has contributed important research, particularly on policy-relevant issues regarding the role of international custodians.[2] The work of John Darby together with Roger Mac Ginty has generated important insights about the impact of violence during peace processes, deduced from a large number of empirical case studies.[3]

This chapter addresses theoretically the internal and external dynamics of spoiling as well as the wider notion of devious objectives in peace negotiations. The analysis of spoiling is based on a negotiation approach, which emphasizes three arguments. First, spoiling is viewed as "situated action"; that is, actors behaving according to situational rationality. Hence the notion of spoiling is associated with some kind of rationality and intentionality, but needs to be analysed within a specific context. In this chapter, spoiling is discussed within the context of what is termed "new intractable conflict and the problem of negotiation", which contains. favourable conditions for spoiling. Second, spoiling is analysed not only in relation to violent action, but also from an inside perspective of negotiation. Hence, the intentions and strategies of negotiators are problematized. Drawing on insights from negotiation theory, the interplay between devious objectives and spoiling are examined. Third, general dynamics of negotiation, which may constrain a peace process, are critically assessed in order to analyse the power and external impact of spoiling.

Favourable conditions for spoiling: "New" intractable conflict and the problem of negotiation

During the 1980s intractable conflict gained increasing attention among conflict researchers. Intractable conflict is depicted as a zero-sum conflict, which is exhausting and costly in human and material terms. Yet societies learn over time to cope and adapt to an abnormal, violent, and insecure environment through various social and psychological mechanisms, which is one of several reasons why conflict becomes intractable. In intractable conflicts, such as the ones on Cyprus and in Israel-Palestine, the parties have accumulated and institutionalized discourses of hatred, prejudice, and animosity towards each other. Collective memories and national myths play a significant role in intractable conflicts, as well as in the reconstruction of self- and enemy images. These perceptions turn into an "ideology" that supports the prolongation of conflict and serves as an identity marker of who we are and who we are not, and thus tends to be resistant to change. As a consequence, the vicious and self-perpetuating circles of violence are "normalized" and become central to everyday life.[4]

The seminal work of John Burton and Edward Azar on deep-rooted conflict had a major impact in the field of conflict research, since many theories at the time were preoccupied with the Cold War and interstate conflict.[5] In contrast, Burton and Azar focused their research on the intercommunal dimension of intractable conflict and relations between identity groups and states. Their main argument and explanation of the intractable nature of conflicts and why they tend to resist efforts to resolve them peacefully was that such conflicts are due to unfulfilled, underlying societal and universal human needs, such as security, identity, recognition, and autonomy.

Since the end of the Cold War we have seen an upsurge of conflicts which some refer to as new wars[6] or wars of a third kind.[7] Even though these conflicts differ in contexts and histories, they share a number of distinct features which make them particularly resistant to settlement through negotiations and traditional diplomacy. These distinguishing characteristics of "new" intractable conflict explain, to a certain extent, why spoiling has become such a recurring phenomenon during contemporary peace processes. According to some scholars, they stand in stark contrast to our traditional understanding of interstate war.[8]

First, the claim to power is frequently made on the basis of a particular identity and ethnic homogeneity. Politics thus tends to be more about labels and tribalist/communalist identity than about politics *per se* (e.g. national interests of states) or ideologies (e.g. principles of democracy or socialism).[9] Hence, it is difficult to distinguish clear strategic goals among the disputants and to identify a shared negotiating formula as an alternative to the continuation of violence.

Second, most of these conflicts are identity-based and constructed on an idealized nostalgic past and myths in order to generate political legitimacy. They draw heavily on discourses of historic enmity, hatred, and insecurity, which trigger basic existential fears of group survival, expulsion, and ethnic cleansing. Paradoxically, in the midst of increasing existential threats and intensified insecurity, identification provides a sense of security in being part of a larger collective.[10] As a consequence, negotiations are frequently framed as a zero-sum game and major risk-taking, since concession-making involves existential questions and concerns of group survival. Whatever is seen as positive in a peace proposal by one side is therefore likely to be interpreted as a loss for the other side. The role of religion as part of the identity construction and justification of violence exacerbates the difficulties in conducting negotiations based on compromise. Religion is about absolute and particularistic values; hence political goals become less visible and incentives to compromise are limited at best or non-existent at worst. The existential framing of negotiation in combination with uncertainty about the direction of a peace process feeds mistrust and fear. A negotiation process by itself may also challenge the disputants' sense of understanding "self" and "other", which is intimately related to conflict. Thus, belief perseverance is further strengthened if there is a continuation of violence. It proves that the other side has not changed, and consequently confirms firmly held enemy images.

Third, these conflicts are distinct from interstate conflicts in that they often take place within collapsing or weak states. The result is anarchy, with an eroding norm system and erosion of the state monopoly of violence. The distinction between civilian and combatant is blurred, as civilians are directly targeted. Civilians therefore constitute the majority of war victims, and any rules of warfare are rendered meaningless. In this anarchic context warlords are the major players, both as instigators of violence and paradoxically as providers of security for some groups. Moreover, warlords in most cases profit economically from the ongoing violence. The privatization of violence leads to an ever-increasing number of conflicting parties and non-state actors. As a result, recognition, legitimacy, leadership, and inclusion/exclusion in a peace process become the decisive and major issues of contention. This is why some parties may accept a negotiation process for reasons (such as recognition and legitimacy) other than reaching a settlement and a sustainable peace.

To be sure, these features of "new" intractable conflicts lead to a number of barriers in a negotiation process which favour and strengthen spoiling activities. The majority of these conflicts are asymmetrical in nature, which is considered by most negotiation theorists as detrimental to efficient negotiations. As William Zartman states, "negotiations under conditions of asymmetry (asymmetrical negotiations) are a paradox, because one of the basic findings about the negotiation process is that it functions best under conditions of equality".[11] The implications of asymmetry in a negotiation process are numerous.[12]

First, asymmetry makes a continuation of unilateral actions more likely and a mutually hurting stalemate, which Zartman defines as a particularly ripe moment for negotiations, less probable.[13] Such a stalemate stipulates increasing symmetrical relations and a situation where the parties are trapped without being able to resort to unilateral strategies. However, asymmetrical conflicts are characterized by gross power inequality in economic, political, and military resources between state and non-state actors. Stronger parties are therefore inclined to use their power superiority to continue unilateral actions, whereas weaker parties mobilize strength and compensate for the asymmetry through a strongly held commitment to armed struggle.[14]

Second, asymmetrical relations are assumed to reflect negatively on the issue of justice in the negotiation process. The rules of engagement about de-escalation and negotiation between stronger and weaker parties are vague or non-existent. Theoretically, justice is done when the parties comply freely and rationally with the contents of an agreement. However, most often stronger parties are inclined to stipulate the rules of the game and impose the conditions of an agreement. As a consequence there will always be some groups who may continue with violent opposition and attempt to derail the peace process, since they assume that the process denies them justice.[15] In addition, weaker parties may be unwilling or unable to fulfil their part of an agreement in the implementation phase, which leads to devaluation of an agreement or, in the worst case, the collapse of a peace process. Few peace agreements contain mechanisms for monitoring adherence.

Third, legal asymmetry between state and non-state actors tends to result in a contest about recognition and legitimacy. For example, who is a valid spokesperson for and a legitimate leader of a non-state actor? Another major question is how to deal with the large number of factional parties in a negotiation process. The quality and legitimacy of leadership – that is, leaders' ability to deliver their followers – are not only decisive in order to reach an agreement but also to implement it. Who are to be included and excluded in the process? What are the consequences of exclusion? Here lies one of the central concerns of the spoiling phenomenon.

According to a number of scholars, these intractable conflicts are non-negotiable. Azar, Burton, Kelman, and others argue for instance that negotiations should be based on an interactive problem-solving approach in order to resolve them.[16] Kaldor provides an extensive critique of the traditional modes of diplomacy and negotiation. In her view, an internationally sponsored peace process generates legitimacy, but sectarian violence should not be rewarded with such recognition. The traditional modes of negotiation have proved limited at best and counterproductive at worst in resolving identity-based conflicts. "Conflict resolution from above" (that is, élite-based negotiations), according to her, has resulted in several unfortunate outcomes.[17] First, inviting war criminals to the negotiating table has given public legitimacy to individuals who are responsible for grave human rights abuses. Second, negotiations and political compromises have often been based on exclusionist and particularistic assumptions, which cannot create stability and long-term workable solutions since such settlements would rely on the power of identity politics. Third, without a mandate to enforce the rule of law, particularly in the implementation phase, any international intervention may lose legitimacy since human rights abuses are likely to continue.

Negotiating in good faith? Credibility and potential spoiling

According to Darby, a peace process must by definition contain the following criteria: the parties negotiate in good faith and are committed to a sustained process; the main actors are included in the negotiations; and the negotiations address the key conflicting issues.[18] Yet very few contemporary peace processes would fit this restricted theoretical definition.

Instead, the definition reflects an "ideal" peace process, which includes the essential prerequisites for a successful one. The lack of these prerequisites partly explains the power spoilers may have, and why spoiling is such a frequent phenomenon in peace processes. The core interest in this section is to problematize spoiling from an inside perspective: the intentions of "potential" spoilers from within the negotiation process. More specifically, this chapter will elaborate on the first prerequisite – that is, the commitment to negotiate in good faith for a sustained peace process.

What does it mean to negotiate in good faith? Obviously, the notion is a general and abstract expression of the good intention, commitment, and willingness (and sometimes risk) to explore negotiations instead of the continuation of conflict. Moreover, such a commitment is likely to be based on an expectation that the other side will reciprocate in a similar vein, which includes an assumption that if an agreement is reached it will be honoured. Thus a commitment to negotiate in good faith assumes some kind of certainty, reciprocity, and predictability about future behaviour and action.[19] Risks of betrayal may be minimized, and trust may come to constitute the essence of a constructive working relationship between the negotiators.

Even though the phrase "negotiating in good faith" is frequently referred to, it is difficult to distinguish any concrete operationalization of the term, just as it is hard to find a precise definition of trust. It is often equated with the notion of willingness to negotiate, which is also mentioned as a prerequisite of a ripe moment for efficient negotiations.[20] Dean Pruitt, for example, attempts to refine ripeness theory as introduced by Zartman by analysing separately the motivation of political leaders. According to him, the goal of achieving mutual cooperation is assumed to be the driving force behind cooperative behaviour, while optimism about the other parties' reciprocity determines the extent to which this goal will affect behaviour. Optimism about a jointly negotiated outcome is necessary, since the danger of unilateral conciliatory efforts might be exploited by the opponent and viewed as weak or even treasonous by one's supporters.[21] In sum, willingness to negotiate in good faith expresses an intention as well as an expectation that the other side will reciprocate to do "what is right". It includes an assumption that the parties will, when reaching an agreement, implement it according to the principle of *pacta sunt servanda*.[22]

The discussion presented above is closely associated with the basic assumptions held in a problem-solving and integrative approach to negotiation. It focuses on a readiness and flexibility to make concessions, but also fundamentally on a joint search for mutually advantageous alternatives to conflict. Thus a problem-solving approach assumes that information is exchanged in an admissible manner about oneself (needs, interests, priorities), and that the conflict is generally framed as a joint problem, a puzzle that should be resolved. By establishing trust and working relations between the negotiators, joint efforts to identify common interests and values will promote a win-win solution. Furthermore, it is assumed that problem-solving negotiations may facilitate long-term exchange between the parties. Thus the other side is not viewed as an opponent but as a partner in the negotiations. The parties will therefore be ready to make compromises on matters of self-interest in order to promote mutual interests and future gains.[23]

Yet the realities of contemporary conflicts have, as discussed above, created tremendous obstacles to traditional negotiations and problem-solving negotiations. As mentioned, they rarely result in ripe moments (mutually hurting stalemate) or enticing opportunity (prospect of future gains).[24] Instead, most peace processes are initiated after heavy international pressures have been exerted on the disputants. As a consequence, the most likely negotiation strategy the adversaries tend to adopt is a competitive one. The key component in a competitive negotiation strategy is power. According to the realism of Hans Morgenthau, negotiation is the art of combining persuasion, compromise, and the threat of force.[25] The dynamics of such a strategy lie in escalation and negotiation. By the use of manipulation, either by sticks (punishment and threat of force) or carrots (rewards), one side may try to change the pay-off structure of the negotiations and the preferences of the opponent in order to get desired concessions and move towards an agreement.[26] Thus a competitive strategy emphasizes self-interests, autonomy, and strategic choice in a negotiation process and the main focus is on the advancement of one side's interests relative to those of the opponent. Accordingly, in competitive negotiations the goals and interests are frequently framed as incompatible, which tends to lead to distrust and obstruct candour and flexibility about preferences and interests.[27] The Israeli-Palestinian negotiations during the period 1996–1998 illustrate how competitive negotiations are pursued and negotiated agreements reached. Without the bridge-building role of US mediation, as a surrogate for the lack of trust between the negotiators, the negotiation process would probably have collapsed.

The notion of commitment has a different connotation in a competitive strategy than in a problem-solving approach. In line with Thomas Schelling's work on the use of commitment, it involves drawing red lines in negotiations – that is, signalling a resistance point where an agreement becomes unacceptable. Hence a commitment is used to send a message to the other side that no further concessions will be possible and, rather than concede, the negotiation process will break down.[28]

In short, a competitive strategy assumes that by issuing rewards and threats one side hopes to influence the other to comply and make concessions, which in the end will result in an agreement. Yet, as Hopmann underlines, "the dilemma of traditional [competitive] bargaining is that the contradiction between cooperative and conflictual tactics may make the negotiation process somewhat schizophrenic, alternating between cooperative moves and conflictual ones. Deceit and manipulative behavior may serve one's short-term or individual interest, but it often detracts from the long-run collective interest in reaching an agreement."[29]

Fred Iklé, in his seminal work on international negotiation, highlights the fact that parties frequently negotiate for side-effects and for other reasons than obtaining peace agreements. He underlines that side-effects may have nothing to do with reaching an agreement between the parties, but rather concern improvement in relations with a third party. Iklé mentions a number of likely side-effects, such as using negotiations to gain international publicity and attention; to prepare for the use of force or to rearm; to gather intelligence; to use negotiations as a sounding board; or to gain prestige.[30] The negotiations between Israel and the Palestinians in Washington in 1992–1993 illustrate clearly how the parties used the negotiation process primarily as a publicity forum.[31] In particular, the Palestinians, who had little incentive to conclude an interim agreement with the Israeli government as long as the PLO (Palestine Liberation Organization) was officially excluded from the peace process, used the negotiations and the media as a platform to put their demands for national self-determination on the international agenda. The charismatic Palestinian spokesperson Hanan Ashrawi described the media as "a partner in my battle for legitimacy" because "they were after the truth and the truth was my ally".[32]

Paul Pillar, in his work on war termination, also underlines that peace negotiations may be used for a variety of reasons other than achieving an agreement. Peace negotiations may be pursued as a way of extending combat in a non-violent form by bringing some of the rules of combat into the negotiations, for example attrition of the enemy's strength and the sapping of its morale. Negotiations may also be conducted primarily as a way of trying to alter the balance of strength, to influence some specific events that would help its war efforts, to include an ally in the war, or to undermine domestic and international support of the enemy while trying to shore up one's own. As a consequence, side-effects may discourage as well as encourage the conflicting parties to negotiate.[33]

Intervention by third parties in "new" intractable conflicts is often perceived as an intrusion by the adversaries. Due to the asymmetrical nature of conflict, they tend to hold irreconcilable expectations of mediation. Stronger parties favour impartial and less-active intervention, whereas weaker parties often desire active and full engagement of mediators as an ally and as a way to compensate for asymmetry.[34] For instance, the Palestinians have repeatedly appealed to the USA as well as the EU and the United Nations for an expanded role of their mediation in order to balance the asymmetry between Israel and the Palestinians. At the same time, inclusion in a negotiation process generates legitimacy and recognition, which are often sought – particularly by non-state actors. It is therefore important that third parties and sponsors of peace processes recognize the fact that parties may hold devious objectives and may use their efforts to facilitate a peace process as a cover for other objectives. Stedman warns: "Mediators, who have vested interest and substantial investment of time, energy, and honor in seeing settlements implemented, tend to interpret acts of noncompliance as being motivated by fear rather than insincerity. Even if they interpret motivation as malign and admit that insincerity is involved, they usually assert that the parties in question are trying to get better settlements, rather than attempting to destroy the settlement."[35] Hence, "mediation efforts should not be offered like buses that come along every fifteen minutes".[36] Oliver Richmond highlights how conflicting parties who hold devious objectives use international mediation in various ways, such as legitimizing their negotiation positions and current status, putting the blame for deadlocks on the mediators, saving face, and avoiding costly concessions by prolonging the negotiation process.[37] For example, Yitzhak Shamir, the Israeli prime minister who accepted the invitation of the USA to attend the Madrid peace conference in 1991, admitted after having lost the elections in 1992 that his decision to accept the invitation was primarily made to avoid American pressure. His intention was also to prolong the negotiation process indefinitely while settling "half a million [Jewish] people in Judea and Samaria [the West Bank]".[38]

In sum, the transition from war to peace is precarious and full of risks and uncertainties. It entails a transition of turning warriors into peacemakers and transforming a culture of violence into one of negotiation. Clearly, such a transition becomes particularly troublesome if it is accompanied by violence. As Darby underlines, any violence during peace negotiations may be interpreted as a confirmation that the transition has failed.[39] What one can delineate from the discussion above is that it is difficult to determine whether a party is negotiating in good faith or whether the aim is to undermine the negotiation process. It is important to differentiate between spoiling as a tactic and spoiling as a strategy. Yet how can one clearly distinguish between competitive negotiation strategies and intentional deception? Furthermore, how can we distinguish calculated efforts to torpedo a peace process from consequential action emanating from a competitive negotiation strategy, or due to a change in objectives during the peace process? One person might view himself or herself as a tough negotiator but with honest intentions while the other side perceives his/her actions as intentional deception. This is what Christer Jönsson refers to as the "problem of credibility". Mistrust and fear of deception are common characteristics of negotiations, leading to distorted credibility judgement.[40] Particularly in "new" intractable conflicts, parties tend to expect and interpret with suspicion the actions and intentions of the other party. The use of threats and escalation during negotiations is a high-risk strategy. Zartman and Faure warn that parties might end up in a "competitive irrationality" because of judgemental bias.[41] The parties may engage in activities that are irrational in terms of possible outcomes. "Accidental" spoiling may be one such plausible outcome, as the parties keep on escalating in the hope that the other side will give in and thus are unable to escape from escalation. Hence, spoiling becomes a consequence of other tactics. It is therefore important to distinguish between initiated and intentional, and consequential and unintentional, spoiling. At the same time, how can we determine spoilers *ex ante*?[42] This enigma is well illustrated in the debate about the credibility of the late Palestinian leader Yasir Arafat as a negotiating partner. From an Israeli and American perspective, Arafat disqualified himself first because of the actions (and non-actions) taken during the negotiations at the Camp David summit in the summer of 2000. Second, Arafat, by his reluctance to confront terror groups such as Hamas and Islamic Jihad, revealed according to this narrative his "true" intention, which was not to negotiate in good faith but to continue the armed struggle indefinitely.

External spoiling and the effects on the negotiation process

This section shifts the focus from an inside perspective of potential spoiling to one that emphasizes the external impact and dynamics of spoiling in the negotiation process. The analysis will be less concerned with the motives and intentions of outside spoilers, and centre more on the implications of their actions. Moreover, external spoiling primarily concerns actors who use violence intentionally to derail a peace process. At the same time it should be stressed that various opposition groups, including those which conduct protests by peaceful means, are inclined to cooperate informally with spoiler groups in their effort to delegitimize a peace process. Incitement, for instance, provides fertile ground for violent actions. Most peace processes are highly divisive, and Pillar underlines that most peace negotiations are accompanied by ongoing violence.[43] Hence a peace process almost by definition produces external spoiling, since it challenges established assumptions of who is a patriot or traitor, enemy or friend. Who is included or excluded from the peace process?

Who becomes the winner or loser when a peace agreement is to be implemented? One decisive factor is leadership – that is, the ability of political leaders to deliver their followers and manage groups associated with violence. Political leaders will have difficulties in leading if their followers are unwilling to go in the same direction.[44] Moreover, leaders who sign agreements are vulnerable to accusations of betrayal and treason, which often works as a powerful deterrent for those who want to promote a peaceful settlement with the enemy.[45]

Violence during such circumstances will feed existing fears and uncertainties among the general public about the direction of the peace process. Opposition groups may convincingly argue that compromise does not lead to peace but to more violence (rewarding and giving in to terror), which limits the mandate and bargaining range of the negotiators. Stedman underlines the complex transition for leaders, who previously were committed to the rhetoric of total war and victory, to enter into a negotiation process and declare willingness to achieve compromise. Since leaders in such circumstances may be accused of cowardice and treachery, they may out of fear talk peace in private and war in public.[46] This exacerbates the credibility problem discussed in the previous section. For instance, Yasir Arafat was accused while negotiating with Israel of speaking with two tongues, one in Arabic which called for *jihad* (interpreted by the Israeli government as terrorism), and one in English calling for "peace of the brave" (referring to peace with Israel). Robert Putnam's two-level game illustrates well how political leaders are Janus-faced in negotiations: they conduct several dialogues simultaneously, influencing interlocutors and domestic and international opinions as well as third parties. Concession-making is therefore intricate in a multilevel game, and it is the interaction between these levels that determines the possibilities and restraints of the negotiations.[47]

To sum up, the power and implications of external spoiling in peace negotiations depend on a number of issues. First, spoiling is more effective at times when the negotiating parties have difficulties in implementing a signed peace agreement, since it increases uncertainties and fears about the outcome and direction of the peace process. The problem of implementation is a widespread dilemma in most contemporary peace processes. For instance, statistics reveal that only one-third of peace agreements in internal conflicts hold for more than five years.[48] The reasons are many and varied. International law specifically refers to *pacta sunt servanda*, but enforcement mechanisms are often absent in many peace agreements. Custodian monitoring has, however, become more frequent in recent years. Custodians are, according to Stedman, international actors who oversee the implementation of peace agreements.[49] For example, in Cambodia the United Nations has acted as a custodian, and the UK and Ireland are joint "internal" custodians of the Northern Ireland peace process. Other obstacles to implementation may be that the agreements have been badly designed, vaguely defined, or intentionally ambiguous if the parties have relied on constructive ambiguity[50] as a way of avoiding deadlocks.[51] Such ambiguity may exacerbate an already fragile situation characterized by suspicion and mistrust, which enhances the effectiveness of spoiling. Consequently, it may create new grounds for hostilities because these ambiguities need to be addressed, interpreted, and agreed upon. A "sceptical scrutiny" of a peace agreement may develop and as a result support for the agreement may significantly weaken.[52]

Second, spoiling is effective when political leaders have publicly declared and made a commitment not to negotiate and make concessions under fire. It is assumed that to negotiate while violence continues signals weakness to the other side, even though in practice it means that the negotiators become hostages to spoilers. Hence, spoilers become the veto holders of the peace process and determine its pace and direction.[53] This is one major difference in the negotiation styles between the two Israeli leaders, Ariel Sharon and the late Yitshak Rabin. Rabin declared after every terror attack in Israel by Hamas and Islamic Jihad that to stop the peace process at such a moment would be to give in to terror and extremism. Sharon on the other hand has consistently refused to deal with the Palestinians as long as the violence continues, which is why every attempt to de-escalate the conflict has failed. The power of spoiling is further enhanced when spoiler groups and extremists on both sides, despite their violent struggle against each other, tend to form a tacit alliance in which they can derive justification from and serve as "external pacers" for each other. For example, a unique coalition between the Palestinian opposition and the Israeli opposition was formed in the early phases of their peace process.[54]

Third, spoilers' capacity to undermine a negotiation process depends on the degree of popular support they enjoy among the public as well on their principled stance to continue an armed and violent struggle. Some spoilers, who Stedman describes as total spoilers (in contrast to greedy and limited spoilers), simply cannot be accommodated or defeated since their demands are non-negotiable.[55] The popular support of spoilers also depends on how the public view the peace process in general and how active or passive war and peace constituencies are. Yet, as Darby soberly points out, peace negotiations rarely result from domestic pressures, despite years of war-weariness.[56]

Finally, negotiations are threatened by spoiling activities if the peace process is framed among a wider public as an élitist and exclusive project. Secret negotiations are still often sought to avoid arousing public anxiety, despite the fact that secrecy is generally seen as being democratically offensive. The sheer fact of being excluded from the process may therefore generate opposition and spoiling. If the negotiations are surrounded by violence and viewed as unjust and illegitimate, concession-making and implementation of an agreement become almost impossible. It is therefore, according to Fen Osler Hampson, important that most of the warring parties are represented in the negotiations.[57] Darby argues for a "sufficient inclusion" – that is, including those with power to bring the peace process down by violence.[58] "Just as the principle of 'sufficient consensus' was adopted in South Africa in recognition of the impossibility of progress if all participants had veto powers, it is necessary to apply a principle of 'sufficient inclusion' in relation to militant organizations."[59]

Conclusion

The problem of spoilers has been a major concern for both practitioners and academics over the last decade, and yet the field of research is rather limited. This chapter has theoretically explored the notion of spoiling, specifically relating to the internal and external dynamics of peace negotiations. Spoiling has been analysed within the context of "new" intractable conflicts in order to understand why so many peace negotiations are difficult to conduct in the first place, as well as the reasons why spoiling is so effective. The dynamics of spoiling have also been discussed as an inside/outside phenomenon. Utilizing negotiation theory, the intentions of negotiators have been explored as well as the interplay between the negotiation process and external spoiling.

A number of conclusions may be drawn from the analysis. First, spoiling needs to be understood as action based on situational rationality since the motives and intentions of spoilers vary greatly. It depends both on the specific context of conflict and on the interplay between inside and outside actors of the peace process. Leadership and the mobilization for a peace process, and the perception by the public that this process is just and inclusive, are critical prerequisites to limit the power of spoiling and extremist violence. Yet, as Darby and Mac Ginty underline, mobilizing for conflict is easier than mobilizing for peace.[60] The role of the international community, for example as custodian, is decisive for the success of sustainable negotiations. At the same time it is important to stress that the international community needs to develop a more critical and sober approach to whatever kind of peace process is supported. There tends to be an exaggerated optimism regarding the extent to which negotiations may resolve intractable and existential conflicts.

There exists a preconceived notion of ending conflict based on a division between war and peace. However, peace processes are rarely ordered so neatly in reality.[61] There are times when other alternatives to negotiations need to be sought in order to de-escalate conflict – international involvement might otherwise result in counterproductive outcomes. Furthermore, the possibility that several negotiating parties may hold devious objectives needs greater recognition. In other words, they may use a peace process as a way to achieve goals other than a peace agreement. The guiding principles and norms established in the preparatory phases of peace negotiations are therefore critical for the ongoing process and for the implementation of a sustainable peace. These norms and principles reflect a deeper understanding of what it means to resolve a conflict.

Second, even if the notion of spoiling highlights a critical problem in most peace processes, it is a value-laden concept to work with. Actors tend to be diagnosed as either for or against a peace process. However, as this chapter demonstrates, it is difficult to distinguish spoiling strategies from competitive negotiation strategies. Furthermore, it is hard to draw a decisive line between intentional and consequential spoiling. For example, the interplay between escalation, manipulation, and negotiation may result in a competitive irrationality, which benefits none of the parties.

Finally, the notion of spoiling tends to be viewed as a rather static phenomenon, whereas in practice it is highly dynamic, as the actors' goals may alter during a peace process. Therefore, the notion of spoiling has some major limitations concerning diagnosis, categorization, and predictability.

Notes

1. Stedman, Stephen. 2003. "Peace processes and the challenges of violence", in John Darby and Roger Mac Ginty (eds) *Contemporary Peacemaking. Conflict, Violence and Peace Processes*. Basingstoke and New York: Palgrave Macmillan, p. 103.
2. See, for example, Stedman, Stephen. 1997. "Spoiler problems in peace processes", *International Security*, Vol. 22, No. 2.
3. Darby, John (ed.). 2001. *The Effects of Violence on Peace Processes*, Washington, DC: US Institute of Peace; Darby, John and Roger Mac Ginty (eds). 2003. *Contemporary Peacemaking. Conflict, Violence and Peace Processes*. Basingstoke and New York: Palgrave Macmillan; see also Höglund, Kristine. 2004. *Violence in the Midst of Peace Negotiations. Cases from Guatemala, Northern Ireland, South Africa and Sri Lanka*, Report No. 69. Uppsala: Department of Peace and Conflict Research, Uppsala University.
4. Bar-Tal, Daniel. 1998. "Societal beliefs in times of intractable conflict: The Israeli case", *International Journal of Conflict Management*, Vol. 9, No. 1; Kriesberg, Louis, Terrell Northrup, and Stuart Thorson (eds). 1998. *Intractable Conflicts and their Transformations*. New York: Syracuse University Press.
5. Azar, Edward and John Burton. 1986. *International Conflict Resolution: Theory and*

Practice. Brighton: Wheatsheaf; Burton, John. 1987. *Resolving Deep-rooted Conflict. A Handbook.* Latham: University Press of America.
6. Kaldor, Mary. 2001. *New and Old Wars: Organized Violence in a Global Era.* Cambridge: Polity Press.
7. Wars of the first kind are institutionalized wars, wars of the second kind concern total wars. Holsti, Kalevi J. 1996. *The State, War, and the State of War.* Cambridge: Cambridge Studies in International Relations.
8. Kaldor, note 6 above; Miall, Hugh, Oliver Ramsbotham, and Tom Woodhouse, 1999. *Contemporary Conflict Resolution.* Cambridge: Polity Press. For a critical view of the distinction between modern and past patterns of violent conflict, see Newman, Edward. 2004. "The 'new wars' debate: A historical perspective is needed", *Security Dialogue*, Vol. 35, No. 2.
9. Kaldor, note 6 above, pp. 77–78.
10. Schulz, Helena Lindholm. 1999. "Identity conflicts and their resolution: The Oslo Agreement and Palestinian identities", in H. Wiberg and C. P. Scherrer (eds) *Ethnicity and Intra-state Conflict. Types, Causes and Peace Strategies.* Aldershot: Ashgate.
11. Zartman, I. William. 1995. "Dynamics and constraints in negotiations in internal conflicts", in I. William Zartman (ed.) *Elusive Peace. Negotiating an End to Civil War.* Washington, DC: Brookings Institution, p. 8.
12. Aggestam, Karin. 2002. "Mediating asymmetric conflict", *Mediterranean Politics*, Vol. 7, No. 1.
13. Zartman, I. William. 1989. *Ripe for Resolution.* New York: Oxford University Press.
14. Zartman, note 11 above, p. 9.
15. Albin, Cecilia. 1999. "Justice, fairness and negotiation: Theory and reality", in Peter Berton, Hiroshi Kimura, and I. William Zartman (eds) *International Negotiation. Actors, Structure/Process, Values.* New York: St Martin's Press.
16. According to them, an interactive problem-solving approach is best advanced in an interactive workshop. In such a setting the participants are able to redefine negotiation away from zero-sum to win-win thinking. These non-binding problem-solving workshops are facilitated by social scientists who encourage the parties to share and exchange information, in a flexible and frank manner, about their interests, needs, and fears. See, for example, Kelman, Herbert. 2002. "Interactive problem-solving: Informal mediation by the scholar-practitioner", in Jacob Bercovitch (ed.) *Studies in International Mediation.* Basingstoke and New York: Palgrave Macmillan.
17. Kaldor, note 6 above, pp. 119–120.
18. Darby, note 3 above, p. 11.
19. Hoffman, Aaron M. 2002. "A conceptualization of trust in international relations", *European Journal of International Relations*, Vol. 8, No. 3, p. 378.
20. See, for example, Stedman, Stephen. 1991. *Peacemaking in Civil War: International Mediation in Zimbabwe 1974–1980.* London: Lynne Rienner; Kleiboer, Marieke. 1994. "Ripeness of conflict? A fruitful notion?", *Journal of Peace Research*, Vol. 31, No. 1.
21. Pruitt, Dean G. 1997. "Ripeness theory and the Oslo Talks", *International Negotiation*, Vol. 2, No. 2, pp. 239–240.
22. Hoffman, note 19 above, p. 379.
23. See further Hopmann, Terrence P. 1995. "Two paradigms of negotiation: Bargaining and problem solving", in Daniel Druckman and Christopher Mitchell (eds) *Flexibility in International Negotiation and Mediation.* Thousand Oaks, CA, London, and New Delhi: The Annals/Sage Periodicals; Pruitt, Dean G. 1990. "Strategy in negotiation", in Victor A. Kremenyuk (ed.) *International Negotiation. Analysis, Approaches, Issues.* San Francisco and Oxford: Jossey-Bass.

24. Mitchell, Christopher. 1995. "The right moment: Notes on four models of 'ripeness'", *Paradigms*, Vol. 9, No. 2.
25. Hopmann, Terrence P. 1996. *The Negotiation Process and the Resolution of International Conflicts*. Columbia, SC: University of South Carolina, p. 25.
26. Zartman, I. William and Guy Olivier Faure. 2005. "The dynamics of escalation and negotiation", in I. William Zartman and Guy Olivier Faure (eds) *Escalation and Negotiation in International Conflicts*. Cambridge: Cambridge University Press.
27. Hopmann, note 23 above; Pruitt, note 23 above.
28. Schelling, Thomas. 1963. *The Strategy of Conflict*. New York: Oxford University Press; Hopmann, note 25 above, pp. 63–64.
29. Hopmann, note 25 above, p. 72.
30. Iklé, Fred Charles. 1964. *How Nations Negotiate*. New York: Praeger, pp. 43–59.
31. Both the Israeli and Palestinian negotiators have attributed the failure of the negotiations in Washington to the high degree of publicity and the complete lack of confidentiality. The negotiations were hampered by constant leaks as well as press conferences in which the parties justified their positions. See further Aggestam, Karin. 1996. "Two-track diplomacy: Negotiations between Israel and the PLO", in *Davis Papers on Israel's Foreign Relations*, No. 53. Jerusalem: Leonard Davis Institute.
32. Ashrawi, Hanan. 1995. *This Side of Peace. A Personal Account*. New York: Simon & Schuster, pp. 143, 195.
33. Pillar, Paul R. 1983. *Negotiating Peace: War Termination as a Bargaining Process*. Princeton: Princeton University, pp. 51–52.
34. Aggestam, note 12 above.
35. Stedman, Stephen. 1996. "Negotiation and mediation in internal conflict", in Michael E. Brown (ed.) *The International Dimensions of Internal Conflict*. Cambridge, MA: MIT Press, p. 369.
36. *Ibid.*, p. 363.
37. Richmond, Oliver. 1998. "Devious objectives and the disputants' view of international mediation", *Journal of Peace Research*, Vol. 35, No. 6, p. 712.
38. Zittrain, Laura Eisenberg and Neil Caplan. 1998. *Negotiating Arab-Israeli Peace. Patterns, Problems, Possibilities*. Bloomington and Indianapolis: Indiana University Press, p. 81.
39. Darby, note 3 above, pp. 52–53.
40. Jönsson, Christer. 1990. *Communication in International Bargaining*. London: Pinter Publishers, pp. 79–87.
41. Zartman and Faure, note 26 above.
42. Zahar, Marie-Joëlle. 2003. "Reframing the spoiler debate in peace processes", in Darby and Mac Ginty, note 3 above, p. 114.
43. Pillar, note 33 above.
44. Darby, note 3 above, p. 121.
45. Iklé, note 30 above, p. 60
46. Stedman, note 35 above, p. 350.
47. Putnam, Robert. 1993. "Diplomacy and politics: The logic of two-level games", in Peter B. Evans, Harold K. Jacobson, and Robert D. Putnam (eds) *Double-Edged Diplomacy. International Bargaining and Domestic Politics*. Berkeley and Los Angeles: University of California Press, p. 71.
48. Licklider, Roy. 1995. "The consequences of negotiated settlements in civil wars, 1945–1993", *American Political Science Review*, Vol. 89, No. 3.
49. Stedman, note 2 above.
50. "Constructive ambiguity" is a frequently used diplomatic term. The intention is to overcome deadlocks by avoiding and postponing detailed interpretations until implementa-

tion. The basic rationale is that the parties will be more committed to a signed agreement, following the device of *pacta sunt servanda*. However, in identity-based conflicts, which often lack established or accepted rules of the game of negotiation, constructive ambiguity frequently becomes destructive and counterproductive.

51. Hampson, Fen Osler. 1996. *Nurturing Peace. Why Peace Settlements Succeed or Fail.* Washington, DC: US Institute of Peace; Aggestam, Karin and Christer Jönsson. 1997. "(Un)ending conflict: Challenges in post-war bargaining", *Millennium*, Vol. 26, No. 3.
52. Ross, Lee. 1995. "Reactive devaluation in negotiation and conflict resolution", in K. Arrow, R. H. Mnookin, L. Ross, A. Tversky, and R. Wilson (eds) *Barriers to Conflict Resolution*. New York: W. W. Norton & Co., p. 34.
53. Darby, note 3 above, p. 118.
54. Aggestam and Jönsson, note 51 above, pp. 778, 780; Iklé, note 30 above.
55. Stedman, note 2 above.
56. Darby, note 3 above, p. 98.
57. Hampson, note 51 above.
58. Darby, note 3 above, p. 118.
59. *Ibid.*, p. 119.
60. Darby, John and Roger Mac Ginty. 2003. "Conclusion: Peace processes, present and future", in Darby and Mac Ginty, note 3 above, pp. 267–268.
61. Coker, Christopher. 1997. "How wars end", *Millennium*, Vol. 26, No. 3.

2

Understanding the violence of insiders: Loyalty, custodians of peace, and the sustainability of conflict settlement

Marie-Joëlle Zahar

When do insiders use violence in peace processes, and what can custodians of peace do to generate insider loyalty to peace? Both questions are crucial to the sustainability of peace agreements. At the end of civil conflicts, peace agreements are premised upon a distinction between two categories of local actors: insiders and outsiders. Insiders are actors who the foreign custodians of peace believe can be brought aboard the transition to peace. By contrast, outsiders are those parties left out of the peace talks. Whatever the reasons behind this judgement call,[1] if it is faulty then the whole edifice crumbles. Yet, as Stedman has cogently argued,[2] the possibility of strategic deception is part and parcel of conflict resolution. Because insiders who spoil peace processes are legion, analysts have until now skirted the question of loyalty.

This chapter focuses on actors who have been invited into peace processes. It asks "When and under what conditions will insiders resort to violence?" and "What can foreign custodians of peace do about this?" In so doing, the chapter steers away from the standard approach to spoiling. Rather than assume that the use of violence necessarily suggests intent to spoil the peace, it starts from the premise that insiders, having already been brought once into the peace process, can therefore presumably be kept in it. It is argued that insiders will only resort to violence if and when the reasons that drove them to accept peace are no more. While some of these reasons are context-specific (availability of resources to restart the war – notably a regional war economy and external patrons[3]), others are process-specific. In other words, the course of peace implementation can generate dissatisfaction among insiders. In order to secure the sustainability of peace, custodians must not only "neutralize" the environment in such a way as to prevent actors from accessing resources that could reignite war, they must also steer peace in such a way as to consolidate insider loyalty to the process. Thus it is contended that, contrary to common wisdom, peace implementation is not a technical matter. It is a highly political act that may, under some conditions, contribute to the promotion of devious objectives that jeopardize the sustainability of peace.

Insiders in peace processes

Insiders are actors of a civil war who have been invited to become parties to the talks that result in a peace settlement. In earlier research the author argued that such actors have different incentives to use violence than actors who are not included in the negotiations. Since peace agreements are in essence élite pacts, insiders are guaranteed political representation in the post-agreement phase.[4] Assuming that insiders are not cornered into signing agreements – as would have happened, for example, had the Rambouillet talks resulted in an agreement between the Serb government and the Kosovo Liberation Front (UÇK) – it is reasonable to assert that they will develop vested interests in the peace agreement.

If such actors use violence in the post-agreement phase, they are usually labelled spoilers and accused of holding devious objectives. While it is true that insiders could have resorted to strategic deception, entering into peace talks to buy time and regroup their military strength,[5] this is not the only possible explanation. Another reason for the use of violence is the existence of a commitment problem. Much has been written about commitment problems.[6] In short, the diagnosis is that all parties are genuinely interested in peace but none can trust the others sufficiently to keep promises. In such situations parties are reluctant to give up their only means of protection against the potential unilateral defection of others, their weapons. Analysts who favour this type of explanation see the commitment problem as a major hurdle to demobilization and disarmament; they believe that only committed foreign custodians of the peace can provide guarantees to all parties and overcome such obstacles.

A final scenario that analysts do not really address highlights the role of custodians in the post-agreement period. Custodians can directly contribute to the disenchantment of insiders with the peace process. Most research on peace implementation takes UN operations as its frame of reference. These missions are described as neutral and their work as technical. Analysts construe foreign intervention in peacebuilding as a positive influence that helps war-torn countries regain peace and stability.[7] This is the legacy of a discourse that cast peacebuilding assistance as "technical aid". Indeed, many of the criteria and guidelines spelled out in specific peacebuilding and post-conflict reconstruction programmes reflect concerns with efficiency and the achievement of concrete goals such as rebuilding the infrastructure of the country, privatizing state enterprises, or transitioning from a state-controlled to a market economy. However, this aid is seldom apolitical. Peacebuilding and post-conflict reconstruction are at heart very political processes.[8] Moreover, peace implementation is increasingly carried out by regional organizations or regional hegemons (NATO in Bosnia and Kosovo, India in Sri Lanka, Syria in Lebanon) which are not necessarily neutral *vis-à-vis* the protagonists. In Lebanon, for example, Syrian forces used military force to deal with initial opposition to the Ta'if Agreement. Syria later used heavy-handed tactics against all types of opposition, violent and non-violent, even when this came from insiders seeking to secure a voice in the process.[9] As argued elsewhere, "this sort of custodianship may heighten the insecurity of [insiders] who do not see the third party as a custodian" but rather see him as a hostile third party.[10] In such instances the custodians may be the source of the commitment problem experienced by some insiders. But custodians can also contribute to the problems of implementation without taking sides. As argued below, the peace implementation strategies that they adopt have a crucial bearing on the type of loyalty to the peace that develops among insiders.

Loyalty and conflict termination

How do you generate loyalty to a peace process? This is the ultimate challenge for custodians of peace concerned with the sustainability of peace agreements. While few analyses of conflict resolution focus on this issue, there is sufficient evidence to surmise that concerns with loyalty influence the custodians' choice of local partners in peace processes. For example, in his account of the Dayton Peace Agreement, American mediator Richard Holbrooke recalls that the decision to exclude the Bosnian Serbs from the process hinged, in part, on the perception that the Serbs were engaging in strategic deception.[11]

It stands to reason that parties to a conflict will only be invited to the negotiating table if they are perceived to be serious enough about finding a compromise solution. This does not necessarily suggest that these parties favour peace, but that, for whatever reason, they are unable to settle the conflict by force and decide to accept the military outcome as the basis for determining the political payoffs accruing to each.[12] If, however, custodians of peace make wrong choices, if the insiders they select end up spoiling the peace, then the consequences can be ominous. Indeed, many a study suggests that the most egregious violence against civilians, for example, follows the return to conflict after a failed peace. To probe the issue of insider loyalty to peace processes and the role of custodians in generating such loyalty, this chapter uses Albert Hirschman's concept of exit, voice, and loyalty.

According to Hirschman,[13] there is an inverse relationship between exit and voice conceived as two standard types of reactions to discontent within organizations. While exit, or the decision to change suppliers, is the typical economic rationale underlying competition between firms, voice is the quintessential political instrument.[14] Both voice and exit are indicators of an organization's performance. Too much voice can disrupt organizational routines and standard operating procedures; massive exit can lead to the disintegration of the organization.[15] In the constant pull and push between voice and exit, loyalty towards the organization may sway the choices of actors.[16]

Loyalty is the third and some would say most important construct in Hirschman's framework. It is an exogenous factor that operates to incite dissatisfied customers to exercise voice and exert pressures to reverse the decline in a given organization. However, loyalty is not a necessary prelude to voice.[17] A person might remain "loyal" to an organization for instrumental reasons (because of the material advantages that the organization provides – in other words, because exit would involve significant material losses) or because he or she perceives the barriers to exit as too great.[18] Though construed as loyalty in the original Hirschman framework, these types of attachment are different from commitment to the goals of the organization, and the differences are consequential enough to be probed further.

Organizational theorists identify three prime factors that enter into organizational commitment.[19] First is a strong belief in and acceptance of the organization's goals and values. This one can label *value-based loyalty*. This kind of loyalty is based on shared commitment. In the world of politics, it is best illustrated by the relationship that nationalism promotes between citizens and the state. Second is a willingness to exert considerable effort on behalf of the organization. This is *process-based loyalty*, where membership in the organization depends on access to the mechanisms of voice. Loyalty is thus a function of participation in the decision-making structures. Third is a strong desire to retain membership in the organization because of the benefits that accrue from this membership.

This *instrumental loyalty* is based on a give-and-take relationship between organization and members akin to the patron-client relations that characterize neopatrimonial societies.

If the first factor represents commitment, the second factor is voice, and the third is attachment, organizational theorists persuasively argue that attachment provides a necessary but not sufficient condition for the transformation of loyalty into commitment, with voice representing the organization's contribution to this transformation by making available the necessary channels and the incentives to use them.[20]

The author has argued elsewhere that the voice-exit framework is useful in thinking about internal conflicts (and by extension peace processes) because it nicely maps on to the greed-grievance debate that has occupied analysts of civil wars and post-conflict reconstruction in recent times. A basic version of the greed-grievance debate reads as follows. There are two types of actors in civil wars: some follow an economic rationale – war to them is a means to an economic end; others follow a political rationale – they fight to attain political objectives. Greedy actors are not interested in peace but in the pursuit of profit, and they stand to lose materially when peace prevails; therefore, they always choose spoiling. Actors with grievances want these grievances addressed and, on this basis, can be brought into peace agreements. In this pared-down version, greedy actors follow economic rationales and always favour exit over voice. Likewise, actors with grievances follow political rationales and therefore favour voice over exit. This highlights a paradox in the literature on spoilers: this literature conflates spoiling and violence, but the conflation is neither necessary nor sound. In fact, actors might use voice or participation in a peace process to pursue devious objectives and spoil the peace. They might use violence to indicate their interest in participating in peace processes.[21]

Three understandings of peace implementation

It is contended here that the notion of loyalty can help shed light on debates surrounding the meaning of peace implementation. In line with Stedman, it is asserted that implementation can mean three distinct things to different actors and observers: compliance, process, or peacebuilding.[22] Compliance emphasizes a legalistic fulfilment of obligations spelled out in the peace agreement; process underscores the commitment to a continuous negotiation of differences; and peacebuilding values the forging of meaningful long-term relationships between former enemies. Compliance is a necessary but not sufficient condition for the transformation of process into peacebuilding, with voice representing the new state's contribution to this transformation by making available channels for participation and incentives to use these channels.

Each of these understandings of peace implementation conceives of peace in a different manner. They also correspond to different strands in the literature on peacebuilding. Compliance is usually paired with a minimalist definition of peace as ending the fighting. Process, on the other hand, is synonymous with institution-building. Analysts who emphasize process have tended to focus on the creation of institutions that secure voice for all parties to the peace process, usually through some form of power-sharing.[23] Finally, peacebuilding tends to privilege a more "organic" approach to reconciliation. In line with the work of Lederach,[24] proponents of this approach highlight the need for a deeper kind of peace, one that reaches through to society.

Peace implementation as compliance: The limits of coaxing

At the minimum, peace agreements seek to elicit compliance. Indeed, more often than not such agreements represent pacts between unwilling partners forced to compromise by their inability to secure a decisive military victory.[25] Actors involved in these pacts negotiate terms that allow them to maximize gains in light of the conditions under which they are negotiating. In other words, peace negotiations occur at a time when both sides, for whatever reason, agree to accept the military outcome, be it symmetrical or asymmetrical, as the basis for determining the political payoffs accruing to each.[26] Peace agreements that elicit compliance are particularly vulnerable to insider spoiling, since attachment to the agreement is a function of expected gains from membership. When expected gains do not become a reality, or when gains from a return to conflict supersede the benefits derived from peace, insiders are likely to attempt to spoil the agreement.

A good illustration of this dynamic is provided by UNITA leader Jonas Savimbi's decision to spoil the Lusaka Accords because of his failure to secure election to the presidency of the Angolan republic.[27] Indeed, even though "Savimbi and UNITA received more from the Angolan settlement than any of the losing parties in El Salvador, Mozambique, Nicaragua, and Zimbabwe received in theirs",[28] Savimbi calculated that electoral results – for the presidency and for provincial governorships, of which UNITA was expected to win four out of 18 – were "too meager a prize to persuade [him] from trying his luck at winning power through war".[29]

Even where the military situation forces compromise, incentives are still required to bring the various factions to the negotiating table. For example, in the conflict in Bosnia and Herzegovina the Serb leadership, whose military power was seriously curtailed by a joint Bosnian-Croat offensive and two weeks of NATO bombings in August 1995, demanded (and secured) the recognition of Republika Srpska, the Serb entity within Bosnia and Herzegovina. Mediators acknowledge that such incentives are not enough to elicit commitment to peace. Problems of credible commitment plague peace implementation, as even actors interested in peace may not be able to trust their interlocutors to keep their promises and may therefore prefer to return to fighting. This is the logic behind the introduction of institutionalized channels for voice most often secured through some sort of power-sharing arrangement.

Peace implementation as process: The problem of exit

By providing institutionalized channels for voice, custodians of peace attempt to elicit a process-based loyalty to peace agreements. However, much depends here on the good functioning of the institutions. If these institutions are unresponsive or difficult to change, then they fail to perform their integrative role. While analysts disagree on the ability of power-sharing to secure long-lasting peacekeeping and a move towards democracy (in other words, the transformation through voice of process-based loyalty into a commitment to the polity or value-based loyalty), the hope is that at a minimum such power-sharing will prove conducive to a continuous negotiation of differences. Under such circumstances the likelihood of insider violence decreases drastically. Only when the power-sharing formula is tampered with, either by a state bent on excluding one of the political actors or by a custodian seeking to reinterpret fundamentally the bases of power-sharing, can we expect insiders to use violence in an attempt to voice their disagreement with the course of peace implementation.

The situation in post-war Lebanon provides a good illustration of the first as well as the second type of obstacle. The Ta'if Agreement sought to include all parties to the conflict in the post-war institutions of the state by formalizing power-sharing. However, peace implementation in Lebanon did not go according to plan. Instead of consensus-based decision-making, the mostly Muslim members of government disregarded strong opposition from Christians on crucial issues such as the content of the electoral law. As a result, Christian political parties and former militias boycotted the first post-war elections in 1992 and hence they were shut out of the institutional channels for expressing their concerns with the implementation of the peace agreement. This was made possible, in part, by the Syrian concerns for order in implementation of the peace process. Syria, the *de facto* custodian of peace in Lebanon, has repeatedly privileged stability over democracy, and consequently kept the lid on serious opposition to its particular interpretation of peace implementation.[30]

Peace implementation as peacebuilding

The third understanding of peace implementation differs sensibly in focus and time span. Peacebuilding is concerned with "the forging of meaningful long-term relationships between former enemies".[31] Focusing on the long term, this approach refuses to eschew the difficult issues of truth, reconciliation, justice, and accountability. Its proponents believe that only catharsis can overcome the horrors of civil war and pave the way for the creation of new identities and relationships. For them, peace implementation is a process rather than an outcome. The societal transformation required on the way to peacebuilding is "a multi-level phenomenon that is dependent on different levels of structural change, stability and equitable social delivery as well as the relationship that ordinary citizens have with structural changes".[32] Herein lies one of the starkest contrasts between this and other approaches to peace implementation. Peacebuilding is an organic approach that seeks to expand the scope of change beyond élite levels and down through the entire population.

There are few, if any, peace processes that fully approximate peacebuilding. While there might be some "peacebuilding" activities in many such processes (the Truth and Reconciliation Commission in South Africa, the *gaçaças* in Rwanda, or the Neve Shalom/Wahat al-Salam experiment between Israelis and Palestinians), their initiators are typically non-governmental organizations that work at the level of society rather than the state.

Insider loyalty in peace processes

There tends to be, in theory as well as in practice, an association between the different understandings of peace implementation sketched above and specific types of loyalty. Peacebuilding seeks to develop value-based loyalty, an attachment to ends such as societal reconciliation. Process engenders process-based loyalty, a loyalty contingent on securing voice in the institutions of the post-conflict state. Compliance is often associated with the least solid type of loyalty, instrumental loyalty.

The last two types of loyalty, instrumental and process-based, are particularly important to investigate in answering the question "when do insiders spoil a peace process?". As argued above, insiders have vested interests in peace processes. Whether those interests are merely material or are political, insiders considering the option of spoiling must assess not only the costs of their actions but also the benefits that accrue to them from a return to conflict. In this cost-benefit analysis, the type of loyalty bears on the insiders' choice of strategies.

Instrumental loyalty and insider violence

When insiders have joined the peace process lured by the gains made at the negotiating table, their loyalty to peace is likely to be instrumental. Such was, for example, the case of UNITA's commitment to the 1994 Lusaka Protocol, which hinged on Jonas Savimbi's perception that he had been promised the presidency of the Angolan republic. When elections failed to secure this outcome, Savimbi and UNITA spoiled the peace process. Another cogent example of instrumental loyalty is the case of RUF leader Foday Sankoh, who joined the peace process in Sierra Leone on the understanding that he would be granted control of the Ministry of Natural Resources, a ministry essential to allow the RUF to go on with its diamond trade in peace as it did in war.

Compliance as a peace implementation strategy tends to generate instrumental attachment to peace, a type of loyalty based on a cost-benefit analysis of gains and losses from staying in the process. When this assessment changes actors prefer to exit, as the costs of staying in become higher than the benefits from exiting the peace. Here, the context of the transition and the commitment of outside custodians can raise barriers to exit. As argued elsewhere, different conflict environments are more or less conducive to exit. Paramount in this respect are those regional factors that affect not only the success or failure of demobilization but also the access of potential spoilers to tradable commodities and financial resources to rekindle the conflict.[33] Where the conflict environment is not conducive to such spoiling tactics and where custodians of peace are willing to follow up on their commitments to deter potential spoilers, peace will have a chance to take root.[34] On their own, however, the cost-benefit considerations that influence actors' choices and strategies cannot generate unswerving loyalty to the process. Insiders who display instrumental loyalty to the process will use violence when an opportunity arises. This constitutes spoiling, because the use of violence is intended to benefit the insiders by ruining the peace. Peace processes based on compliance dynamics are therefore likely to be the most fragile and the most vulnerable to devious objectives.

Process-based loyalty and insider violence

When insiders to the peace process have joined negotiations because of institutional arrangements that guarantee they will not be excluded from politics in the post-conflict polity, their loyalty is likely to be process-based. As was convincingly argued by Timothy Sisk:

from South Africa to Sri Lanka, from Bosnia to Burundi, from Cambodia to Congo, it is difficult to envisage a post-war political settlement that does not, or would need to, include guarantees to all the major antagonists that they will be assured some permanent representation, decision-making power and often autonomous territory in the post-war peace. Indeed, the gist of international mediation in such conflicts is to encourage parties to adopt power-sharing in exchange for waging war.[35]

Power-sharing has been advocated as a means of defusing group insecurity and obtaining the parties' commitment to peace.[36] It is said to encourage factions to commit credibly to a peace settlement by providing guarantees against exclusion.[37] Arguments in favour of power-sharing focus on the security dilemma inherent in negotiations; once this is overcome, the theory expects parties to the peace process to be reassured about their fate in a post-conflict setting and to exhibit commitment to the peace process.

But is this assumption well-founded? The preferred outcome of war élites[38] is to win and impose their own terms on any given settlement. This preference is illustrated by the fact that 85 per cent of civil wars end in the military victory of one side over the other. In the remaining 15 per cent of cases it has been suggested that warring factions come to the negotiating table upon recognition of their inability to achieve a decisive military victory. Peace settlements are thus default options, and many a warring party has attempted to spoil a negotiated peace once its military power was replenished.

In the early stages of a peace agreement the risks that the parties may not abide by the negotiated deal are particularly high. As mentioned earlier, leaders may not be serious about their interest in peace. They may use peace negotiations as a subterfuge to restock their military arsenals. Leaders may also seek a whole range of benefits from the cessation of hostilities. However, peace dividends usually require a certain length of time to become tangible. If the expected dividends from peace do not come through, leaders may calculate that the payoffs from war, especially payoffs tied to the war economy, are higher.[39] In such a situation they may be less reluctant to use violence in order to spoil the peace process.

Parties to power-sharing settlements have also sought to manipulate the terms of power-sharing to the advantage of the faction they represent. A long tradition of instrumental approaches to ethnic conflict has established that political élites can play important roles in mobilizing masses and triggering conflict.[40] A stark illustration of this dynamic would be the issue of refugee returns to Republika Srpska. Consecutive RS governments have invoked lack of control at the ground level and fear of incidents involving refugees returning to their homes in Republika Srpska to account for their delay in complying with the provisions of Annex 7 of the Dayton Peace Agreement (DPA) concerning the issue of refugee returns. Meanwhile, the Bosnian Serb élites have also attempted to curry favour with the electorate by pointing to their position on refugee returns as proof of their commitment faithfully to represent Bosnian Serb voters. In such instances the insiders seek to derail the process even though the method used is non-violent. Though non-violent, this is clearly a devious objective and deserves the label "spoiling".

Lastly, insiders might object either peacefully or violently to attempts by other insiders or by the custodians of peace at modifying the power-sharing agreement. This raises the thorny issue of the transformation of power-sharing into other forms of government. Analysts and practitioners currently conceive of power-sharing as a necessary transitional security guarantee for parties to enter into an agreement with former enemies. However, the question is still open as to the conditions under which the rigid structures of power-sharing can "wither over time to the point where the guarantees for group security they contain are no longer necessary".[41] While this transition seems to have occurred smoothly in South Africa,[42] attempts to modify the institutional structure in Bosnia and Herzegovina have met with varying degrees of resistance on all sides,[43] and they have outright failed in places such as Lebanon.[44]

How do we understand the use of violence by insiders attempting to object to the modification of institutional structures set up in the peace accords? Much depends on the manner in which such modifications are introduced. Much also depends on the environment in which these modifications are proposed. The case of the electoral law in Lebanon is highly illustrative of both aspects of this question. The Ta'if Agreement, which brought Lebanon's civil war to an end, required that a new electoral law have the support of two-thirds of Lebanon's cabinet members, thus effectively allowing a dissenting minority to exercise a veto right. Yet the electoral law was adopted at a session where the Christian opposition representatives were absent and in total disregard of their opposition to its content. Moreover, elections were held in spite of a provision in the Ta'if Agreement to the effect that Syria should withdraw its 35,000 armed forces from Lebanon prior to the first post-war electoral exercise. For the Lebanese Christian opposition, no free and fair elections could be held under the umbrella of such a large foreign presence in the country. A majority of Christian voters thus boycotted the first post-conflict elections in 1992, withdrawing legitimacy from Christian parliamentarians who participated in the electoral exercise. Christian political forces were left with little to no access to the formal structures of power because of this boycott.[45] While the Christian opposition elected not to use violence to object to this modification to the terms of the Ta'if Agreement, would it have stood to reason to call violence, had it occurred, spoiling? Neither the manner in which modifications were introduced nor the environment in which elections were held could have been characterized as respectful of the terms of the peace process. Should the use of violence to steer the course of implementation back in the "right" direction and to secure voice for insiders fearing marginalization be construed as spoiling? It is argued here that it should not, thus making an analytical distinction between methods and ends.

In summary, distinguishing different types of loyalty to the peace process allows the analyst to provide a more nuanced discussion of the question of insider violence. As argued above, the use of violence is but a method; it is the ends to which this method is used that matter in determining who is a spoiler and who is not. When violence is used to right a wrong one may ask whether there were other avenues, but one may not automatically blame the party that is wronged for reacting to the course of events.

The role and responsibilities of custodians

How does this relate to the role of custodians in moving peace implementation along? While all three meanings of implementation can definitely coexist in a given post-agreement environment, only the first two correspond to actual strategies adopted by custodians in the framework of peace implementation.[46] If, as argued above, every choice of strategy corresponds to privileging a specific loyalty type, and if different types of loyalty affect the conditions under which insiders would consider the use of violence, the custodians' choices in this matter bear consequences for the sustainability of peace.

The politics of peace implementation

Peace implementation is a costly process that is not financed off the regular budget of the United Nations. To raise funds for peace implementation missions, international organizations, regional organizations, and concerned third parties have increasingly relied on pledges of aid. "During the 1990s, the international donor community pledged more than $100 billion in aid to three dozen countries recovering from violent conflict."[47] Such large amounts raise the issue of mobilizing and maintaining assistance[48] at a time when many (primarily Western) donors are facing economic crisis at home and renegotiating the social contract with their citizens with a view to retrenching the "welfare state".

Custodians of peace must also justify putting nationals in harm's way. The issue of "body bags" and the trauma of Viet Nam and Somalia have been widely discussed in connection with the deployment of US soldiers on peace implementation missions. Less discussed but increasingly important is the security of civilian staff of such missions. While not a post-civil-war context, the current situation in Iraq and the repeated kidnappings and murders of foreign nationals highlight the difficulty for governments to justify getting involved in messy situations.

Two consequences deriving from such pressures deserve to be underlined. First is the insistence on "exit strategies", or the definition of benchmarks for success that will allow the civilian and military components of a peace implementation mission to pack up and leave. Second is the growing talk among analysts and policy-makers about the need for resolve in the face of "spoilers" and the increasing militarization of peace implementation, a trend dating back to NATO's interventions in the Balkans and one which finds increasingly positive echoes in the post-11 September world.

The pressures of "early exit": Privileging compliance and process over peacebuilding

While there are good reasons for the insistence on exit strategies (if only domestic pressure on decision-makers and the need to deal with simultaneous crises around the world), it is also important to investigate the impact of such considerations on the peace implementation strategies and tactics favoured by the custodians of peace. The constraints facing custodians of peace lead them to privilege compliance and process over peacebuilding.

Compliance and process are short- to medium-term peace implementation strategies that define clear goals. Compliance focuses on the implementation of the letter of a peace agreement; process seeks to establish specific institutions and ensure their good functioning. They provide custodians with definable benchmarks and the possibility of defining an end-state. It is no wonder, then, that many analysts and policy-makers have sought to focus on the first post-war election as such a benchmark.[49] The holding of national elections to establish a legitimate and functioning government can be read as proof of compliance with the peace process. It can alternatively be read as the re-establishment of a democratic process of negotiating differences. But elections hold the potential of destabilization if one or more insiders (also outsiders, but the latter are left out of this analysis) have been brought into the process with the promise of an electoral gain that does not materialize (Angola is a case in point) or if the process is not considered "fair and free" (Lebanon and Bosnia and Herzegovina provide cogent illustrations).

As discussed earlier in this chapter, power-sharing arrangements can provide a way around the instability of electoral outcomes. This explains the favour that such arrangements curry with the international community. However, the decision to rely solely on power-sharing arrangements can seriously limit the transformability of peace implementation as process into peacebuilding. Despite expectations to the contrary, power-sharing often tends to institutionalize "peace" rather than "conflict".[50] In other terms, power-sharing arrangements are seen not as a means of teaching groups to live together and negotiate the issues over which they disagree; rather, they are privileged as a means of stopping violence by outsiders who are not willing to commit to stay the course. The hope is that the power-sharing formula will stabilize the conflict zone and that, in time, peace will prevail. However, the problem with power-sharing is that it tends to create vested interests that can only be modified by consensus. If one of the actors refuses to budge, and since power-sharing formulae often give the actors a veto power, there is no peaceful way to resolve differences and the entire process can be at risk. The custodians' focus on stability in the short term thus privileges the choice of stabilizing strategies bent to increase instability, and is unlikely to generate loyalty to peace in the long term.

The pressures of "early exit": The dangers of coercive implementation

Whether custodians favour compliance or process, they have a choice as to methods by which to reach their objectives. This choice bears consequences for the sustainability of peace processes and for the nature of insider loyalty.

Faced with parties that do not trust one another or do not really display much interest in cooperation, custodians of peace must decide on a course of action. Do they let parties simply walk out and risk, in the process, the unravelling of peace? Do they provide further material incentives to insiders in order to achieve progress? Do they, finally, resort to force or the threat of force to see to it that peace implementation proceeds apace?

These are not easy questions and the answers are not straightforward, as demonstrated by impasses such as the demobilization crisis that beset the Northern Ireland peace process. It is highly unlikely for custodians to let peace unravel, particularly where they have already invested human and financial resources. The dangers of early exit have been highlighted by none other than former US mediator in Bosnia and Herzegovina, Ambassador Richard Holbrooke:

> we must be very careful when we talk about exit strategies not to confuse them with exit deadlines. We agree that it is highly preferable that peacekeeping operations have an end-state and not be absolutely open-ended. But an exit strategy must be directed towards a defining, overall objective – not an arbitrary, self-imposed, artificial deadline. Artificial deadlines encourage belligerents to outwait the outside intervention, delay and wait until the international community goes away, at which point they can resume doing what they had been doing before. Artificial deadlines give hope to warlords, criminals, and corrupt officials that they can outlast the international community.[51]

Custodians are also aware of the potential for blackmail should they give in to the temptation to reward insiders for every act of cooperation. Concessions to blackmail can only exacerbate problems. This was one lesson of UNPROFOR's experience in Bosnia and Herzegovina, where the UN Protection Force was blamed for giving in to Serb blackmail and therefore losing credibility. This and other situations have brought to the fore a debate on the need to show resolve.

The current tendency among policy-makers to showcase the need for resolve plays itself out in the debates on armed humanitarianism[52] and political conditionality. While military and political resolve can be credited for progress in peace implementation in places such as Bosnia, this raises the thorny issue of ownership of the process. To quote Darby and Mac Ginty, "Some peace processes are largely creatures of the international community. They reflect the desired outcome of key states in the international community rather than the wishes of local communities."[53] The Bosnian peace process is a case in point, as illustrated by the role of the Office of the High Representative in taking decisions for Bosnians in order to avoid paralysis. Observers suggest that, almost 10 years after the Dayton Peace Agreement, the loyalty of all Bosnians to a united Bosnia and Herzegovina is still open to question.

Conclusion

While this chapter does not claim to offer easy answers, it argues that, in the last analysis, the sustainability of peace depends on the loyalty of insiders. It distinguishes between three types of loyalty that create different kinds of barriers to spoiling. While insiders who have joined the peace process lured by material benefits are highly likely to resort to violence if these benefits do not materialize, parties that have gained representation in the political system are less likely to forgo such gains. These same parties, however, might resort to violence to express dissatisfaction with the course of peace implementation.

This has led to an investigation of the role of custodians in creating conditions favourable to sustainability. It is argued that custodians can understand peace implementation in one of three ways: compliance, process, or peacebuilding. In practice, however, only the first two meanings of peace implementation find echoes in the politics of intervening third parties. This the author believes to be detrimental to stability because of the relatively short time span of such strategies. Further, the custodians' obsession with exit strategies compounds the problem, because it often translates into a willingness to use "force" when faced with bottlenecks. However, such methods are unlikely to forge meaningful long-term relationships between former adversaries and create a strong belief amongst them in the goals and values of conflict resolution. Whether outsiders can generate the kind of conflict transformation envisaged by the proponents of peacebuilding seems unlikely at the present time.

Notes

1. Whether such actors are nearing military exhaustion, or whether they are political moderates, or simply whether they can be offered incentives to agree to a negotiated solution to the conflict.
2. Stedman, Stephen J. 2003. "Peace processes and the challenges of violence", in John Darby and Roger Mac Ginty (eds) *Contemporary Peacemaking: Conflict, Violence and Peace Processes*. Basingstoke: Palgrave Macmillan, p. 107.
3. Zahar, Marie-Joëlle. 2005. "Political violence in peace processes: Voice, exit and loyalty in the post-accord period", in John Darby (ed.) *Violence and Reconstruction*. Southbend: Notre Dame University Press.
4. See *ibid.*; Zahar, Marie-Joëlle. 2003. "Reframing the spoiler debate in peace processes", in John Darby and Roger Mac Ginty (eds) *Contemporary Peacemaking: Conflict, Violence and Peace Processes*. Basingstoke: Palgrave Macmillan, pp. 118–121.
5. See Horowitz, Donald. 1985. *Ethnic Groups in Conflict*. Berkeley, CA: University of California Press; Stedman, note 2 above.
6. Walter, Barbara. 1997. "The critical barrier to civil war settlement", *International Organization*, Vol. 51, No. 3; Fearon, James. 1998. "Commitment problems and the spread of ethnic conflicts", in David Lake and Donald Rothchild (eds) *The International Spread of Ethnic Conflict: Fear, Diffusion, and Escalation*. Princeton: Princeton University Press.
7. Stedman, Stephen J. 1997. "Spoiler problems in peace processes", *International Security*, Vol. 22, No. 2; Walter, *ibid.*
8. Brynen, Rex. 2000. *A Very Political Economy: Peacebuilding and Foreign Aid in the West Bank and Gaza*. Washington, DC: US Institute of Peace Press.
9. Zahar, Marie-Joëlle. 2002. "Peace by unconventional means: Lebanon's Ta'if Agreement", in Stephen Stedman, Donald Rothchild, and Elizabeth Cousens (eds) *Ending Civil Wars: The Implementation of Peace Agreements*. Boulder, CO: Lynne Rienner.

10. Zahar, note 4 above, pp. 116–117.
11. Holbrooke, Richard. 1999. *To End a War*. New York: Knopf.
12. Kecskemeti, Paul. 1970. "Political rationality in ending war", in William T. R. Fox (ed.) *How Wars End*. Philadelphia, PA: Annals of the American Academy of Political and Social Science.
13. Hirschman, Albert O. 1970. *Exit, Voice, and Loyalty: Responses to Decline in Firms, Organizations, and States*. Cambridge, MA: Harvard University Press.
14. Hirschman, Albert O. 1978. "Exit, voice, and the state", *World Politics*, Vol. 31, No. 1.
15. That is every organization but the state. Indeed, while exit was and remains common in stateless societies, the consolidation of states has been accompanied by a growing restriction of the conditions for lawful secession. See Hirschman, Albert O. 1974. "'Exit, voice, and loyalty': Further reflections and a survey of recent contributions", *Social Sciences Information*, Vol. 13, No. 1.
16. The loyalty concept is the most under-researched aspect of the voice-exit-loyalty model. Some perceive loyalty as an attitude that moderates exit and voice; others interpret it as a distinct behavioural response to dissatisfaction, on a par with exit and voice.
17. Barry, Brian. 1991. *Democracy and Power: Essays in Political Theory, I*. Oxford: Clarendon Press.
18. Cannings, Kathleen. 1992. "The voice of the loyal manager: Distinguishing attachment from commitment", *Employee Responsibilities and Rights Journal*, Vol. 5, No. 3.
19. Mowday, R. T., R. M. Porter, and L. W. Steers. 1979. "The measurement of organizational commitment", *Journal of Vocational Behavior*, Vol. 14, No. 2; see also Mowday, R. T., R. M. Porter, and L. W. Steers. 1982. *Employee-Organization Linkages*. New York: Academic Press.
20. Cannings, note 18 above.
21. Zahar, note 3 above.
22. Stedman, note 2 above.
23. Lijphart, Arend. 1969. "Consociational democracy", *World Politics*, Vol. 21, No. 2; Lijphart, Arend. 1977. *Democracy in Plural Societies*. New Haven: Yale University Press; Lijphart, Arend. 1991. "The power-sharing approach", in Joseph V. Montville (ed.) *Conflict and Peacemaking in Multiethnic Societies*. New York: Lexington Books.
24. Lederach, John Paul. 1997. *Building Peace: Sustainable Reconciliation in Divided Societies*. Washington, DC: US Institute of Peace Press.
25. Peace settlements are in essence élite pacts established as a transitional strategy towards democratic regimes or outcomes. See Sisk, Timothy D. 1996. *Power Sharing and International Mediation in Ethnic Conflict*. Washington, DC: US Institute of Peace Press; Hartzell, Caroline and Donald Rothchild. 1997. "Political pacts as negotiated agreements: Comparing ethnic and non-ethnic cases", *International Negotiation*, Vol. 2; Wood, Elisabeth Jean. 1999. "Civil war settlement: Modeling the bases of compromise", paper presented to the Annual Meeting of the American Political Science Association, Atlanta, 2–5 September.
26. Kecskemeti, note 12 above.
27. Lyons, Terrence. 2002. "The role of postsettlement elections", in Stephen Stedman, Donald Rothchild, and Elizabeth Cousens (eds) *Ending Civil Wars: The Implementation of Peace Agreements*. Boulder, CO: Lynne Rienner.
28. Stedman, Stephen J. 1996. "Negotiation and mediation in internal conflict", in Michael Brown (ed.) *The International Dimensions of Internal Conflict*. Cambridge, MA: MIT Press, p. 370.
29. Ohlson, Thomas and Stephen J. Stedman. 1994. *The New is Not Yet Born: Conflict Resolution in Southern Africa*. Washington, DC: Brookings Institution, p. 193.

30. Zahar, note 9 above; Zahar, Marie-Joëlle. 2005. "The dichotomy of international mediation and leader intransigence: The case of Bosnia and Herzegovina", in Ian O'Flynn and David Russell (eds) *Power Sharing: New Challenges for Divided Societies*. London: Pluto Press.
31. Stedman, note 2 above.
32. Hamber, Brandon. 2003. "Transformation and reconciliation", in John Darby and Roger Mac Ginty (eds) *Contemporary Peacemaking: Conflict, Violence and Peace Processes*. Basingstoke: Palgrave Macmillan.
33. Pugh, Michael, Neil Cooper, and Jonathan Goodhand. 2003. *War Economies in Regional Context: The Challenges of Transformation*. Boulder, CO: Lynne Rienner.
34. Zahar, note 3 above; Zahar, note 4 above.
35. Sisk, Timothy. 2003. "Power-sharing after civil wars: Matching problems to solutions", in John Darby and Roger Mac Ginty (eds) *Contemporary Peacemaking: Conflict, Violence and Peace Processes*. Basingstoke: Palgrave Macmillan.
36. Consociationalism and its variants are the most widely accepted and promoted power-sharing formulae. Consociational power-sharing rests on four principles: a grand coalition or power-sharing executive, segmental autonomy involving territorial or non-territorial forms of self-government, proportionality as a principle of political representation, and minority veto.
37. Lijphart, Arend and Carlos Waisman (eds). 1996. *Institutional Design in New Democracies: Eastern Europe and Latin America*. Boulder, CO: Westview.
38. As the conflict develops, positions harden; the warring factions increasingly view the situation in zero-sum terms and leaders who attempt to extend bridges and promote compromise are cast as traitors. At the end of a civil war old élites with prior experience of accommodation are typically sidelined to the advantage of new war élites consisting primarily of successful military commanders or charismatic politicians with unyielding positions on the issues at stake.
39. Berdal, Mats and David Malone. 2000. *Greed and Grievance: Economic Agendas in Civil Wars*. Boulder, CO: Lynne Rienner.
40. Bates, Robert. 1974. "Ethnic competition and modernization in contemporary Africa", *Comparative Political Studies*, Vol. 7; Bates, Robert. 1982. "Modernization, ethnic competition, and the rationality of politics in Africa", in D. Rothchild and V. Orlorunsula (eds) *Ethnic Conflict in Africa*. Boulder, CO: Westview; Riker, William. 1993. *Agenda Formation*. Ann Arbor: University of Michigan Press; see also Horowitz, note 5 above.
41. Sisk, note 35 above.
42. Sisk, Timothy and Christoph Stefes. 2005. "Power sharing as an interim step in peace building: Lessons from South Africa", in Philip G. Roeder and Donald Rothchild (eds) *Sustainable Peace: Power and Democracy after Civil Wars*. Ithaca, NY: Cornell University Press.
43. Zahar, note 30 above.
44. Zahar, Marie-Joëlle. 2005. "Power sharing in Lebanon: Foreign protectors, domestic peace and democratic failure", in Philip G. Roeder and Donald Rothchild (eds) *Sustainable Peace: Power and Democracy after Civil Wars*. Ithaca, NY: Cornell University Press.
45. Bahout, Joseph. 1993. "Liban: Les élections législatives de l'été 1992", *Monde arabe Maghreb Machrek*, Vol. 139, January–March; Krayem, Hassan. 1998. "The Lebanese civil war and the Ta'if Agreement", in Paul Salem (ed.) *Conflict Resolution in the Arab World*. Beirut: American University of Beirut Press.
46. Because forging long-term meaningful relationships is a long-term objective rather than a short-term strategy, this is left out of the discussion.
47. Forman, Shepard and Stewart Patrick. 2000. "Introduction", in Shepard Forman and

Stewart Patrick (eds) *Good Intentions: Pledges of Aid for Postconflict Recovery*. Boulder, CO: Lynne Rienner, p. 1; see also Brynen, note 8 above.
48. Brynen, *ibid*.
49. Kumar, Krishna (ed.). 1998. *Postconflict Elections, Democratization and International Assistance*. Boulder, CO: Lynne Rienner.
50. Chinchilla, Fernando. 2003. "Preventing new waves of violence: Assessing international intervention in Angola and Mozambique", PhD dissertation, Université de Montréal.
51. Holbrooke, Richard C. 2000. Ambassador Richard C. Holbrooke, US Permanent Representative to the United Nations, Statement in the Security Council on "Exit Strategies in Peacekeeping Operations", 15 November, available at www.un.int/usa/00_173.htm.
52. O'Hanlon, Michael. 1997. *Saving Lives with Force: Military Criteria for Humanitarian Intervention*. Washington, DC: Brookings Institution Press.
53. Darby, John and Roger Mac Ginty. 2003. "What peace, what process?", in John Darby and Roger Mac Ginty (eds) *Contemporary Peacemaking: Conflict, Violence and Peace Processes*. Basingstoke: Palgrave Macmillan, p. 4.

3

The linkage between devious objectives and spoiling behaviour in peace processes

Oliver Richmond

The starting point for this chapter is the proposition that compromise solutions to conflicts and wars are not necessarily viewed by disputants as the optimum rational outcome of a peace process. Consequently, spoiling behaviour – activities designed to undermine any existing negotiating process, and possibly to prevent any future accommodation by any party – towards a peace process represents a form of rejection of some aspect of that process by some groups within it and their constituencies.[1] Paradoxically, disputants often realize that a peace process is still valuable to them, even if they do not agree with the sort of compromise agreement being suggested by third parties. Disputants therefore hold "devious objectives" not necessarily related to a liberal peace compromise, which is assumed to be the most desirable outcome of a peace process.[2] They may continue their participation even if only to reject any proposals. Yet peace processes, and most academic and policy analysis of them, rest on the assumption that any outcome will conform with the liberal peace model, which embraces democratization, self-determination, some form of social justice, a territorial settlement, human rights and the rule of law, and a market democracy in a globalized setting. Spoiling behaviour and devious objectives indicate that disputants may not have accepted aspects of this as the basis for their desired solution. Devious objectives on the part of disputants may indicate that they value a peace process for certain resources it may provide, but do not envisage the sort of outcome the international community or third parties desire. This may herald the emergence of spoiling behaviour. This may partially explain why some peace processes become extended, as in the cases of Cyprus (from 1964 until the present), Sri Lanka (from 2000 until the present), and the Middle East (from the early 1990s), or falter, as in the case of the Rambouillet Accords and the more recent efforts over Kosovo (starting in 1999). Indeed, extended peace processes actually appear to be the norm. If devious objectives can be identified early on, it is possible that such a progression can be better understood, addressed, and perhaps prevented.

The standard set of assumptions brought to a peace process by third parties are predicated upon the belief that some form of balancing and trade-off will occur between disputants as a result of the process. This should be underpinned by a mutual acceptance by the main actors of the liberal peace model.[3] Yet many of the case studies in this volume suggest that this may not be the case. From Cyprus to Sri Lanka, Bosnia, Kosovo, and the Middle East, disputants have sought to reproduce their own version of a peace settlement, which often incorporates ethno-nationalist or nationalist dynamics, while receiving as much control of the state and territory as they can through the peace process itself. This indicates that for some actors pre-negotiation objectives are only very reluctantly given up, and the peace process can become a continuation of the conflict by other means.

It is the contention of this chapter that adopting an "outside-in" view of a peace process clarifies this tendency. Furthermore, understanding such devious objectives may provide a prescriptive capacity towards the prevention of spoiling behaviour. Until fairly recently the view of the disputants in a peacemaking process had received little attention, unless in the context of official negotiating positions. The emergence of the literature on spoiling and the work of others on obstacles to peacemaking have attempted to explore this gap.[4] Most of this literature, and the peacemaking literature in general, implicitly accepts that the liberal peace is the standard by which peacemaking processes, settlements, and the roles and actions of disputants, internationals, and custodians can and should be measured. The liberal peace model provides a normative basis for making peace, though this is not unproblematic from the disputants' perspective and may partly explain spoiling behaviour. Consequently, it is important to develop our understanding of how disputants view, value, and think strategically about a peace process, the role of third parties, and the interrelationship of the peace process with their own range of objectives, spanning their pre-negotiation objectives to their considered notion of a future peace agreement. This chapter develops this line of thought by examining the disputants' views of peacemaking, and the subsequent implications of devious objectives, as an aid to pinpointing actors who are blocking a solution, or to identify spoiling behaviour. This capacity is important for custodians of peace processes if they are to defend the liberal peace, prevent spoiling behaviour, and make sure that disputants comprehend the responsibilities they are placed under in such a process.

Devious objectives and peace processes

Traditional approaches to peace processes have tended towards an omniscient, neutral, impartial, external perspective of a specific conflict, and have tended to assume that a *compromise* solution is the objective of all parties concerned.[5] They assume that upon the introduction of a peace process and a third party into a conflict through some form of peacemaking the negotiating positions of the disputants are immediately modified. No longer are they aiming for victory on the battlefield or through various other forms of violence, but for a compromise around a negotiating table. The latter is generally argued to represent a significant break with past practice and thinking during conflict, and a change in attitudes. The parties are, as result of a hurting stalemate or a crisis, persuaded that a peace process with the objective of a compromise must be pursued, and are thus committed to flexibility with respect to making concessions. To achieve this a third party has three alternative approaches: to facilitate communication; to provide alternatives for resolution; or to use more or less coercive tactics aimed at gaining concessions.[6] Such orthodox thinking assumes peacemaking is a mediated and coercive bargaining process fitting into a power-political framework and assuming rationality.[7] The power-political framework assumes that the disputants have made a simple choice between violent conflict and compromise, the disputants choosing the latter as victory is perceived to be out of their grasp. Yet this is where traditional analyses break down.

As many of the chapters of this study attest, the establishment of a peace process does not necessarily mean the end of violence, nor that disputants have fully accepted a mediated compromise around a negotiating table. Instead, they may intend either to win a victory around the negotiating table by tactics designed to force further concessions from the opposition, or to disrupt negotiations completely and bring them to an end. Peace processes become marred by endless rounds of inconclusive talks and sporadic outbreaks of violence, and become hostage to the internal political processes (including elections and changes of leadership and of negotiating teams) of the disputants. Peace processes can span the entire careers of diplomats, UN officials, and state representatives, as has now been the case from Sri Lanka to Cyprus and Northern Ireland. The intent to use disruptive strategies indicates the existence of devious objectives, and represents spoiling behaviour on the part of actors who may be normatively judged to be "spoilers" in the context of the broader expectation of an imminent liberal peace brought about through the peace process. In other words, compromise and non-violence are not necessarily implicit aspects of peacemaking when viewed from the internal perspective of disputants, internal factions, and constituencies. Thus, in order to understand the lack of progress and the lack of success in implementation of peace agreements, it is important to disaggregate the different components within each party, and to have a clear idea of their interaction or lack thereof. The same also holds true for third-party custodians of a peace process. Thus, in the context of the Cyprus case, both Greek and Turkish Cypriot communities have used the peace process to advance their own zero-sum objectives rather than to accept the compromises suggested by the UN special representative. Fully aware of this, the United Nations has continued the process, even if this means merely "going through the motions".[8] In Sri Lanka, the use of a "facilitator" rather than a mediator signalled both the LTTE's and the government's intentions not to be faced with external suggestions they might have to refuse or accept.[9]

Such an inside-out perspective indicates that disputants may indeed be guided by objectives unrelated to finding a compromise solution. At the same time disputants may be aware of the need to be seen to be cooperating with the third party. Through such a perspective it becomes clear that disputants are unlikely to shift from violent conflict aimed at victory to a discussion aimed at achieving a compromise if they perceive an alternative approach which involves minimal costs and concessions on their part, but allows the struggle to be continued at a low level. From this point of view, the disputants may value the assets and resources a peace process brings to a conflict more than a compromise solution. In this way, the peace process itself, and the role of any third parties, become a new battleground where disputants do their utmost to retain the associated resources such as legitimacy, credibility, alliances, recognition, and time to regroup. They engage in a process of acceptance and then rejection, in which they attempt to manipulate the process in their own favour without losing the resources it brings to them, but also without having to make the concessions the process is predicated upon.

This indicates that an understanding of both perception and misperception forms one analytic avenue through which devious objectives and spoiling behaviour can be understood. Factors that shape and distort perception, such as stereotyping, selective perception (where the receiver singles out information that supports a prior belief), projection (in which an individual projects his or her own beliefs on to others), and perceptual defence (which results in the screening out of threatening information) caused by the perceiver's own needs, motivations, and personal experiences, are significant.[10] It is partly through such factors that a peace process may come to be viewed by disputants as a tool for devious objectives, in the same way that third parties may see their role as an opportunity to construct a version of the liberal peace where it had not existed before. Devious objectives may be defined as any involvement in a mediation or peacemaking process on the part of a disputant that is not committed to a compromise.

A second avenue for understanding the basic stimulus for devious objectives may arise from the problem of the relative symmetry or asymmetry of disputants' and peacemakers' status, representation, and resources. If it is indeed incorrect to assume that decision-makers tend to perceive the world accurately, as Robert Jervis argues,[11] and that there are "multiple realities", then it must be asked how likely it is that two parties locked in a dispute will commit to a peace process and turn to a third party when this may involve costly compromises. This is highlighted by the fact that all conflict is basically asymmetric. Yet analyses of peacemaking generally assume a relative symmetry between the disputants, giving rise to the dictum that a peace process is most likely to succeed in a situation of a hurting stalemate. This is a gross simplification, as no two parties or sets of resources are alike; defining them and their relative proportions is difficult, as conflict is a result of initial and continuing *asymmetries* within the multiple aspects of the disputants' relationship. If we assume that conflict and disputants' positions are always asymmetric, both practically and perceptually, this reinforces the proposition that disputants will tend to view a peace process as zero-sum and an extension of the disputants' efforts to "win", or at least to avoid defeat.[12] In a conflict with identity components, this scenario becomes all the more complex because of the fact that one party may represent an internationally recognized entity, and therefore control all of the machinery of a state, while the other is viewed as rebel, secessionist, or insurgent. This may be further complicated by the tendency of the two sides to find allies in neighbouring states, often dependent on ethnicity. Such obvious and hidden asymmetries are indicative of the reasons why peace processes actually become discursive frameworks through which disputants mediate their own pre-negotiation objectives with their imagined peace, and therefore attempt to negate their antagonist's claims, and even those of the third party.[13] In this way a peace process consists of a set of multiple negotiations, between disputants, interveners, custodians, and their interpretations of the past, present, and future environments, being both practical, symbolic, and existential. In such a complex environment it is not surprising that devious objectives emerge, being rather more subtle than the traditional power-political or liberal peace framework.[14] The following section extends this analysis by examining some of the key areas in the relationship between disputants, third parties, and the peace process. Taking the liberal peace as the assumed objective of a peace process, and any behaviour, non-violent or violent, which deviates from this framework as indicative of devious objects and the potential for spoiling behaviour, this approach provides significant insight into the conditions necessary for the development and identification of devious objects and spoiling behaviour.

Devious objectives and the third party

In order to develop this understanding of devious objectives, and to be able to identify their existence as a first step towards the identification of spoiling behaviour, problems related to asymmetry and perceptions of disputants must be examined in the context of how they perceive the peace process and the role of the mediator. It may be the case that the mediator and the adversaries hold conflicting views and expectations about the objectives of a peace process. Thus, what follows assumes that there may indeed be a relationship between the above elements and the potential success of the process of mediation, and therefore that the disputants' perceptions of these elements must also be significant, as are their beliefs about the world and images of other actors. Therefore, as a disputant's estimations of others' goals and beliefs influence decision-making, it is essential that they are accurate. Yet accuracy is difficult to assess, and may be coloured by preconceptions that influence decision-making or misperceptions.[15]

It is necessary to ascertain as a starting point what the pre-negotiation objectives of disputants and third parties are. Generally speaking the former will denote some kind of clear-cut victory while the latter will be framed by the general conditions of the liberal peace. It is then necessary to ascertain what the mediator's role and objective are perceived as being. If the mediator is perceived as aiming for a compromise resolution of the conflict, should it be regarded as a facilitator, a manager,[16] an ally, or an agent of empowerment or legitimation? Similarly, another important starting point will be to examine whether the mediator is perceived as being directive or facilitative, judgemental or non-impartial, and whether these perceptions have been altered at any point in the process (and by what) and if this has had a direct or indirect effect on the process of negotiation. Both sets of views are continuous and may undergo change, and both are relevant to their assessment of the mediator's past record, objectives, bias, and ability to find a solution. It may well be that the very presence of a third party is enough for some or all disputants to begin to harbour devious objectives, and therefore that the exis-

tence of a peace process is simply sufficient condition for sp(
iour to emerge on the part of certain actors or subgroups. 1
an insight into the commitment of the disputants to the peac(
its end goal of conflict settlement, and might explain why peace processes often become extended or remain unimplemented, as with aspects of the processes in Cyprus, the Middle East, and Northern Ireland.

It must also be asked how the conflict environment shapes the decision of the disputants as to the role they expect the mediator to play, and whether this role is aimed at achieving the greatest practical gain for the adversaries or a compromise. There are few interactions where two adversaries understand each other's goals, fears, beliefs, and perceptions, and likewise where they are fully conversant with those of a third party. It does not, therefore, seem to be overly simplistic to study the question of whether the introduction of a third party into a dispute arises because both sides perceive this as a way of obtaining help in understanding each other's positions, fears, and aspirations, *or* because they may perceive the mediator as being able to help them in their particular and possibly inflexible goals. This was the case in Cyprus when the UN Security Council mandated a peace process in 1964. Both sides believed that the peace process should support their cases, rather then entail compromise.[17] This also seems to be reflected in the current situations in Sri Lanka, where the government has tried hard to limit the function of the peace process, and in Kosovo, where the internationals and custodians of the peace process, under the umbrella of UNMIK, have worked to prevent any discussion of the final status of Kosovo until a set of standards have been met.[18]

One particular factor in a peace process, that of perceptions, appears more amenable to change than the power relationships which may dictate such inflexible goals contained within it. In other words, it can be assumed that perceptions play an important, if not a greater, role in motivating decisions than realities.[19] The relationships between the negotiators and the mediator, and the rewards and costs that emanate from the complete process of mediation, are in part a product of the perceptions of the two parties, and in this way can only be properly explained by themselves.[20] The implication of this is that the perceptions of the three parties as to each other's position and power, aims and relationships, plus the process of mediation are vital determinants not only of the role that the disputants want the mediator to play, but also of the "success" of the process. As the fate of a mediator depends on more than just personal qualities or actions, but also on the disputants' initial requirements, the mediator's perceived fairness, and its perceived ability to aid the process and support its outcome, the conflicting parties' perceptions of a mediator must be expected to evolve throughout the process. It is through the filter of those perceptions that the negotiators calculate what their objectives are and whether they want to cooperate during the process of mediation, or hinder or reject it. This *inside-out* perspective of peacemaking and mediation, from the point of view of the disputants, provides significant insights into the process of mediation, and seems to challenge several of the underlying assumptions often made about mediation (as well as peace processes).

Reasons for the emergence of devious objectives

The disputants' relative resources and status are directly related to their capacity for devious objectives and spoiling. In asymmetric conflicts the parties are differentiated by the control of most of the official resources of the state on the part of the government side, a tendency to see the conflict as a fight to the death, and the need to make alliances with sympathetic external powers on the part of the "rebels", ethno-nationalists, or other identity groups. Clearly, there are a number of very sensitive issues here. These involve retaining or attaining sovereignty and not giving direct or indirect recognition to the opposition, and retaining or acquiring control of resources, privileges, funds, and territory. This indicates how the opening of a channel of communication inherent in a peace process may be perceived as a major concession, and why a peace process often becomes a site for the contestation of resources, legitimacy, and recognition. The assumption of a compromise is so often of only secondary concern.

The acceptance of a peace process, and its associated third parties, is the equivalent to consenting to external intervention in the affairs of a state.[21] When issues such as these dominate both sides' perceptions of the problem, it is likely that a hurting stalemate is necessary in order to provide a third party with a stable situation to assess and reorganize the two sides' positions on these issues at a point where the issues themselves are static. A hurting stalemate does not necessarily imply symmetry, but it does imply that neither side views the costs of attempting to win as acceptable, and the current situation is uncomfortable. The core of the argument of the "hurting stalemate" model is that the only circumstances in which adversaries will seek a negotiated settlement are those in which "no party can envision a successful outcome through continuing current strategies, nor an end to increasingly unbearable costs". The "entrapment model" in which opposing leaders are trapped into a pursuit of victory by a perception of the costs of the conflict as an investment, and the "enticing opportunity model" in which leaders suddenly see mediation as a more cost-effective method of achieving their goals, also provide significant insights into the disputants' views of mediation, and into their tendency to harbour devious objectives.[22] This adds credence to Kissinger's belief that only a war without victory or defeat could contain the seeds of a settlement. During the October war between Israel and Egypt in 1973 he constantly switched his support from side to side in order to exhaust them, leaving them little choice but to negotiate.[23]

The threat of further violence may prevent disputants from finding the stalemate too comfortable, but this is not to say that a policy of empowerment of the weaker side through the peace process can succeed in bringing them to a stalemate. Furthermore, if such a stalemate is to be artificially created (as occurred in the case of Bosnia in the mid-1990s) this may not provide fertile ground for a sustainable peace process, and may exacerbate devious objectives and spoiling behaviour. As in Bosnia, and more generally in the Balkans, the use of force in the 1990s by third parties and local disputants has led to a number of peace agreements which subsist on strong international sponsorship, as with the role of the internationals and the ICTY in Serbia, UNMIK in Kosovo, and the Office of the High Representative in Bosnia.[24] As Assefa points out, empowerment would entail bringing about a perceived but *untested* power parity, whereas a stalemate suggests that the two sides' positions and parity have already been tested by a violent conflict which has led them to a painful situation of not being able to lose or win.[25] This is a situation in which one or both sides would view the process as intrinsically valuable, but where there is also room for manoeuvre. While a peace process can reduce the costs of a conflict, a compromise solution may still be perceived as too expensive, as continues to be the case in the Cyprus dispute.

If disputants are harbouring devious objectives they will see the peace process as a means to a particular end, not necessarily associated with a compromise solution. They may try to limit the role the third party can play (as in the context of Cyprus, and in Sri Lanka where disputants rejected the right of the third party to make proposals), and therefore see the process as only being legitimate if it helps them in their objectives. This may result in a continuation of the dispute at a low level, especially if disputants expect empowerment, legitimization, or internationalization to occur as a result of a peace process. At the same time the disputants need to offer the international community the hope that the peace process may lead to a compromise in order to continue harvesting its indirect benefits. It is also clear that devious objectives may arise because disputants do not have the capacity, will, or support actually to make the concessions necessary for a compromise. In such cases it is likely that, as has been the case in Cyprus, Northern Ireland, Kosovo, and Sri Lanka, the peace process will become protracted.

A contributing factor to the emergence of devious objectives is that disputants are rarely a coherent group: there is a tendency for them to be divided between those who want compromise and those who want to work towards their pre-negotiation objectives. Any devious objectives on the part of the disputants may be the result of a trade-off between these factions. From this point of view the disputants may value the resources the peace process provides, leading them towards devious objectives that actually undermine attempts to arrive at a compromise. This has certainly been the case with UN peacemaking in Cyprus, and was also the case on a far more overt level in the US-brokered negotiations between Israel and Egypt leading to the Camp David Agreements, although in the latter case a compromise did arise as a consequence of a US guarantee and offer of substantial enticements.

One of the major areas of contestation within a peace process is recognition and legitimacy, whereby disputants become engaged in a recognition game that needs to be resolved before any meaningful progress can be made. Sometimes these games span decades, as can be seen in Northern Ireland, Cyprus, Sri Lanka, Kosovo, and the Middle East. Non-state actors in particular will contest their unrecognized status, and governments will contest claims for "proto-political status".[26] This is obvious terrain in which the assumption of a compromise is not present, and is thus open to spoiling behaviour.

Previous attempts at mediation or involvement during different phases of the same conflict play an important role in forming the disputants' views of the mediator. The disputants' evaluation of the third party's record, objectives, and resources are vital in their calculation of their own objectives and determining how sincere they are in the search for a compromise solution, which is the basic assumption of all mediation. The disputants' perceptions, or misperceptions, of the third party play a significant role in the process; mediation is a dynamic and interactive process. Understanding how the disputants view the peace process and the third party may therefore enable a better understanding of their objectives, devious or not, and of the likelihood of their cooperation as opposed to spoiling the peace process. This may also allow for a clear understanding of what areas of the process may contravene the pre-negotiation objectives of the disputants, and therefore what form their spoiling behaviour may take. It will also provide a clearer picture of exactly why the disputants may value the peace process, and what types of resources, direct or indirect, they may benefit from.

There are also difficulties raised by the depth in which the third party becomes involved in the dispute itself, or in the *status quo*. If the mediator is indirectly associated with the *status quo*, possibly in terms of the legitimation or recognition of one side, this may lead to complex obstacles arising from the fact that one side may have been prevented from attaining victory, or have been saved from defeat, by the initiation of mediation. This problem is related to the level to which the mediator interferes with the disputants' independence, sovereignty, and legality, which may often be unavoidable, and is therefore also related to the mediator's impartiality and control of the process. By extension this leads us to the proposition that a mediator can become part of the conflict and may become a party to be bargained with, and may indeed be viewed as such by adversaries who see mediation as a tool for the continuation of their dispute at a non-violent level. Ultimately, the parties may come to hold perceptions of what the mediator may achieve which are unrelated to the mediator's objectives of a compromise. In this sense, devious objectives and spoiling can be said to emanate from any of the parties involved in a peace process, even including the mediator. Even more problematic are the cultural and normative issues that may result in disputants failing to accept that the liberal peace package which essentially lies behind any mediation effort on the part of the United Nations and many other international actors is universal and applicable to their particular case. In this case devious objectives may be rather more radical than simply influencing a peace process in favour of one side or another. Spoiling activities may be aimed at the objective of ending a process which one or other disputant or faction perceives will never allow them to achieve their objectives. This appeared to be the case in Somalia during the collapse of the UN nation-building efforts in the early 1990s,[27] and with Serb attempts to avoid any discussion of the Kosovo issue during the period after the Dayton Accords.

Such approaches can lead rapidly to a stalemate, as all sides will have a tendency to give as little as possible while searching for the best possible return. This fragile situation once again returns the debate to *realpolitik*, in that progress depends on the balance of power. If the mediator enters this relationship with its own resources, this will rapidly lead to perceptions of bias. If it refrains from doing so, perhaps because of a lack of such resources, it will rapidly became associated with the stalemate and be open to accusations of ineffectiveness. Furthermore, it may become a scapegoat for the disputants, their constituencies, and even its own constituencies. However, even in this situation the fact that the disputants are still talking rather than fighting (albeit without significant progress) may reflect positively on the mediator, who will under these circumstances display a tendency to try to focus the attention on minor areas of the dispute where the two sides can move forward in the hope that this will lead to progress. Finally, this tactic can also lead to negative perceptions of the peace process, as it could be construed as an attempt to bring about a new and less satisfactory partial solution. Clearly, the methods used by third parties aim at the construction of a liberal peace in the best-case analysis, and at merely the continuation of the process itself in the worst-case analysis. It is in this latter instance that devious objectives are most likely to be held, and for spoiling activities to emerge as a consequence. If, therefore, a peace process is subject to a lot of procedural negotiation over the types of activities the third party can undertake, it is likely that the disputants are not committed to a compromise solution and may be harbouring more devious goals, and even considering spoiling tactics.

The disputants should ask themselves what it is they have to gain from asking a particular third party to assist in a peace process, and whether their notion of peace relates clearly to the international norms and regimes the third party would expect a peace process to promote. Despite the difficulties outlined above and the sensitivities of each party on the issue of bias, it is likely that they will expect the process to add credence to their positions and demands with the opposing party and also have the weight to be able to reinforce their position. This means that they will choose a third party on the basis of what it can offer them, resulting in the finding of a third party that has something to offer both sides or disagreeing on the choice of a mediator. Thus, as Bercovitch points out, access to resources rather than impartiality may be more important.[28] The next best alternative after this would be to choose a mediator who professes neutrality, but even in this case it is likely that the opposing parties will expect their own agenda to receive the mediator's support while being sensitive to bias favouring the opposition. According to Princen, third parties are invited into a conflict in order to persuade the other side of one's rightful position, but also to persuade constituencies of the necessities of compromise and concession.[29] But this must work for both sides, and both must have a similar perception of the mediator or it will not be accepted. If, therefore, the mediator is seen to be pressuring one side only, this would be perceived as being unfair by that side and they may withdraw their support, unless this was perceived as likely to produce a worse outcome. Thus it is probable that the third party the disputant would be most likely to choose and accept would be the one whose interests are most closely aligned to those of the disputant. This means that the disputants would perceive the third party as not just being a neutral facilitator, but as an ally. Beyond this, the disputant would look for someone whose interests were partially aligned and so was an "agent". The next stage, if the former were not available, would be to choose a third party whose interests were at least not aligned with those of the opposing party. Finally, as a last resort, a neutral third party may be chosen. Princen argues that this line of reasoning can be pushed a step further, resulting in the acceptance by a disputant of a third party who is clearly antagonistic. This depends on the disputant making the calculation that alternatives to mediation are worse than accepting a clearly biased mediator.[30] It is only necessary, therefore, to assume that both sides must perceive the intervention as more beneficial to themselves than all the other alternatives. These factors underline, however, that if one adopts an inside-out view of a peace process, and of the disputants' expectations, then devious objectives seem to be a logical possibility, and that such objectives may motivate spoiling behaviour. This will not necessarily be aimed at ending a peace process, but at shaping it to the advantage of one or other disputant, thus allowing them to have continued access to the resources a peace process gives them.

In the case of an imposed peace process, the disputants may show a clear tendency towards devious objectives if they perceive the process as having prevented them from attaining victory. In this case the aggrieved party will tend not to negotiate in good faith, and will concentrate on persuading the mediator that its negotiating positions are fair. In both phases of the Cyprus case, in 1964–1965 and since 1974, the Greek Cypriot side has put much effort into interpreting and moulding the third parties' position. Clearly this tends to be the norm for disputants, as the position of the third party is vital in terms of their calculation of their official and unofficial objectives. In situations such as the negotiations at Dayton in 1995, or at Camp David in the late 1970s, the third party (in both cases the USA) was able to impose both the peace process itself and its outcome through a complex system of rewards and conditionalities. Yet, in both cases, devious objectives clearly emerged: the Serbs redirected their attention to the "forgotten" territory of Kosovo, and both the Israelis and the Egyptians established a "peace of convenience" while continuing other aspects of their wider conflict. Even powerful third parties, and peace processes that have wide international acceptance and legitimacy, are open to devious objectives and subsequent spoiling behaviour.

Linking devious objectives and spoiling

What this chapter has shown, through the adoption of an inside-out view of a peace process, is that disputants may value a peace process for a variety of reasons, not all of which are necessarily associated with the general assumption that a peace process rests on the trading of concessions until a compromise is arrived at. In fact, given that most conflicts are asymmetric, and that third parties bring their own interests to any peace process, it is quite likely that disputants will harbour objectives in line with their pre-negotiation positions rather than wanting a compromise solution in which a third party would expect to fulfil the normative and institutional requirements of the liberal peace. Where such objectives are present, within either the negotiating teams, factions, or constituencies, it is quite possible that spoiling behaviour will emerge, as disputants will tend to experiment with different tactics that may place the very process into doubt. At the very least this may compromise the liberal peace outcome to which peace processes generally aspire.

The key to understanding devious objectives, and their connection with spoiling behaviour, is to identify what views, perceptions, or misperceptions the disputants formed from their understanding of the peace process and third party, and how these have influenced their expectations. This provides an insight into whether or not there is a confluence between the liberal peace objectives of the process and third-party sponsors and the disputants' objectives. This would provide a clearer understanding of the type of assets the peace process and the third party may be able to bring to bear which will be of significant value to the disputants. Disputants may see a peace process as providing them with an opportunity to lobby and manipulate other actors in order to arrive at a solution close to their original objectives. They may see it as providing them with status, recognition, and access to diplomats, officials, or international and regional organizations and their resources. They may see it as being open to the threat of their withdrawal, and thus manipulable. They may see violence or the threat of violence as an acceptable strategy, depending on their assessment of the coercive resources third parties are willing to deploy and the third parties' desire to continue the process at any cost. A peace process may simply become a stage for the continuation of the dispute while avoiding both the costs and the concessions of warfare.

The disputants' objectives regarding a third party within a peace process can thus be identified in terms of empowerment or disempowerment; an ally; an agent of internationalization or legitimization; face-saving; or a directive or facilitative mediator. What they perceive to be "symbolized" by the process and the presence of a third party must also be understood. Whether they perceive the mediator as neutral or biased in terms of its use of coercive or facilitative methods should provide an insight into the development of their views, and would also raise the question of why the disputants continue to cooperate with the mediator if they view it as biased against them. Do the disputants perceive the mediator as having the ability, either physically or theoretically, to bring about a compromise solution, or do they view the mediator as being able to bring about an outcome other than a compromise which they view as being more in line with their objectives? Is there an element of both perspectives contained in the disputants' views of the mediator? Finally, do the disputants view the peace process as a channel through which to continue the conflict at another, possibly less costly, level? If the disputants' views seem to be incompatible with the mediator's search for a compromise solution along the lines of a liberal peace, then why do they continue to interact with it? Again, a possible explanation may be to continue the dispute as another, less costly, level, or to accrue indirect benefits from the process. The question must therefore be asked if we should view the initiation of a peace process as an indication of a marked deviation in the disputants' objectives, in that they move from aiming at a victory to aiming at a compromise?

Some preliminary observations are made here on how devious objectives can be identified and avoided, so avoiding a conflict developing the characteristics of intractability. It must be impressed upon the parties that a compromise entails concessions in practice, rather than just on paper, and that if a commitment to concessions is not observed, the third party will be able to do little more than facilitate discussion and the peace process may even be ended, as was seen in the negotiations over Kosovo before the NATO intervention of 1999. Third parties should calculate whether disputants would welcome a return to the battlefield or would view this as an outcome worse than a compromise involving concessions, and in the event of the former would probably have to consider a military response on the part of the international community, as was the pattern during the Balkan wars of the 1990s. If the disputants have not ruled out the use of violence as a method for attaining a solution, and are still committed to their pre-negotiation objectives, they must not be able to use a peace process to regroup, but instead must face the consequences of the choice between further violence, compromise, or losing control of the political outcome of their dispute. If devious objectives are identified the custodians of the peace process must act immediately, otherwise the negotiations will continue on a futile level of legalist or procedural discussions and the possibility of conflict will not recede, as has been the case with UN peacemaking in Cyprus from 1964 to the present time.

In such cases, the third party's priority is the continuation of the peace process and warding off a reversion to violence. This is particularly important if there can be no recourse to a Chapter VII enforcement operation, or to unilateral or coalition-based intervention. In this scenario, a peace process must be managed in such a way as to "do no harm". It should not bring resources, direct or indirect, to disputants until they have committed themselves to the trading of concessions and compromise, and indeed have made significant gestures in this direction. Strategies relating to empowerment or disempowerment can be discussed if it is clear which parties are blocking progress, and various diplomatic strategies related to "proto-political" recognition (as seen in Northern Ireland and Kosovo) may have to be considered to overcome the ubiquitous recognition problem. It should be recognized that peace processes, particularly before they become widely accepted and institutionalized in a negotiating culture, are normally susceptible to devious objectives, and that spoiling behaviour is subsequently likely to result. By being aware of these possibilities, third parties are provided with explanatory and normative resources in order to prevent such dynamics overpowering moderate voices who may well concur on the overall goal of a liberal peace across the dividing lines of a conflict.

Conclusion

Understanding the phenomenon of devious objectives provides indications of the likelihood of spoiling behaviour of all types emerging in a peace process. Disputants may calculate that any compromise solution can be influenced in their favour according to the resources, qualities, past record, bias, and interests of third parties. In the extreme, the peace process may be valued for the resources and possibilities it gives rise to – possibilities which are not directly associated with a genuine commitment to a compromise settlement within the framework of a liberal peace. Where such calculations are identifiable, spoiling behaviour becomes plausible, particularly as this may be a more rational approach for disputants who see a peace process as a rational method through which to attain at least some of their original objectives. Juxtaposed to the liberal peace framework within which third parties assume a settlement will emerge, spoiling behaviour may result from a perception that peace undermines or threatens the claims of one or more disputants in any particular area. In this sense, the identification of devious objectives aids in understanding non-violent and violent spoiling behaviour, factionalization within negotiating teams and constituencies, and understanding what motivates total or limited spoiling – whether it stems from opposition to one facet of the political, economic, and social dimensions of the liberal peace, greed, misperception, or simple misunderstanding. Such dynamics may result in attempts by disputants to introduce complications into negotiation processes, make implausible claims, avoid negotiation, threaten constituency unrest, demand changes in third-party personnel, use targeted or limited violence, sign agreements but not implement them, play for time, or search for new alliances or resources while negotiations are ongoing. It must be remembered, however, that where outright spoiling and the ending a peace process are not the objective, disputants may feel they are gaining sufficient benefits from the existence of even an inconclusive process that they will not want to upset it. They must tread a fine line between attempting to influence a process in their favour and keeping it alive and legitimate. Understanding such dynamics may aid third parties in their goal of guiding a peace process to a point of agreement where disputants are committed to a settlement which will be implemented, and which also conforms to the international and custodian expectations associated with a liberal peace.

Notes

1. Some sections of this chapter draw upon a previously published article developing the concept of "devious objectives". See Richmond, Oliver P. 1998. "Devious objectives and the disputants' views of international mediation: A theoretical framework", *Journal of Peace Research*, Vol. 35, No. 6. This early framework also provided the basis for a case study on the Cyprus conflict from 1964 to 1994. See Richmond, Oliver P. 1998. *Mediating in Cyprus*. London: Frank Cass. See also Stedman, Stephen John. 1997. "Spoiler problems in peace processes", *International Security*, Vol. 22, No. 2; Zahar, Marie-Joëlle. 2003. "Reframing the spoilers debate", in John Darby and Roger Mac Ginty (eds) *Contemporary Peace Making: Conflict, Violence, and Peace Processes*. Basingstoke: Palgrave Macmillan.
2. For more on this notion of the liberal peace as an assumed outcome of peace processes and peacebuilding, see Richmond, Oliver P. 2005. *The Transformation of Peace*. London: Palgrave, especially Chapters 3–5.
3. See, among others, Held, David. 1995. *Democracy and the Global Order*. Cambridge: Polity; Clark, Ian. 2001. *The Post-Cold War Order*. Oxford: Oxford University Press; Ikenberry, G. John. 2001. *After Victory*. Princeton: Princeton University Press; Duffield, Mark. 2001. *Global Governance and the New Wars: The Merging of Development and Security*. London: Zed Books; Paris, Roland. 2004. *At War's End*. Cambridge: Cambridge University Press.
4. See Richmond, "Devious objectives", note 1 above.
5. From this perspective, the United Nations as a mediator would have much to contribute. For example, John Burton assumes that the bargaining positions of the adversaries are *not* modified or restrained by the introduction of UN peacemaking. Burton, John. 1986. "The history of conflict resolution", in J. Burton and E. A. Azar (eds) *International Conflict Resolution: Theory and Practice*. Boulder, CO: Lynne Rienner, p. 156.
6. See Touval, S. and I. W. Zartman (eds). 1985. *International Mediation: Theory and Practice*. Boulder, CO: Westview.
7. Jabri, Vivienne. 1995. "Agency, structure and the question of power", *Paradigms*, Vol. 9, No. 2.
8. Diplomatic source, personal interview, UNFICYP Headquarters, Nicosia, Cyprus, 11 November 2003.
9. See Perera, Jehan. 2002. "Appreciating the president's lament", *NPC Weekly Report*, 3 March, p. 2.
10. Lewicki, Roy J., Joseph A. Litterer, David M. Saunders, and John W. Minton. 1994. *Negotiation*, 2nd edn. Burr Ridge, IL: Irwin, pp. 184–190.
11. Jervis, Robert. 1976. *Perception and Misperception in International Politics*. Princeton, NJ: Princeton University Press, pp. 3–7.

12. See Aguirre, Francisco Javier Guerrero. 1995. *Power, Asymmetry and Negotiation: A Theoretical Analysis*, available at www.kent.ac.uk/politics/research/kentpapers/paco1.html. Also see Habeeb, William Mark. 1988. *Power and Tactics in International Negotiation; How Weak Nations Bargain with Strong Nations*. London: Johns Hopkins University Press, p. xi.
13. See Debrix, François. 2003. "Introduction", in François Debrix and Cynthia Weber (eds) *Rituals of Mediation: International Politics and Social Meaning*. Minneapolis: University of Minnesota Press.
14. For more on this see Jabri, note 7 above.
15. An example of this is provided by the assurances that both the UK and Germany gave each other before the First World War as to their good intentions towards each other, which only made matters worse because of their misperception of each other's goals and beliefs, and strong images. Jervis, note 11 above, pp. 74–75.
16. Bercovitch, J. and J. Langley. 1993. "The nature of the dispute and the effectiveness of international mediation", *Journal of Conflict Resolution*, Vol. 37, No. 4, p. 671.
17. See UN Security Council Resolution 184, 4 March 1964. See also the Galo Plaza Report, UN Doc. S/6253, para. 8. Plaza wrote: "I gained the impression that the Governments of both Cyprus and Turkey, both of which had requested the General Assembly to discuss the Cyprus problem, each expected the Assembly to support its respective stand and would not yield to any substantial compromise until a decision had been taken by the Assembly."
18. "Standards for Kosovo" was supported by the Security Council in presidential statement S/PRST/2003/26, 10 December 2003. This was also confirmed by confidential personal interviews with officials in UNMIK and the EU, Pristina, 13–14 January 2005.
19. Kaufman, S. and G. T. Duncan. 1992. "A formal framework for mediator mechanisms and motivations", *Journal of Conflict Resolution*, Vol. 36, No. 4, p. 691. However, Jervis argues that perceptions are slow to change, and do so only when images fail badly, leading to "perceptual satisficing". Jervis, note 11 above, pp. 191–192.
20. Wall, J. A. 1981. "Mediation", *Journal of Conflict Resolution*, Vol. 25, No. 1, p. 163.
21. Touval, S. 1993. "Gaining entry to mediation in communal strife", in Manus Midlarsky (ed.) *The Internationalisation of Communal Strife*. London and New York: Routledge, p. 255.
22. Mitchell, C. 1995. "The right moment: Notes on four models of ripeness", *Paradigms*, Vol. 9, No. 2.
23. Stoessinger, J. G. 1992. *Why Nations Go To War*, 6th edn. New York: St Martin's Press, pp. 165–166.
24. See, for example, Paris, note 3 above; Cousens, Elizabeth M. 2001. "Building peace in Bosnia", in Elizabeth M. Cousens and Chetan Kumar (eds) *Peacebuilding as Politics*. London: Lynne Rienner; Caplan, Richard. 2004. "International authority and state building: The case of Bosnia and Herzegovina", *Global Governance*, Vol. 10, No. 1, p. 15; O'Neill, William G. 2002. *Kosovo: An Unfinished Peace*. Boulder, CO: Lynne Rienner, pp. 37–40.
25. Assefa, H. 1987. *Mediation of Civil Wars*. London: Westview Press, p. 18. Assefa makes the important point that if the balance of power exists merely at the perceptual level, the conflict is likely to escalate in order to test the limits of the balance. In his opinion, stalemate is the optimum point of entry for the mediator.
26. Mitchell, C. 1993. "External peacemaking initiatives and international conflict", in Manus Midlarsky (ed.) *The Internationalisation of Communal Strife*. London and New York: Routledge, p. 277.
27. For more on this see UN Security Council Resolution 814, 26 March 1993.

28. Bercovitch, J. 1996. "Introduction", in J. Bercovitch (ed.) *The Theory and Practice of Mediation*. Boulder, CO: Lynne Riennes, p. 3.
29. Princen, T. 1992. *Intermediaries in International Conflict*, Princeton: Princeton University Press, p. 9.
30. *Ibid.*, pp. 61–62. Princen gives the example of Egypt after the 1973 war with Israel. Egypt viewed the USA as being biased against them, but accepted their mediation offer as it was perceived as being better than attempting to maintain a cease-fire and suffering domestic unrest.

4

Terrorism as a tactic of spoilers in peace processes

Ekaterina Stepanova

While the notion of a "peace process" is rather vague, the term is generally used to define a process centred on the goal of achieving and implementing a workable peace agreement (as distinct from the more general terms of "conflict resolution" or "conflict management"). More specifically, the task of arranging, facilitating, and managing peace negotiations is commonly referred to as *peacemaking*. But while broadly used and generally accepted, the term is far from non-controversial, mainly due to the tendency to extend mechanically the positive understanding of "peace" to apply to the notion of a "peace process". Thus a peace process is often seen as something benign by definition, inherently positive, and an end in itself to be backed at any price (consequently, anyone who opposes a peace process is automatically listed as an "enemy of peace").

The downside of this approach is that it tends to create heightened expectations about the potential outcome of a peace process. Moreover, it runs against the record of the outcomes and general effectiveness of peace processes, which remains extremely mixed. While the end of the Cold War stimulated some very short-lived optimism about the global prospects for peace processes, the longer-term trends are much less encouraging. Over the last 50 years half of the peace processes in the world have collapsed,[1] leading to re-escalation of violence – often in more intensive and lethal forms than before the peace process started. Moreover, many conflicts in the world do not lead to *any* formal peace processes or *any* formal peace agreements (they either drag on or the solution is imposed or enforced, not negotiated). Out of 72 internal armed conflicts that started between 1940 and 1992, only 51 per cent led to peace negotiations (peace processes); and of those, 43 per cent of peace agreements were never implemented and the combatants returned to fighting.[2] It is quite symbolic that, for much of the 1990s to the early 2000s, the state of the so-called Oslo peace process – the main follow-up to the first Arab-Israeli agreements of the 1970s that produced the term "peace process" – could be more accurately described in terms of continuing confrontation, failure, and deadlock than in terms of peace. The mixed and often disappointing outcome of many "peace processes" has even somewhat compromised the term itself, particularly in those parts of the world that have lived through the "peace processes" and seen them fail or produce little positive impact. It even led to some attempts to deconstruct the term – to divorce "peace" from "process". As stated in one of the typical critiques of the notion, "a peace process can drag on endlessly. By definition, so long as there is a 'peace process', there is no peace."[3]

Still, all the mixed outcomes of and complications related to "peace processes" hardly render the notion useless. The term is a useful one as long as it is defined in a more functional way: literally as nothing more and nothing less than "a road to peace", and not given any inherent evaluative meaning.

After an agreement is reached, actors unwilling to accept it and undertaking policies and actions aimed at undermining its implementation are commonly characterized as "spoilers". However, as a spoiler is primarily identified and defined on the basis of its position towards a peace agreement, in order to understand, explain, and effectively counter spoiling behaviour it is logical to start with the *substantive* nature of the peace process in general and of a concrete peace agreement. In other words, attention should be paid not just to the fact of negotiations, but to their substance. Do any negotiations amount to a peace process, and what are the criteria that make negotiations qualify as a peace process?

Unlike more technical negotiations, peace talks are meant to identify and address the basic incompatibilities between the parties: those fundamental issues about which the conflict has been fought in the first place. Certainly, no one expects all these issues to be resolved by a peace agreement, and the final decisions on the most contentious issues may be deferred until the peace process is consolidated (that is, until a cease-fire and confidence-building measures are firmly in place). However, if too many of the central issues are left over for the future renegotiation process – for an endless series of follow-up interim agreements, as in the case of the Oslo process – that in itself maybe a recipe for failure. In sum, a "peace process" that does not address most of the critical issues at dispute can hardly qualify as such, and those that postpone them indefinitely may qualify as such but have all the chances of failure. The same refers to the inclusiveness of a process: in most contemporary conflicts there are more than two parties involved, and a process that does not involve the main armed opposition group, or the key militant actors in the area who have sufficient capability to destabilize a peace process if they are left out, may be doomed to failure from the beginning.

Do all negotiations referred to as "peace processes" stand up even to these two basic criteria – the need to address the key issues at dispute and the inclusiveness of the process? Should reaching a peace agreement always be seen as an end in itself, to be achieved at any price, or is it the nature and substance of a peace agreement, its inclusiveness, and its relevance to the central issues of the conflict that matter? What if a peace agreement ignores the critical issues at dispute, delays their solution, or excludes one of several main parties to the conflict? In that case, would it qualify as peace process at all or could it still be seen as such, albeit carrying the seeds of its own destruction and failure?

After a peace agreement has been reached, actors unwilling to accept it and undertaking overt or less-explicit policies and actions aimed at undermining its implementation are commonly characterized as "spoilers". In the research literature, the so-called "spoiler problem" pretends to assume the focal role for discussions on why peace processes fail and on the role of violence in peace processes. The spoiler-centred approach has both its shortcomings and its advantages.

The main disadvantage of this approach is that it tends to reduce challenges posed by violence to peace implementation to the existence of the "spoilers". The presence and activities of spoilers are not, however, the only explanations of why peace processes are disrupted: inability of the parties to agree on the main issues at dispute, a lack of progress towards political settlement, and a lack of trust between the parties may be more significant in the failure of a peace process than the "spoiler problem". Also, the excessive focus on spoilers brings us back to the somewhat simplified vision of a peace process as being something inherently positive and of all those actors who, for various reasons, may oppose a particular peace process as being "spoilers". Clearly, not much needs to be done to spoil something that is inherently flawed or perceived at least by one or several key parties to the conflict as inadequate, biased, unjust, and/or imposed entirely from the outside with little regard to realities on the ground and interests of the main protagonists. A peace agreement that does not reflect certain objective realities on the ground (such as the stalemate between the main parties to the conflict) and is driven solely by the urgency of the problem, the scale of violence, and/ or by the strategic interests of the outside powers might be doomed to failure even with a lack of concrete and identifiable "spoilers". In that case the presence of spoilers – the so-called "spoiler problem" – might not necessarily be a problem in itself or the source of failure of a peace process, but an indication or manifestation of more fundamental, inherent flaws of the peace process and of unaddressed critical issues of the conflict.

Against this background, rather than referring to a "spoiler problem" it might be more accurate to use the term "spoiler behaviour". Also, the formal identification and classification of "spoilers" on the grounds of their position on a certain peace agreement (as "pro-peace" or "anti-peace" actors) should always be preceded by and based on a detailed analysis of the nature and driving forces of the peace agreement itself and of the peace process in general. Finally, before dealing with the role of "spoilers" in peace processes, it might be useful first to qualify and evaluate local and regional players on the basis of their positions on the central issues at dispute.

A peace process may fail even if it *does address* the key issues of the armed conflict and represents a genuine attempt to move forward to resolve them. A peace process can both fall victim to factors external to the process itself (such as changes in international environment) and suffer from several "internal" design flaws, procedural defects, and other faults. One of the common flaws of peace processes is inadequate attention paid to the *subjective dynamics* of the conflict: characteristics that are more closely and directly related to the parties themselves than to the key issues of disagreement between them or to the underlying causes of violence. Effective resolution of the key issues of the violent conflict is an absolute essential, but not necessarily sufficient prerequisite for the peace process to succeed unless the subjective dynamics of the conflict are also adequately addressed. In this context, the main advantage of the focus on the role of "spoilers" in peace processes is that it draws attention to the "subjective dynamics" of the conflict and to the parties themselves. An additional advantage of the *spoiler-centred, actor-oriented approach* is that it emphasizes the dynamic nature of violent conflicts and peace processes rather than the more static "objective" causes of violence.

The role of violence in peace processes

One of the main immediate goals of the peace process is to end armed fighting, but violence almost never stops with the start of negotiations and often continues during peace implementation. Still, there is the image that a halt of violence (say, in the form of a cease-fire) should precede any serious peace negotiations. In practice, declaring a cease-fire may help negotiations to get started, but cease-fires are neither necessary prerequisites for negotiations nor easily sustainable, particularly during the earlier stages of negotiations. Violence is neither antithetical nor alien to peace processes – it accompanies peace processes.[4] In particular, violence tends to increase before, during, or immediately following such key turning points in a peace process as, for instance, the signing of a peace agreement. A period immediately after the signing of a peace agreement is one of the most risky stages of the peace process, when the scale and intensity of violent incidents can temporarily increase. After the signing of the Oslo Agreement, particularly in 1994–1996, Israeli civilians were killed by radical Palestinian groups at a higher rate than in the course of the previous *intifada*.[5] Thus acts of violence by parties and factions, including acts designed specifically to disrupt negotiations, should be expected and taken into account in the very design of the peace process.

How and to what extent do acts of violence affect the peace process? The effects of violence on negotiations and peace implementation are multiple and diverse. The most obvious impact is that of destabilizing (spoiling) negotiations or peace implementation, which may stall the peace process or even threaten re-escalation of the armed conflict. While this is certainly the most common scenario, it is not the only one. At times violence, on the contrary, appears to be counterproductive, in the sense that it seems to force the parties to start or restart negotiations, serving as a catalyst for the peace process. Also, while in some cases acts of violence can discourage external actors and mediators from getting involved, in other cases violence may actually raise the profile of a conflict and conflict management effort, raise the level of external interest in the conflict, and encourage external actors to intervene more actively in the process. In extreme cases it may result in external parties intervening militarily to enforce peace, but more often in them intervening politically to reactivate negotiations.

Even in a most basic two-party negotiation model, incidents of violence can affect one or both sides of negotiations, as well as local actors outside the negotiation process, and may influence the external/international custodians and intermediaries (by increasing or decreasing their interest in a peace process). It should also be noted that different actors may perceive the impact of violence differently – acts of violence do not influence their cost-benefit considerations in the same way, and the level of their determination to go on with the peace process despite acts of violence may vary.

Also, in the context of a peace process, violence often appears in modified forms and may involve a variety of motivations, tactics, and goals, different from those that had been put forward before negotiations started. Such new motivations may include attempts to block or reverse the peace process, to prevent one's own marginalization as a result of a peace process, or to engage in intra-group violence as a result of violent splits over intra-party disagreements on whether or not to join the political process. These new motivations and tactics do not, however, fully replace the previous ones: some actors, particularly those excluded from or retaining reservations about the political process, may still use violence for the same purposes they had pursued before the process started (to destroy or seriously weaken an opponent by violent means). Thus an ongoing peace process may be accompanied by a complex mix of various forms of violence, some of them modified by the peace process itself. Consequently, it is important to distinguish between different kinds of violence during a peace process, including the different tactics employed (in particular, between guerrilla warfare, terrorism, and other forms of political violence).

In sum, the dynamic interaction of force and talks not only serves as a background for a peace process, but can even be viewed as an almost essential characteristic common to most peace processes. Moreover, violence is one of the most objective indicators of the soundness and sustainability of a peace process. One of the main strengths of the peace process is not the absence of violence since negotiations started (few peace processes would not be accompanied by acts of violence) – it is whether the peace process can continue despite incidents of violence, whether violence is not allowed to spin out of control.

Terrorism and its functions during and after conflict

Any peace process is directly related to violent conflict, as it is aimed at bringing the violence to an end and achieving lasting peace after conflict. In contrast, not everything called terrorism is related to an armed conflict. While the phenomenon of terrorism is a multifaceted one and can mean very different things to different people, the tendency, dramatically reinforced by the events of 11 September 2001, to use terrorism as a synonym for almost all existing forms of violence in the world (from criminal and punitive to all known forms of political violence) is a misleading and unhealthy one. While a more narrow, meaningful, and focused definition is certainly needed, there is always a risk of leaving aside some of the important features of elements of "terrorism in all its forms and manifestations", as it is referred to within the UN system. This problem can be solved only by recognizing that there are different forms (types) of terrorism with quite disparate causes and foundations, and that any meaningful definition of terrorism at least partly depends on which type of terrorism it refers to.

As the focus here is on the process of managing violent conflict, of primary interest are only those forms of terrorism that are directly related to or generated by armed conflict. Thus neither the recent phenomenon of the so-called "super-terrorism" (high-profile terrorist activities by groups and networks with a global outreach or vision, such as Al-Qaeda[6] or Aum Shinrikyo, that have non-negotiable and *unlimited* goals and may be ready to use *unlimited* means, such as weapons of mass destruction, to achieve them) nor the use of terrorist means by left-wing, right-wing, ecological, and other extremists at a time of peace will be covered by this chapter, as these forms of terrorism may manifest themselves regardless of and independently from concrete local or regional violent conflicts.[7]

Unlike these forms of terrorism, the so-called conflict-related, or conflict-generated, terrorism is used as a tactic (a mode of operation) by militant groups which tend to identify themselves openly with a certain political cause in a particular armed conflict, and are thus directly tied to the political agenda of that conflict. Their cause may be quite ambitious (to seize power, create a new state, fight against foreign occupation), but normally it does not go beyond a local or regional context. Thus, these groups' goals and agendas, by and large, remain *localized*, even if some of their fund-raising, logistical, propaganda, or even planning activities may be internationalized – that is, conducted in and from the territory of several states beyond the conflict area (as in the case of the Tamil Tigers). In sum, terrorist activities are carried out by these groups for *limited political goals* and, not surprisingly, by *limited means* (weapons and materials used in terrorist activities of this type do not have to be very advanced, tend to be standard and relatively available, and are sometimes even quite primitive, such as the unstable bombs used by Palestinian suicide bombers).

As armed conflict involves various forms of violence, it is particularly important to distinguish conflict-related terrorism from other types of violence with which it is commonly confused. There are three main criteria distinguishing conflict-related terrorism from other forms of violence: if a certain act of violence fits all three criteria, it can with a great deal of certainty be characterized as a terrorist act.

The first criterion distinguishes terrorism from plain crime, including organized crime. While an act of terrorism is certainly a crime, it is always more than just a crime. What makes it something more than plain crime is its *political goal*[8] (interpreted very broadly, so that it can range from a very concrete to a more abstract one; while such a goal may include ideological or religious motivations or be formulated in ideological or religious categories, it always has a political dimension). Terrorism, however, is not the political goal itself, but a tactic to achieve that goal (thus it makes sense to refer to "terrorist means" rather than "terrorist goals"). For groups engaged in conflict-related terrorism, a political goal is an end in itself and not just a secondary instrument or a "cover" for advancement of other interests (such as illegal accumulation of wealth, as in the case of organized criminal groups).

A second criterion that distinguishes terrorism from other forms of politically motivated violence employed in the course of asymmetric armed conflict (particularly from guerrilla warfare, with which it is most commonly confused in the context of an armed conflict[9]) is the primary *target of violence*. While guerrilla warfare implies the use of force primarily against governmental military and security forces, terrorism is directed *against civilian populations and objects* or *intentionally indiscriminate*. This does not mean that a certain armed group cannot use both guerrilla and terrorist tactics at the same time, or switch from one to the other and back. This makes the dilemma of "terrorists or freedom fighters" almost irrelevant, as it is possible for the same organization to use different modes of operation at once and to attack different targets to achieve its political goals – the same organization can *both* be a national liberation/insurgency/guerrilla movement *and* resort to terrorist means. In fact, many organizations active today in conflict and post-conflict settings engage in both guerrilla warfare *and* terrorist activities (be it Hamas or the Islamic Movement of Uzbekistan or Harakat ul-Mujahiddin in Kashmir or the Liberation Tigers of Tamil Eelam). It is this combination of these two different modes of operation used by the same organization that is the main conceptual and practical problem in dealing with conflict-related terrorism.

While this criterion is by no means a relative one, as in some cases it might be difficult to identify a target of violence or threat of violence as civilian and to distinguish between combatants and non-combatants in a conflict area, it is still useful to be kept in mind. Among other things, the choice of the target of violence has serious implications from the point of international humanitarian law: guerrilla attacks against government military and security targets are not internationally criminalized, while deliberate attacks against civilians (including terrorist attacks) are.[10]

While civilians remain the most immediate targets of terrorism – a specific tactic that always necessitates a victim – the victim is usually not the end recipient of the message. Terrorism is a deadly performance that involves the use of or threat to use violence against civilians, but is staged specifically for someone else to watch – most often the *state* (or a group/community of states) – and is meant to blackmail the state and make it to do or abstain from doing something. The state as the ultimate recipient of the terrorists' message brings one to the third defining criterion: the *asymmetrical nature of terrorism*.

There may be various forms of politically motivated violence against civilians in an armed conflict (in addition to rebel attacks against civilians or civilian objects, intercommunal sectarian violence or repressive actions by the state itself may meet the first two criteria mentioned above). What distinguishes terrorism from other forms of politically motivated violence against civilians is its *asymmetrical nature* – terrorism is used as a weapon of the weak against the strong, a weapon of the weaker side in an asymmetrical confrontation. It is the asymmetrical nature of terrorism that explains the specifics of this mode of operation – the need to attack civilians. Thus, terrorism serves as a force multiplier compensating for conventional military weakness: a militant group cannot hurt the state by conventional military means, so it tries to strike at the state "where it hurts most", by non-conventional means (attacks against civilians and civilian infrastructure). Terrorism is a weapon of the weak to be employed against the strong – it is neither a weapon of the strong to be employed against the weak (repressive actions by states), nor a weapon of the weak to be employed against the weak (sectarian violence between followers of various Sunni *madrassas* in Pakistan, or local clashes between Muslims and Christians in various parts of Indonesia, or interethnic strife in many African states would hardly qualify as terrorism precisely because they are symmetrical).

It is important to note that the asymmetrical nature of terrorism implies not merely a gap in capabilities between the parties involved (which goes without saying), but first and foremost an asymmetry of level and status of the main protagonists. The simplest and most basic form of such *status asymmetry* is the use of terrorist means by a non-state (substate) actor as a mode of operation in an asymmetrical confrontation with a functional, established, or at least identifiable state to influence its actions or policy by committing or threatening violence against the civilian population. A more complex form of such status asymmetry would, for instance, be an asymmetrical confrontation between a non-state network(s) and a group of states (or a community of states, or an international organization representing states and nations).

As follows from the main characteristics of conflict-related terrorism listed above, terrorism is a specific tactic employed by "non-state" actors in an asymmetrical equation. Deliberate use of force by the state against its own or foreign civilians is not included in the definition of conflict-related terrorism used in this chapter, as *it is not applied by a weaker actor in an asymmetrical armed confrontation*. This, of course, does not make the use of indiscriminate force by the state against civilians less of an international crime from the point of view of international humanitarian law, which explicitly forbids such activities by the state and defines them, depending on the scale and the domestic or international context of atrocities, as either "war crimes" or "crimes against humanity".[11]

This definition does not exclude the possibility of the state/government itself (particularly parts of the state security apparatus) acting as an "inside" spoiler to a particular peace agreement or sabotaging a peace process as a whole. Nor does it exclude state support for terrorist activities by non-state actors.

Certainly, the combination of criteria listed above is just the minimal common denominator for a certain incident of violence to qualify as a terrorist act. This list is not necessarily final or exhaustive in covering all and every manifestation of terrorism in an armed conflict. This can be demonstrated, for instance, by the problem of the so-called "loyalist violence" that may be directed both at anti-state militants and at the broader population seen as their "supporters".

Among other things, the asymmetrical nature of terrorism means that it can be employed as a mode of operation not in any armed conflict, but only in one that at least has a clear asymmetrical aspect and involves a confrontation between actors of a different status, such as between a non-state militant group(s) and the government (the IRA versus the UK government in Northern Ireland) or between a foreign state(s) often viewed as an occupier and local armed groups (such as Israel for Palestinians or the USA and its coalition partners for Iraqi resistance). In some cases the asymmetrical use of terrorist tactics (against civilians, but ultimately directed against the state) provokes a "symmetrical" response in the form of paramilitary violence directed against groups employing terrorist means and their alleged popular base ("loyalist violence"). Against this background, where would the "symmetrical" use of violence by groups declaring their general loyalty to the state, but using uncontrolled violence against "the enemies of the state" (that may include civilians) fit? Clearly, there is an important distinction between guerrilla groups that operate in opposition to the state and paramilitary groups that operate to reinforce the state by conducting operations the state itself cannot (does not want to) perform. One of the possible ways to address this problem analytically is to view activities by those groups that act in close cooperation with the state in the context of "state support to terrorism" by non-state actors. The problem of loyalist violence is more complex, though: it can also be seen as a symmetrical way to confront "asymmetrical" threats posed by anti-state groups, whether sponsored by the government or existing in its own right – this is the way loyalist groups in Northern Ireland, some of the radical militant groups in Indonesia (Front Pembela International, Laskar Jihad), allegedly connected to the government and used by it against Christian separatists, and the AUC (self-defence forces) in Colombia have operated. In any case, the phenomenon of "loyalist violence" is not just fully compatible with but entirely dependent on asymmetrical confrontation between a state and an anti-state group, as it in itself is a "symmetrical" reaction to anti-state violence.

Finally, to conclude the discussion of the asymmetrical nature of terrorism, it is interesting to note that the "asymmetric conditions" most favourable for conflict-related terrorism are not necessarily the most favourable circumstances for international peacemaking or externally driven peace processes to take place, and are even less typical for international peace operations to be carried out to implement peace accords or monitor a cease-fire.[12] In an asymmetrical conflict between a state (particularly a relatively powerful one) and a domestic or foreign non-state actor(s), as long as the state remains more or less in control of the situation (and as much part of the problem as part of the solution), it may not welcome any formal international peacemaking efforts. These constraints, coupled with a steadily growing number of *internally managed peace processes*,[13] mean that in addressing spoilers' behaviour in peace processes it is no longer sufficient to focus on international peacemaking and externally managed peace processes only. More specifically, the link between conflict-related terrorism and the peace process is no less, if not more, relevant for national efforts to negotiate and ensure a lasting peace than for internationally managed peace processes.

Terrorist means can be used at all stages of armed conflict and for different purposes. There are three main functions of conflict-related terrorism that roughly correspond to different stages of the armed conflict itself.

At a pre-conflict stage or at the early stages of violent conflict, terrorism can be employed *as a means of escalation of violence* in order to provoke broader armed confrontation (as a catalyst for violence). In this case terrorism often takes the form of several "symbolic" attacks designed to serve as trigger events to spark a full-scale violence, rather than of a consistent mode of operation. More commonly, however, terrorist means are employed at more advanced stages of violent conflict.

At the stage of an ongoing armed confrontation (before the start of a peace process or after its collapse), terrorism is most typically employed by the main parties to the conflict *as a mode of operation*, as one of their violent tactics. As, in this case, terrorism is used in the context of a broader armed confrontation, it is likely to be practised by groups that might enjoy some level of local popular support in a conflict area, ranging from very limited to quite substantial. Also, terrorism is not likely to be the only violent tactics employed by these groups – they often combine it with guerrilla tactics (rebel attacks against security or military targets), and sometimes even with non-violent activities, including social, humanitarian, religious, and other functions. In sum, while groups employing terrorist means as one of their main modes of operation in an armed conflict are commonly referred to as "terrorist organizations", it would probably be more correct to refer to them as "groups involved in terrorist activities". A classic case in point would be Hamas, which combines guerrilla and terrorist tactics with extensive social work and has enjoyed no less than 30–40 per cent public support among Palestinians in the course of the second (Al-Aqsa) *intifada*.

When used at an active stage of the armed conflict, terrorist means are likely to serve various operational purposes: while terrorist acts undertaken outside of the conflict area itself (e.g. by Lashkar-e-Tayiba and Jaish-e-Mohammad in New Delhi rather than in Kashmir proper, or by the IRA in London rather than in Ulster, or by Chechen groups in Moscow rather then in Chechnya) are generally meant to be of rather symbolic nature and importance and serve the purpose of blackmailing the state and terrorizing and shocking the society, terrorist activities carried out within a conflict area may also serve the purpose of causing as much direct damage to the "enemy" as possible in order to make the costs of governing an area untenable.

Finally, terrorist means can also be employed at the stage of an ongoing peace process (often at the end of the conflict, during the lull(s) in the fighting, or after a preliminary cease-fire or a formal peace agreement has already been reached). At this stage, terrorism appears to be a tactic best suited for spoilers and one of the easiest ways to disrupt ongoing peace negotiations and destabilize a peace process: while the use of terrorist means can hardly help achieve a lasting peace agreement,[14] it can be very effective in ruining a peace agreement.

In sum, terrorist means can be used both at the "peak" stage of an ongoing armed confrontation, when terrorism becomes one of the main modes of operation of violent groups, and at the concluding stages of conflict, when a group feels the growing need to resort to increasingly asymmetrical forms of violence as the range of other options for resistance becomes more limited, the peace process gains momentum, and more moderate groups become part of the peace process. While it is in the latter context that the link between terrorism and peace processes is most evident, a resort to terrorist means by spoilers with a goal of disrupting an ongoing peace process is not necessarily delinked from the way terrorist tactics had been applied for other purposes and at other stages of violent conflict. For example, if terrorism had already been used as a major mode of operation during the active stage of the armed confrontation (prior to the beginning of a peace process), potential spoilers may be more inclined to use it as spoilers' technique after a formal agreement has been reached.

"Spoilers that matter": Countering terrorist activities by major parties to the conflict

Spoilers have usually been identified and categorized on the basis of their perceived or declared *goals and intentions vis-à-vis* a peace process (see, e.g. Stedman's classification of spoilers as limited, greedy, and total).[15] While categorizing spoilers on the basis of their declared intentions *vis-à-vis* a peace process may help identify actual spoilers, it does not help to address the problem of so-called potential spoilers. It is also unclear who has the right to make the judgement about whether the spoiler's demands are legitimate and should be accommodated as part of the peace process (particularly if spoiling behaviour indicates strong opposition of a major party to the conflict to the way a peace process has been managed or dissatisfaction with the contents of a process).

In fact, it is spoilers' *capabilities* to disrupt a particular peace agreement or a peace process, if they so decide, that may be no less, if not more, important than the evidence about their intentions available at the time. A capabilities-centred approach may allow us to identify spoilers not just *post hoc*, but also *in advance*, and thus to address the problem of both actual and potential spoilers. In sum, spoilers can and should be classified not only on the basis of their goals or intentions but also with regard to a number of more specific prerequisites for conflict-related terrorist activities. It is on the basis of spoilers' capabilities to disrupt a peace process by terrorist means that the spoilers could be categorized as follows.

- "Spoilers that matter": major parties to a conflict that are not satisfied with the nature and/or handling of a peace process and do or may undertake terrorist acts to disrupt actual or potential peace negotiations (such as Hamas, Islamic Jihad, and some other radical Palestinian groups or Hizbullah in Lebanon).
- Smaller and more radical spoiler groups (that are often radicalized factions or offshoots of larger organizations that might have already signed or are likely to sign a peace accord or a cease-fire/confidence-building agreement). For these groups, terrorism is often the main or the sole violent tactic employed and they are likely to enjoy less (or no) popular support than their parent organizations. More radical splinter groups stand to gain little from the peace process themselves and might even become an embarrassment for the larger movements of which they used to be part and which have lost control over their more radical elements. These splinter groups normally become more active at the stage when some preliminary or more formal agreement with the main parties has already been achieved (the classic example is that of the Real IRA, Continuity IRA, and other offshoot groups in

Northern Ireland after adoption of the Mitchell principles on democracy and non-violence by the IRA in 1997).

These two types of spoilers that do or may use terrorist means to disrupt peace processes may require different, or at least significantly nuanced, strategies to deal with them. The first category of spoilers identified above are the parties that have already employed terrorism as a major mode of operation in the course of the armed confrontation, and continue to carry out terrorist activities as the most efficient and most immediately available means to disrupt peace negotiations which they view as harmful to their interests and/or security. For key parties to an armed conflict that choose to use terrorist means with a specific purpose of disrupting the ongoing negotiations involving other parties, a decision to employ terrorist means is not just a matter of choice. Whatever the purpose of the use of terrorist means by spoilers of this type, they tend to be effective only when employed by a sufficiently *capable* and highly *determined* opponent, using terrorism as a highly *rational* operational strategy.[16]

The capability and determination, essential for a major militant actor to employ terrorist means effectively, are characteristics more closely related to the type and character of violent non-state actors themselves. Even with an explosive combination of a feeling of injustice, violations, or lack of civil and political rights, the high degree of desperateness of the situation or the brutality of government repression does not necessarily provoke a reaction by a non-state actor in the form of terrorism unless the state is faced by a sufficiently *capable* and highly *determined* opponent.

In this context, "capability" cannot be reduced to or merely substituted by the so-called technical capabilities (such as access to arms, money, and the availability of trained professionals). Rather, it is more closely associated with the structural model employed by these groups and their organizational competence: their *structural/organizational capabilities* to mount terrorist attacks. The more flexible, diffuse, and fragmented is the organizational structure of groups involved in conflict-related terrorist activities, the closer it is to a horizontal/network model, particularly to its complex "matrix-type" version, the more informal are the ties between its various units, the greater its capacity to employ terrorist means effectively – both as a major mode of operation in an asymmetrical armed conflict with a state (as a classic hierarchy) and as a violent tactic specifically aimed at disrupting peace negotiations and implementation.

To justify the use of or threat to use violence against innocent civilians, for whatever purpose, a high level of determination, indoctrination, and justification of the use of terrorism is required. Such indoctrination and justification are facilitated and provided by *extremist ideologies*. Structurally, shared ideological beliefs, goals, and values are also the key dominants that help bring together various informally interconnected elements of these groups and serve as their structural "glue". In the post-Cold War era it is a combination of radical nationalism with religious extremism[17] that has proved to be most conducive for conflict-related terrorism.

In sum, it is the structural capabilities and extremist ideologies of major armed parties to a conflict – the two more specific prerequisites for effective use of terrorist means – which make terrorism a strategy of deliberate choice for armed actors and explain why it is not every asymmetrical armed conflict that generates terrorism and why, even in the same conflict or post-conflict area, some groups may resort to terrorism (whether as a major mode of operation or as a spoilers' technique) while others refrain from terrorism. The armed actors' structural capabilities and extremist ideologies are also their main comparative advantages in an asymmetrical confrontation. At the stage of a peace process, as long as spoilers of this type keep specific organizational/structural capabilities and extremist ideologies, they will retain the capability to disrupt seriously or even undermine negotiations and peace implementation by terrorist means, if and when they wish and decide to do so. Even if these armed actors have not yet acted like spoilers, they still remain potential spoilers that can put both peace negotiations and peace implementation at risk. Even partial accommodation of their concerns would not necessarily prevent them from acting as spoilers, unless their capabilities to mount terrorist attacks are also neutralized.

From the structural perspective, the most logical way to neutralize spoilers' capabilities to mount terrorist attacks and to deprive them of their main structural advantage is both to introduce some elements of network organizational design into existing or emerging state structures (for instance, through more active interagency cooperation) and to find ways *to formalize the informal links within spoiler organizations and turn decentralized horizontal networks into hierarchies.* At the stage of ongoing peace negotiations and the search for political accommodation this imperative becomes all the more pressing, as the structural model typical for many of these groups complicates centralized strategic decision-making and coordination of actions by their different elements, putting under question their adherence to any formal or informal agreements that could be achieved.

The most logical and standard way to achieve this objective is to encourage both general demilitarization of politics and, more specifically, *political transformation* of the armed groups themselves, by stimulating them to get increasingly politicized and involved in non-militant activities, and to form distinctive and fully fledged political wings (rather then merely civilian "front organizations" for fund-raising/propaganda purposes), so that these political wings could gradually develop a stake in greater legitimization, develop into political parties, and eventually be incorporated into the political process.

That said, it has to be stressed that for spoilers of this type a peace process and the political transformation that it requires pose a major strategic dilemma. Moreover, a political transformation of these groups can itself pose a number of new security risks to the peace process and for an emerging or existing political system at large. An evolution of a violent non-state group into a legal political party could be extremely painful and may be preceded by or lead to violent splits within groups and intensification of internal and sectarian violence. In fact, in some cases such a split can drive more radical factions to resort more actively to terrorist means, in an increasingly irrational manner. Conflicts between moderates and extremists within an "inside spoiler" may even weaken its position and legitimacy at negotiations by revealing divisions within the group.[18]

Also, while the positive effects of a political transformation of militant groups, including those employing terrorist means, for peace negotiations and peace implementation to succeed can hardly be underestimated, this process may have other, less direct, often unexpected, and potentially destabilizing implications for the political system as a whole, particularly in those conflict and post-conflict areas where this system is still functioning or has been essentially recreated despite all the damage caused by protracted hostilities (as in war-torn Lebanon throughout the 1990s). Indeed, a problem of potentially adverse implications of a political transformation of key militant parties, at times acting as spoilers, and their integration into the post-war domestic political context, often fragile and based on a delicate balance of local political forces and interests (e.g. in the case of Hizbullah's strategic decision fully to join the Lebanese political system), is rarely addressed or taken into account by managers or monitors of peace processes and deserves greater attention. Furthermore, it should be realized that, in some cases, it is the imperfect, unjust, sectarian, inefficient, and corrupt nature of the political system that remains dominant or re-emerges in a conflict or a post-conflict area which may serve as a strong disincentive for some key parties to a conflict to become fully politicized and integrated into this system, providing them with another reason to retain their armed capabilities and at times pushing them to act as spoilers.

Nevertheless, it is political transformation of militant actors that, however painful, is the most effective way to widen the gap between more moderate elements within a spoiler organization that could evolve into a legal political entity and underground "hard-liners" (or more radical "splinter"/offshoot units), making them easier to isolate, marginalize, and delegitimize and potentially even facilitating their ultimate "freeze", relocation to other countries, dissolution, or destruction (as was the case for many PLO and PFLP offshoot groups). In sum, while the process of political transformation would not necessarily result in a group's rejection of violence once and forever, it could facilitate and contribute to marginalization of its most radical elements.

Despite all the problems and risks potentially associated with the transformation of key armed actors into legal political entities, these are risks worth taking in order to undermine the capacity of spoilers of this type to disrupt the peace process. Unlike the more radical "splinter" groups, spoilers of the first category are the key armed players in the local context that are likely to enjoy support of parts of local population. These groups cannot be ignored and left out of the peace process without fundamentally damaging the process itself. A strategy of isolation and exclusion is badly suited for dealing with spoilers of this type, as it might radicalize the movement as a whole and strengthen hard-liners within the organization, rather than marginalize and weaken them, which is the ultimate way of countering spoilers of the second type – smaller and more radical offshoot or "splinter" groups.

Countering terrorist activities by splinter groups: Marginalization and isolation

The following are some of the main characteristics of *spoilers of the second category*:
- more radical or "splinter" groups acting as spoilers may be more inclined to use terrorism irrationally (i.e. when the use of terrorist means appears inefficient or even counterproductive for achieving their broader declared political/ideological aims)
- these groups are more likely to be personality-driven
- they tend to enjoy less public support than spoilers of the first category and some of them can even operate with a lack of significant local public support
- with a lack of broad popular support (popular legitimacy), spoilers of this type are more heavily dependent on the need to draw upon cultural/historical legitimacy as a means to legitimize their actions
- they are also more likely to depend more heavily on criminal activities as a means of self-financing and enjoy closer relationship with criminal groups; some of them may even degenerate into criminal organizations
- the gap between the group's declared political/ideological goals and undeclared pragmatic objectives widens – some such groups might in fact

have lost their initial ideological goals and, unable to adjust to the postwar environment, depend on violence and terrorism to maintain themselves.

Against this background, the key issue is whether spoilers of this type have the capability to a strike a decisive blow to undermine a peace process, rather than cause it limited damage. While there are few doubts that more radical or "splinter" spoilers can mount violent attacks (including acts of terrorism), even while acting without solid popular support and driven primarily by their own undeclared survival strategies rather than by declared political/ideological causes, it remains highly questionable if their violent activities are sufficient to disrupt fully a solid, properly managed, and widely popular peace process.

A classification of spoilers on the basis of their capabilities to disrupt a peace process is clearly one of the most complicated and controversial tasks: not every armed group easily lends itself to categorization as a spoiler of either of the two types mentioned above. In any case, all efforts should be made to "polarize" the "spoiler spectrum" to a maximum extent possible, so that actual or potential spoilers could fall into either of the two broad categories. While the problem of dealing with *"spoilers that matter"* (key armed actors on the ground acting or retaining a capacity to act as spoilers and use terrorist means) cannot be addressed, let alone solved, at the operational level only and requires a more fundamental, structural solution, terrorist activities by *more radical "splinter" groups* might be countered primarily at the operational level. Challenges posed by major parties to a conflict that have all the necessary capabilities to undermine a peace process if and when they decide to do so require at least partial accommodation of their concerns, preferably as part of a peace agreement itself, and a strong emphasis on political transformation of such organizations. In contrast, more radical "splinter" groups should be further marginalized and isolated to a point when they could be either effectively destroyed (preferably by their own local rivals) or forced to leave the area and seek refuge abroad. As far as the prospects for ultimately integrating a particular spoiler into the peace process are concerned, one of the potential strategies that may be relatively noncontroversial from both anti-terrorism and peacemaking perspectives could be to target and leave out of the political process individual terrorists responsible for ordering, planning, and carrying out terrorist attacks, and those hard-line (often offshoot or "splinter") units and groups in whose activities terrorist means consistently prevail over all other activities, rather than the broader movements or "parent organizations" that cannot and should not be simply isolated or marginalized.

Whether the smaller, more radical groups are able and will be allowed to ruin the peace process by resort to terrorist means depends, more generally, on the nature and management of the peace process itself and, more specifically, on the link between peace process and anti-terrorism, which is the subject of the concluding section of this chapter.

In lieu of conclusion: Anti-terrorism and peacemaking

Whether terrorism is used as a major mode of operation in an armed conflict and/or serves as an instrument of destabilization of the ongoing peace negotiations or peace implementation, a link between peacemaking and anti-terrorism is self-evident. The extent to which this link should be politically established and recognized is, however, less clear. Should reaction to terrorist attacks or anti-terrorism concerns in general be politically dissociated from the peace process for the practical purposes of effective war termination? Or, alternatively, should the two be interlinked to the point of one being fully dependent or conditional upon the other?

The strategy of separating anti-terrorism from ongoing political negotiations and from the peace process in general (by restraining reaction to terrorist attacks or keeping it low profile) might seem to offer the parties to a conflict a way out of the vicious circle of violence and the need to respond to it. This approach can certainly be used as a conflict resolution tool to create a short-term "window of opportunity" when politico-military conditions, for whatever reason (such as a change of leadership in one side in a conflict, or international developments), seem to be favourable for a decisive breakthrough in a peace process. But while not necessarily a one-time tool, this approach can only be applied for a limited number of times. Unless decisive progress is quickly achieved, de-linking the political process from anti-terrorism concerns is not an effective long-term strategy, as most vividly demonstrated by the handling of the Oslo peace process by Israeli governments in the early and mid-1990s.[19] In fact, it can seriously undermine both anti-terrorist efforts and public support for the peacemaking efforts. However, the approach at the opposite extreme – that of tying the peace process and anti-terrorism too closely together, to the point of making one entirely conditional upon the other – can neither lead to a lasting peace settlement nor effectively address the security challenge posed by terrorism to peace negotiations and implementation.[20]

In sum, while anti-terrorism cannot be separated from the peace process because the two are inherently intertwined, linking the former directly to the latter can also create problems. Some standard political and diplomatic techniques (for instance, recognizing a certain group as a negotiating partner on condition that it puts a temporary moratorium on its terrorist activities) may be used to address this problem, but, as noted above, not all spoiler groups might even be interested in joining the political process. In sum, there is a need to link anti-terrorism to peacemaking in a way that is sufficiently indirect not to make one entirely conditional upon the other.

The nature and management of the peace process itself might provide one of the potential solutions of this problem. Actions by groups and factions designed specifically to disrupt negotiations (including terrorist acts) should be taken into account in the design of the peace process, and the latter should be structured in such a way that it contains some in-built hedges against potential disruption by terrorist means.

First of all, a peace agreement should be a result of detailed and intensive negotiations on most critical issues of concern. In many cases a peace agreement itself (or a set of peace agreements at the regional level) is a necessary precondition for partial or complete political transformation of armed resistance groups. While resolution of some central issues at dispute may be deferred until procedural or confidence-building measures are agreed or implemented, most of the critical issues of the armed conflict should be included or at least mentioned in a peace agreement. While the discussion of some of these issues may be left as a subject for further negotiations and further interim agreements may be needed, the initial agreement should be of a fundamental, rather than of largely symbolic, nature. As demonstrated by the extended phased Oslo confidence-building process, postponing many or most of the critical solutions for a series of follow-on interim agreements can undermine the confidence-building process itself. The very process of attempting to settle a number of post-Oslo interim disputes frequently served to erode confidence on both sides, and each new round of the peace process recreated conditions that facilitated the disruption of the peace process by high-profile acts of terrorism or sustained terrorist campaigns.

Secondly, a peace agreement should contain some measures to end violence, such as *cease-fire and confidence-building provisions* that may also precede the conclusion of a formal peace agreement. Cease-fires alone, though, are unlikely to eliminate violence completely. It takes more consistent and long-term confidence-building efforts to achieve full demilitarization and political transformation of the key armed actors that are acting or have the potential to act as spoilers (as noted above, such a strategy might be less relevant for dealing with smaller and more radical offshoot groups and units).

While, ultimately, such a political transformation may be viewed as a long-term confidence-building strategy in itself, it can only evolve as a result of the combined impact of a full range of more specific confidence-building measures. In this context, the use of terrorist means (rather than other violent or non-violent disruption or obstruction techniques) by spoilers is an additional complication, as, in this case, the main problem in building confidence often remains precisely whether and to what extent the integration and recognition of militant groups that are or have been involved in terrorist activities can be politically and publicly acceptable, particularly within the domestic context. It is at the stage of ongoing peace negotiations that a group's involvement in terrorist activities, even if it was limited to the use of terrorist means as one of the violent tactics at the stage of a full-scale armed confrontation, can become a major, often unsurpassable, stumbling block.

To ease such concerns on the part of the major armed groups and the population at large, a combination of military (security) and political, legal, and other "civil" confidence-building measures is required.

First of all, a cease-fire can include and be supplemented by security *measures of constraint*, such as the establishment of demilitarized zones, cessation of military flights, deactivation of weapons systems, and gradual reintegration or disbandment of irregular forces, reinforced by a range of other moves introduced primarily as confidence-building gestures for the armed parties themselves, including *measures of transparency* (extraordinary information exchange; notification of certain military activities; plans for acquisition/deployment of major weapons systems), measures for *monitoring compliance and evaluation* (inspections, observation of military activities), and other joint actions (liaison teams; establishment of direct lines of communication; joint expert crisis management teams etc.).[21] In areas re-emerging from asymmetric conflicts, a combination of such measures appears to be workable when unilateral actions by a stronger side (as a first step) are immediately followed by comparable confidence-building steps by the other side (a non-state actor). As demonstrated by recent research, a sub-area of particular relevance to political transformation of armed actors, effective war termination, and the success of the peace process is demobilization and reintegration of combatants,[22] whose impact goes far beyond the security implications. As pointed out earlier, a former party to a conflict may remain a potential, if not an actual, spoiler as long as it retains an armed capability to undermine a peace process (in terms of structure, personnel, arms etc.). While such security measures as monitoring and verification activities (whether internationally administered or jointly undertaken by the parties themselves) may help prevent a potential spoiler from taking military advantage of groups undergoing demobilization and from taking control over demilitarized areas, the task of reassuring a spoiler's concerns about its own security (that prompt it to keep some armed capability for self-defence purposes) may also be facilitated by a series of non-military confidence-building measures.

The scope of *non-military* (political, legal, civil society, and other) *confidence-building tools* and strategies that can be undertaken at the operational level, with the goal of facilitating the transformation of major local armed actors (spoilers of the first type) into political parties, ranges from amnesties and prisoner releases (that could be made part of peace agreements) to introduction of new anti-terrorism legislation (with proper oversight and accountability provisions) or modification or review of the previous rigid and repressive legislation. The latter may itself pose a major challenge for a full political transformation of armed actors (as in the course of the Sri Lankan peace process, when the LTTE *de facto* operated openly in a political capacity while, in accordance with the Sri Lankan anti-terrorism law, individuals were still detained for their previous association with the LTTE).

In sum, demilitarization of politics and transformation of warring parties into political actors should be seen as priority tasks for both anti-terrorism and peace implementation. Only in so far as significant progress in demilitarization and political transformation of key local armed actors is achieved through a coordinated approach, combining military/ security, political, legal, and other means and undertaken both at a shorter-term operational level and at a longer-term strategic level, can some of the more ambitious *normative tasks* be effectively addressed in a post-conflict environment, such as protection of human rights and democracy-building. It does not mean that all human-rights-related issues should be deferred until the peace is firmly implemented. Moreover, a peace agreement explicitly outlawing discrimination may serve as an anti-terrorist tool itself, as it is the lack of, or mass violations of, political and civil rights that appears to be one of the few factors that has a direct positive correlation with the resort to terrorism.[23] At the same time, formal human rights commitments are unlikely to be implemented unless the general demilitarization and basic political transformation of the key armed actors are achieved, and attempts to apply high standards of human rights to war-torn environments where there is no way to guarantee these rights may discredit democracy-building and further undermine confidence between the parties or between the parties and international custodians.

The same applies to the goal of rapid democratization, often pursued in parallel to a peace process. A need for caution here is even more pressing in those conflict and post-conflict areas where terrorism has been used, whether as a mode of armed resistance or as a spoiler's technique. The relationship between terrorism and democracy in general may be quite ambiguous: while democratic states may be more dramatically hit by attacks on their civilians (as they value the lives of their civilians more than other regimes), established democracies rarely give pretext for large-scale domestic, home-grown terrorism as a result of internal conflict. The link between conflict-related terrorism and democracy can be even more problematic. Most of the existing research suggests that terrorist means used as a mode of operation in a violent conflict tend to be more effective (and the resort to them is most rational) when they are used against a certain type of a state – neither too weak, nor too strong (semi-democratic regimes and states in transition are more exposed to conflict-generated terrorism than either established democracies or rigid authoritarian regimes). In unstable war-torn environments in particular, attempts to implant democratic mechanisms and institutions prematurely can in fact facilitate uncontrolled mobilization of political frustration and violence.[24] This might be particularly relevant for areas that have long experienced authoritarianism or prolonged periods of state failure (state collapse) and are undergoing a painful political transformation and modernization. While democracy may be identified as a long-term goal to be achieved, in such an environment demands for fast democratic changes may be both premature and counterproductive for the success of the peace process. For instance, while human rights groups have widely criticized the predominance of armed groups and their patronage networks in civil administration in Tamil-populated areas of Sri Lanka, the full political transformation of the LTTE in Sri Lanka, essential for the success of the peace process, implies a leading role for the LTTE in civil administration in Tamil-populated areas.[25]

While measures aimed at facilitating political, structural, and, ultimately, ideological transformation of the key armed actors are best tailored for dealing with actual or potential spoilers of the first type, the most far-sighted political strategy for dealing with spoilers of the second type should be focused on their further marginalization. The latter may be achieved by engaging, integrating, and transforming the structure and ideology of the more moderate elements of broader movements and, above all, by depriving the radicals of whatever limited social support they might still enjoy by *making peace widely popular.* In this context it should be noted that, in some cases, the very excesses of such radical groups (including highly lethal and particularly horrific terrorist attacks) might help to reduce support for them further (and also indicate that terrorist means are used by them in an increasingly irrational manner).

In this context, the perceived *legitimacy of the peace process* in general and of a concrete peace agreement in particular accounts for much of their popularity (in contrast to negotiation outcomes based on pure calculation). Among other things, such legitimacy depends on whether all the key local actors and forces (including potential spoilers of the first type) are included in negotiations. As for international legitimacy of a peace process, it is critically important for internationally managed peace negotiations and implementation, but can hardly be decisive for internal peace processes (while often sought and desirable). Similarly, external pressure and regional and international developments may play an important role in an organization's decision to refrain from the use of terrorist means, whether as a major mode of operation or as a spoiler's technique. External influences alone, however, are never sufficient to prevent a group from using terrorist means in the long term: in the constantly changing international environment, outside pressures on groups acting or retaining the capacity to act as spoilers may fade with time.

The link between armed conflict and terrorism cannot be reduced to a strictly causal dependence, when terrorism is generated by conflict and is used as a form of violent resistance in that conflict. When employed as a spoiler's technique to undermine an ongoing peace process, terrorism is aimed at re-escalation of violence and can itself regenerate armed conflict.

On the one hand, sustained or high-profile acts of terrorism should not be allowed to impede the peace process. On the other hand, rigid counterterrorist measures, if undertaken separately from the peace process and with little regard to war termination priorities, might almost as easily interfere with the peace process as terrorist acts by spoilers. Ironically, the so-called "collective impact" measures undertaken as part of counterterrorist campaigns, while not particularly successful as specific anti-terrorist tools,[26] can be very efficient in undermining whatever confidence-building efforts had been in place (as most vividly demonstrated in the course of the Israeli-Palestinian conflict).

One of the ways to address this dilemma is by trying to distinguish, to the extent possible, between mainstream paramilitary groups retaining the capabilities to undermine the peace process and smaller and more radical offshoot or splinter groups, and to polarize further the spectrum of spoilers and reinforce the distinctions between these two categories of armed actors. The optimal strategy for dealing with spoilers of the first type and undermining their capabilities to disrupt the peace process is to encourage the transformation of their more moderate leaders, members, bodies, and currents into political entities.

As for the spoiling behaviour of the more radical "splinter" groups (which often takes the form of terrorism), whether it would be allowed to disrupt a peace process depends primarily on the resilience, legitimacy, and popularity of the process itself, on whether it includes all the parties to a conflict that enjoy significant popular support and retain the capabilities to disrupt peace negotiations and implementation, and, ultimately, on whether the peace sought is perceived as a product of resolution of key issues of conflict rather than as a goal *per se*, to be achieved at all costs.

Notes

1. Intervention by I. William Zartman at the conference on Pathways Out of Terrorism and Insurgency: Comparative Analysis of Peace Processes, Priverno, Italy, organized by the Center for Studies on Terrorism and Political Violence (Latina) and Gino Germany Center for the Study of Crisis, Conflict and Socio-Political Instability (Rome), April 2002.
2. Walter, Barbara F. 2002. *Committing to Peace: The Successful Settlement of Civil Wars*. Princeton: Princeton University Press.
3. Whitbeck, John. 1999. "Peace, process or worse", *Al-Ahram Weekly*, No. 461, 23–29 December, available at http://weekly.ahram.org.eg/1999/461/op1.htm.
4. For general discussion of this point see, for instance, Darby, John and Roger Mac Ginty (eds). 2000. *The Management of Peace Processes*. New York: Macmillan Palgrave/St Martin's Press; Stedman, Stephen J. 1997. "Spoiler problems in peace processes", *International Security*, Vol. 22, No. 2.
5. *Intifada* means "uprising" in Arabic.
6. E.g. Al-Qaeda's super-terrorist network, strategy, and operations were truly global, reached out both to the developed world (the West) and to underdeveloped states, and were as extensive in areas of peace as in areas of conflict. It is important to stress that while Al-Qaeda's super-terrorist network has, for instance, served as one of the donors to several local groups engaged in conflict-related terrorism, these and other potential links between super-terrorism and conflict-related terrorism still do not make one a mere substitute or outgrowth of the other, or fully dependent or conditional upon the other – each of these two types of terrorism retains a great degree of autonomy and its own logic and dynamics.
7. For more detail on distinction between various types of terrorism, see Stepanova, Ekaterina. 2003. *Anti-terrorism and Peace-building During and After Conflict*, SIPRI Policy Paper No. 2. Stockholm: SIPRI, pp. 3–5, available at http://editors.sipri.se/pubs/Stepanova.pdf.
8. On political motivation as a key defining characteristic of terrorism, see e.g. Hoffman, B. 1998. *Inside Terrorism*. New York: Columbia University Press, pp. 13–44.
9. For more detail on distinctions between terrorism and guerrilla warfare as modes of operation in an armed conflict, see Ganor, Boaz. 1998. *Defining Terrorism: Is One Man's Terrorist Another Man's Freedom Fighter?* Herzliyya: International Policy Institute for Counter-Terrorism.
10. According to Protocol I to the Geneva Conventions, "the Parties to the conflict shall at all times distinguish between the civilian population and combatants, and between civilian objects and military objectives, and accordingly shall direct their operations only against military objectives". See Protocol Additional to the Geneva Conventions of 12 August 1949, and Relating to the Protection of Victims of International Armed Conflicts (Protocol I), 8 June 1977, Article 48. Similarly, the international law regulating non-international armed conflict (Protocol II to the Geneva Conventions) does not prohibit members of rebel forces from using force against government soldiers or property provided that the basic tenets governing such use of force are respected.
11. The approach chosen by the author of this chapter is fully in line with the position of the UN High-level Panel on Threats, Challenges and Change and with the emerging consensus on this issue among experts working on the draft Comprehensive Convention Against Terrorism. Recognizing that the use of force by the state against civilians does not fall under the definition of terrorism as such, they called for recognition, in the preamble of the convention, that "State use of force against civilians is regulated by the Geneva conventions and other instruments, and, if of sufficient scale, constitutes a

war crime by the persons concerned or a crime against humanity". See, for instance, United Nations. 2004. *A More Secure World: Our Shared Responsibility*, Report of the Secretary-General's High-level Panel on Threats, Challenges and Change. New York: United Nations, para. 164a, p. 52.
12. For more detail see Stepanova, Ekaterina. 2004. "Linking anti-terrorism and peace operations: Specifics and constraints", in *Peace Support Operations, Parliaments and Legislation*. Moscow: Geneva Center for Democratic Control of the Armed Forces; Center for Political and International Studies.
13. Most of the 38 formal peace accords signed between 1988 and 1998 dealt with conflicts that may have involved some form of external influence and involvement but were concentrated within national boundaries, as distinct from wars between neighbouring states. For more detail see e.g. Darby, John and Roger Mac Ginty. 2000. "Introduction: Comparing peace processes", in John Darby and Roger Mac Ginty (eds) *The Management of Peace Processes*. New York: Macmillan Palgrave/St Martin's Press, pp. 2–3.
14. See e.g. a reference to the Khasav-Yurt agreement in the concluding part of this chapter.
15. Stedman, note 4 above.
16. For more detail see Crenchaw, Martha. 1990. "The logic of terrorism: Terrorist behaviour as a product of strategic choice", in Walter Reich (ed.) *Origins of Terrorism: Psychologies, Ideologies, Theologies, States of Mind*. Cambridge: Cambridge University Press.
17. Particularly if supported, in some cases, by certain local socio-cultural norms and traditions, e.g. remnants of clan-based society, such as blood feuds or slavery.
18. For a discussion on effects of intraparty tensions on negotiations see Hoglund, Kristine. 2001. "Violence: Catalyst or obstacle for conflict resolution?", paper prepared for research seminar, Department of Peace and Conflict Research, Uppsala University, Uppsala, 26 September, pp. 14–15.
19. See e.g. Karsh, Efraim (ed.). 1997. *From Rabin to Netanyahu: Israel's Troubled Agenda*. Portland, OR: Frank Cass, pp. 117–262; Ganor, Boaz. 2002. *Israel's Counter-Terrorism Policy, 1983–1999: Efficacy Versus Liberal Democratic Values*. Herzliya: International Policy Institute for Counter-Terrorism.
20. This was most dramatically demonstrated by the link between terrorism and the peacemaking process in the context of the internal conflict between Russia's federal centre and Chechen radicals in the mid-1990s. It was the two high-profile terrorist attacks by Chechen militants (the raids on hospitals in Budenovsk in June 1995 and in Kizlyar in January 1996) that forced the federal government to sign the hasty and inherently problematic Khasav-Yurt agreement, which was backed by neither political will nor economic resources and did not lead to effective peace implementation.
21. For a comprehensive and detailed list of security confidence-building measures see, for instance, OSCE Forum for Security Cooperation, 1992. *Stabilizing Measures for Localized Crisis Situations*. Vienna: OSCE.
22. For more detail on the importance of demobilization for war termination see Stedman, Stephen J. 2001. *Implementing Peace Agreements in Civil Wars: Lessons and Recommendations for Policy Makers*, International Peace Academy Policy Paper Series on Peace Implementation. New York: IPA, p. 16. On reintegration programmes as anti-terrorism tools in post-conflict environments see Stepanova, note 7 above, pp. 37–38.
23. For more detail on this see, for instance, Kueger, Alan and Jitka Maleckova. 2002. "Education, poverty and terrorism: Is there a causal connection?", report for World Bank Annual Conference on Development Economics, Washington, DC, April.
24. For more detail on the ambiguous relationship between democracy and terrorism see

Rupeshinge, Kumar. 1992. *Internal Conflict and Governance*. New York: St Martin's Press, pp. 1–26.
25. See e.g. Human Rights Watch. 2002. *Sri Lanka: Human Rights and the Peace Process*, Human Rights Watch Background Briefing, July. New York: Human Rights Watch, pp. 2, 8.
26. For more detail on the negative impact of collective-impact counterterrorist measures for conflict and post-conflict areas see Stepanova, note 7 above, pp. 13, 32–33.

5

Spoilers or catalysts? The role of diasporas in peace processes

Yossi Shain and Ravinatha P. Aryasinha

War is not an independent phenomenon, but the continuation of politics by different means ... The aggressor is always peace-loving; he would prefer to take over our country unopposed.
Carl von Clausewitz[1]

... the key to peace is the achievement of mutual agreement, which can only occur when each party sacrifices something they previously believed to be essential. To the contemporary mindset, the true "peacemaker" is the person who is willing to put aside his own ideas of history, justice and morality – in whose name wars are inevitably fought – in the interest of goodwill and nonviolence.
Shalom Levin[2]

The real triumph is that it has shown that representatives of four great Powers can find it possible to agree on a way of carrying out a difficult and delicate operation by discussion instead of by force of arms, and thereby they have averted a catastrophe which would have ended civilization as we have known it.
Neville Chamberlain[3]

To the realist, peace represents a stable arrangement of power; to the idealist, a goal so pre-eminent that it conceals the difficulty of finding the means to its achievement. But in this age of thermonuclear technology, neither view can assure man's preservation. Instead, peace, the ideal, must be practiced. A sense of responsibility and accommodation must guide the behavior of all nations. Some common notion of justice can and must be found, for failure to do so will only bring more "just" wars.
Henry Kissinger[4]

Three days ago I decided the United States should join our NATO allies in military air strikes to bring peace to Kosovo. In my address to the nation last Wednesday, I explained why we have taken this step – to save the lives of innocent civilians in Kosovo from a brutal military offensive; to defuse a powder keg at the heart of Europe that has exploded twice before in this century with catastrophic results; to prevent a wider war we would have to confront later, only at far greater risk and cost; to stand with our NATO allies for peace.
Bill Clinton[5]

This chapter, viewing the issue of spoilers in peace processes through the prism of diasporas, seeks to explore a number of questions. Who is a peace "spoiler"? Which types of conflicts/peace processes are vulnerable to spoiling due to diaspora influence? What is at stake for diasporas in such conflicts/peace processes? What determines a diaspora's capacity to influence such conflicts/peace processes? What modalities are used by diasporas in influencing such conflicts/peace processes? And what suggestive evidence is available on the diaspora-conflict link?

Peace "spoiler"

In the authors' understanding, the term "spoiler" must not be regarded as self-evident. Certainly it implies an attempt to undermine the achievement of peacemaking at all costs, yet it should also include those who enter peace processes without genuinely seeking such results, and even those who prematurely seek peace at all cost notwithstanding the evidence that by engaging in the process of peace they may in fact exacerbate the conflict. In turn it becomes imperative that the success of a peace process depends upon effective mechanisms to manage spoilers.

Early research relating to peace spoilers centres around the work of Stedman, who defines "peace spoilers" as "leaders and parties who believe that peace emerging from negotiations threaten their power, worldview, and interests, and use violence to undermine attempts to achieve it".[6] He argues that spoilers differ by the goals they seek and their commitment to achieving those goals. Three types of spoilers have been identified: "total spoilers", whose goals are immutable and "who see the world in all-or-nothing terms"; "limited spoilers", who have specific goals that may or may not be negotiable; and "greedy spoilers", whose goals "expand or contract based on calculations of cost and risk". Darby seeks modification of this typology in order to encompass all former militants whose violence may threaten a peace process, including those who are engaged in negotiations and those who may undermine it unintentionally through their violent activities.[7] He identifies four types of spoilers:

"dealers", those prepared to make a deal; "zealots", those whose goal is to spoil the process by bringing it down through violence; "opportunists", violent groups that may be persuaded under some circumstances to end violence; and "mavericks", those groups whose violence is primarily motivated by personal rather than political objectives. Zahar proposes an alternate "spoiler" typology that focuses on the relationship between "intent", the reasons that may motivate groups or individuals to spoil, "capability", the resources available to groups and individuals to this end, and "opportunity", the constraints on spoiling posed by the presence and commitment of foreign interveners.[8]

With reference to diasporas the authors believe that it is more meaningful that the act of "spoiling" be viewed as lying along a continuum that ranges from high levels of support (when diasporas act as catalysts) to extreme levels of hostility (when diasporas act as spoilers) towards a negotiating process or settlement. As the quotes opening the chapter suggest, the authors believe that there is a need to broaden the interpretation of the term "spoiler" and the act of "spoiling" in order to analyse meaningfully their effect on peace processes and, more so, the attainment of an enduring peace. This would require a more nuanced interpretation of the term that would permit, as the earlier quotations reflect, not only acts of sabotage but also acts of appeasement in the search for peace to be considered as acts of "spoiling".

Given the state-centric treatment found in much of the field of political science/IR literature which ascribes sanctity to state sovereignty, there has been the tendency in recent conflict studies literature to associate the term "spoiler" with only sub-state or non-state actors who pose obstacles to peace processes, disregarding state actors. This chapter rejects the notion that only non-state actors can be peace spoilers. It suggests that "spoilers" of peace processes could be of three types:
- those who totally oppose the "reasonable" resolution of a conflict (e.g. the Palestinian Hamas, which reject any "reasonable" peace deals with Israel)
- those who enter into superficial peace settlements for purposes of expediency, disregarding the serious issues that are needed to resolve a conflict and generate a durable peace (e.g. as Chamberlain did in 1938)
- those who object to a particular peace deal and/or procedural issues involving such a process (e.g. the IRA's resistance to decommissioning weapons, the Armenian diaspora's views on relations between Armenia and Turkey, and the Sri Lankan Tamils regarding securing an interim administration in north-east Sri Lanka prior to agreeing to a final settlement).

This chapter focuses only on the last category, where spoiling cannot be regarded as automatic (as in the first category above) or as resulting from unintended consequences of actions by the parties involved (as in the second category).

Peace processes vulnerable to spoiling

One can identify four types of conflict and related peace processes:
- state-to-state conflicts which deal primarily with resources or boundaries, where neither side is seeking to eliminate the other (e.g. Eritrea-Ethiopia or India-Pakistan)
- state-to-state conflicts that have a distinct minority dimension (e.g. Armenia-Azerbaijan on Nagorno-Karabakh)
- intrastate conflicts where a minority is seeking secession/irredentism (the Sri Lankan Tamils, the UK Northern Irish Catholics, the Moro in the Philippines, the Kashmiris/Sikhs in India, the Turkish Kurds, and the southern Sudanese are good examples)
- intrastate conflicts which have the limited objective of regime change and do not question the legitimacy of the state or its boundaries. Such conflicts involve political exiles, who by definition would expect to return home once the conflict ceases (exiles from Iraq prior to the downfall of Sadam Hussein, Iranian exiles, or anti-Castro Cubans in Miami).

It is argued that where sizeable diasporas and organized diasporas might be present, such conflicts are more vulnerable to diaspora influence.

Diaspora involvement

For the purpose of the present study, a diaspora is regarded as a people with a common origin who reside outside their country of origin or real or symbolic "homeland" (kin-state), whether independent or not.[9] They regard themselves, or are regarded by others, as members or potential members of the national community of their "homeland", a standing retained regardless of the actual status of their citizenship inside or outside their homeland.[10] Here a distinction must be drawn between "far-removed diasporas", who are affected largely in an ideational sense through family ties, and "affected diasporas", who are influenced by the conflict directly and indirectly and in turn have a direct impact upon it.

Diasporas cannot be viewed simply as a domestic constituency within their host states, but rather as constituting a complicating analytical category in IR theory that operates at a distinct third level and plays an independent role between the interstate and domestic levels. Despite the growing acknowledgement that diasporas represent communities with transnational bonds and play a significant role in issues concerning their homelands (kin-states or aspiring kin-states), few have focused on the specific impact diasporas have on peace processes between their kin-states and their rivals. Those who do tend to view diasporas mostly as detrimental and at times as helpful to such processes, often failing to take cognizance of the complexities concerning the negotiation of identities of diasporas in such processes. Normatively, given that managing spoilers is essential to the effective implementation of peace processes, it is hoped that a study of diasporic involvement in conflict/resolution will allow us to consider whether and how diaspora support for conflict escalation can be prevented, or at least minimized, how diasporas can be mobilized for peace processes, and who is best equipped to do so and to what effect.

What motivates diasporic involvement in conflict/peace processes?

How pivotal or marginal diasporic involvement is in determining the direction and trajectory of a conflict is a crucial question. It has been suggested that when compared with their homeland kin, diasporas are seemingly more hard-line nationalistic and as a result more maximalist in conflicts at "home". Writing in 1860, English politician and historian Lord Acton[11] observed that "exile is the nursery of nationality" and that "nationality" arose from exile, when men could no longer easily dream of returning to the nourishing bosom that had given them birth. Certainly, many political exiles and their diasporic constituencies have historically played an integral part and often led in the struggle for political independence in their claimed homelands. Exiles have influenced the shaping of new nation-states that were born out of wars (noticeably exiles during the First World War) or the nature of post-war governments in already established states (such as Iraq after Saddam Hussein). Their success has been ensured mostly by their alliance with foreign victors (the Western Allies in Europe during the First World War or the Americans in Iraq today).[12]

Political exiles who wish to return to their native land are only one segment of a diaspora. Even those who wish to reside away from the real or historic homeland are often driven towards involvement in homeland-related affairs, and particularly wars. Byman *et al.* argue that, motivated by ethnic affinity, communities abroad often feel a genuine sympathy for the struggles of their brethren elsewhere.[13] At times they may also feel a sense of guilt that they are safe while those left behind are enmeshed in bloody conflict. Further, "some case study evidence suggests that diasporas harbor grievance for much longer than resident populations", and that "the reason why diasporas are predicted to affect the risk of conflict is financial". Being much wealthier than resident populations in the countries they have left, they are much better able to finance conflict. In addition, "diasporas do not themselves suffer any of the costs of conflict, and so have a greater incentive to seek vengeance than the resident populations".[14] Wiebe believes that when homelands are well-established states, kin communities abroad are less inclined to channel their ethnic identity into diasporic activity.[15] But when the homeland territory is not governed by the ethno-national community, or in cases of new and weak states, or when the national identity was "held in trust" by the diaspora during the years of foreign domination, diasporic involvement is intensified. In the case of the Sikhs, the people's distinct identity and the struggle for a separate Sikh homeland of "Khalistan" was initiated and is sustained by the Sikh diaspora almost a decade after militancy in the Punjab was crushed. Appadurai regards Khalistan as "an invented homeland of the deterritorialized Sikh population of England, Canada and the United States",[16] while Tatla opines that the diaspora continues to "redefine Sikh ethnicity in terms of an ethno-national bond".[17] This chapter identifies four possible factors which are at stake and could motivate a diaspora to seek to influence negotiations for peace with its enemies: issues of identity, visions of the conflict and compromise, organizational and bureaucratic interests, and economic interests in the homeland.

Issues of identity

The ethnic identity of a diaspora group is made up of elements that are shared with their kin in the homeland (historical, social, and cultural ideals) as well as other elements that are unique to the diaspora and derive from its separate experiences. The diaspora's identity is also affected by the degree to which its leaders (and members) are actively engaged in the domestic affairs of the homeland. Many symbols of homeland sovereignty – a currency, stamps, the military, a flag, and the like – are ingredients that may reinforce the identity of the diaspora kin just as they cultivate and sustain the national identity of the homeland's citizens. The "wholeness" or inviolability of the homeland's territory is also a key marker of the nation's well-being for the diaspora. Thus an interstate conflict or internal separatist movement generally becomes a major ingredient in diasporic identity. A threat to the homeland's survival from conflict always serves as an important mobilizing force for diasporic communities, enabling them to build institutions, raise funds, and promote activism among community members who might otherwise allow their identity to fade to the level of mere ethnic "folk ways". This is especially true for diasporas that are part of the rich and accommodating tapestry of open and pluralist societies like the USA.

Indeed, the open nature of US society has led many ethnic Americans to lose much of the "content" of their ethno-cultural and religious identity and create instead "a highly individualized ethnic identity". This dynamic "further erodes commonality of experience, the 'mutual understandings and interpretations' that are the substance of 'thin' ethnic content".[18] In these circumstances the fate of the homeland's violent conflict can play an important role in the diaspora community's ability to mobilize, maintain, and nourish its own ethnic identity in the country of domicile. Thus the strong relations between American Jews and Israel have been constantly reinforced by the perpetual security challenges faced by the Jewish state. When diaspora communities identify with their homelands as a place they can always move to if the conditions in their countries of residence (host lands) become unfriendly, the diaspora involvement in problems in the homeland increases significantly. This also tends to occur when homelands, in turn, regard themselves as defenders of their "people" (inside or outside the homeland). This has been the case with Israel (with its Zionist ideology) and Jewish communities outside Israel, many of which have been targeted by acts of terror and anti-Semitism, allegedly because of their affinity with Israel. When in July 2004 Prime Minister Sharon of Israel called on "our brothers in France [to] move to Israel, as soon as possible, to flee the wildest anti-Semitism there", some leaders of the French Jewish diaspora joined President Jacques Chirac in rebuking Sharon for inserting Israel's own struggles and the rhetoric of Zionist aspirations into the French arena in a manner that may allegedly undermine the standing of Jews inside France. Even the Israeli daily *Ha'aretz* wrote that although Zionism's offer to all Jews to have Israel as their home always remains, "it is not feasible for Israel to push against the wall Jews who are citizens of other countries, and force them to choose between loyalty to their country and their identification with Israel and their need for it".[19]

Vision with respect to the conflict and compromise: Who speaks for the people?

For a diaspora, the vision with respect to homeland conflict and compromise is often rooted in the collective memory (immediate or generational) of the state, or the "people" who were forced out of their land as part of a historic trauma. Such memories do not necessarily reflect the challenges faced in the context of developments that have taken place since the trauma occurred. Yet, besides current threats, it is the maintenance of the memory of catastrophic events – such as the Armenian genocide or the Jewish Holocaust – that instructs nations' behaviour and has the capacity to become a rallying cry in the mobilization of the people (inside and outside the state). Traumatic memories are particularly critical for diasporic identity, enabling diaspora organizations and leaders to build institutions, raise funds, and promote activism, with significant consequences for kin-state diplomacy. In such a context peace deals that compromise a diaspora's key memory could appear a double-edged sword: on the one hand threatening a diaspora's public perception of grievance and justification for struggle; but on the other, when congruent with the hyphenated identities in their host countries, such memories would be seen as positive influences, consistent with the host state's creed. Thus some have argued that the Holocaust has now become part of American memory and serves Jewish mobilization on behalf of Israel. Even more significant has been the critical role played by diasporic Armenians in the USA and France in shaping the foreign policy of these countries towards the Caucasus, with relevance to the possibility of a peace settlement between Armenia and Azerbaijan. This influence exemplifies how national images and policies of states are affected by a powerful diasporic community. While the Armenian genocide is the most central issue to diasporic identity and its organizational agenda, it is less important to the homeland community, which for the most part escaped the trauma of the event. Moreover, while no diasporic Armenians in the West are from Nagorno-Karabakh, the issue matters to the diaspora in light of the historical memory of losing lands and lives to Turkish nationalists throughout eastern Anatolia between 1915 and 1923.[20]

Indeed, the answer to the question of who has the right to legitimate and authoritative representation of the people (inside and outside the homeland) remains a point of debate, and may vary according to the balance of material and intellectual power between the kin-state domestic population and the diaspora. It is also influenced by the networks that have emerged among the multitude of political forces inside and outside the homeland.

Until the 1970s the Armenian genocide was for the most part ignored around the world, and Armenian claims for national rights went virtually unnoticed. Inspired by "third world" ideology and the international attention given to political terrorism in the Middle East and Europe, young Armenians in Lebanon established the Armenian Secret Army for the Liberation of Armenia (ASALA). In numerous acts of terrorism against Turkish facilities and diplomats (as well as against Western targets allegedly associated with the "fascist regime in Turkey"), ASALA's violence re-energized the Armenian cause in the international arena. The organization's visibility posed a challenge to the Dashnak leadership, and the diasporic party responded by establishing its own terrorist arm known as the Justice Commando for the Armenian Genocide (JCAG).[21] Terrorism won the Armenian cause international attention, and helped in rallying the largely dormant diaspora – whose members tended to unite around conservative political and religious organizations – to demand international recognition of the genocide. Tololyan has written that "the true audience of Armenian terrorism [was not Turkey and its NATO allies but was] the Armenian diaspora, whose fraying culture is constituted to a remarkable degree by old stories".[22]

Moreover, if a homeland government chooses to pursue reconciliation with a historical enemy, diaspora communities may even feel that their identity as historical victims of that enemy is under threat. To the extent that an Armenian rapprochement with Turkey requires de-emphasizing the genocide issue, for example, it threatens the identity of diaspora Armenians. As Kachig Tololyan and Krikor Beledian aptly remark, "The diaspora ... has the Genocide as its point of departure. It clings to the memory of the Catastrophe; the more distant the memory becomes, the more the diaspora seems to write about it."[23] If the Armenian state, the international embodiment of "Armenianness", decides to put the genocide lower down on its list of national priorities, it is by implication devaluing diaspora Armenians as part of the transnational Armenian community.

The debate (inside and outside the homeland) about whether diasporic segments "have the right" publicly to oppose an official position of the homeland's elected government – in favour or against – on a peace deal with its external enemies is always contentious. Anderson opines that while diasporas "find it tempting to play identity politics" with respect to their home states, "this citizen-less participation is inevitably non-responsible – our hero will not have to answer for, or pay the price of, the long-distance politics he undertakes".[24] There are many who claim that those who do not reside inside the homeland and do not send their children to serve in its army should stay out of the homeland's high politics. When it comes to Israel and American Jewry, for example, diasporic politics (left and right) often reflect Israeli political divisions regarding foreign policy and peace deals with the Palestinians, and the question of whether American Jews should publicly criticize Israeli official policy or automatically support its government decisions often split the diaspora and intensify division between its activists and their counterparts inside Israel who often recruit them.

This split recently alarmed Rabbi Dr David Luchins, a prominent leader of America's Jewish Orthodox community – which tends to hold right-wing positions when it comes to yielding territory in peace deals between Israel and the Palestinians. In an unusual move, Rabbi Luchins criticized those in his camp who rallied in New York against Sharon's decision to pull out from settlements in Gaza. His criticism of his diasporic compatriots was based not only on his conviction that diaspora members do not have the right to be "players" but only "audience" in the homeland's politics, but also derived from his fear that when a Jew criticizes Israel for its policies the outside world cannot understand the nuances of criticism based on affinity and concern for the homeland well-being. Comparing Israeli politics to a baseball game and Israeli citizens to the teams, he said: "American Jewish Zionists have box seats, and we have the right and obligation to support our team. But we are not playing. Only members of the team, even those who are benched, have the right to take part in the team meetings. We fans talk strategy, but the only ones with the right to decide matters are the team members."[25]

This position, however, is not shared by many other diaspora activists; even more interesting, homeland decision-makers tend to implicate diasporas in their decisions on peace negotiations and even endow the diaspora with an authoritative voice. For example, famous Jewish-American diplomat Dennis Ross, the former chief negotiator for the US Middle East peace team who now chairs the Institute for Jewish Policy Planning founded by the Jewish Agency, recently called on Prime Minister Ariel Sharon and the state of Israel to grant diaspora Jewry an official consulting status when it comes to Israeli foreign policy that affects the entire Jewish people.[26] This is a far cry from the vision of Israel's founder David Ben-Gurion, who always stressed the centrality of the state over the "temporary" existence of the diaspora. Yet Ross's message is now endorsed, at least rhetorically, by the Israeli government itself. Thus when Ariel Sharon addressed Jewish leaders in New York shortly after becoming prime minister in 2001 he told them that "if Israel weakens or God forbid disappears" their comfortable lives as American Jews "would not be the same". He added that diaspora Jews should raise their voice in defence of Jerusalem, since "the future of Israel [and Jerusalem] is not just a matter for Israelis who live there: Israel belongs to the entire Jewish people. And Israel would not be what it is today if it were not for the efforts of all Jews worldwide."[27]

Organizational or bureaucratic interests

Just as the threat to the homeland is a powerful tool in galvanizing faraway communities, funding diasporic organizations, and engaging diasporas in the politics of their countries of domicile (the host state), the end of the conflict in the homeland can reduce diasporic interest and recruitment potential and may even threaten the viability of diasporic organizations. After the signing of the Oslo Agreement in September 1993, Arthur Hertzberg wrote that, with peace in the Middle East, Israel would no longer remain Jewish America's "secular religion", and the diaspora would have to reshape its identity and institutions to meet domestic US challenges.[28] Certainly the eruption of mass violence in the Middle East in the autumn of 2000, which was followed by a new wave of anti-Semitism, deeply affected the thinking and organizational efforts of the majority of Jewish Americans. Jewish-American organizations that had spent the better part of the 1990s learning to focus inward on domestic challenges and searching for new roles in the changed political environment produced by the Oslo accords quickly reverted to their pre-Oslo programming and rallied to Israel's side as the extent of the danger to Israel became clear. Mort Zuckerman, chairman of the Conference of Presidents of Major Jewish Organizations, commented at the time that "one of the things Arafat has accomplished is a greater degree of unity among Jews in Israel and [the USA]. There is a wider degree of support and unanimity within this community than has existed in a long time."[29] This new posture of Jewish unity has also generated a significant resurgence of Jewish donations to ensure Israeli security and economic viability.

The Armenian case is also telling and perhaps more dramatic. Since September 1991, following the restoration of Armenian statehood, a complex and difficult interaction developed between Armenians inside and outside the state regarding the most basic questions of identity. When Armenia's first president, Levon Ter-Petrossian, formulated a foreign policy that avoided the genocide as a central issue, it was quickly inserted by the diaspora into Armenia's domestic politics and deeply affected the bilateral relations between Turkey and Armenia. How to address the genocide legacy also remains a key factor in Armenia's ability to reach an agreement with Azerbaijan over Nagorno-Karabakh. From his first day in office and throughout four years of negotiations with Azerbaijan (a cease-fire was established in 1994), Ter-Petrossian earned the ire of the strong diasporic community. This was caused by his attempts to reconcile with Turkey and resolve the war with Turkish Azerbaijan, in part by means of downplaying the genocide issue. Ter-Petrossian's so-called "realist-pragmatist" policy meant that "the steps of the Armenian people must be proportionate to the degree of [their] strength".[30] This reasoning dictated that "the Armenian genocide should be left off Armenia's political agenda". Ter-Petrossian prescribed normal relations with Turkey instead of dreams based on "radical interpretations of the past". He posed the rhetorical question: "Let's say that all states and the United Nations were to recognize that they slaughtered us; what then?" The president also maintained that if Armenia wished to achieve political democracy and real independence from Russia, it should open up to

Turkey. It was in his opinion an illusion that Russia can ensure the security of Armenia. Consequently, Ter-Petrossian refused to recognize the self-declared independence of Nagorno-Karabakh, rejected calls for its annexation, and insisted that the conflict was between local Armenians and the government of Azerbaijan.

The diaspora-led Dashnak Party (a transnational, pan-Armenian organization that views itself as the guardian of Armenian nationalism) and other diasporic organizations criticized Ter-Petrossian for abandoning the national cause. They funded newspapers and other organs to galvanize domestic Armenian opinion against his "treasonous" handling of the Nagorno-Karabakh negotiations. Ter-Petrossian was ultimately forced to resign in 1998, and the diaspora was highly instrumental in his removal. The newly installed president, Robert Kocharian, who recognized the power of the diaspora in defining Armenia's national goals, made the pursuit of genocide recognition an integral part of Armenia's foreign policy agenda. Ronald Suny has written:

Almost immediately the new government reverted to a more traditional nationalism, one more congenial to the diaspora and in line with the hard-line position adopted by the Nagorno-Karabakh government. Armenia ... reemphasized the Genocide issue, always a source of pain and emotion for Armenians and a powerful wedge between Armenia and Turkey. As a consequence, a profoundly risky attempt to reorient the national discourse ultimately failed before intractable obstacles both domestic and foreign ... The power and coherence of the Armenian national identity, the popular projection of the images of Genocide onto the Nagorno-Karabakh conflict, and the closing off of the Turkish option all contributed to the fall of a once-popular national leader, whose move beyond the limit of Armenian identity choices and national discourse did not bring the expected political payoff, i.e. stability, economic well-being, integration in the region, etc.[31]

Indeed, Armenian diasporic organizations have been in the forefront of presenting the genocide case to the Western media, academic community, and governments. In recent years diasporic lobbies have succeeded in pushing European parliaments and American legislators to pass genocide resolutions despite Turkey's denials, protests, and diplomatic efforts to thwart such pronouncements. As much as President Kocharian recognizes the critical role of the diaspora, his administration has found itself squeezed between the great potential advantage of improving relations with Turkey and the diasporic veto power. It is also evident that as much as Kocharian contemplates the idea of striking a deal with Turkey that will give attention to the genocide in a manner that ultimately removes the issue from the political realm, he fully understands that without the high profile the genocide gives the Armenians, his country may not receive the international attention for which it yearns.

Certainly many homeland Armenians are likely to welcome "new realism" in foreign policy, as they resent the fact that their ongoing suffering is not felt by the diaspora. As Mehmet Ali Birand, a leading Turkish observer, has written: "What bothers the Armenians in the shops and markets is not whether Turkey will accept the Genocide allegations or not. They are more concerned with how to fill their stomachs and how to win their daily grind."[32] Furthermore, in many respects the attention given to the genocide today is much more internationally significant then the attention given to Armenia altogether. To some extent one can argue that, in the minds of the diaspora, Armenia as a homeland has served more as a notion, perhaps a mythical vision, than as a concrete sovereign state. This vision, so entangled with the memories of the genocide, has been interjected into the weak Armenian state to such a degree that it now dominates its foreign policy decisions.

Economic interests in the homeland

For a diaspora, economic interests in the homeland could also become a countervailing consideration in judging peace settlements, given the prospect such agreements hold for the protection of their current assets and possible future investment in their homelands. In kin-states which are coming out of long years of backwardness and adversity, diaspora members who acquired skills abroad may have a relative advantage in playing a guiding role in the emerging state. In this context, the role played by the Americans for a New Irish Agenda (ANIA), which comprised Irish-American businessmen, in helping facilitate the Good Friday Agreement with respect to the conflict in Northern Ireland becomes instructive. This was projected as an exercise of thinking "outside the box", a theory traditionally applied to the business world. Goldman observes that membership of the ANIA included IBM executive Kim Reilly, Mutual American CEO Bill Flynn, and the reclusive billionaire Chuck Feeney who owned virtually every duty-free shop in the world.[33] While the Irish members of the ANIA were "stakeholders serving their homeland, which had been torn apart by violence", "their motivations were not completely altruistic", as a "peaceful Ireland would also open the door to lucrative investments". It is noteworthy that second- and third-generation Irish Americans had moved up the corporate ladder to such an extent that by the mid-1980s approximately 30 per cent of the CEOs of *Fortune* magazine's top 500 companies were Irish.

Furthermore, diasporas' role in post-conflict reconstruction has also been alluded to with reference to the Bosnian and Eritrean diasporas in Europe: recent fieldwork amongst both communities indicates how links with their countries of origin that extend beyond the political dimension (to include trade and social networks) help to herald peace processes, or alternatively spoil them.[34] Koser and Van Hear suggest there is anecdotal evidence that in Sri Lanka too, since the cease-fire in March 2002, Tamils abroad have been visiting in large numbers and many were investigating the possibilities of reviving or investing in businesses in Jaffna and elsewhere.[35]

Determinants of a diaspora's capacity to influence conflict/peace

A diaspora operates as a "triangular relationship" that concerns the diaspora itself, the "society of settlement" (host state), and the "society of origin" (home state).[36] To this we should add a fourth dimension – the prevailing trends in the global political economy,[37] which result from the forces of economic globalization, demographic pressures, and the challenges posed by the new global security environment. Aryasinha has emphasized that this added fourth dimension is necessary in integrating the experiences of "recent" diasporas compared to the trajectory of "earlier" diasporas.[38] One can elaborate on these four dimensions.

First, the extent to which a diaspora is able to act as a "spoiler" reflects the organizational strength of diasporic institutions and individual members in their host society and their capacity collectively to enjoy relative autonomy of action (agency). Different groups within the diaspora community could have diverging views about the appropriate direction of the homeland's foreign policy. If the community is divided, its influence weakens, or it might be applied in different directions. The Sri Lankan Tamils have been spared much of the interorganizational rivalry that has plagued most other recent diasporic communities, such as the Sikhs and Kurds in the West. The degree of hegemony maintained by the Liberation Tigers of Tamil Eelam (LTTE) over the Tamil diaspora community is comprehensive, and permeates through not only the political life of the community but also the economic, social, and educational spheres. However, a ramification of this monolithic leadership role of the LTTE as the vanguard of the Sri Lankan Tamil diaspora has been that the Tamil diaspora community has lost much of its "agency" role and is often seen as a tool in the hands of the LTTE.

Second, the propensity as well as the longevity of diasporic support depend heavily on the character of the host states and their attitude to "outsiders". Here it is assumed that diasporic activism is possible largely in host states that are democratic polities. Such polities, however, may vary greatly in terms of their willingness actively to police diasporic activists, and in their willingness to assimilate "outsiders" in their midst. This point has been particularly evident in the case of Germany *vis-à-vis* its Kurd and Croat communities. Germany generally stymied Kurdish diasporic struggles but permitted Croats residing in the country to struggle for independence and ultimately influence its own foreign policy. In the early 1990s, even before the Yugoslav federation had begun to disintegrate, Croats of the diaspora heeded the homeland's call and returned to fight in the war that broke out in 1991. Other diaspora members raised money (as much as $30 million had been mustered by 1991) while at the same time lobbying hard in Germany, which in turn pushed the European Union into early recognition of the new state. Croat diasporic nationalists also raised over $4 million for the 1990 election campaign of Franjo Tudjman, Croatia's arch-nationalist president, and eventually were awarded representation in parliament. After the country won its independence, 12 out of the 120 seats in the Croatian parliament were allotted to diaspora members. At the same time, only seven seats were set aside for Croatia's ethnic minorities.[39]

Fuglerud, who studies the Tamil diaspora in Norway, claims that maintaining relationships with the Norwegian people was not a major concern for the Tamil refugees.[40] Instead, the situation in the homeland and maintaining connections to fellow countrymen were of far greater importance for them. Fuglerud opines that "the future of Eelam depends on the Tamil diaspora as much as the future of the diaspora, in a certain sense, depends on the fate of Eelam". Discussing the relationship between space, time, and national identity, he argues that in the Sri Lanka Tamil diaspora one finds two different conceptions of Tamil culture: the "traditional" and the "revolutionary".[41] He observes that the latter serves as a basis for Tamil separatism, and that by propagating this and being seen to be espousing the cause of its home community the diaspora has gained greater attention and also a degree of moral high ground in its host states. With reference to Canada's role as a host state, Ignatieff cautions "the disturbing possibility is that Canada is not an asylum from hatred, but an incubator of hatred".[42]

It is not clear, however, whether diaspora members are likely to be galvanized more if they are allowed to assimilate into their adopted countries or are prevented from doing so. Sometimes integration into host societies empowers diaspora activists, who feel more confident to advance their homeland agenda within their host state, while at other times such integration has stymied their passion. Yet at other times diaspora members who are prevented from integrating or fail to integrate into a hostile environment are pushed to channel their alienated energies towards homeland-related struggles. Moreover, if militants among a diaspora are prevented from controlling their kin-communities, involuntary support is likely to decrease. In the case of the USA, Shain has observed that the power of a diaspora relies heavily on its organizational ability to justify homeland-related actions in terms of American national interests and values.[43] Indeed, the American interest in the conflicts in Northern Ireland and Cyprus, and between Armenia and Azerbaijan, India and Pakistan, and Israel and its Arab neighbours, is all heavily influenced by the strength of well-organized ethnic diasporas in US politics. Finally, even the adversaries of kin-states may recognize and try to confront or work with diasporic forces involved in the homeland conflict to advance their own cause. After the defeat of the Labour government in Israel's 1996 elections, the PLO reached out to liberal Jews in the USA to try to sustain the progress of Palestinian autonomy in the West Bank and Gaza. However, the efforts of Palestinians and other Arab officials to use Jewish Americans as a lever on the US executive branch, the Congress, or the Israeli government were undermined when Arafat lost all credibility as a result of the collapse of the Oslo peace process.

Third, a diaspora's capacity also depends on the situation in the kin-state. These capacities may be circumscribed when kin-states violate norms that are valued by the host state, resulting in the diaspora being implicated or held accountable morally and politically for actions taken by the kin-state's players. The US government and perhaps even the US public may expect diaspora leaders to persuade or pressure their homeland governments/communities to alter their policies in a more congenial direction. As a rule of thumb, the "weaker" the homeland is, both in terms of need for diasporic assets and in terms of permeability to societal pressures, and the more cohesive the diasporic community is, the greater influence the community will exert on the homeland.

Since diasporas may provide critical material and symbolic resources for their kin-states, and since the homeland authorities' own survival may be contingent on the availability of these resources, diasporas may earn a strong voice in their kin-states' most critical decisions. When diasporic communities are much more developed – institutionally, economically, and culturally – than their co-nationals inside the homeland, and when the relative strengths of the diaspora *vis-à-vis* the homeland's authority and society are so patent, diasporic institutions are likely to dominate the production and appropriation of national symbols and the collective memories of the entire nation (inside and outside the homeland), in a manner that gives the diaspora the power to determine the ideological parameters of a homeland conflict and the requirements for a termination of hostilities. Armenians in the USA and France, for example, are responsible for instilling into the Armenian-Azeri conflict an echo of the Armenian genocide. Ultimately, the genocide also became the central "chosen trauma" of the Armenian state. It was increasingly invoked when Turkey extended its support to Azerbaijan, another Turkic country. Richard G. Hovannisian has said that Turkish moves to support Azerbaijan in the Karabakh conflict were seen by the diaspora "as the logical continuation of a long-term policy to keep Armenia helpless and vulnerable ... [so that] at a convenient moment it can, perhaps, seize upon an excuse to eliminate the little that was left of the historic Armenian territories".[44]

Fourth, the prevailing trends in the global political economy resulting from the twin effects of globalization and global security also determine a diaspora's capacity. Presently, the strong bearing globalization has on the international system enables diasporas to reach higher levels of activity on the basis of the flow of people, the flow of capital, and the flow of information. The human capital of a diaspora (its skills and professional expertise) and diasporic financial capital have impacted greatly on kin-states. Diaspora members, in turn, have been harnessed and rewarded by their governments, including being given the right to vote. Yet "globalization's evil offspring", to borrow Jim Hoagland's phrase, also enables political entrepreneurs, like Osama bin Laden, to exploit radical Islamism to recruit and activate alienated migrants to engage in terrorism in a way that transforms traditional diasporic struggles associated with nationalist affinities into transnational utopian religious movements that ultimately seek to undermine altogether the nation-state and modernity. Sheffer notes that "out of the fifty most active terrorist organizations and groups, twenty-seven constitute either segments of ethnonational or religious diasporas or are supported by such diasporas".[45] These terrorists are more lethal and more agile in instances where a diaspora is under the hegemony of such organizations.[46]

Indeed, attitudes that were generally receptive to receiving "outsiders" in the Western liberal democracies have also undergone considerable change in recent years, initially due to demographic pressures but also because of security issues. With reference to the Sri Lankan Tamil diaspora, McDowell draws attention to a repatriation programme offered to Tamil asylum-seekers by Switzerland in 1996, one of the first of its kind in Europe, which sought to stem the flow of Tamil refugees to that country in the face of their engaging in violence.[47] In 1998 Norway and Denmark, and in 2000 Germany and most recently the UK, deported to Colombo those whose asylum applications had been rejected. According to Robert Evans MEP: "The UK government and the other European governments are presently trying to work out a common European Asylum Policy that will provide an opportunity and assistance for those wishing to return to Sri Lanka to resettle. But there will not be any forced repatriation."[48] Munz and Weiner, in a comparative study of the interaction between migrants and refugees with that of the foreign policies of the USA and Germany towards resident diasporas' countries of origin, note that, faced with growing resistance to admitting foreigners into their countries, both governments have been using foreign policy instruments in an effort to change the conditions in the refugees' countries of origin that forced them to leave.[49] The study addresses questions such as which policies can influence governments to improve their human rights, protect minorities, end internal strife, reduce the level of violence, or improve economic conditions so that large numbers of people need not leave their homes.

The level of global security concerns that prevail at a given time further influences the level of national security threat a country feels towards diaspora groups living in its midst. This results in the imposition of country-based security measures. Smith notes with respect to the conflict in Sri Lanka that in the post-9/11 period up to US$4 billion of LTTE funds have been frozen. Such actions may clearly constrain the capacity of diasporas.[50] Indeed, since the public outrage in the West following 9/11, the loyalty of diasporas has become increasingly suspect and there has been a tendency to view political activities of diaspora communities in support of homeland causes with considerable alarm. In the USA, Canada, the UK, France, Australia, and many other countries scrutiny of diaspora activities has increased, particularly in the transfer of funds. This has resulted in an increased propensity by diasporas to dissociate themselves and/or to seek to nudge community-related organizations away from extremism. This is no doubt in order to avoid the difficulties presently faced by Islamic communities and other diasporas which are regarded to be supporting terrorism. At the same time diasporas have sought to overcome these obstacles. A recent challenge by Sri Lankan Tamil and Kurdish diaspora groups[51] to the US Patriot Act's prohibition on providing "expert advice or assistance" to foreign terrorist organizations was upheld by the District Court of California. This is likely to reduce the inhibitions Tamil diaspora organizations in the USA, as well as their members, felt in providing funds for fear of possible prosecution.[52]

Means used by diasporas to influence conflict/peace

This chapter identifies four means used by diasporas in influencing conflict in home states: direct participation in conflicts, propaganda support, funding, and influencing foreign policy-making towards the home state by the host state and other players in the international arena.

Shedding blood for the homeland is not commonly associated with diaspora members – who are in fact often perceived as "standing on principle" from afar while their homeland kin pay the physical price. Yet in recent years we have witnessed direct participation by diaspora members in violent homeland conflicts, including active participation in the kin-state military or homeland insurgencies. Members of the Kosovar Albanian, Croat, and Sri Lankan Tamil diasporas are reported to have returned to participate in the respective struggles of their homelands. Other forms of diasporic input to homeland conflicts are abundant. According to the Independent International Commission on Kosovo: "It was the Kosovar Albanians in the diaspora who became the most radicalized part of the Kosovar Albanian community and were to create the KLA."[53]

The importance propaganda and communications play in mobilizing diaspora is highlighted by Byman *et al.*, who note that "some of the most significant diasporas of today, like the Indians and Sri Lankan Tamils, have begun to exercise unprecedented clout in the affairs of their home countries, akin to the Jewish diaspora in the US", and that "the more activist elements among these larger immigrant communities ... have more rapid and visible means of calling attention to issues of interest in their home countries than ever before thanks to the communication and information technology revolution".[54] Jeganathan, who analyses the specific impact of the internet with respect to the Sri Lankan Tamil diaspora and pro-Eelam websites, observes that these sites "preserve the form of the nation as territory for the LTTE and those who want to believe in its mission", and that "this works for all those nationals of Tamil Eelam who click on to ⟨eelam.com⟩ from New York, Oslo, Sydney or Amsterdam, who have no wish to return to Eelam, no wish to live there, but who must believe in it if they are to keep living where they are".[55] He observes that "for them, Eelam is real; it is lived – not as a place but as an image. And for them, eelam.com exists at the intersection of cyberspace and Eelam, at the intersection of an extraordinary technology or representation and the imagi-nation." The net result of this plethora of sources of information, as articulated by one Tamil activist, is that "Tamils are no longer dependent on any established mass media telling us what is going on in the world about ourselves". Speedier communication has also been vital in diasporas playing a catalytic role in drawing attention to crisis situations back home, benefiting from the increased propensity on the part of the international community to support the protection of human rights, and also enabling greater intervention in internal situations. Based on research carried out on Croatians and Slovenians in Australia, Skrbis observes how they reacted to nationalist upheaval in their respective homelands in recent times, and specifically deals with the transmission of ethno-nationalist sentiments across migrant generations.[56] He argues that ethno-nationalist sentiments in the ethnic homelands can draw their strength, ideas, material support, or simply nationalist enthusiasm from diaspora settings, while the reverse is also possible.

Homeland organizations often actively play on this sympathy and guilt to secure critical financial support, at times even by resorting to coercion against kin members at home. This has been the case in Eritrea, the Punjab, and Sri Lanka. Shain and Sherman, who consider the impact of diasporic transnational financial flows on national identity in the case of Israel and the Jewish-American diaspora, conclude that "diasporic communities may not only be the result of international volatility but, through financial flows, may be an important stimulus for identity shifts and the changing role of the state in the international system".[57] Benedict Anderson notes that "the IRA survives not only because of its local nationalist appeal and its ruthless methods, but because it has gained political and financial support in the United States and inside England, weapons in the international arms market, and training and intelligence from Libya and the Near East".[58] On the basis that approximately 1 million Tamils live in the diaspora, it is estimated that, with an average annual contribution of US$100 for each Tamil, international fund-raising amounts to over US$1 billion.

The important role diasporas play in lobbying foreign governments and INGOs on issues concerning their home states is well known. Such influence generally results in aid, legislation/statements supportive of the cause of the diaspora, and greater freedom to carry on their propaganda activities. Canada's Foreign Minister Bill Graham, who has often espoused the Tamil cause and kept the conflict in Sri Lanka on Canada's foreign policy agenda, has 6,000 eligible Tamil voters in his Toronto constituency; while the need for Tamil diaspora votes in the Woodspring borough of Dr Liam Fox, the former Under-Secretary of State at the British Foreign and Commonwealth Office, in 1997 on the eve of a general election contributed to sealing what came to be regarded as the "Fox Accord" in Sri Lanka. This sought to replicate the framework for bipartisan consensus, which prevailed in the UK with regards the Northern Ireland problem, between the leaders of the ruling PA and the opposition UNP in Sri Lanka in responding to the LTTE and the ethnic problem.

While Tatla attributes poor bilateral relations between home and host states as giving a diaspora space for manoeuvre,[59] Shain emphasizes that the power of diaspora activists in the USA relies on the ability to justify their causes and actions in terms of American national interests and values.[60] He observes that the participation of ethnic diasporas in shaping US foreign policy is mostly a positive phenomenon, and argues that ethnic groups, despite residual attachments to their homelands, do not betray American political values and ideals. On the contrary, their involvement in homeland-related affairs has been instrumental in disseminating those values inside and outside the USA. By contrast, Smith[61] and Huntington[62] view diaspora influence on the foreign policy of the host state negatively. Huntington cites instances where diasporas supporting their home governments against the USA become sources of spies to gather information for their homeland governments and serve as a corruptible influence in the US electoral process. He claims that, as with commercial interests, American national interest is increasingly being eroded as a result of US foreign policy being driven by ethnic interests.[63]

From the point of view of international stability, Collier warns that "the global effort to curb civil wars should focus on reducing the viability – rather than just the rationale – of rebellion", adding that "governments of rich nations should keep the behavior of diaspora organizations in their borders within legitimate bounds".[64] Collier also argues that governments in both post-conflict countries and the international community should develop strategies for reducing the damage done by diasporas in post-conflict societies, in order to reduce the risk of conflict repetition. Such strategies might focus upon cooptation, persuasion, and penalties.[65]

The diaspora-conflict link

As seen above, the conventional wisdom is that diasporas are more likely to be confrontational and nationalist and thus serve as "spoilers", exacerbating conflict and thwarting peace efforts. According to this view their non-compromising position is the luxury of absentee fighters who dwell on old memories, nourished by nationalist passion and assuaging the guilt of separation by replacing it with an overblown sense of loyalty to a faraway cause. In numerical terms, of the separatist struggles launched in various parts of the world, Marshall and Gurr note that only five internationally recognized states have been born as a result of armed separatist conflicts during the last 40 years:[66] Bangladesh (1971), Slovenia (1991), Croatia (1991), Eritrea (1993), and East Timor (2002). On the basis of available data, this does curb the aspirations of diasporas to create their own states.

Aryasinha has noted that of the 20 major armed conflicts ongoing in 1999, a majority were secessionist in nature and all had sizeable diasporas spread across the globe.[67] These groups include the Armenians, Kashmiris, Assamese, Sri Lankan Tamils, Kurds, Palestinians, Kosovars, Shi's, Basques, Irish, and Chechens. Collier and Hoeffler, who investigated the causes of civil war and tested "greed" and "grievance" theories using a new dataset of 78 large civil conflicts that occurred in the period 1960–1999, note that besides dependence on primary commodity exports, the presence of a large diaspora substantially increases the risk of conflict.[68] After five years of post-conflict peace the risk of renewed conflict is around six times higher in societies with the largest diasporas in the

USA than in those without US diasporas. Presumably this effect works through the financial contributions of diasporas to rebel organizations. Byman et al., who consider contributions to insurgencies by external actors (states, diasporas, refugees, and other non-state actors such as religious/political organizations), find that, with the exception of state entities that continue to support such causes, diasporas are the most potent force, "making a significant contribution in terms of money, limited contribution in terms of diplomatic backing and minor contribution with respect to arms, training, intelligence and inspiration".[69] The study notes that in fact, in insurgencies involving the Algerian Islamists, Egyptian Islamists, Indian Sikhs, Chechens, Sri Lankan Tamils, Kurds, and Northern Irish Catholics, diaspora support sustains or has sustained these struggles, which have had no sponsorship by any state actor.

With reference to the ethnic conflict in Sri Lanka, in discussions with the Norwegian facilitators and Sri Lanka government spokespersons in August 2002 the authors found no evidence to suggest that the Tamil diaspora at large had any influence in promoting or seeking to sustain the Norway-facilitated peace process during either the Kumaratunga or the Wickremesinghe periods.[70] In fact it has been observed that in the aftermath of the LTTE's pledge in November 2000 to work towards evolving a political settlement to the problem, "opinions expressed on the internet reveal the alarm that has spread through the Tamil community, from Canada to Australia, at the Norwegian peace initiative", and that the LTTE was "under tremendous pressure from Tamils living abroad to continue the armed struggle for an independent state".[71] Tololyan's complaint that in Armenia "they want service and money from diasporans, not thoughts or opinions" appears equally true for the Sri Lankan Tamil diaspora.[72] Lindsay Beck[73] observes that, despite its rhetoric, "thanks for the cash, we'll take it from here [is] may be the message overseas Tamils are hearing, as peace talks deepen between the government and the Tamil Tigers". The report notes "the Tigers' enduring power over the community makes it hard to determine just how the hundreds of thousands who moved abroad as fighting terrorized civilians and crippled the economy, see the peace process or their role in peacetime Sri Lanka". It quotes Kevin Shimmin, a human rights activist who works for the Sri Lankan community in Toronto, as observing that there is quite a bit of frustration, "for the ones who truly support the peace process are the ones asking the difficult questions". However, Cheran believes that the Tamil diaspora has today become a major player in the politics of Sri Lankan Tamil nationalism, and argues that "some of the narratives that are prevalent among Tamil diaspora communities in Canada and Europe are challenging the dominant and often militant variety of Tamil nationalism, and that the multiple forms of Tamil-ness that emerge in the diaspora can play a healthy role in checking and countering the vicissitudes of contemporary Tamil nationalism".[74]

Against these many observations stands another body of evidence that shows the role of diasporas as "catalysts" in peace processes. For instance, during the years of the Oslo peace process many Jewish-American groups acted as unofficial emissaries in the efforts to open new diplomatic channels to countries that had no diplomatic relations with Israel. They lobbied to lift the Arab boycott, rewarded Arab and Islamic states which normalized relations with the Jewish state, and encouraged others to do the same.[75] These missions were not always commenced with the prior approval of the Israeli government; indeed, at times organized members of the Jewish-American diaspora have undertaken international political initiatives that conflicted with the desires of Israeli governments. Further, through financial flows Jewish Americans provided an important stimulus for identity shifts and the changing role of the Jewish state in the international system. This, in turn, impacted on the negotiation of peace deals. When in June 2004 the United Jewish Communities, the umbrella organization of all local Jewish federations in the USA, refused to invest their donations in the West Bank and Gaza, in order not to interfere in Prime Minister Ariel Sharon's plan to disengage from some of these territories, they were rebuked by Sharon's leading right-wing opponents as "Jewish traitors". On the Irish diaspora, Goldman has detailed the role played by the ANIA, comprising Irish-American businessmen, which helped open up channels of communication between the conflicting parties as well as involving the US government in facilitating the Good Friday Agreement with respect to the conflict in Northern Ireland.[76] Commencing with the facilitation of a brief visit to the USA by Gerry Adams of Sinn Féin in January 1994, the ANIA was able to secure an assurance from the Clinton administration that in return for a complete cessation of violence, Adams would have unrestricted access to the USA and be given permission to raise funds. This resulted in the Northern Ireland peace process getting under way, with the IRA on 31 August 1994 issuing a statement announcing a complete cessation of military operations in a bid to move towards legitimacy.

Some tentative conclusions

The survey and analysis provided here allude to a very mixed picture regarding the impact of diasporas on conflict and conflict resolution and the role they play as peace spoilers or catalysts. A few observations would be pertinent.

In the resolution of state-to-state conflicts (with or without a distinct minority dimension), kin-states must address both domestic and far-removed constituencies that may promote or hinder a political settlement. During negotiations with external enemies, political debates that take place within the nation-state often include diasporic constituencies that are geographically removed from the homeland and yet have a strong voice and interest in the conflict and its outcome. The diaspora activists who are *outside the state but inside the people* have weight on the international scene because of their stature, means, institutions, and connections (inside their kin-state, in their countries of domicile, and in other international domains). Moreover, the fact that third parties which are not ostensibly connected to the conflict may see diaspora activists as potential allies in advancing their own causes further enhances the diaspora's stature. Such visibility and prominence, which may have an impact on conflict resolution or perpetuation, also comes at a price: if the conflict flares up, the diaspora may be seen as culpable.

The interaction between diasporas and homeland constituencies (pre- or post-statehood) in conflict resolution is dynamic. In many ways diasporas are not merely contractors, fulfilling the homeland leaders' orders; they are often architects and initiators of policy – especially, but not exclusively, in intrastate conflicts when a minority are seeking secession/irredentism. Sometimes both parties to an international conflict have diasporic constituencies that may play a positive role as facilitators or may have a negative role in raising obstacles to dialogue. Diaspora leaders on both sides may also open a channel of negotiations. The diasporas' propensity to play a role as facilitators or spoilers of negotiations both depends and impacts on the homeland government's (or aspirants') readiness to compromise or continue the conflict. Homeland governments that are permeable to diasporic influence always have to calculate to what extent the diaspora will support or oppose their policies. In some cases the diaspora is not just the homeland's tail, but may dominate the wagging. The understanding that diasporas are important players in the conflict brings third parties to address them and their interests.

The diasporas' own identity issues with regard to the homeland and their countries of residence shape their understandings of the conflict. These understandings fluctuate in accordance with their concern for current and pragmatic agendas or the saliency of history and memory in their communal identity. Some may argue that the diaspora has the luxury of dwelling in the past while at home governments and people must occupy themselves with issues of day-to-day existence. Yet others maintain that the diaspora's faithfulness to issues of kinship identity reminds the homeland of its historical obligations to preserve certain values which if sacrificed would undermine the national entity's true *raison d'être*. In applying their own identity concerns to the homeland's policy, diaspora elements may consider how the homeland may be a source of pride abroad, or alternatively how it may become a source of embarrassment. This observation is valid regardless of the individual's position about the conflict and regardless of his investment in his kinship identity.

Finally, it seems to the authors that emphasizing one or the other trend of diasporic involvement as spoilers or catalysts in conflict or conflict resolution is too simplistic. Whether diasporas "spoil" or whether they act as "catalysts" in supporting a peace processes remains a more complex issue that is closely tied to the representation and leadership of the homeland. Who speaks on behalf of the homeland's well-being and the people (inside and outside the homeland) is always contested, and extends far beyond the boundaries of the homelands. The extent to which diaspora members are empowered over the homeland voices is a function of many elements of the host state, home state, economics, and the viability of organization – all of which have an impact upon the direction of diasporic influences. It is evident that "a diaspora's role in homeland conflict perpetuation and conflict resolution can be [at times] so powerful, that homeland leaders would ignore diaspora preferences at their own peril".[77] Moreover, finally one must consider seriously the view that a diaspora and its leaders are not just careless nationalists. In fact they may be better placed to view the conflict in the homeland precisely because of their remoteness and being outside the range of fire. This argument considers diasporic voices as more realist, and therefore at times less willing to accept "false" compromises. In the latter case their alleged spoiling is in fact an eye-opener for saving their kin in the homeland from themselves; a view which was expressed by key Jewish leaders in the USA who opposed Oslo because of the risks involved. All in all, the larger the disapora and more diverse in its perspectives, the greater is the likelihood that its members produce conflicting views that are more likely to mirror debates in the homeland, rather than dictate them.

Notes

1. von Clausewitz, Carl. 1873. *On War*, trans. Colonel J. J. Graham. London: N. Trübner. Originally published in German by Dümmlers Verlag, Berlin, 1832.
2. Levin, Shalom. 1994. "The peace ideal and the school's contribution to its actualization", in Rachel Pasternak and Shlomo Tzidkiyahu (eds) *A New Era or Losing the Way: Israelis Talk About Peace*. Tel Aviv: Eitav (in Hebrew).
3. British Prime Minister Neville Chamberlain in his "Peace in our time" speech given in defence of the Munich Agreement. *Parliamentary Debates, Commons*, Vol. 339, 3 October 1938, available at www.wwnorton.com/college/history/ralph/workbook/ralprs36.htm.
4. Henry Kissinger in his acceptance speech of the Nobel Peace Prize 1973, available at www.nobel.se/peace/laureates/1973/kissinger-acceptance.html.

5. President Bill Clinton, radio address to the nation, Washington, DC, 27 March 1999.
6. Stedman, Stephen John. 1997. "Spoiler problems in peace processes", *International Security*, Vol. 22, No. 2, pp. 10–11.
7. Darby, John. 2001. *The Effects of Violence on Peace Processes*. Washington, DC: US Institution of Peace, p. 47.
8. Zahar, Marie-Joëlle. 2003. "Reframing the spoiler debate in peace processes", in John Darby and Roger Mac Ginty (eds) *Contemporary Peacemaking. Conflict, Violence and Peace Processes*. Basingstoke and New York: Palgrave Macmillan.
9. Perusal of the historical pattern of the use of the term "diaspora" makes it clear that an agreed definition is lacking.
10. Shain, Yossi. 2005. *The Frontier of Loyalty: Political Exiles in the Age of the Nation-state*, revised edn. Ann Arbor: Michigan University Press.
11. Dahlberg-Acton, John. 1967. *Essay in the Liberal Interpretation of History*. Chicago and London: University of Chicago Press, p. 134, quoted in Anderson, Benedict. 1998. *The Spectre of Comparisons; Nationalism, Southeast Asia, and the World*. London: Verso, p. 58.
12. Shain, note 10 above.
13. Byman, Daniel, Peter Chalk, Bruce Hoffman, William Rosenau, and David Brannan. 2001. *Trends in Outside Support for Insurgent Movements*. Santa Monica, CA: Rand.
14. *Ibid.*, p. 9.
15. Wiebe, Robert H. 2002. *Who We Are: A History of Popular Nationalism*. Princeton: Princeton University Press.
16. Appadurai, Arjun. 1990. "Disjuncture and difference in the global cultural economy", in M. Featherstone (ed.) *Global Culture: Nationalism, Globalization and Modernity*. London: Sage.
17. Tatla, Dharshan Singh. 2001. "Imagining Punjab: Narratives of nationhood and homeland among the Sikh diaspora", in C. Shackle, G. Singh, and A. S. Mandair (eds) *Sikh Religion, Culture and Ethnicity*. London: Curzon Press.
18. On this point see Gitelman, Zvi. 1998. "The decline of the diaspora Jewish nation: Boundaries, content and Jewish identity", *Jewish Social Studies*, Vol. 4, Winter, p. 128.
19. *Ha'aretz*. 2004. "Editorial: Jews between Israel and France", *Ha'aretz*, 21 July.
20. This point was made by Khachig Tololyan, editor of *Diaspora*, in a letter to Yossi Shain, 4 October 1999.
21. Kruz, Anat and Ariel Merari. 1985. *ASALA – Irrational Terror or Political Tool*. Jerusalem: Jaffee Center for Strategic Studies/*Jerusalem Post*; Boulder, CO: Westview Press, p. 118.
22. Tololyan, Khachig. 1987. "Martyrdom as legitimacy: Terrorism, religion and symbolic appropriation in the Armenian diaspora", in Paul Wilkinson and Alasdair M. Stewart (eds) *Contemporary Research on Terrorism*. Aberdeen: Aberdeen University Press.
23. Tololyan, Khachig and Krikor Beledian. 1998. Interview by Arpi Totoyan in *Haratch* (Paris), 2–3 July; reprinted in Lima, Vincent. 2000. "Fresh perspectives on Armenia-diaspora relations", *Armenian Forum*, Vol. 2, No. 2, 20 December, available at www.gomidas.org/forum/af3c.htm.
24. Anderson, Benedict. 1992. "The new world order", *New Left Review*, No. 193.
25. Cited in Bronson, Sarah. 2004. "Orthodox leader: US Jews have no right to criticize Israel", *Ha'aretz*, 2 August.
26. See *Maariv International*, 24 June 2004.
27. Shain, Yossi and Barry Bristman. 2002. "The Jewish security dilemma", *Orbis*, Vol. 46, No. 1, p. 52.
28. Hertzberg, Arthur. 1993. "Less religious on Israeli matters", *Ha'aretz* (Hebrew edn), 10 October.

29. Quoted in Radler, Melissa. 2001. "Presidents conference chairman: Arafat has unified the Jews", *Jerusalem Post*, 13 July.
30. Cited in Astourian, Stephen H. 2000. "From Ter-Petrosian to Kocharin: Leadership change in Armenia", Working Paper 2000_04-asto, Berkeley Program in Soviet and Post-Soviet Studies, available at http://repositories.cdlib.org/iseees/bps/2000_04-asto.
31. Suny, Ronald Grigor. 1999. "Provisional stabilities: The politics of identities in post-Soviet Eurasia", *International Security*, Vol. 24, No. 3.
32. Birand, Mehmet Ali. 2001. *Turkish Daily News*, 2 February.
33. Goldman, Michael. 2002. "Diplomacy outside the box: Behind the Good Friday Agreement", *Swords & Ploughshares*, Vol. 11, No. 1.
34. Black, Richard, Khalid Koser, and M. Walsh. 1997. "Conditions for the return of displaced persons", Final Report. Brussels: European Commission Secretariat General, Justice and Home Affairs Task Force.
35. Koser, Khalid and Nicholas Van Hear. 2003. "Asylum migration and implications for countries of origin", UNU/WIDER Discussion Paper No. 2003/20, March. Helsinki: WIDER.
36. Sheffer, Gabriel (ed.). 1986. *Modern Diasporas in International Politics*. London: Croom Helm.
37. Aryasinha, Ravinatha. 2004. "Earlier vs recent diaspora and protracted separatist ethno-nationalist conflict in home state", paper presented at the International Studies Association-American Political Science Asssociation Northeast Annual Conference, Boston, MA, November.
38. By "recent" diasporas is meant groups where the bulk of the diaspora has been generated in the last quarter of the twentieth century. By "earlier" diasporas is meant both the "classical" diasporas such as the Jews and Armenians, established in antiquity or in the Middle Ages, and "modern" diasporas such as the Croats, Slovaks, and Irish, whose presence dates to the post-industrial age. The category of "recent" diaspora has benefited from less-stringent immigration processes that do not require assimilation.
39. See *The Economist*. 2003. "Special report. 'Diasporas: A world of exiles'", *The Economist*, 4 January.
40. Fuglerud, Oivind. 1999. *Life on the Outside: The Tamil Diaspora and Long Distance Nationalism*. London: Pluto Press, p. 3.
41. Fuglerud, Oivind. 2001. "Time and space in the Sri Lanka-Tamil diaspora", *Nations and Nationalism*, Vol. 7, No. 2.
42. Ignatieff, Michael. 2001. "The hate stops here", *The Globe and Mail*, 25 October.
43. Shain, Yossi. 1999. *Marketing the American Creed Abroad: Diasporas in the US and Their Homelands*. Cambridge and New York: Cambridge University Press.
44. Hovannisian, Richard G. 2000. "On historical memory and Armenian foreign policy", lecture, Haigazian University, Beirut, 31 July, available at www.haigazian.edu.lb/announce/pressrelease.htm.
45. Sheffer, Gabriel. 2005. "Diaspora, terrorism, and WMD", *International Studies Review*, Vol. 7, No. 1, pp. 160–161.
46. Adamson, Fiona. 2004. "Displacement, diaspora mobilization and transnational cycles of political violence", in John Tirman (ed.) *The Maze of Fear: Security and Migration After 9/11*. New York: New Press.
47. McDowell, Christopher. 1996. *A Tamil Asylum Diaspora: Sri Lankan Migration, Settlement and Politics in Switzerland*. London: Berghahn Books.
48. *Tamilnet*. 2002. "British MPs tour Jaffna, Vanni", *Tamilnet*, 16 October, available at www.tamilnet.com/.
49. Munz, Rainer and Myron Weiner. 2002. *Migrants, Refugees and Foreign Policy: US and German Policies Toward Countries of Origin*. London: Berghahn Books.

50. Smith, Chris. 2003. *In the Shadow of a Cease-fire: The Impacts of Small Arms Availability and Misuse in Sri Lanka*. London: Small Arms Survey.
51. *Tamilnet*. 2003. "Cole, Chang lead US Patriot Act challenge by Tamils", *Tamilnet*, 5 October, available at www.tamilnet.com/art.html?catid=79&artid=10034.
52. *IPS*. 2004. "US court ruling seen as aiding Tamil rebels", *IPS*, 16 January. See "District Court California HLP II *et al.*, Vs John Ashcroft *et al.*, 22 Jan 2004, Court Ruling on Patriot Act"; "District Court California HLP II *et al.*, Vs John Ashcroft *et al.*, 3 March 2004, Amended Court Ruling", available at www.tamilnet.com/art.html?catid=13&artid=11380.
53. Independent International Commission on Kosovo. 2000. *The Kosovo Report; Conflict, International Response, Lessons Learned*. Oxford: Oxford University Press.
54. Byman *et al.*, note 13 above, pp. 43–49.
55. Jeganathan, Pradeep. 1998. "eelam.com: Place, nation and imagi-nation in cyberspace", *Public Culture*, Vol. 10, No. 3.
56. Skrbis, Zlatko. 1999. *Long Distance Nationalism: Diasporas, Homelands and Identities*. Brookfield, VT: Ashgate Publishers.
57. Shain, Yossi and Martin Sherman. 2001 "Diasporic transnational financial flows and their impact on national identity", *Nationalism and Ethnic Politics*, Vol. 7, No. 4.
58. Anderson, note 24 above.
59. Tatla, note 17 above.
60. See argument made in Shain, note 43 above.
61. Smith, Tony. 2000. *Foreign Attachments: The Power of Ethnic Groups in the Making of American Foreign Policy*. Cambridge, MA: Harvard University Press.
62. Huntington, Samuel. 1997. "The erosion of American national interest", *Foreign Affairs*, Vol. 76, No. 5.
63. Huntington, Samuel. 2004. *Who Are We? The Challenges to America's National Identity*. New York: Simon & Schuster.
64. Collier, Paul. 2003. *Breaking the Conflict Trap: Civil War and Development Policy*, World Bank Policy Research Report. Oxford: World Bank and Oxford University Press, pp. 22–44.
65. Collier, Paul. 2000. "Policy for post-conflict societies: Reducing the risk of renewed conflict", paper presented at The Economics of Political Violence conference, Princeton University, 18–19 March.
66. Marshall, Monty G. and Ted Robert Gurr. 2003. *Peace and Conflict 2003; A Global Survey of Armed Conflicts, Self-Determination Movements, and Democracy*. College Park, MD: University of Maryland.
67. Aryasinha, Ravinatha. 2002. "The scope and limits of external influence in the resolution of protracted separatist ethno-political conflict", paper presented at the Thirtieth Conference on South Asia, University of Wisconsin-Madison, November.
68. Collier, Paul and Anke Hoeffler. 2002. "Greed and grievance in civil war", Working Paper 2002-01. Oxford: Centre for the Study of African Economies, available at www.csae.ox.ac.uk/workingpapers/pdfs/2002-01text.pdf.
69. Byman *et al.*, note 13 above.
70. Based on personal interviews conducted in August 2002 by one of the authors with key figures in the current peace process from the Sri Lanka and Norwegian governments.
71. Subramanium, Nirupama. 2000. "Tamil diaspora for nothing less than Eelam?", *The Hindu*, 23 November.
72. Tololyan, Khaching and Krikor Beledian. 2002. Interview for Armenian Forum: Fresh Perspectives on Armenian-diaspora Relations, available at www.gomidas.org/forum/af3c.htm.

73. Beck, Lindsay. 2003. "Tamil diaspora in limbo over role in Sri Lanka peace", Reuters, 6 January.
74. Cheran, Rudhramoorthy. 2001. *The Sixth Genre: Memory, History and the Tamil Diaspora Imagination*, Marga Monograph Series on Ethnic Reconciliation No 7. Colombo: Marga.
75. See Zacharia, Janine. 2001. "The unofficial ambassadors of the Jewish state", *Jerusalem Post*, 2 April.
76. Goldman, note 33 above.
77. Shain, Yossi. 2002. "The role of diasporas in conflict perpetuation or resolution", *SAIS Review*, Vol. 22, No. 2, p. 115.

6

"New wars" and spoilers

Edward Newman

The relationship between the nature of armed conflict and the spoiler phenomenon – how the dynamics of a particular conflict relate to the impact and nature of spoiling – is a key issue in conflict resolution and peacebuilding. This is both a conceptual and a policy challenge. A clear understanding of the nature of different types of violent conflict is necessary in order to anticipate and address spoiling and spoilers. Ultimately, therefore, an understanding of the relationship between the nature of conflict and the nature of spoiling is important for achieving a viable peace process and settlement.

This chapter will consider if certain types of contemporary conflict – especially types of civil wars – give rise to patterns of spoiling by actors who have little interest in peace because they have incentives in the continuation of violence, public disorder, and the political economy of war. The protagonists in such conflicts – sometimes described as "new wars" – exploit the political economy of conflict for material gain, and only a peace process which holds significant material gains would be acceptable. Is spoiling behaviour endemic amongst protagonists in conflicts which are driven, or significantly characterized, by a "war economy" – that is, so-called conflicts of "greed" rather than "grievance"? If this is the case, do such conflicts defy conventional conflict resolution approaches? The chapter considers the relevance of "new wars" literature for the spoiling phenomenon in contemporary civil wars. It concludes that a number of the observations and arguments associated with the "new wars" thesis are useful and interesting, but that the distinction between "modern" forms of conflict and wars of "earlier" times is overdrawn and in some instances does not stand up to scrutiny. Moreover, the tendency in the new wars scholarship to identify common patterns in all contemporary civil conflicts ignores differences amongst them.

Nevertheless, the "new wars" literature indicates a reality of violent conflict: it is wrong to assume that all – or even most – conflict situations can be resolved by an accommodation of conflicting interests, or that a peace settlement is a process of finding consensus amongst parties that basically all seek peace. Some groups have clear and rational incentives for the continuation of violent conflict, even without a final "victory". There is evidence that certain environmental variables (such as the nature of peace settlements, the role of external actors, the political economy of conflict, the presence of disputes over natural resources, and the presence of significant diaspora groups) give rise to certain types of spoiling activity. Amongst these factors, the existence of powerful and violent groups whose primary intent is economic aggrandizement must be addressed by tactics which may be different from conventional conflict resolution methods.

The "new wars" debate

Since the end of the Cold War a number of analysts have argued that qualitative changes have occurred in the nature of violent conflict and that it is now possible to think in terms of "contemporary" or "modern" conflict, and particularly civil war, as a departure from "earlier" forms of conflict.[1] This argument holds that "One of the most dramatic ways in which the post-Cold War world differs from the Cold War international system is in the pattern of violence that has been developing."[2] Moreover, "The new wars can be contrasted with earlier wars in terms of their goals, the methods of warfare and how they are financed."[3]

A number of variables can be used to approach the concept of the "changing nature of conflict". For example, firstly one could consider the main protagonists and units of analysis of war, such as states or non-state actors, public or private actors, terrorist groups, or warlords. A second variable is the primary motives of protagonists, such as ideology, ethno-nationalism, territorial secession, or material aggrandizement. Third is the spatial context: interstate, "civil", regional, or global. Fourth is the technological means of violence – the weapons and strategies of war. Fifth is the social, material, and human impact of conflict, including patterns of human victimization and forced human displacement. Sixth is the political economy and social structure of conflict. "New wars"

analysts argue that most contemporary conflict displays an evolution in all of these factors, as detailed below.
- Most wars today are intrastate rather than interstate; and interstate wars have declined in number whilst intrastate wars have increased in number.
- New wars are characterized by state failure and a social transformation driven by globalization and liberal economic forces. This gives rise to competition over natural resources and illegal commercial entrepreneurship, private armies, and criminal warlords, often organized according to some form of identity.
- New wars are more likely to be characterized by ethnic and religious conflicts rather than political ideology.
- Civilian casualties and forced human displacement are dramatically increasing as a proportion of all casualties in conflict, especially since 1990.
- Civilians are increasingly deliberately targeted as an object of new wars; atrocities and ethnic homogenization are key hallmarks of contemporary conflict.
- A breakdown of public authority blurs the distinction between public and private combatants, and between combatants and civilians.

In terms of the main protagonists and units of analysis of "new wars", the basic argument is that interstate wars have declined in number relative to civil wars. A common expression of this idea is presented in the report of the International Commission on Intervention and State Sovereignty: "The most marked security phenomenon since the end of the Cold War has been the proliferation of armed conflicts within states."[4] Violent civil conflict is generally linked with a social environment that features a range of non-state as well as state actors. The weakening or undermining of the state is central to this environment, seen in the context of neo-liberal economic forces and globalization which erode state capacity, authority, and public goods. In turn, a pattern of violence by private – often criminal – groups emerges in this vacuum of state authority and power, often associated with ethnic allegiances and often vying over natural resources or criminal opportunities. Thus, according to this argument, the spatial context of contemporary wars is generally within, rather than between, states, although usually with regional spill-over processes at work. The global context is the decline of bipolar power and ideology, and in this vacuum the (re)emergence of identity politics and criminality. And the actors are insurgency groups, criminal gangs, diaspora groups, ethnic parties, international aid organizations, and mercenaries, as well as regular armies. One of the most interesting, perhaps counterintuitive, observations in this literature is the idea that international aid and intervention by the "international community" exacerbates new wars: "mafia-style economies and protracted internal warfare are often a result of international interventions which are actually claiming to foster the establishment of market structures and democracy".[5] This has the interesting implication that "provisions to provide a minimum of social security contradict their purposes in sustaining military *insecurity*".[6] There are clear implications here for "spoiling" by certain actors who gain profit from a conflict environment.

Within the new wars and the mafia economy, the "warlord" has pride of place, competing for control of parts of the illegal war economy, often based upon the control of an area of territory. Warlords are armed combatants who defend their interests through the use of violent force. Their objectives may be material or identity-based, or sometimes ideological – and often a combination of all three. The idea of set-piece battles and conventional armies is far from this scene.[7]

The social and economic context of new wars is characterized by weak or failed states, a collapse of the formal economy, and rivalry between criminal groups over natural resources or illegal commercial activities. Globalization is an important component in the political economy of new wars, and the starting point is that "the age of globalization is characterized by a gradual erosion of state authority" and accompanying "violent war economies".[8] As Kaldor puts it, "the processes known as globalization are breaking up the socio-economic divisions that defined the patterns of politics which characterized the modern period. The new type of warfare has to be understood in terms of this global dislocation."[9] Thus, neo-liberal economic forces have resulted in a weakening of state capacity and a weakening of the provision of public goods. So "the 'failure' of the state is accompanied by a growing privatization of violence ... the new wars are characterized by a multiplicity of types of fighting units both public and private, state and non-state, or some kind of mixture".[10]

In the most extreme cases the state itself is criminalized, as it becomes little more than a means to exploit state revenue and natural resources. Competition for control of the state is in reality a competition for control over the power to exploit. The decline of state legitimacy and power gives rise to rivalry amongst non-state actors and the distinction between public and private authority is blurred. Within this context, violence is effectively privatized as the state's control and monopoly over violence declines as an extension of the erosion of state capacity: "The new wars occur in situations in which state revenues decline because of the decline of the economy as well as the spread of criminality, corruption and inefficiency, violence is increasingly privatized both as a result of growing organized crime and the emergence of paramilitary groups, and political legitimacy is disappearing."[11] This is a "globalized war economy": fighting units finance themselves through plunder and the black market or through external assistance. These are sustained through violence, so "a war logic is built into the functioning of the economy".[12] According to Duffield this logic is self-sustaining and rational, rather than an expression of breakdown or chaos.[13]

Much of the new wars literature has argued that economic motives and greed are the primary underlying driving forces of most contemporary violent conflict. Indeed, the violence itself creates opportunities for entrepreneurship and profit; the continuation of violence rather than military "victory" is primary. In this context Keen has suggested that:

Conflict can create war economies, often in the regions controlled by rebels or warlords and linked to international trading networks; members of armed gangs can benefit from looting; and regimes can use violence to deflect opposition, reward supporters or maintain their access to resources. Under these circumstances, ending civil wars becomes difficult. Winning may not be desirable: the point of war may be precisely the legitimacy which it confers on actions that in peacetime would be punishable as crimes.[14]

Other analysts have put this into the context of globalization, which "creates new opportunities for the elites of competing factions to pursue their economic agendas through trade, investment, and migration ties, both legal and illegal, to neighboring states and to more distant, industrialized economies".[15] Some authors specifically relate civil war in certain societies to the intensification of transnational commerce in recent decades, drawing a distinctly "modern" picture of conflict in the late twentieth century.[16] Paul Collier argues that "economic agendas appear to be central to understanding why civil wars start. Conflicts are far more likely to be caused by economic opportunities than by grievance."[17] Not surprisingly, there is evidence that many civil wars are therefore caused and fuelled not by poverty but by a "resource curse".[18]

In sum, globalization represents two processes in the new wars thesis. It underpins changes in the state – particularly an erosion of state authority and public goods – which results in social vulnerability. Secondly, globalization generates increased opportunities for economic motives in civil war as a result of transborder trade, both legal and illegal. Again, there are clearly implications here for spoilers who seek to exploit the economic incentives of an ongoing conflict situation.

The social and economic context is also closely linked to the primary motives of protagonists and combatants in conflict. The new wars literature focuses mainly on economic and identity-based motives. Snow suggests that "new internal wars" seem "less principled in political terms, less focused on the attainment of some political ideal ... these wars often appear to be little more than rampages by groups within states against one another with little or no ennobling purpose or outcome".[19] Indeed, the lack of clear political objectives and the absence of a discernible political ideology to justify actions are a common theme of new wars analysis. Kaldor suggests that "The goals of the new wars are about identity politics in contrast to the geo-political or ideological goals of earlier wars."[20]

The new wars thesis also makes certain claims regarding the social, material, and human impact of conflict, including patterns of human victimization and forced human displacement. This relates to absolute numbers of fatalities and displaced people, deliberate or inadvertent targeting of civilians, and the relative proportion of combatant to civilian casualties. The literature on new wars is unanimous in the view that "an unhappy trend of contemporary conflict has been the increased vulnerability of civilians, often involving their deliberate targeting".[21] Thus "new wars" are characterized by the deliberate targeting and forcible displacement of civilians as a primary objective of violence, and the "importance of extreme and conspicuous atrocity".[22] Systematic rape as a weapon of war, ethnic cleansing, the use of child soldiers, and a high proportion of civilian to combatant casualties are prominent features of these civil wars. As Snow points out, "In places like Bosnia, Somalia, Liberia, and Rwanda, the armed forces never seemed to fight one another; instead, what passed for 'military action' was the more or less systematic murder and terrorizing of civilian populations."[23]

The Carnegie Commission on Preventing Deadly Conflict described the "strategies and tactics that deliberately target women, children, the poor, and the weak", claiming that "In some wars today, 90 per cent of those killed in conflict are non-combatants, compared with less than 15 per cent when the century began."[24] Kaldor states a similar idea: "At the beginning of the twentieth century, 85–90 per cent of casualties in war were military. In World War II, approximately half of all war deaths were civilian. By the late 1990s, the proportions of a hundred years ago have been almost exactly reversed, so that nowadays approximately 80 per cent of all casualties in wars are civilian."[25]

In terms of forms of warfare, "Behaviour that was proscribed according to the classical rules of warfare and codified in the laws of war in the late nineteenth century and early twentieth century, such as atrocities against non-combatants, sieges, destruction of historic monuments, etc., now constitutes an essential component of the strategies of the new mode of warfare."[26] The UN High Commissioner for Refugees *State of the World's Refugees* report follows a similar line of argument in terms of forced human displacement, which is closely related to victimization in times of war. It suggests that there have been "changing dynamics of displacement" and describes "the changing nature of conflict".[27] It observes the "devastating civilian toll of recent wars", stating that "in the post-Cold War period, civil wars and communal conflicts have involved wide-scale, deliberate targeting of civilian populations".[28] The UNHCR states that "Refugee movements are no longer side effects of conflict, but in many cases are central to the objectives and tactics of war."[29] Again, amongst many academics, a common theme is that "the global dynamics of flight and refuge are changing" in the context of the "changing nature of conflict".[30] The data presented by the UNHCR appear at first to support this.[31] As of 31 December 1999 the total number of people "of concern" to the UNHCR – comprising refugees, asylum-seekers, returned refugees, and internally displaced persons – was over 22 million. The estimated number of refugees by region for the period 1950–1999 shows an almost perfectly linear increase in refugees from 1951 to the end of the century. Kaldor concludes that "the distinctions between external barbarity and domestic civility, between the combatant as the legitimate bearer of arms and the non-combatant, between the soldier or policeman and the criminal, are breaking down".[32]

"New wars" and spoiling

The literature of the "new wars" provides a great service in explaining patterns of contemporary conflict, and especially in drawing attention to the social and economic aspects of conflict and the relationship between security and development. However, much of this is not new; all of the factors that characterize new wars have been present, to varying degrees, throughout the last 100 years. The actors, objectives, spatial context, human impact, political economy, and social structure of conflict have not changed to the extent argued in the new wars literature. The difference today is that academics, policy analysts, and politicians are focusing on these factors more than before, and they are understanding the underlying dynamics of conflict – and especially the social and economic factors – to a greater degree than in the past.[33]

Nevertheless, the literature has generated a range of insights which are relevant to the analysis of spoiling and spoilers. The new wars thesis describes the social and economic context of many wars as one of weak or failed states, a collapse of the formal economy, and rivalry between criminal groups over natural resources or illegal commercial activities. This is sometimes put into the context of international pressures for deregulation and privatization. Consequently, the primary motives of many protagonists in certain types of conflict are economic self-aggrandizement and the consolidation of power, often based upon ethnic identity. The idea of a "new war economy" – where the conflict environment enables illegal economic activities and some combatants do not necessarily seek military victory – has been a strong element of conflicts in cases such as Bosnia, Sierra Leone, and the Democratic Republic of the Congo (DRC). This economic dynamic does not explain the motivations and tactics of all protagonists in these conflicts, and certainly not in all civil wars in the post-Cold War era. Thus the "war economy logic" is not a general phenomenon or overriding explanatory variable in contemporary civil war. But it does raise interesting insights in terms of spoiling potential in many contemporary and recent conflicts. New wars theory thus helps to explain spoiling in some, but not all, conflicts. It therefore also suggests that an analysis of spoiling cannot be divorced from the specific nature of a conflict.

An implication of the "new wars" thesis is that globalization, neo-liberal economic pressures, and even the intervention of humanitarian agencies contribute to the incentives that give rise to spoiling activities. The political economy of violence – a mainstay of the "new wars" theory – would appear to be key to spoiling in a number of recent and ongoing conflicts.

Sierra Leone

The conflict in Sierra Leone in the 1990s is regarded by many observers as the archetypal "war economy", marked by a set of complex networks which allowed certain parties to profit from violent conflict.[34] Few analysts would disagree that the exploitation of diamonds by both sides played a crucial role in fuelling the decade-long conflict, which saw three failed peace agreements and claimed almost a million lives. Opinions are often divided, however, on whether the conflict was fought *over* diamonds or merely *with* diamonds. It is difficult to find exact estimates of the funds that the rebel Revolutionary United Front (RUF) was able to procure through illicit diamond trading, but they were at one point enough to support 3,500–5,000 combatants.[35] The country's official diamond exports in 1999 accounted for only $1.5 million, compared to what one study estimates as $68.5 million lost to illicit activity.[36] Diamonds were smuggled to neighbouring countries such as Guinea and especially Liberia, or, in what is known as "parallel financing", exchanged for arms and drugs. On the government side, diamond revenues were used to employ private security companies. The line between governmental and RUF forces was blurred, as they often colluded for economic rewards – a key characteristic of the war economy idea.

The war economy dynamic was clearly reflected in the Lome peace agreement of 1999. The agreement made RUF leader Foday Sankoh chairman of the Strategic Mineral Resources Commission and thereby gave him official control over the country's diamond resources. Clearly the spoils of war were a central issue at the negotiating table. Away from the negotiating table, the continuation of violence during and after the "peace process" demonstrated the link between the spoils of war and spoiling.

Angola

Angola provides another example of conflict characterized in part by a war economy in which the country's natural wealth contributed to the onset of violence and its perpetuation and intensification. In addition, the war economy on numerous occasions also directly undermined peace efforts on different levels. The two most important resources are the vast oil reserves found off the western coast and in the north-western region, and the eastern diamond fields. Both these resources were used to a large extent to fund arms purchases.[37] It was largely the illicit diamond trade that attracted international attention as a destabilizing factor, especially since the mid-1990s. This is reflected in the number of UN Security Council resolutions[38] passed on the specific issue and other international measures that have been deployed in order to tackle the problem of "blood diamonds" or "conflict diamonds", such as the monitoring system known as the Kimberley Process launched in January 2003. Moreover, the struggle to control the diamond fields presents a very clear illustration of how mineral wealth elicits resource-driven, predatory, or rent-seeking behaviour in all parties involved.

In the case of Angola it is relevant that the most abundant diamond fields were close to the borders with the DRC and Uganda, countries which are themselves unstable and through which illicit trade can occur. UNITA, along with a large number of independent local *garimpeiros* (prospectors), foreign nationals, and MPLA military personnel, joined the prospecting explosion in the early 1990s, although often on an individual rather than an organizational basis.[39] It is telling that there was an increase in the levels of military strikes and low-intensity fighting at the beginning of the 1991 peace agreements, as these talks only included the MPLA and UNITA and not the various lower-level players.[40] Savimbi's return to war after the 1992 elections can also be explained in large part as being due to the fear of losing these valuable resources: the result was a clear victory for the MPLA and defeat for UNITA, meaning an absolute majority for the government.[41] In effect this meant that the MPLA would not have to concede any lucrative ministerial power-sharing deals in a future government, and a return to large-scale violence by UNITA was the result. Control over the diamond fields played a role again a few years later, when an impasse over territorial control in the Lundas caused serious friction between the rebels and the government.

Effectively UNITA was unwilling to remove its presence from the diamond fields until it was granted legal mining concessions, which, in turn, the government was unwilling to grant until UNITA had withdrawn its forces. And again, in 1997 the MPLA's operations to "remove illegal *garimpeiros*" in the Lundas while peace negotiations were reaching their final stages in mid-1997 were used to limit UNITA's mining activities in the region.

While diamond mining created opportunistic predation and violence, it also created its opportunistic truces. There are accounts of UNITA and government soldiers, as well as local parties, tolerating each other's mining activities on neighbouring soil and even engaging in trade with one another.[42] Seemingly paradoxical, this seems to be a characteristic of war economies, and was probably exacerbated by the narrow international focus on outlawing UNITA diamonds. It has been argued that the Kimberly Process increased the occurrence of internal diamond sales and led to increased collusion between UNITA and government officials, who would then sell the "verified" diamonds on the international markets.[43] An analysis of the economy driving the Angolan civil war must also take into account the huge oil revenues reaped by the MPLA élite, which in comparison dwarf those obtained through illegal trade in diamonds by UNITA. In 1999 the MPLA made an estimated US$3.3 billion – a figure which is only marginally lower than what UNITA is believed to have acquired through diamond sales in their entire most lucrative period between 1993 and 1998.[44] After this the government started a major counteroffensive and drove the rebels out of the Lundas, reducing their annual profits to around US$200 million from 1999 until their defeat in 2002.

Bosnia

Most contemporary scholars describe the war in Bosnia and Herzegovina from 1992 to 1995 as one fuelled by ethnic differences and tribalism, sometimes collectively referred to as "Balkanization". According to this theory, the conflict was dominated by nationalist parties and agendas vying for control of territory and ethnic homogeneity. Yet, as Mary Kaldor suggests,[45] such as approach does not account for the chequered character of the front lines of this war, and the large amount of inter-ethnic co-operation in commercial activity. During the war, Croatians were said to have maintained "customs" duties of 30 per cent for any delivery of humanitarian aid and other supplies to the geographically isolated and heavily besieged Muslim territories in central and eastern Bosnia.[46] However, the war economy as an explanatory factor of the conflict is best seen in the local forces of all sides engaged in their own rent-seeking behaviour whenever the opportunity for private gain arose. This was in large part a result of the extensive criminalization of the fighting forces that occurred among all the warring parties. Bosnian Muslims, being cut off from supply routes and lacking any form of organized army to oppose the vastly better equipped and organized Serb forces, were heavily reliant on criminal syndicates and local gangs for the defence of towns and cities in the absence of a standing army, as was the case in Sarajevo.[47] The use of criminals in paramilitary units was also tactically employed by the Serb government in the initial stages of the war in Croatia and Bosnia.[48] In addition, military criminalization of all parties involved was the driving factor behind the preservation of the supply lines that allowed for Croat and Muslim resistance in numerous isolated enclaves around the country, without which they would have probably broken down in a very short time. Sarajevo again provides a good example, being probably the strategically single most important location of the conflict: had it not been for the clandestine trade in arms and other vital supplies that crossed ethnic lines it is doubtful whether the city would have lasted over three years.[49]

The acquisition of arms, food, and other vital supplies via clandestine smuggling channels helped repel Serb forces and enabled the city to survive for months before international aid materialized. However, as much as this was necessary for survival in the initial stages of the war, the large-scale incorporation of criminals predictably also had its down sides: first of all, illegal and predatory economic behaviour was associated with human rights abuses and harmful activities, including human trafficking. In addition, there is evidence that political motivations were weak or non-existent amongst the actors in the criminal underworld – a further key characteristic of the war economy concept. Criminal groups had few qualms about ignoring political or nationalist war aims, and some realized soon enough that they could do better business in times of war than they could in times of peace. Thus the refusal of some forces to bow to any politically brokered agreement regarding the fate of the city of Mostar, for example, can be linked to the economic benefits that the absence of a state apparatus presented for some of its commanders and their ties to the criminal underworld.[50] Crime syndicates, vital in the initial defence of towns and cities, were also consistently unwilling to integrate themselves into the official armed forces, resulting in the need to conduct violent purges in urban centres during wartime.[51] To this day criminal elements remain heavily embedded in and occupy vital position inside the state apparatus of the fledgling nation. Indeed, the EIU estimated in 2005 that most of the 40 per cent of officially unemployed population in Bosnia have some means or other of sustenance through clandestine, non-regulated channels, showing how deeply entrenched the war's legacy of a shadow economy has become.[52]

Chequered front lines and the involvement of criminal elements in defence and supply networks provided incentives for independently operating crime syndicates, with their own clandestine international networks of supply and demand, to exacerbate hostilities or at times obstruct peace processes. Thus, despite their not being at the centre of the aggression, it is necessary to keep an eye on the opportunistic and often predatory economics if one wants to explain the duration, course, and conclusion of this conflict.

Democratic Republic of the Congo

The Democratic Republic of the Congo is perhaps the worst epitome of a war economy in terms of its scope and impact. The fact that this war has been termed the "seven nation war" gives some indication of the number of actors involved on the state level alone: according to an International Crisis Group report there are currently "five foreign civil wars and one interstate war being waged on DRC territory".[53] In addition, there are about a dozen non-state active armed groups.[54]

Most of the fighting has focused upon access to the valuable mineral-rich regions of eastern Congo rather than on any political goals as such,[55] despite the claims of the rebel groups and the DRC's neighbours, and it is here that approximately three-quarters of the deaths and 90 per cent of population displacement have taken place.[56] It is telling that Rwanda, a direct backer of RCD-Goma (Rassemblement Congolais pour la Démocratie-Goma, a major faction), established a "Congo Desk"[57] to deal with resources extracted from Congolese soil; and President Paul Kagame described the war as "self-financing".[58] From there it is only a small step to reach the conclusion that "the activities funded by revenues generated by the Congo Desk strongly shape Rwanda's foreign policy and directly influence national decision making".[59] A UN panel of experts identified a system of personal enrichment through looting, something it referred to as "élite networks" which are well structured on both Ugandan and Rwandan sides. Both Uganda and Rwanda have reported marked increases in exports of valuable minerals, primarily coltan, gold, and diamonds,[60] of which the countries themselves have no actual reserves.[61] And despite Rwandan and Ugandan troop withdrawals since late 2002, "the necessary networks have already become deeply embedded to ensure that the illegal exploitation continues independent of the physical presence of foreign armies".[62] Intervention by Angola, Zimbabwe, and Namibia on behalf of the DRC government has also been attributed to economic interests, and was in some ways proven to be so by the takeover of Gecamines, the DRC's national mining company, by Zimbabweans and the granting of access to Congolese oil reserves to Angola.[63]

Economically motivated predatory interests do not operate only at the state level. A number of armed non-governmental groups are involved, vying for a piece of the action. It is no surprise that in this environment no comprehensive power-sharing arrangement has been concluded to which all can agree and which incorporates satisfactorily all these groups' ambitions. There is also increasing evidence of "enemies" cooperating with one another to benefit from this lucrative trade in Congolese minerals or simply to increase the number of points used to levy "road taxes".[64] Cross-recruitment – whereby combatants move from one armed group to another – makes it increasingly difficult to differentiate forces of the various armed political and ethnic groups,[65] leaving little but economic exploitation to be contended as a driving factor behind the violence. Extensive military commercialism is also evident: minerals are directly traded for arms.[66]

The actors who may have had an active interest in the continuation of conflict also fall beyond the borders of the DRC, and the lack of sustained efforts to achieve a lasting peace and return to a resemblance of territorial integrity in Congo may be influenced by economic considerations, at least at the regional level. For example, it is now widely accepted that revenues from predatory diamond and coltan extraction on Congolese soil have played a significant role in the economies of some neighbouring countries.[67]

The Expert Panel on the Exploitation of Natural Resources in the Democratic Republic of Congo was set up by the UN Security Council in 2000 and presented its final report to the Council in 2002. A number of states have been directly implicated in predatory economic exploitation,[68] and 85 international companies were reported by the panel to be in breach of OECD standards through their practices in the DRC. Dena Montague's findings suggest an ongoing spoiling situation associated with economic predation: "As long as rebel movements can flourish by establishing lucrative commercial relationships with international corporations, democratization will not take root."[69]

Conclusion

There is considerable evidence that the nature of spoiling – in terms of its prevalence, impact, and the measures needed to address it – can be a condition of certain *types* of violent conflict. The "war economy" is now a well-established aspect, or even a driving force, of many types of conflict in terms of the motivations and conduct of actors. There is also evidence – although often anecdotal or intuitive – that spoiling can be directly connected to the incentives and "spoils" of the war economy. Thus spoiling behaviour is an extension of the incentives that certain actors have in the continuation of conflict because this provides an environment in which illicit and profitable activities can be pursued. As a corollary, the implementation of a peace process may be deliberately or inadvertently obstructed if certain actors perceive that the benefits of an ongoing conflict environment outweigh the potential payoff of peace.

This suggests a number of lines of enquiry in terms of dealing with spoiling in this context. Most importantly, it is wrong to assume that all – or even most – conflict situations can be resolved by an accommodation of conflicting interests or that a peace process is a process of finding consensus amongst parties that basically all seek peace. In certain types of armed conflict some groups have "rational" incentives for the continuation of conflict and contesting peace itself. The political economy of conflict, natural resources, and significant illicit entrepreneurial activities in the "war economy" can be associated with a certain type of recalcitrant spoiling.

Therefore, it may be unrealistic to bring every armed group into a peace process, but this should not necessarily be allowed to obstruct or disrupt the process. Material "rewards" for compliance with a peace process may be inevitable, but it is essential to be aware that some armed groups see this as their primary goal, and there is a danger that their demands may not be appeased for long. Similarly, donors must be conscious, in bringing material resources to the conflict, that there is a danger of becoming a part of the problem rather than the solution. Finally, spoilers who exploit war economies usually rely upon some form of transborder exchange. It is therefore essential that in regions of violent conflict, illicit cross-border commercial exchanges are scrutinized and targeted for interdiction, and that certain commodities – such as diamonds, coltan, or oil – are promptly subject to international legal sanctions to prevent their exploitation by spoilers.

Acknowledgements

The author would like to thank Niklas Keller and Elsje Fourie for their assistance in preparing this chapter.

Notes

1. This section draws upon Newman, Edward. 2004. "The 'new wars' debate: A historical perspective is needed", *Security Dialogue*, Vol. 35, No. 2.

2. Snow, Donald M. 1996. *Uncivil Wars. International Security and the New Internal Conflicts*. Boulder, CO: Lynne Rienner, p. 1.
3. Kaldor, Mary. 2001. *New and Old Wars: Organized Violence in a Global Era*. Cambridge: Polity Press, p. 6.
4. ICISS. 2001. *The Responsibility to Protect: Report of the International Commission on Intervention and State Sovereignty*. Ottawa: International Development Research Centre, p. 4.
5. Jung, Dietrich. 2003. "A political economy of intra-state war: Confronting a paradox", in Dietrich Jung (ed.) *Shadow Globalization, Ethnic Conflicts and New Wars: A Political Economy of Intra-State War*. London: Routledge, p. 12.
6. *Ibid.*, p. 14.
7. Duffield, Mark. 2001. *Global Governance and the New Wars: The Merging of Development and Security*. London: Zed Books, p. 14.
8. Jung, Dietrich. 2003. "Introduction: Towards global civil war?", in Dietrich Jung (ed.) *Shadow Globalization, Ethnic Conflicts and New Wars: A Political Economy of Intra-State War*. London: Routledge, p. 2.
9. Kaldor, note 3 above, p. 70.
10. *Ibid.*, p. 92.
11. *Ibid.*, p. 5.
12. *Ibid.*, p. 9.
13. Duffield, note 7 above, p. 14.
14. Keen, David. 1998. *The Economic Functions of Violence in Civil Wars*, Adelphi Paper 320. Oxford: Oxford University Press for the International Institute for Strategic Studies, pp. 11–12.
15. Berdal, Mats and David M. Malone. 2000. "Introduction", in Mats Berdal and David M. Malone (eds) *Greed and Grievance. Economic Agendas in Civil Wars*. Boulder, CO: Lynne Rienner, p. 3.
16. Reno, William. 2000. "Shadow states and the political economy of civil wars", in Mats Berdal and David M. Malone (eds) *Greed and Grievance. Economic Agendas in Civil Wars*. Boulder, CO: Lynne Rienner; Snow, note 2 above.
17. Collier, Paul. 2000. "Doing well out of war: An economic perspective", in Mats Berdal and David M. Malone (eds) *Greed and Grievance. Economic Agendas in Civil Wars*. Boulder, CO: Lynne Rienner, p. 91.
18. de Soysa, Indra. 2000. "The resource curse: Are civil wars driven by rapacity or paucity?", in Mats Berdal and David M. Malone (eds) *Greed and Grievance. Economic Agendas in Civil Wars*. Boulder, CO: Lynne Rienner; Ross, Michael L. 1999. "The political economy of the resource curse". *World Politics*, Vol. 51, No. 2.
19. Snow, note 2 above, p. 57.
20. Kaldor, note 3 above, p. 6.
21. ICISS, note 4 above, p. 4.
22. Kaldor, note 3 above, p. 99.
23. Snow, note 2 above, p. ix. See also Allen, Chris. 1999. "Warfare, endemic violence and state collapse in Africa", *Review of African Political Economy*, Vol. 26, No. 81; Shawcross, William. 2000. *Deliver Us From Evil. Peacekeepers, Warlords and a World of Endless Conflict*. New York: Simon & Schuster.
24. Carnegie Commission on Preventing Deadly Conflict. 1997. *Final Report*. Washington, DC: Carnegie Commission on Preventing Deadly Conflict, pp. xvii and 11.
25. Kaldor, note 3 above, p. 100. Chesterman concurs with this basic trend: Chesterman, Simon. 2001. "Introduction", in Simon Chesterman (ed.) *Civilians in War*. Boulder, CO: Lynne Rienner, p. 2.
26. Kaldor, note 3 above, p. 8.

27. UN High Commissioner for Refugees. 2000. *The State of the World's Refugees: Fifty Years of Humanitarian Action*. Oxford: Oxford University Press, Chapter 1 and pp. 276–280.
28. *Ibid.*, p. 277.
29. *Ibid.*, p. 282.
30. Schnabel, Albrecht. 2001. "Preventing the plight of refugees", *Peace Review*, Vol. 13, No. 1, p. 109.
31. UN High Commissioner for Refugees, note 27 above, pp. 306–310.
32. Kaldor, note 3 above, p. 5.
33. For a critical view on the idea of "new wars" see Newman, note 1 above.
34. Richards, Paul. 2003. *The Political Economy of International Conflict in Sierra Leone*. The Hague: Netherlands Institute of International Relations, Clingendael; USAID. 2000. "Diamonds and armed conflict in Sierra Leone: Proposal for implantation of a new diamond policy and operations", working paper. Washington, DC: USAID Office of Transition Initiatives; Smillie, Ian, Lansana Gberie, and Ralph Hazleton. 2000. *The Heart of the Matter: Sierra Leone, Diamonds and Human Security*. Ottawa: Partnership Africa Canada.
35. Perez-Katz, A. M. 2002. "The role of conflict diamonds in fuelling wars in Africa: The case of Sierra Leone", *International Affairs Review*, Vol. 6, No. 1, p. 65.
36. OTI. 2000. "Diamonds and armed conflict in Sierra Leone: Proposal for implementation of a new diamond policy and operations", working paper, 8 May. Washington, DC: USAID Office of Transition Initiatives.
37. Thompson, Lauren. 2000. "Angola: Opportunity missed", *The Professional Jeweler*, available at www.professionaljeweler.com/archives/news/2000/angola.html.
38. For example Security Council Resolutions 1173 (1998) and 1295 (2000), and subsequent resolutions.
39. Dietrich, Christian. 2000. "Power struggles in the diamond fields", in Jakkie Cilliers and Christian Dietrich (eds) *Angola's War Economy – The Role of Oil and Diamonds*. Pretoria: Institute for Security Studies.
40. Dietrich, Christian. 2000. "Inventory of formal diamond mining in Angola", in Jakkie Cilliers and Christian Dietrich (eds) *Angola's War Economy – The Role of Oil and Diamonds*. Pretoria: Institute for Security Studies, p. 145.
41. Dixon, Norm. 1993. "Civil war threatened as Angola rejects UNITA", *Green Left Weekly*, available at www.greenleft.org.au/back/1992/75/75p17.htm.
42. Dietrich, note 39 above.
43. Reno, William. 2000. "The real (war) economy of Angola", in Jakkie Cilliers and Christian Dietrich (eds) *Angola's War Economy – The Role of Oil and Diamonds*. Pretoria: Institute for Security Studies.
44. Hodges, Tony. 2002. "The role of resource management in building sustainable peace", available at www.c-r.org/accord/ang/accord15/10shtml.
45. Kaldor, Mary. 1999. "Bosnia-Herzegovina: A case-study of a new war", in Kaldor, note 3 above.
46. Cooper, N. and M. Pugh with J. Goodhand. 2004. *War Economies in a Regional Context: The Challenges of Transformation*. Boulder, CO: Lynne Rienner.
47. *Ibid*.
48. A number of reports indicate that Serbia even released selected prisoners and sent them across the border into Yugoslavia for the purpose of joining these paramilitary units. See Kaldor, note 45 above.
49. Cooper, Pugh, and Goodhand, note 46 above.
50. Bjelakovic, N. and F. Strazzari. 1999. "The sack of Mostar, 1992–1994: The politico-military connection", *European Security*, Vol. 8, No. 2.

51. For example, in Sarajevo 1,300 members of the "armed forces" were imprisoned and a number of officers with high-level criminal connections were killed. Cooper, Pugh, and Goodhand, note 46 above.
52. Economist Intelligence Unit. 2005. *Country Report: Bosnia and Herzegovina*, available at www.eiu.com.
53. International Crisis Group. 1999. "Africa's seven nation war", 21 May, available at http://129.194.252.80/catfiles/1325.pdf.
54. The largest are the APC (Congolese People's Army), the FDD (Forces for the Defence of Democracy – a Burundian rebel group), the SPLA (Sudanese People's Liberation Army), the RCD-Goma (Congolese Rally for Democracy – Goma), the RCD-ML (Congolese Rally for Democracy – Movement for Liberation), the RCD-National (Congolese Rally for Democracy – National), the UPC (Union of Congolese Patriots), the Interahamwe (mainly Rwandese Hutu militia), and the Mayi-Mayi (self-financing Congolese militia), as well as numerous local warlords and splinter groups of these factions.
55. See for example Olsson, Ola and Heather Congdon Fors. 2004. "Congo: The prize of predation", *Journal of Peace Research*, Vol. 41, No. 3; Global Witness. 2004. "Same old story: A background study on natural resources in the Democratic Republic of Congo", June, available at www.globalwitness.org/reports/show.php/en.00054.html.
56. Amnesty International. 2003. "Democratic Republic of Congo: 'Our brothers who help kill us'", Special Report AFR 62/010/2003, April, available at http://web.amnesty.org/library/pdf/AFR620102003ENGLISH/$File/AFR6201003.pdf.
57. A UN panel of experts estimates that "The Congo Desk's contribution to Rwanda's military expenses would ... have been in the region of US$320 million." United Nations. 2002. "Final Report of the Panel of Experts on the Illegal Exploitation of Minerals and Other Forms of Wealth in the Democratic Republic of Congo", S/2002/1146, October, p. 15.
58. *Ibid.*, p. 27.
59. *Ibid.*, p. 15.
60. Global Witness, note 55 above.
61. Olsson and Congdon Fors, note 55 above, p. 326.
62. United Nations, note 57 above, p. 25.
63. International Crisis Group, note 53 above.
64. See for example "Network war: An introduction to Congo's privatized conflict economy", available at www.totse.com/en/politics/the_world_beyond_the_usa/167160.html; United Nations, note 57 above.
65. Amnesty International, note 56 above.
66. "Network war", note 64 above.
67. Reno, William. 2000. "War, debt and the role of pretending in Uganda's international relations", occasional paper, Centre of African Studies, University of Copenhagen.
68. UN Security Council. 2002. "Report on the Exploitation of Resources of Democratic Republic of Congo is Challenged in Security Council", SC/7561, 5 November.
69. Montague, Dena. 2002. "Stolen goods: Coltan and conflict in the Democratic Republic of Congo", *SAIS Review*, Vol. XXII, No. 1.

Part II
Cases

7

Northern Ireland: A peace process thwarted by accidental spoiling

Roger Mac Ginty

The Northern Ireland peace process was constructed with spoilers in mind. Seven previous British government political initiatives aimed at staunching the conflict ended in failure between 1972 and 1993. Various factors accounted for these failures, but the initiatives all shared the common trait of excluding powerful veto holders (many of them capable of engaging in spoiling). Rather than excluding groups and constituencies prepared and capable of making any new political dispensation unworkable, the peace process of the 1990s deliberately sought to include veto holders. As a result, opportunities for spoilers were drastically reduced. This makes the Northern Ireland case particularly interesting *vis-à-vis* the spoiling debate for at least two reasons. First, Northern Ireland may be in a position to offer lessons to other peacemaking processes on structural and procedural factors that limited spoiling. Second, spoiling behaviour in Northern Ireland often adopted subtle forms, thus raising questions on the conceptual boundaries of spoilers and spoiling behaviour.

Much depends on our interpretation of spoiling, and for the purposes of this chapter broad and narrow interpretations are juxtaposed to illustrate the often textured and subtle forms of spoiling. The narrow interpretation of spoiling conforms with much current literature on spoilers and spoilers. According to this view, spoiling constitutes deliberate attempts to undermine a peace process or accord and usually employs violence or coercion. The broader interpretation of spoiling recognizes that peace processes and accords are often challenged and undermined by actors who abjure the use of violence. Such "peaceful spoiling" can be no less damaging to a peace process or accord than activities by militants. The debate on spoiling also needs to recognize that many peace processes and accords have been undermined by "accidental spoiling", or an activity that erodes support for a peace process or accord as a *by-product* of its primary intention. Thus post-peace-accord crime or intra-group feuding can puncture the political and public optimism required to sustain a peacemaking process. The phenomena of peaceful and accidental spoiling require the deployment of the broader interpretation of spoiling.

The conflict and the peace process

A brief sketch of the contours of the conflict[1] and the peace process[2] should help illuminate later discussion of spoilers. The Northern Ireland conflict, despite a long and complex history, is essentially a modern political contest between exclusive nationalist projects. On the one side, an Irish nationalism largely specific to the Catholic community within Northern Ireland favours political unification of the island of Ireland. On the other side, a form of British nationalism specific to the Protestant community wishes to maintain Northern Ireland's constitutional position within the UK. Although the conflict itself is not about religion *per se*, religion is the fissure along which the clash between nationalisms is most visible. Two broad politico-cultural blocs have developed (Protestant-unionist-loyalist versus Catholic-nationalist-republican), each with an updateable memory bank of real and perceived grievances, and each with an acute understanding of the location and immutability of boundaries between in-groups and out-groups. The relative strength of each group (53.1 per cent Protestants and 43.8 per cent Catholics in 2001[3]) has meant that both were prone to suspicion and chronic insecurity.

Northern Ireland is a classic deeply divided society, with ethnic voting patterns, high levels of residential segregation, and a confessional schooling system. By the standards of many other conflict societies, absolute levels of political violence have been low, but Northern Ireland's small size and low population have meant that the conflict has had a wide impact.[4] Political violence has been a constant feature of Northern Ireland's experience, ranging from communal street violence in the 1920s and 1930s to an organized guerrilla campaign by the Irish Republican Army (IRA) in the late 1950s. There was also a good deal of structural violence, with the loyalist state apparatus limiting political and cultural expression by the pro-united-Ireland minority.[5] By the late 1960s Catholic-nationalist disquiet, mainly over poor social conditions, had become more vocal and prompted reactionary responses from the Northern Ireland government and the loyalist majority. The resulting instability led to the prorogation of the Northern Ireland Parliament and the institution of direct rule from London. Catholic-nationalist demands for civil rights gave way to a more nationalist "Irish unity" agenda.

From the early 1970s onwards a three-cornered low-intensity conflict developed between the British state and its local agents, Irish republicans, and pro-UK loyalists. Irish republicanism, although prone to occasional splinters, was dominated by the IRA, an organization that jealously guarded its pre-eminent position with its core constituency – an important factor in the limiting of spoiler activity in later years. Although employing the rhetoric of a "war of liberation" against Britain, the IRA's campaign often had a sectarian flavour, deepening intercommunal tensions. The British state maintained up to 30,000 troops in Northern Ireland and many areas were effectively "garrisoned", often fuelling grievances among Catholic nationalists and constantly reinjecting a fresh dynamic into the conflict. Aiding the British Army was a locally recruited militarized police force, the Royal Ulster Constabulary (RUC), and a militia army, the Ulster Defence Regiment (UDR). Membership of both organizations was overwhelmingly Protestant, again reinforcing the sectarian nature of conflict. The final part of the conflict triumvirate was comprised of loyalist militant organizations, principally the Ulster Volunteer Force (UVF) and the Ulster Defence Association (UDA). Notionally targeting the IRA, these organizations more often preyed on politically unconnected Catholics. Successive British governments used the loyalist militants as proxies, storing up further nationalist resentment towards the British state.

While majorities of both Catholic nationalists and Protestant unionists disdained violence by either republican or loyalist militants, a culture of ambivalence towards violence by the in-group did develop.[6] Indeed, this ambiguity towards violence has done much to shape Northern Ireland politics, and goes some way to explaining the troubled implementation of the Belfast Agreement. By the mid-1990s over 3,500 people had been killed in a conflict that seemed as interminable as it was vicious. The precise origins of the peace process are hotly debated, but a number of factors can be prioritized: war-weariness and a growing recognition by all sides of a "mutually hurting stalemate",[7] and the impact of dialogue between the leaderships of Irish republicanism and nationalism in raising the former's awareness of the opportunities held by constitutional politics and the political costs of civilian casualties.[8] Crucial too was the development of a working relationship between the British and Irish governments. The governments' strategic aim was to engineer a settlement that would attract support from majorities in both communities, thus delegitimizing political violence.

The key therefore was to broaden both the appeal of any peace accord and the constituency involved in its negotiation. The crucial question was whether the circle of peace negotiations could be widened to encompass militant actors. Given that both governments had invested immense energy into demonizing violent actors, the inclusion of militant actors was problematic and directly contradicted the "surround sound" chorus of condemnation that had comprised the bulk of ministerial activity for the previous decade. Yet Margaret "I won't talk to terrorists" Thatcher initiated subterranean talks with republicans to assess their seriousness with regard to a nascent peace process. For Northern Ireland's unionist majority in particular, the inclusion of republicans in negotiations would continue to pose a dilemma: accept what they saw as "unreconstructed terrorists" in negotiations (and eventually government), or risk self-exclusion from negotiations.

The peace process developed tentatively. The inclusion of militant organizations was not at any price: first they must declare cease-fires and demonstrate (by word and deed) a genuine interest in peace negotiations. Loyalist and republican militant organizations declared cease-fires in 1994, thus clearing the way for formal negotiations between their political representatives and the British and Irish governments. By September 1997, after many false starts and cease-fire breaches, multi-party talks were convened between all major political parties with the exception of the Democratic Unionists (DUP), who found abhorrent the inclusion of Sinn Féin, political cousins of the IRA. The Belfast (or Good Friday) Agreement, reached in April 1998, saw the British and Irish governments realize their dream of a comprehensive peace accord that could attract support from violent veto holders.[9] The political representatives of the IRA and the main militant loyalist groups felt able to commend the agreement to their constituencies.

Under the agreement, Northern Ireland's constitutional position within the UK was recognized, but so too was the right of Northern Ireland to unify with the Republic of Ireland should a majority of its citizens elect to do so in a referendum.[10] A devolved power-sharing Assembly would be established in Northern Ireland, to run concurrently with a British-Irish Council and a North-South Ministerial Council, creating a set of interlocking institutions that would deal with political relationships throughout the British Isles.[11] As part of the agreement prisoners from militant organizations on cease-fire would be eligible for early release, and there was to be major reform of the policing and judicial systems.

The agreement attracted 71 per cent support from Northern Ireland's electors in a referendum (comprising an overwhelming majority of Catholics and a bare majority of Protestants), and elections to a power-sharing Assembly were held in June 1998. The infant years of the Assem-

More than two warring parties	Yes/No
One of the parties fighting for secession	Yes
Coercion involved in peace accord	No
More than 50,000 soldiers	No
State collapse	No
Easily identifiable spoilers	Yes
Neighbouring states oppose the accord	No
Valuable, easily marketable spoils	No

Figure 7.1 The presence/absence of Stedman's eight factors complicating the ending of civil war in Northern Ireland

bly were beset with difficulty, much of it stemming from chronic mistrust between unionists and republicans, exacerbated by the IRA's reticence to engage in the (public) decommissioning of its weapons' stocks. By late 2002 the Assembly had been suspended four times. Unionists in particular were disaffected with the peace process and implementation of the agreement, often interpreting it in terms of unionist concessions and nationalist gains. Northern Ireland limped from political crisis to political crisis, and often required the ministrations of the British and Irish prime ministers. Yet despite the political crises, they were not accompanied by large-scale political violence.

To the extent that spoilers were present, they failed to attract widespread support, were incapable of derailing an inclusive peace process, or were so interested in pecuniary spoil that they had minimal political impact. Stedman identifies eight factors that complicate the ending of civil wars, only two of which are fully present in Northern Ireland (Figure 7.1).[12] To take his points in turn, while there were more than two warring parties they were aligned with only two political projects: the maintenance of Northern Ireland's constitutional position within the UK, or Irish unification. One of the parties was fighting for secession, or more precisely unification with another state, but this goal was watered down as part of the peace process to unification by consent. Violent coercion was not involved in reaching the accord, and the total number of combatants did not exceed 50,000. Rather than state collapse, the safety net of direct rule from London meant that government functioned largely as normal in terms of the provision of basic public goods despite the backdrop of political violence and the inability of local parties to share power.

Spoilers were easily identifiable, but that did not automatically translate into capability to spoil the peace process. Instead of opposing the peace accord, the Republic of Ireland was its guarantor, and developed an extraordinary partnership with the British government from the mid-1980s onwards. Finally, Northern Ireland did not have the valuable and easily marketable spoils such as diamonds or timber that were present in other conflict areas. This is not to deny an economic dimension to the conflict and spoiling (though the greed thesis of conflict causation is to be treated with caution[13]); rather it is to note that the spoils were of a different order – extortion, control of drug importation and distribution, and cross-border cigarette and fuel smuggling. Crucially, while there were profits to be made in the illicit economy, non-state militant groups invested heavily in the licit economy. The essential point to make, having reviewed Stedman's "complicating conditions", is that in comparison with other contemporary conflicts the conditions for the pacific management of conflict in Northern Ireland were propitious.

Narrow and broad interpretations of spoiling

The identification of spoilers and spoiling behaviour involves the adoption of normative positions on a peacemaking process. The term "spoiler" is inherently condemnatory and makes no pretence at terminological neutrality (if such a state were possible). The ability to deploy "explanatory rhetoric"[14] suggests the possession of a social power aligned with a moral and political code that identifies certain types of behaviour as deviant or acceptable. In simple terms, the identification of certain groups as spoilers suggests a moral judgement on the righteousness of a peace process. Critical analyses of peace processes have attempted to caution against the blithe acceptance of a peace process as a good thing.[15] These suggest that many peace processes are merely problem-solving, often ministering to the manifestations of conflicts without addressing underlying conflict causes and latent development needs. Moreover, orthodox peace processes may actually reinforce protagonists at the expense of more accommodationist parties, legitimize their stark analyses of the conflict, and prioritize the economic mores of international financial institutions rather than the needs of citizens in war-torn societies.

The key point is that political processes associated with the label "peace" do not necessarily enhance human security and well-being. The word "peace" is capable of mobilizing tremendous moral energy, but it may also camouflage or license the continuation of war by other means. Indeed, the Western liberal optimism often automatically associated with peace initiatives may not always travel intact, and its local reception is heavily dependent on political and cultural contexts.

Despite concerns over the normative implications of peace processes in general and spoilers in particular, violence during peace initiatives is a real phenomenon and is worthy of serious study.[16] Clearly we cannot view violence during peace processes as an undifferentiated category; it has different origins, motivations, and impacts. Yet we do need to move beyond conceptual paralysis. This chapter will adopt, in turn, a narrow and a broad view of spoilers in relation to Northern Ireland. Under the narrow definition, spoilers are "leaders who believe that peace threatens their power, worldview and interests, and use violence to undermine attempts to achieve it"[17] and operate "in relationship to a given peace agreement".[18] A broader view will accept that spoilers need not necessarily employ violence and that spoiling, in the sense of thwarting or complicating the reaching or implementation of a peace accord, can be a by-product of other activities. In other words, peace processes can be spoiled by accident. This broader view stretches the existing accounts of spoiling behaviour.

Spoilers in Northern Ireland: The narrow view

The inclusion in the peace process of the main loyalist militant organizations and the IRA was not without moral and practical difficulty for the governments and Northern Ireland's constitutional political parties. By 1994 the UDA, UVF, and IRA had all declared cease-fires and authorized their political representatives to engage in negotiations with the British and Irish governments and other parties. There followed a painstaking shadow dance in which each tentative move by any party was scrutinized for signs of strength or weakness, gain or loss. The developing peace process presented all parties with dilemmas and pressures. For members of militant organizations, many of whom had been insulated from the necessity to engage in political calculation, the most pressing dilemma was whether continued involvement in a peace process whose outcome was far from clear was likely to pay dividends. The principal arguments against pursuing the peace process fell into three categories: ideological, rational political calculation, and spoils. The "zealots"[19] maintained that the ideological purity of their political project was incompatible with involvement in the peace process. The rational-choice militants saw violence and negotiation as tactical tools to be employed whenever each was likely to extract maximum advantage. Those more interested in accumulation through their association with militant organizations calculated whether the peace process or a reversion to violence offered more opportunities for pecuniary advantage. Matters were complicated by the fact that individual militants could simultaneously hold one or more of these positions, and shift from position to position.

The IRA and its political representatives, Sinn Féin, were constantly aware of the republican history of schism and split. As a result they invested immense energy in consulting with their core constituency, careful not to stretch the elasticity of their movement beyond breaking point. Yet over the course of the peace process the mainstream republican movement diverged considerably from many of its key objectives. Central here was its acceptance of the state of Northern Ireland, even if only as an interim entity that could become unified with the Republic of Ireland if a majority of citizens consented. This marked an enormous *volte face* only made possible by a process of internalization and rationalization marshalled by the Sinn Féin leadership. In retrospect, the real story here was the lack of splits within republicanism – but this is not to say that dissent and splits did not occur, nor that republicans did not engage in spoiling.

If we accept the narrow view of spoilers as actors who use violence to thwart a peace process, then the IRA decision to rescind its cease-fire between February 1996 and July 1997 can be interpreted as a case of spoiling. The case is not absolutely clear, though, and, as with much else in the spoiler debate, is heavily dependent on interpretation. Through 1995 most actors in the conflict declared themselves willing to engage with the peace process sponsored by the British and Irish governments: republicans, constitutional nationalists, loyalists, many unionists, and civil society all expressed interest in the peace process. But no one vision of how the peace process should proceed, or how it should culminate, prevailed. The IRA, frustrated by what it saw as the slow pace of the British government in initiating multi-party negotiations, exploded a lorry bomb at London's Canary Wharf in February 1996.

For the next 17 months the IRA carried out attacks in Northern Ireland, but its campaign was qualitatively different to that which it had suspended in 1994. The volume of attacks was of a lower level than in the previous campaign. Doubtless this was partially due to successes by state forces in Northern Ireland and the Republic of Ireland, but it also reflected a change in tactics on behalf of the IRA. Greater care was taken to avoid civil casualties, and attacks were mainly targeted on the security forces (rather than loyalists), particularly the British Army, to give the impression of conflict between two "armies". What became clear was that the IRA was using violence in a tactical sense; as a means to gain re-entry into the peace process, but a reconstituted peace process more ready to recognize republicans' sense of urgency and their issue agenda. In the eyes of the other parties engaged in the peace process, the IRA was guilty of classic spoiling behaviour and was disrupting a conflict transformation process. The IRA view was quite different: at the most the organization aimed to thwart the peace process at a particular moment in its development but did not want to cause the complete derailment of the process. The calibration of the intensity of violence was designed to leave the door open just enough for its own readmittance to the peace process. In its own view it was involved in short-term tactical spoiling, while others interpreted its actions as strategic spoiling. This "controlled spoiling" constituted an enormous risk on the part of the IRA, in that it was dependent on other actors limiting their frustration and remaining committed to the peace process.

Two other republican groups can be identified as spoilers with greater confidence: the Real IRA (RIRA) and the Continuity IRA (CIRA). Both were mainly comprised of disaffected members of the IRA who felt that the peace process strategy as pursued by the Sinn Féin leadership was a delusion and could not deliver the principal republican objective of Irish unification. Neither organization was able to mount a military campaign similar in scale to that of the mainstream IRA, nor were they able to muster large numbers of activists or supporters. The Real IRA (colloquially called the "cokes", a play on Coca-Cola's "It's the *real* thing" advertising campaign) emerged in November 1997, and did succeed in attracting support from a small number of key militants in the IRA, including its chief bomb-makers. The CIRA first came to prominence in July 1996. The IRA, anxious to maintain the cohesiveness of its membership and arms stocks, warned its members against joining the new rivals to the "true" republican mantle. Once Sinn Féin had been admitted to political negotiations it was also aware of the sensitivity of the British government and Northern Ireland's unionists to republican violence. Thus the RIRA and CIRA found themselves on the margins of republicanism. Unable to attract large numbers of IRA personnel, they increasingly relied on inexperienced recruits – an advantage in that many of these operatives were unknown to the state security forces on either side of the border. They also had to establish new arms supply routes (often originating in the Balkans) and money-raising enterprises. The latter replicated the IRA's well-established schemes of armed robbery, cross-border smuggling, and donations (mainly from the USA). Some CIRA and RIRA members were involved in Northern Ireland's growing drugs trade – a trade that the mainstream IRA had discouraged, to the extent of assassinating suspected drugs dealers under the cover name Direct Action Against Drugs.

As the peace process developed, both the CIRA and RIRA launched military campaigns. The attacks were notable for at least three reasons. First, the sporadic nature of the attacks betrayed the essential weakness of the organizations, unable to mount widespread campaigns and unable to rely on the wider resources, including community support, enjoyed by the IRA. Second, CIRA and RIRA attacks had a high failure rate, suggesting infiltration by the security forces and again illustrating that the republican constituency lacked the stomach for a return to war. Third, despite widespread condemnation of both groups as mindless wreckers, their target selection suggested some sophistication. Between September 1997 (when multi-party talks including Sinn Féin commenced) and April 1998 (when the Belfast Agreement was reached) the CIRA and RIRA detonated eight large car bombs in Protestant-majority towns across Northern Ireland. A number of other attacks were thwarted. Ascribing motivations to secretive groups with poorly articulated political platforms can never be an exact science, but the regularity with which Protestant-majority towns were targeted suggested that the primary aim of the attacks was to goad Northern Ireland's Protestant community into pressurizing unionist politicians to withdraw from the peace talks. While it was an attempt to spoil the peace process, it was also an attempt to make it seem as though unionists were to blame by withdrawing from the talks. The physical destruction wrought by the bombs was merely collateral; the real target was political. Moreover, the attacks had the added advantage of embarrassing mainstream republicans, who were discomforted by the prospect having to condemn violence by fellow republicans.

But the campaign of bomb attacks on market towns went too far. On 15 August 1998 a RIRA bomb exploded in the centre of Omagh, killing 29 civilians. It was the worst single incident in the Troubles, and coming just months after the Belfast Agreement had been ratified by a majority of Northern Ireland's population it had additional poignancy. The political impact of the attack was dramatic, mobilizing Northern Ireland's nationalist and republican community – many of whom may have entertained agnosticism towards political violence – into a rejection of the spoilers. Three days after the bombing the RIRA announced a cease-fire; it was also subject to intense security action that disrupted its operations. Although the CIRA did not announce a cease-fire it suspended its operations for a time, re-emerging in 2000 and 2001 with a series of bomb attacks in London, including a rocket attack on the MI5 headquarters in London. CIRA attacks also resumed in Northern Ireland in 2000, mostly in the form of bombings on security installations. Some RIRA members joined the CIRA when the former declared a cease-fire.

Dissident republicans did not develop political platforms capable of articulating a rationale for their violence. One pressure group, the Thirty-Two County Sovereignty Committee, was linked in the media with the RIRA, but the group did not contest elections. The absence of publicly available statements meant that observers were left to infer motivations and aims following acts of violence. Even if the CIRA and RIRA were in a position to articulate their aims publicly, it is unlikely that the message would be coherent. In all probability their members entertained a complex mix of motivations spanning ideological purity, rational political calculation, and access to spoils.

Security concerns were central to the repeated collapse of the power-sharing Assembly. By November 2002 it had collapsed for a fourth, seemingly terminal, time. Interestingly, unionist concern was overwhelmingly focused on the mainstream IRA rather than the dissident republican groups. The IRA's niggardly approach to the decommissioning of its arms stocks and alleged breaches of its cease-fire were the principal cause of unionist mistrust of republicans, rather than deliberate spoiling by republican splinters. So not only were the republican spoiler groups ineffectual in preventing the reaching of the peace accord, but they were unable to claim credit for the post-accord difficulties.

Identifying loyalist spoilers is complicated by the ambiguous attitude of the two main loyalist militant groups, the Ulster Volunteer Force and Ulster Defence Association, to cease-fires and the promiscuity with which loyalist groups adopted different names. The most prominent loyalist spoiler group, the Loyalist Volunteer Force (LVF), was formed in 1996 from disaffected members of the UVF. The LVF was very much the creature of Billy Wright, a former UVF leader vehemently opposed to the cease-fire and peace process strategy. The organization was limited in terms of membership (barely reaching three dozen at its high point) and geographical area of operation (mid-Ulster), but it did engage in a number of sectarian murders of Catholics. To the extent that the LVF engaged in a conscious effort to influence the direction of the peace process, these attacks may have been an attempt to draw the IRA into its traditional self-assumed role of defender of the Catholic community. If this happened, Sinn Féin would be barred from political negotiations. But the intensity of the LVF campaign was relatively limited and the IRA largely avoided being drawn into a sectarian conflict once the peace process was up and running. A major motivation for the LVF's actions was the venting of anger, reflecting the view of many loyalists that the peace process was following a republican and nationalist agenda. The organization made no attempt to articulate a political rationale for its violence. In a sense it engaged in "frustration spoiling", or the violent expression of a disapproval of the peace process.

The LVF served two further purposes. First, its name offered the UDA (on cease-fire from October 1994 until 2001) a flag of convenience under which it could continue violence while the integrity of its cease-fire appeared intact. This action, though, heaped further pressure on the already strained relations between the UVF and the UDA, contributing to a full-blown feud from 1999 onwards. The second purpose was as a vehicle for the accumulation of spoils. LVF leader Billy Wright was shot dead by a republican faction while in prison in December 1997; thereafter the organization degenerated into drug dealing. The LVF was able to control, and profit from, the supply of drugs to selected loyalist communities.

Spoilers in Northern Ireland: The broader view

Thus far this discussion of spoilers and spoiling in Northern Ireland has been premised on two assumptions: that spoilers use violence in their attempts to imperil a peace process, and that spoilers set out deliberately to undermine a peace process. In Northern Ireland it is possible to identify actors who were opposed to the peace process but did not use violence. Furthermore, it is also possible to identify actors who undermined the peace process as a by-product of other actions. While they may have been accidental spoilers, their impact was no less real than those of groups which deliberately attempted to undermine peacemaking efforts. If we accept the broader interpretation of spoiling (actors committed to thwarting the peace process but doing so by non-violent means, and actors who spoil the peace process by accident) then the list of spoilers in the Northern Ireland peace process expands considerably.

To take the issue of peaceful spoilers first, the Democratic Unionist Party was perhaps the most strident opponent of the peace process. The basic DUP position was that the peace process was nationalist in origin and design and would lead to an erosion of Northern Ireland's position within the UK. It was forthright in its opposition to Sinn Féin, regarding the latter's inclusion in talks as incompatible with non-violent democratic politics. The DUP boycotted the multi-party negotiations leading to the Belfast Agreement, campaigned for a "no" vote in the referendum on the agreement, and, although a part of the power-sharing government, refused to attend executive committee meetings because of the presence of Sinn Féin. Unionist disenchantment with the agreement deepened in the post-accord period, to the extent that the DUP won most seats in the November 2003 Assembly elections and had stunning success in the 2005 Westminster election. Its election campaign was unashamedly anti-peace-process, claiming that "The Belfast Agreement is wrecking Northern Ireland" and that "Sinn Féin/IRA's ... so-called ceasefire is a mere illusionary tactic, used to advance its long-term aims and objectives. The long and varied list of terrorist activity over the last five years and beyond demonstrates that the IRA has not gone away but is continuing to re-arm and perpetrate terror, even when in government."[20] Entitled to the First Minister's post following its 2003 election victory, the DUP refused to re-enter the Assembly unless the agreement was renegotiated, thereby acting as an effective brake on the further implementation of the Belfast Agreement. Yet it was able to do so without recourse to violence, and its power to spoil ultimately came through the ballot box.

While the DUP was largely clear in its opposition to the peace process, other parties were opposed to the peace process more sporadically, often in reaction to particular issues. This was not surprising, since the Northern Ireland peace process was both comprehensive and long-lasting, covering a range of sensitive issues. At times the objections were procedural, relating to the pace or style of negotiations, while at other times fundamental matters of principle were raised. If a party objected to an issue that had the potential to inhibit the further development of the peace process, did this make it a spoiler?

To illuminate further this issue of parties blocking the peace process (if only temporarily), the cases of Sinn Féin and the Ulster Unionist Party can be considered in tandem. At various times during the peace process and the post-accord implementation phase each party adopted obdurate stances that inhibited the other's engagement with the peace process. Despite eager rhetoric, each party was guilty of a good deal of foot-dragging and cynicism. In the case of Sinn Féin, its continued links with the IRA, and the IRA's reluctance to disarm, were interpreted by the UUP as an indication of ambiguity in committing to exclusively peaceful means. From the Sinn Féin perspective, the reluctance to decommission was part of the negotiation process and designed to extract maximum advantage from a bargaining chip. For others, though, the weapons issue represented a departure from the terms of the peace accord and undermined confidence in the peacemaking process.

Similarly, the UUP adopted stances that inhibited others' full participation in the peace process. The party adopted an ultra-cautious approach for most of the peace process, anxious to remain in the process and explore any opportunities it may offer, but also anxious to limit concessions to nationalists and republicans. On the whole the UUP approach to the multi-party negotiations could be described "slow minimalist", favouring a deliberate and measured pace on a tightly defined agenda, while the nationalist and republican approach was "speedy maximalist", with an emphasis on quickening the pace of the process and expanding its agenda. The UUP did not embrace the peace process; instead it took a *realpolitik* decision that the British and Irish governments, together with nationalists and republicans, were aligned in a political process that could have profound consequences for the future of Northern Ireland. To remain outside of that process risked the imposition of a new political dispensation that eroded the unionist position. In specific terms the UUP stance involved – at different periods – refusing direct contact with Sinn Féin, excluding Sinn Féin ministers from meetings of the North-South Ministerial Council, and withdrawing from the Assembly.

The cases of Sinn Féin and the UUP illustrate the subjectivity at the heart of the spoiler debate. Both parties "spoiled" the peace process by offering each other a cold shoulder rather than a warm handshake. All other participants, including the British and Irish governments, adopted tough stances at one stage or another during the peace process. Many of these positions were held in good faith, and reflected the unease of their core constituencies. To consider these cases of peaceful spoiling requires stretching the meaning of spoiling to the point of distortion, but their impact on the Northern Ireland peace process was more profound than that of deliberately targeted spoiler violence.

The second type of spoiling behaviour to be considered under the broader interpretation of spoiling in peace processes is inadvertent spoiling. In this case actors do not deliberately set out to destroy or disrupt the peace process, but the peace process becomes undermined as a by-product of their activities. The activities of the main loyalist militant groups, the UVF and UDA, fall into this category. Although on cease-fire and represented in the 1997–1998 multi-party negotiations, many loyalists felt that the peace process and subsequent peace accord were more beneficial to nationalists and republicans than unionists and loyalists. Unable to build a political base to mirror that of Sinn Féin, loyalist resentment that the peace process was one-way traffic developed in the face of apparent (and highly visible) concessions to republicans in the form of troop withdrawals, police reform, and the inclusion of Sinn Féin in government.

In a context of dissatisfaction with the peace process, the loyalist militant organizations fissured into gangs organized around individual commanders. Parts of Belfast in particular became the personal fiefdoms of loyalist militant leaders who controlled the drugs and other illegal trades. Tensions developed between some local commanders, and any pretence of maintaining a coherent political strategy evaporated. In short, many loyalists lost interest in the political process and the Ulster Democratic Party, linked with the UDA, was dissolved in 2001. In July 2001 the UDA withdrew its support from the Belfast Agreement but announced that its cease-fire was still intact. This was not the case. Some units within the UDA orchestrated major rioting and engaged in a campaign of intimidation against Catholic householders in interface areas of Belfast (where Catholics and Protestants live in close proximity). Yet these attacks, which forced many Catholics from their homes and reached a high point in summer 2001, were not part of a wider political campaign designed to undermine the peace process. Certainly they were fuelled by dissatisfaction with the perceived imbalance of political change, but also by local-level frustrations and sectarianism. A number of politically uninvolved Catholics were also murdered, and the British government intervened in October 2001 to declare the UDA and UVF cease-fires over.

Another source of significant loyalist violence was feuding between the UDA and UVF, and within the UDA. The feuds, which claimed over a dozen lives and led to the intimidation of hundreds of loyalists out of their homes, had no discernible political element and were largely motivated by clashes of egos and contests over control of territory and spoils. The security threat emanating from the feud was largely localized to Belfast and its surrounding areas, and to members and associates of loyalist organizations. Wider political developments connected with the peace process were largely incidental to the feud, yet such violence undermined public confidence in the peace process. At the very least it led the pro-peace constituency, both unionist and nationalist, to question the quality of peace delivered by the peace process.

In a similar manner to which loyalist feuding and racketeering harmed the peace process as a by-product, non-political crime also contributed to public frustration with the peace process. Northern Ireland, in line with many other societies emerging from protracted violent conflicts, experienced a post-accord crime surge[21] in which crime rates showed a sharp rise.

Discussion and conclusion

Spoilers, in the sense of violent actors deliberately seeking to thwart a peacemaking process, have had a limited impact on the Northern Ireland peace process. They failed to mount and sustain large-scale violent campaigns, failed to attract widespread community support, and ultimately failed to prevent the reaching of a major peace accord. Post-accord problems owed little to the deliberate strategies of violent spoilers. Three spoiler-limiting factors were at work. First, the inclusive peace process strategy adopted by the British and Irish governments meant that the main actors capable of using political violence were involved in the peace process, at least in the crucial phase of negotiations leading up to the April 1998 Belfast Agreement. The premise of the peace process as organized by the British and Irish governments was that veto holders with the power to bring down any peace accord from without must be included in the formulation of that accord.

Second, and related to the previous point, was the development of penalties for the use of violence. Again this was largely a function of cooperation between the British and Irish governments and their ability to set the parameters and ground rules of the peace process. Participants in the multi-party negotiations were obliged to sign up to principles of non-violence, on the understanding that breaches would result in exclusion from the peace talks. In the post-accord period the governments established an Independent Monitoring Commission to adjudicate on alleged cease-fire breaches and recommend appropriate penalties. It must be said, though, that both governments were prepared to accept a certain level of violence from the main militant groups in order to keep them in the process. The backdrop of "acceptable violence", even at a low level, had serious consequences in the erosion of public faith in the peace process and subsequent accord.

The third factor limiting spoiling in the Northern Ireland peace process was environmental. Many of the elements present in other conflict societies that facilitate spoiling were absent in Northern Ireland. Crucial here was the absence of external spoilers (or sponsors of spoilers), and the absence of portable marketable goods such as diamonds.

If we look beyond overt spoiler behaviour, though, and accept broader interpretations of spoiling (peaceful spoilers and inadvertent spoilers), then Northern Ireland did witness considerable spoiling behaviour. One political party (the DUP) was able effectively to block the further implementation of the Belfast Agreement in 2003 through the ballot box. The label "spoiler" appears to convey automatically an image of a violent wrecker of a peace initiative, and thus seems inappropriate to describe the pursuit of democratic politics. Yet the effect of the DUP was similar to that achieved by violent spoilers in other peacemaking processes. At other stages during the peace process, virtually every participant (including both governments) adopted positions that acted as a brake on political movement. In effect they were engaging in spoiling behaviour, albeit limited and tactical spoiling as they tended to object to elements of the peace process rather than the peace process itself.

The peace process also witnessed significant levels of inadvertent spoiling, whereby actors involved in feuding, intracommunity "policing", and criminal accumulation contributed to a generalized attitude that the peace process was tolerant of ambiguity in relation to law and order. This was crucial in sapping the morale of the pro-peace constituency. While the feuding and extortionist militant groups did not deliberately embark on a campaign to derail the peace process, their impact was similar. It was, for all intents and purposes, spoiling by accident.

By way of conclusion, it is possible to reach seven propositions on spoiling. While primarily referring to Northern Ireland, the propositions may have applicability to other cases.

Spoiling can be violent and non-violent

The focus on violent spoiling behaviour is understandable, especially if it threatens a fragile cease-fire and the public optimism invested in it. Yet spoiling can adopt more subtle and at times insidious qualities. This non-violent spoiling can be similar to violent spoiling in effect. By disdaining the use of violence, non-violent spoilers have often avoided being identified as "spoilers" in public political discourse and avoided facing the moral pressure heaped on violent spoilers.

Spoiling can be intentional and unintentional

Just as violent spoilers are often the recipients of media and political attention, so too does most attention focus on intentional spoilers. Yet unintentional spoiling is commonplace, whereby peace processes and peace initiatives are endangered as a by-product of the actions of political or militant actors. Perhaps the most damaging aspect of inadvertent spoiling is its ability to undermine public faith invested in a peace process. If citizens are unable to experience an improved quality of life as a result of the peace process then it becomes irrational for them to support it.

Spoiling will vary in potential at different stages of a peace process

While there is no typical peace process model, a number of peace processes have followed a pattern in which tentative approaches between antagonists give way to more structured and – in some cases – institutionalized relationships. Confidence may be built along the way, with the result that a peace process may be able to endure greater instability after its initial stages. This was certainly the case in Northern Ireland, where the peace process adopted dynamics of its own and was able to withstand significant spoiler pressure once initial hurdles were overcome. It is difficult to generalize, however, on the existence of a relationship between the longevity of a peace process and its ability to withstand spoiling. The quality of the peace process and its ability to withstand spoiling are more important than the duration of a cease-fire and peace negotiations.

Intentional spoiling is often sophisticated in its choice of targets

Despite condemnation of spoilers as "mindless wreckers", their choice of targets and timing of attacks is often sophisticated. It relies on provoking a reaction from political and military opponents who may be members of the in-group or out-group. The spoiling activities may thus be calculated to have a gratuitous or symbolic element, designed to goad or shame opponents into reaction. Integral in the planning of the spoiling activity may be a calculation of possible reactions by opponents.

Attention given to violent veto holders can have a negative impact on the quality of any peace resulting from a peace process

In many peace processes, those who shout loudest and hold the most weapons get the most attention. For understandable reasons, potentially violent veto holders may be treated with sensitivity and additional efforts may be invested in attempting to retain them in a peace process and persuade them to moderate their behaviour. Yet there is a danger that other sectors in society, which may not be armed and may not be prepared to engage in violent spoiling, may be overlooked. Moreover, strategies to include at all costs potentially violent veto holders may compromise the nature of any peace that may result from the peace process. The over-attentive courting of violent veto holders may alienate other non-violent actors who are essential for the pacific development of a post-peace-accord society, such as civil society or external investors. Maintaining this delicate balance of inclusion is perhaps the most difficult task facing the organizers of a peace process. In the case of Northern Ireland, the British and Irish governments were prepared to overlook a certain level of violence by militants connected with political parties in the peace process. But transmitting a message that there is an acceptable level of spoiling is a dangerous policy. It risks encouraging boldness among potential spoilers and disaffection among those committed to peaceful approaches.

The greed thesis is unlikely to offer a stand-alone explanation of spoiling

The attractions of the greed thesis are obvious, in that it offers a ready-made narrative of warlords, bandits, and profiteers. Moreover, this narrative often suits a political agenda that wishes to delegitimize and depoliticize those labelled as "spoilers", at once banishing their cause from the political sphere and branding their activities as criminal. Yet just as the greed thesis is of limited explanatory worth in relation to conflict causation (and much less so for conflict maintenance), caution is required when it is applied to spoiling. Those engaged in spoiling activity may have a complex set of motivations, and it is difficult to disaggregate one element (pecuniary gain) from another. Moreover, motivations are likely to be fluid, and to vary among individual members of the same organization.

Absolutism makes for a poor peace

There is no such thing as total peace. Instead, a contested peace attended by uneasy compromises, ragged cease-fires, "devious objectives",[22] and misunderstandings is more likely. The lens offered by terms such as "good" and "evil", fashionable again thanks to the war on terror, is extremely unhelpful here. It is crucial that those involved in a peace process (at both the élite and the grassroots levels) internalize this notion of a contested peace and use it when rationalizing spoiling behaviour. Crucial to the reaction to spoiling tactics is the tolerance threshold of the participants in the peace process. Participants guided by absolutism and an expectation of the perfect observance of non-violence during a peace process are likely to be disappointed. This is not to justify spoiling, merely to recognize that competition, violence, and spoiling have been integral parts of many contemporary peace processes. Nor is it advocacy of a *laissez-faire* attitude towards violent spoiling: action can be taken to discourage violent spoilers (such as the benchmarks of non-violent behaviour adopted for entry into political negotiations in Northern Ireland).

Notes

1. Recommended accounts of the conflict include Whyte, J. 1989. *Interpreting Northern Ireland*. Oxford: Clarendon Press; McGarry, J. and B. O'Leary. 1994. *The Politics of Antagonism*. London: Athlone Press.
2. More detailed accounts of the peace process can be found in Cox, M., A. Guelke, and F. Stephen (eds). 2000. *A Farewell to Arms? From "Long War" to Long Peace in Northern Ireland*. Manchester: Manchester University Press; Mac Ginty, R. and J. Darby. 2002. *Guns and Government: The Management of the Northern Ireland Peace Process*. Basingstoke: Palgrave Macmillan.
3. Northern Ireland Statistics and Research Agency. 2002. *Northern Ireland Census 2001: Key Statistics*. Belfast: Stationery Office, pp. 20–21.
4. Fay, M. T., M. Morrissey, and M. Smyth. 1999. *Northern Ireland's Troubles: The Human Costs*. London: Pluto.
5. Farrell, M. 1976. *The Orange State*. London: Pluto.
6. The 2003 Northern Ireland Life and Times survey of political attitudes found that 23 per cent of Protestant respondents had a lot or a little sympathy with the reasons for loyalist violence and 30 per cent of Catholics had a lot or a little sympathy with the reasons for republican violence. Survey details can be found at www.ark.ac.uk.
7. Zartman, I. W. 2003. "The timing of peace initiatives: Hurting stalemates and ripe moments", in J. Darby and R. Mac Ginty (eds) *Contemporary Peacemaking: Conflict, Violence and Peace Processes*. Basingstoke: Palgrave Macmillan.
8. Good accounts of internal machinations within the republican movement can be found in Maloney, E. 2002. *A Secret History of the IRA*. London: Pinto; Mallie, E. and D. McKittrick. 1996. *Fight for Peace: The Irish Peace Process*. London: Heinemann.
9. *Agreement Reached in the Multi-Party Negotiations*. Belfast: Stationery Office, 1998.
10. Mac Ginty, R., R. Wilford, L. Dowds, and G. Robinson. 2001. "Consenting adults: The principle of consent and Northern Ireland's constitutional future", *Government and Opposition*, Vol. 36, No. 4.
11. Details of the agreement can be found in Wilford, R. (ed.). 2001. *Aspects of the Belfast Agreement*. Oxford: Oxford University Press.
12. Stedman, S. J. 2001. "Implementing peace agreements in civil wars: Lessons and recommendations for policymakers", IPA Policy Paper on Peace Implementation, May. New York: International Peace Academy.
13. For a critique of the greed thesis see Mac Ginty, R. 2004. "Looting in the context of armed conflict: A conceptualisation and typology", *Third Word Quarterly*, Vol. 25, No. 5.
14. Marsh, P., E. Rosser, and R. Harré. 1978. *The Rules of Disorder*. London: Routledge & Kegan Paul, p. 6.

15. Darby, J. and R. Mac Ginty. 2003. "Introduction", in J. Darby and R. Mac Ginty (eds) *Contemporary Peacemaking: Conflict, Violence and Peace Processes*. Basingstoke: Palgrave Macmillan; Chandler, D. 1999. *Bosnia: Faking Democracy After Dayton*. London: Pluto. See also Said, E. 2001. *The End of the Peace Process*. New York: Pantheon Books.
16. Darby, J. 2001. *The Effects of Violence on Peace Processes*. Washington, DC: US Institute of Peace Press.
17. Stedman, S. J. 1997. "Spoiler problems in peace processes", *International Security*, Vol. 22, No. 2, p. 5.
18. Stedman, S. J. 2003. "Peace processes and the challenges of violence", in J. Darby and R. Mac Ginty (eds) *Contemporary Peacemaking: Conflict, Violence and Peace Processes*. Basingstoke: Palgrave Macmillan, p. 108.
19. Darby, note 16 above, p. 54.
20. DUP. 2003. *DUP Assembly Election Manifesto*. Belfast: DUP, pp. 6–7.
21. See Call, C. 1999. "Crime and peace: Successful peace processes produce the world's most violent countries", paper presented at the Annual Conference of the International Studies Association, Washington, DC, February.
22. Richmond, O. 1998. "Devious objectives and the disputants' view of international mediation: A theoretical framework", *Journal of Peace Research*, Vol. 35, No. 6.

8
Why do peace processes collapse? The Basque conflict and the three-spoilers perspective

Daniele Conversi

Peace activists and negotiators face a particularly daunting task in areas where violence functions as a tool for reinforcing ethno-national boundaries and maintaining group cohesion. In such an environment, support and justification for violence exist as a distinct reality, separate from political practice. Promoters of peace and conciliation therefore face the tremendous challenge of tackling this "culture of violence", trying to integrate it and, eventually, transform it into a viable "culture of peace". More ambitiously, as militarism and violence remain intrinsically antithetical to culture, the broader goal should be to devise some sort of "alchemy" capable of transforming violence into culture. This kind of intergroup dynamics is palpable in the enduring conflict between radical Basque nationalism and the Spanish state. It is a condition highly conductive to the emergence of spoiling activities on the part of those who bear arms.

The use of the concept of "spoilers" in this chapter covers a broader spectrum than most other contributions. The chapter identifies three types of spoilers:
- the conventional hard-core group of intransigent "*militant nationalists*", unwilling to renounce their maximalist goals
- *state actors*, taking advantage of the existence of terrorism as a way to consolidate their grip on power by adopting a rigid non-negotiation programme
- extra-territorial actors moving in the *international* arena and exerting a powerful influence upon state governments.

Accordingly, in the Spanish case the three groups are identified in the following ways. ETA's younger militant generations fall into the first type, at least until the fall of the neo-conservative government in 2004. Spain's neo-conservative government falls into the second type. Finally, the international context created by the US-led "war on terror" – which, as will be demonstrated, exasperated inter-ethnic and centre-periphery tensions within Spain – characterizes the third type.

This chapter is divided into two sections. The first part will chart the rise and fall of peace initiatives in the Basque country (1975–2000), identifying a "culture of violence" that has materialized during years of conflict. The second will explore the highly negative effects of an overwhelming external context (namely the US-led "war on terror") on the Basque peace process from 2001 to 2004, disrupting the process, and the consequent radicalization of nationalist politics throughout Spain. The broad aim is to verify if, and how, the concepts of "spoilers" and "spoiling" can be applied to the study of the Basque peace process both at the state and at the international level.

Etiologies

It is hardly possible to resolve an ethnic conflict without attempting to identify its causes, however complex these may be. Such an understanding should be an intrinsic part of any mediation, arbitration, or conflict resolution effort.[1] As a first step, this chapter identifies two distinct sets of causes or etiologies.
- Roots and sources: the causes initially leading to the choice of armed struggle.
- Continuity patterns: the causes of its persistence in a changed environment.

These two "moments" should be clearly separated. Accordingly, two interconnected sets of questions will be attached to each moment.
- Why did Basque activists decide to engage in political violence in the first place? How did it happen? Why did it happen in that particular historical moment? What were the conditions which led to this choice?
- Why has armed struggle remained an available option (even though it may be so only for a minority) once these conditions had greatly changed?

As will become apparent, the responses to the two groups of questions can be altogether different; that is, the structural constraints and historical conditions which once spawned the conflict can change so dramatically that a whole set of new questions would need to be asked to explain its persistence.

A previous book has explored the first set of questions,[2] thus the bulk of this chapter will focus on the second point, dealing more directly with the past failures to achieve peace since the 1980s. The lack of cultural freedoms and collective rights under the Francoist dictatorship could be identified as the original catalyst of conflict. Thus, if the causes which gave rise to the conflict have now been removed, why does the conflict persist? This is a common problem which policy-makers have often confronted, even after large concessions have been granted by the strongest party (usually the state). In such instances the key question will inevitably be "Why does violence still continue in such a changed environment?"

An answer to this question lies in socio-cultural factors. The creation of an armed organization inevitably spawns its own identity, which becomes associated with the group like a trademark through its logo. Hence a logic of self-perpetration emerges as part and parcel of this identity. The organization's identity is made up of words as well as deeds. Actions typically speak louder than words, but are always wrapped in a specific discourse which tends to persist despite political change. In post-Francoist Euskadi the persisting discourse of state oppression was revived at every sign of ill-treatment or mishandling by the security forces, however feeble, and was accordingly adapted to justify the continuation of armed struggle, itself essential to the continuity of an oppositional and antagonistic identity. It is therefore important to chart the historical evolution and itinerary of violence, particularly focusing on how it changed and expanded.

The historical sources of violence

ETA (acronym for Euskadi Ta Askatasuna – Basque Homeland and Freedom) was secretly founded in 1959 by a group of nationalist students and activists.[3] It was originally devoted to political debate, working as an underground cultural forum for the expression of a Basque identity as this was being suffocated by the Francoist dictatorship (1939–1975). The first premeditated political murder occurred in 1968, but a true escalation towards violence took place only after the assassination of Admiral Carrero Blanco (1973), the proposed successor of Franco. From the early 1970s, coinciding with the demise of the *ancien régime*, ETA applied its theory of the "action-repression-action spiral", which the theorists of violence used as a unifying process: its confrontational policy led to fierce repression by the Francoist state, which, in turn, reinvigorated popular Basque consciousness. Thus provoking systematically the state's security forces became an expedient for bringing the struggle for Basque identity continuously to the fore; this also assured a constant increase in ETA's membership figures.

After the death of the dictator Francisco Franco in 1975 the Transition (1975–1982) represented the first historical opportunity for Spain to reconfigure itself as a pluri-national and multicultural state, departing from a centralist tradition lasting over two centuries which had tried to destroy minority cultures as politically viable entities. The 1978 constitution recognized both the unitary "essence" of Spain and the right of each self-defined region to be granted an autonomy statute.[4] It was overwhelmingly approved by referendum throughout Spain, except in the Basque country where a radical minority forcefully boycotted it and even moderate nationalists abstained. However, a statute of autonomy (the Statute of Guernica) was granted to the Basque country in 1980, in the footsteps of its Catalan predecessor (after a popular referendum from which radical nationalists again abstained).[5] The peak of violence had been reached in the previous year, when over 100 people were murdered in ETA-related violence. The Statute of Guernica was an essential tool to inaugurate the demilitarization of Euskadi. Its first military result was the abandonment of armed struggle by one of the two major competing guerrilla organizations, ETA-politico-militar (ETA-pm). Once Euskadi was granted the autonomy statute, ETA-pm, then the main branch of ETA, decided to drop armed struggle altogether, while ETA-militar (henceforth simply ETA) opted for the continuation of its violent strategy. Together with a relevant sector of the local Communist Party, ETA-pm's former members set up in 1976 the electoral alliance EE (Euskadiko Ezkerra – Basque Left), which participated in the 1977 elections. Thus the granting of autonomy was the first bold (and by far the boldest) leap forward in the direction of peace. As a result, violence steadily declined and the popular support which ETA enjoyed before autonomy also waned. However, the most radical faction of ETA (formerly ETA-militar) refused even to consider abandoning armed struggle before achieving its maximalist goal of "self-determination", which was tantamount to separation from Spain. Since the granting of autonomy was at the core of any peace process, the continuation of ETA's violence can be seen as a spoiling activity in itself *vis-à-vis* the possible normalization process: in this historical phase ETA-m as a whole became the key "spoiler".

Violence in the Basque country reached its peak in the late 1970s and thereafter receded, while persisting. Support for armed struggle, as inferred from surveys, opinion polls, and other data, also peaked in that period and then receded.[6] An explanation for this surge of support in the Transition years (1975–1982) and subsequent decline must hence be found, together with an explanation for its slow demise later on.

A second coalition openly seeking Basque independence emerged during the Transition years: in April 1978 a plethora of loosely connected organizations adopted the name of Herri Batasuna (Popular Unity). Like ETA, HB never had a proper leader or central figurehead, and was characterized by an unparalleled flexibility in the recruitment of its cadres.[7] A distinctive trait has always been its ideological heterogeneity. Marxists, environmentalists, gay activists, neo-traditionalists, anti-nuclear activists, cultural revivalists, punks, pacifists, feminists, unemployed, priests, small-town businessmen, students, peasants, and every other imaginable sector from both urban and rural *milieux* were all well represented in what was probably one of the most unorthodox, unconventional, and *sui generis* parties in Europe. What united all these groups was the rejection of both the Spanish constitution and the autonomy statute, and the aspiration to independence. What kept their disparate interests within a single front was the confrontational character of the struggle, the blanket division of the world into oppressor(s) and oppressed. Violence and counterviolence turned into the leitmotifs and the glue of this multitude of social actors. Since independence was the key goal, all ideological differences were momentarily put aside. Therefore, HB had most probably a vested interest in the persistence of violence and in ETA's continuing activity.

Herri Batasuna is often identified as the political arm of ETA, like Sinn Féin in relation to the IRA. It does indeed support ETA's political programme, rejecting parliamentary democracy in favour of direct democracy based on peoples' assemblies (although it participates in both local and national elections). HB's demands include fully fledged independence, socialism, and monolingualism. Without ETA's actions and the state's predictable reactions, Herri Batasuna and its successors would probably cease to exist, since what binds together this plethora of small left-wing groups is the climate of radicalization induced by ETA.

Moreover, the main coordinating agency within the broader movement of support for radical nationalism is the KAS (Koordinadora Abertzale Sozialista – Patriotic Socialist Coordinating Council), which is in itself a very loose coalition of different organizations.[8] Both HB and ETA are members of the KAS, but ETA's role is something more than one of *primus inter pares*. Since it is the only armed organization, and thus the only one which controls offensive weapons, its influence inside the coalition cannot be challenged. No open condemnation of ETA's actions is possible within HB, and ultimately all key decisions need to pass through the filter of ETA's armed men and women. ETA's actions (*ekintzak*) have played a binding role within the movement, due to the latter's fragmentary nature. In short, the KAS was the organizing medium for a broad front whose military vanguard remained ETA. The KAS therefore functioned as the channel of communication between ETA and the wider oppositional movement. Both the latter and HB's political strategy were controlled by ETA. Key HB members were accused of being directly dependent on ETA, an accusation reiterated by Javier Solana in 1987.[9] The use of violence as a binding mechanism indicated the persistence of a likely "spoiler" profile and potential vested interests in blocking peace processes.

Herri Batasuna was renamed Euskal Herritarrok in 1998, and later again simply Batasuna.[10] However, the most important party in the Basque country remained the PNV (Partido Nacionalista Vasco – Basque Nationalist Party), a centrist party founded in 1895 by Sabino de Arana.[11]

Static images of the enemy and the culture of radical violence

In order to understand fully the spoiling attitudes and activities of the radicals, one may need to focus on the rhetoric and language of the armed factions. Most importantly, one should apprehend how the rhetoric has maintained some constant refrains, especially in the vocabulary of radical fringes, from which potential spoilers may emerge. For instance, in their press releases and communiqués the radicals have consistently claimed that "nothing has changed since the end of the dictatorship" and that the Spanish state remains an eternal threat and agent of oppression. Most external observers are naturally sceptical about these claims: the overwhelming evidence is that things have indeed changed. But any evidence of change was firmly rejected during the Transition in favour of a dogmatic idea of the perennial unchangeability of the "oppressor" state. The idea of the state's alleged incapacity to transform itself has been used as a rationale to avoid any ideological or political change within the organization: dogmatic and intransigent claims notably serve an internal purpose of group cohesion.[12] The entire logic of armed struggle and radical nationalism is built upon the "static" image of the enemy as perpetual oppressor. Ethnoradicalism hence functions as a "mirror image" of state centralism.[13] To argue the contrary, that the state has changed, and to recognize that it has granted some crucial rights to the Basques since 1978 would be tantamount to weakening the image of the enemy, and hence one's own image. As armed struggle unfolded, the enemy's vista became an intrinsic part of the radicals' very self-image. The perception of the foe is hence pivotal in the determination to "fight on" which is characteristic of potential spoilers in peace processes.

At the same time, the continued use of violence was advocated by important, although decreasingly so, sectors of Basque public opinion which uncompromisingly vowed to achieve independence. Because the Spanish state was still perceived as the main enemy, the whole democratization process was seen only as a façade disguising a perennial Spanish attempt to eliminate Basque identity. This was the "sectarian view that the elections were a stunt 'to legitimise fascism' [and that] ... Spanish tyranny was now masked by the trappings of a fraudulent democracy".[14] Notwithstanding the autonomy concessions, the radical leftists declared that the Basques were "persecuted more than before".[15] Indeed, the "occupation forces" were still massively present in the region as a reminder of Madrid's past attempts to crush Basque aspirations. Hence, important sectors saw the severing of all ties with Spain as the only viable solution. In order to achieve this goal, ETA's actions were considered not only justified but necessary.

Therefore, one should always stress the role played by a *culture of violence* in largely foreseeable spoiling activities.[16] This should be conceptualized as a boundary-building process in which violence is utilized in a near-ritual way to stress the boundary between insiders and outsiders.[17] This basic twofold distinction can probably be generalized to other violent ethnic conflicts, such as the Kurds, the Eritreans, the Ambonese/Moluccans, the Tamils, and other cases where leaders routinely use violence to bind the group around their goals.

In general, the major spoilers in peace processes tend to be *veto holders*, of which there are normally two: the paramilitaries and the government.[18] In the Basque case, neither of the veto holders was interested in bringing forward the peace process. The factors obstructing a conflict settlement (that is, "spoilers" and "spoiling" groups and tactics) are not only to be sought among the radical factions and forces shaping the most violent fringes. A far more important protagonist which often actively seeks to hinder or undermine conflict settlements is the state – a set of binding and generally legitimate institutions which operate within a shared and recognized legal framework. Formally, all political parties rhetorically advocate the cessation of hostilities and violence, as well as the need for peace negotiations – although some of the main political forces have not been formally engaged in the peace process.

Marginalization and radicalization: The production of vocational spoilers

The elimination of ETA figures – by exile, imprisonment, or killing – created a vacuum that was soon filled by younger and more radical elements. In cases when the leaders were not killed, their remoteness in prison or exile made it impossible for them to exercise a leading role. For instance, in 1986 "Txomin", *aka* Domingo Iturbe Abasolo, at the time ETA's number one, was forced into exile. This action spurred a new climax in the process of distancing the older leadership (the so-called *históricos*) from the emerging militant base.[19] New radical elements were swiftly incorporated into ETA's executive committee to replace the *históricos*. More ruthless and determined, the new guerrillas could move much more freely and safely across the border to France, while the known *históricos* could hardly deceive the French intelligence services. In this way, the latter became increasingly displaced by the former inside ETA. In ETA "it was impossible to be a militant while living abroad".[20] By being abroad, the older leaders lost many of their contacts with the closely knit social networks of Basque resistance and the information and protection they provided. New, ambitious young militants were eager to replace them in a process which was regulated by unrelenting internal competition.

Paradoxically, while the police exulted over the elimination of ETA's leaders, moderate nationalists expressed serious concerns about further uncontrollable violence.[21] In fact, ETA's history has shown that the young *arrivées* are unmistakably more radical, more uncompromising, and less prone to negotiate. Thus Txomin's expulsion in 1986 hampered the progress of peace talks, since he was one of the leaders most favourable to negotiations.[22] The following year Txomin died in a car accident in Algeria, a country which had hosted serious peace negotiations. The elimination of the old guard in 1986 can also explain why some of the most bloody terrorist acts occurred in 1987, such as the attacks on the Hypercor supermarket and the Zaragoza *guardia civil* barracks.[23]

During the transition to democracy (1975–1982), popular mobilizations had largely depended on ETA's actions. Each *ekintza* (ETA action) had a deep impact among the youth. But, most of all, ETA was also a means through which the Basque-Madrid conflict, and the oppositional identity related to it, were kept alive.

Setting up the basis for peace (1980–2001): From the autonomy statute to the cease-fire

The foundations for bringing political violence to a total end were probably laid as soon as nationalists and non-nationalists began jointly to work to restrain the terrorists and their sympathizers. On 12 January 1988 the Pact of Ajuria Enea was signed in Vitoria by all political parties represented in the Basque Parliament, with the exception of HB. It stressed the importance of the autonomy statute as a framework for conflict resolution and as the key institution for carrying the peace process forward. All the signatories committed themselves to operate within a climate of democratic and legally binding consensus. It was assumed that peace could only be achieved by respecting the choices and wishes of all sectors of the Basque electorate.

The pact's intrinsic optimism was based on a few precedents. In the past, individuals and even entire groups (such as ETA-pm) had renounced armed struggle and eventually became involved in day-to-day politics. These precedents provided a puissant inspiration for the signatories. Most important, the pact stressed the need to rehabilitate those former terrorists who would eventually repudiate armed struggle and abide by the rules of the democratic game. On a more security-oriented level, the pact proposed coordination between the judiciary and security forces, as well as international cooperation and a negotiated solution.

Outside the officialdom of party politics, civil society also began to mobilize: in 1992 Elkarri was founded as a "movement for dialogue and agreement" to promote a peaceful and consensual solution to the Basque conflict. Its 3,000 grassroots members, with 800 voluntary activists, were articulated through over 100 self-funded local workshops in towns and suburbs of the Basque Autonomous Community and Navarre, as well as in Madrid, Barcelona, and Brussels.[24]

Ten years after the Pact of Ajuria Enea a new deal was motioned, this time with the inclusion of radical nationalists. Inspired by the positive example of the Northern Ireland peace agreement, the Lizarra Declaration (12 September 1998) was subscribed to by all nationalist forces. Indeed, the declaration highlights that "the British government and the IRA were aware that neither of the two sides could win a military victory and, due to this, accepted the fact that the conflict could go on for a long time if nothing was done to alter this situation".[25] The Irish peace agreement was clearly embraced as *the* model of conflict resolution. The Lizarra Declaration was based on an open *entente* between radical and moderate nationalists and marked the beginning of ETA's unilateral cease-fire (September 1998–December 1999). The latter was, however, never recognized as such by the central government. Hence the moderate nationalists had to pay a heavy price for joining forces with the radicals: the agreement dramatically deepened the gap between the nationalist forces (which had signed the pact) and the "Spanish" forces (which had not). The exception was IU (Izquireda Unida), which thus remained the only Spanish-wide coalition bridging the divide between Basque nationalist and all-Spanish parties.

For mainstream nationalists, and particularly for the PNV, the fallout proved to be unprecedentedly self-damaging. After ETA renounced the cease-fire, the PNV's failure to rein in the radicals backfired. In the process, mainstream moderate nationalism had to become more radicalized by sharing a clause on "the sovereignty of the citizens of the Basque Country" (again indicating the example of Northern Ireland's path to "self-determination"). From the central government's viewpoint, it was possible now to criminalize the entire Basque nationalist spectrum. The unilateral cease-fire declared by ETA lasted from September 1998, following Lizarra, to December 1999. However, as we shall see, the gap between Madrid and Basque politics became even wider after the beginning of the global "war on terror" (2001).

The end of the cease-fire

By 2000 Spain had become one of Europe's most politically stable countries, as well as one of the most economically prosperous. The 12 March general elections ratified the right-wing administration of the Popular Party (Partido Popular) led by Prime Minister José María Aznar López. Aznar was re-elected with an unexpected outright majority, defeating the leftist electoral coalition of former communists and socialists. However, this victory heralded the beginning of an unexpected decline in the standards of Spanish democracy. With 52 per cent of the vote and 183 seats (up from 156 seats) in the lower house of Parliament (Congreso), the Popular Party (PP) could command an absolute majority. This gave the government enormous leverage in dealing with the opposition, and especially with ETA.

The cease-fire had been broken a few months before, and by early 2000 ETA had returned to terrorism. Following the murder of the Spanish Army's Lieutenant-Colonel Pedro Antonio Blanco García, nearly a million Spaniards took to Madrid's streets in protest at the killing. The right-wing government successfully capitalized on this consensus. Despite popular outrage, several assassinations and random acts of violence continued in the following months, including the murder of a journalist and local politicians from the PP and the opposition Socialist Party (PSOE). On 7 August four ETA members were blown up in a car loaded with guns and explosives in Bilbao. One of the four killed, Patxi Rementeria, was the chief of ETA's most ruthless Commando Vizcaya. The radical nationalists' instinctive reaction was to blame the state's security forces, and a wave of vandalism and arson attacks spread across the northern Basque provinces.

In order to prove that the blow had not impaired its organizational capacity, ETA engaged in a dramatic crescendo of violence. On the following day a Basque business executive was killed near Bilbao, and nine people were injured near Madrid's Chamartin train station. The spate of attacks increased in the following months. The deadliest episode was the killing of a Spanish Supreme Court judge, José Francisco Querol Lombardero, with his driver and bodyguard in Madrid on 30 October; 64 passers-by were also wounded, one of whom later died. Three days later two people were injured in Barcelona's Clara Campoamor park, where Aznar was due to speak. Terrorism spread to the south, and in Andalusia hit-squads gunned down two local councillors and carried out other attacks. On 21 November Ernest Lluch, the country's former health minister under the first Spanish socialist government (1982–1986), was assassinated in Barcelona. This killing was designed to mark the twenty-fifth anniversary of the monarchy, which the terrorists regarded as one of their main targets.

Aznar's military crackdown on ETA and his refusal to negotiate resulted in a spate of arrests over the years. Police achievements, however, have not apparently deterred the organization, nor have they altered its capacity to reproduce itself in more radical outgrowths: throughout its history, the group has repeatedly shown it can survive the loss of senior leaders at the price of further radicalization. At the same time, ETA's leadership is now said to include many women.[26]

But the random killing of journalists and other public figures overstepped a new threshold with the designation of new targets. Hitherto the only "legitimate targets" were members of the police and armed forces. Once local and national politicians began to be attacked, the climate of terror reached a new peak. Despite the popular mood against it, with the end of the cease-fire ETA tended to become even more ruthless and indiscriminate: with over 20 assassinations, ETA's death toll in the year 2000 became the highest since 1992. But the strength of civil society in Spain, and particularly in the Basque country, was confirmed by the gargantuan level of attendance at protest marches against terrorism, with crowds swelling up to a million.[27]

By the year 2000, on the twenty-fifth anniversary of the Transition's beginning, Spain was still hailed as a remarkable success story and an international model in the annals of democratization, particularly for its skilful management of ethno-national conflicts. However, the PP government's incapacity to resolve the problem of terrorism would soon reveal itself in a dramatic crescendo of confrontational politics.

Factors in the cease-fire: International models versus domestic pressures

Among the international processes which influenced the Basque aborted settlement was the Anglo-Irish Agreement of 15 November 1985.[28] It was initially very important in encouraging radical activists by providing an ideal framework, a distant reference point, and hope for success. But it turned out to be an external "model" with mere circumstantial and inspirational influence, rather than practical effect.[29] The conditions were dissimilar, and the Spanish state's response differed altogether from the response of the British state.

In this instance, could Aznar's incumbent government be identified as a key "spoiler" in the peace process? The spoiling tactics used by the government were mostly non-collaboration and/or withdrawal from further negotiation. Already, in 1999, the conservative government had acted in a spoiling capacity with an unprecedented and puzzling gesture: during the only secret negotiations with ETA in Zurich, President Aznar's government leaked the names of the mediators and Madrid's security forces arrested one of the two ETA interlocutors. Hence the government was not genuinely interested in adopting those measures of "confidence-building" which are necessary for any peace process to progress. This occurred in the midst of the cease-fire declared by ETA. Judge Joaquim Navarro later accused Aznar of having "lost the best opportunity which had ever been to achieve a definitive peace".[30]

Initially, the conservative government's spoiling tactics were made easier by its capacity to play on the climate of popular uproar against terrorism. In the 1990s the majority of Basque civil society had erupted in mass demonstrations against terrorism and the mood was ripe for a wide consensual settlement. However, the government did at some point choose to take advantage of this popular exasperation to further its own power base. By reasserting a nearly dogmatic intransigence and a stern refusal to accept "terrorist blackmail", Aznar's government gained considerable benefits from the ensuing political impasse. Aznar himself had survived a car-bomb attack while opposition leader in 1995 and seemed to play on his unexpected "heroic" credentials, adopting a personal attitude of revenge. As the terrorists became increasingly ostracized, the government's anti-terror rhetoric was genuinely believed by many to harbour a solution to the problem.

Then, in the post-9/11 crusading climate, this trend became more pronounced, leading to acts of wider criminalization of the entire Basque movement in which non-violent activists began to feel persecuted. The Spanish government's collusion with American interests occurred first of all at the expense of Basque civil liberties, and consisted mostly of a media campaign aimed at preparing the Spaniards for the onslaught: on 20 February 2003, in a major break with the post-Francoist democratic consensus, a National Court judge ordered the closure of the daily *Euskaldunon Egunkaria* – the only daily newspaper entirely written in Basque – and the arrest of 10 prominent staff and employees. All the arrested were held incommunicado under new "anti-terrorist legislation" and taken to Madrid's National Court.[31] This unprecedented attack on free expression was the signal to many liberals and democrats that Spanish democracy was now being taken hostage by the very conservative government which used the fight on terrorism as a cover to subvert democracy. The role of the global "war on terror" in this self-defeating decision will be assessed later. Although nearly all political parties had initially agreed with the government's attempt to isolate ETA's support basis, nationalist parties from all regions, and from left to right, were quick to identify the government's move as a throwback to the dark years of Francoism. The very Francoist roots of the conservative party in power (PP) were now laid bare to see and were rediscovered as an argument of popular polemics. Pasqual Maragall, the socialist mayor of Barcelona, strongly condemned the closure of *Egunkaria*, and for this reason he was accused of "anti-patriotism".[32] The most noticeable consequence of the government's repressive move was to strengthen radical nationalism throughout the country. Various and new forms of separatist nationalism gained a yet unquantifiable number of sympathizers, while resentment against Spain's role in America's "crusade" spread even among ordinary Spaniards. Although ETA was far too isolated and unpopular to take full advantage of the post-9/11 discontent with central government, Spain's participation in the "war on terror" has made the atmosphere immensely more radicalized.

Secret negotiations: Who opposes peaceful settlement?

Research on spoilers suggests that one or more group or institution may take advantage of the continuation of violence.[33] One could easily identify the radical nationalists gravitating around HB as belonging to this category. Moreover, if the government is included in this definition, it may well not use physical violence to pursue its goals, but simply legal measures. The 2003 imprisonment of Basque activists fits this description. The government's exploitation of the US "war on terror" did not help the anti-terrorist cause: indeed, as a result of post-2001 government actions, mass anti-terrorist marches and demonstrations declined, even though most of the blame for the continuation of violence still fell on ETA.[34]

It is worth remembering that ETA has a loose, leaderless organizational structure made up of cells which, at least in the past, had limited relations with each other. Police operations have periodically decimated the organization, which regularly resuscitated itself with renewed vigour. These internal dynamics also led to internal splits, after which the most radical elements usually seized control of the organization. This has been a pattern recurring throughout ETA's history.

There is no official date when the peace process was initiated. Underground talks had been carried out for several decades since the end of Francoism. Some forms of negotiations had occurred throughout various post-Francoist Spanish governments.[35] Robert Clark identifies the earliest Spanish government attempts to negotiate with ETA as occurring between 1975 and 1980, culminating with the pacification of ETA-pm and the ensuing period of "social reintegration" (1981–1983). Then followed a period of crisis and rediscussion, with the emergence of new protagonists (1982–1983), and a second, aborted, attempt at "social reintegration" (1984–1986). Finally, Clark distinguishes two phases in the "Algerian Connection" (1986–1987 and 1987–1988), of which more later on.

In all, there are no neatly identifiable "spoilers" within ETA: the organization as a whole keeps on reproducing itself through violence, despite its increasing isolation. Therefore, it is possible to argue that the organization itself has acted as a "spoiler". In fact, those within the organization who did not wish to carry on with violence were most often identified and marginalized. During the early years of ETA many left the organization and were relatively free to do so. But more recently even influential individuals within ETA have been murdered simply because they had adopted a less intransigent, more conciliatory line, or because they have decided to leave the organization. Two cases stand out. A brilliant strategist and activist, Pertur (Eduardo Moreno Bergareche), was among the inspirers of ETA-pm's move to abandon armed struggle. His goal was to create a leftist party devoted to combining revolutionary socialism with Basque nationalism. Pertur disappeared mysteriously in July 1976, possibly kidnapped and assassinated by a hard core of "preemptive spoilers". But the murder of such an influential man caused a "blowback" effect, reverberating so deeply that ETA-pm ended up adopting Pertur's proposals in its Seventh Assembly (September 1976) and abandoning armed struggle.

The assassination of Yoyes (María Dolores Katarain), former director of ETA, caused even more emotional strains throughout Basque society, so much so that a movie about her life (*Yoyes*, directed by Helena Taberna) was released in Spanish cinemas in 2000. She was assassinated in 1986 after returning from exile, following accusations of high treason by ETA's leadership. This "execution" was aimed precisely at discouraging any militants from abandoning the organization. Beyond ETA's rhetoric of negotiations, such an internal "corrective" against pro-peace trends seems to point to the existence of an in-built mechanism of "pre-emptive spoiling" within the organization.

After all, the name ETA is used as a trademark, and until today its powerfully evocative logo has been associated with the years of heroic struggle against Francoism. No wonder that it is not easily surrendered, and nor can the identity born out of its association with armed struggle be easily relinquished.

Rather than simply pointing the finger at possible "spoilers", the concept of a "culture of violence" may be more useful, as it does not refer simply to the internal dynamics of the organization but also to its social surrounding, which remains the terrain for recruitment. Low-level street violence (*Kalle borroka*), with acts of sabotage and vandalism, has declined, but remained the most fertile recruiting ground for the reproduction of violence and the continuing input of militants. An entire culture had been built around it.

9/11 and the neo-conservative authoritarian turn

The importance of international factors in local conflicts has begun to receive the attention it deserves.[36] More recent developments in Spain have been characterized by the intrusion of an unusual element of conflict. A new external actor could probably be identified as "spoiling" in the Spanish peace process and it is indeed a very powerful one: the US government. In the summer of 2001, in preparation for a major global onslaught on terror, the US Secretary of State, in consultation with the Secretary of the Treasury, the Attorney General, and the Secretary of Homeland Security, included ETA in the list of international terrorist organizations having committed, or posing a significant risk of committing, "acts of terrorism that threaten the security of U.S. nationals or the national security, foreign policy, or economy of the United States". But, most importantly, Executive Order 13224 after 9/11 designated ETA as including Batasuna, Euskal Herritarrok, and Herri Batasuna, since "those entities were formed at ETA's direction and functioned as part of ETA".

Following semi-secret deals and negotiations between the Bush administration and Aznar's government, the USA promised sponsorship to Aznar's own "war on terror". In turn, he was to prove himself one of the most faithful allies in US foreign policy. Aznar was indeed led into a *cul-de-sac* with his embarrassing policy of visionless support for the invasion of Afghanistan and Iraq. As elsewhere, the US "war on terror" has been largely unpopular, and by 2002 over 90 per cent of Spaniards opposed the war on Iraq.[37]

Madrid's pro-US government could only compensate for its legitimacy deficit by emphasizing Spanish "patriotism" as an easy escape valve. This in turn led to an exacerbation of ethno-nationalism throughout the peninsula, because the government's increasing patriotic appeals negatively galvanized public opinion among minority nations. On the other hand, US-style accusations of "anti-patriotism" began to be directed against all opposition groups, including the conservatives' main rivals, the socialists.[38]

Shortly after his controversial electoral "victory", President Bush travelled in search of potential allies for what was already shaping itself as the "war on terror".[39] Three months before 9/11, in June 2001, Bush visited Madrid, declaring that "our government is committed to stand side by side with the Spanish government as it battles terrorism here in Spain".[40] Such profferings of help were warmly welcomed by the Spanish conservative government, led by Aznar. An alliance of intents took shape in which Madrid's government found more than rhetorical support. The following paragraphs will examine the consequences of this *entente* and, in particular, its consequences on centre-periphery and inter-ethnic relations within Spain.

In the 12 March 2000 general elections Aznar had been re-elected with an outright majority, not least because he looked "tough" on ETA. But the US embrace came at a very high price for Spanish sovereignty. Ultimately the reframing of the Spanish war against local terrorist networks as part of an international crusade against global terror largely backfired. With a spate of bloody attacks in Madrid on 11 March 2004, pan-Islamic terrorism struck for the first time on European soil. The scale of the Madrid atrocities (nearly 200 dead and 1,400 were injured) turned them into the most murderous act of terrorism in Spanish history. Despite the government's attempt to blame the attacks on ETA, their occurrence revealed a link with the existing wars in Iraq and Afghanistan – a fate sealed by Aznar's meeting with Bush and Blair at the Azores summit, when the order to invade Iraq was released.

The government's obstinate denial and attempt to hide all evidence of this linkage were at first reiterated by neo-conservatives throughout the world, who did not hesitate to echo Aznar's words and define this as the "new Guernica".[41] However, public revulsion at the slaughter was channelled into a new indignation against a government not only incapable of protecting its people, but also actively trying to conceal the truth about the massacres – a spontaneous sense of anger mostly conveyed by young people via text messages and e-mails in spite of the neo-conservative government's grip on the media.[42] The government was aware of the Spaniards' deep hostility to the global "war on terror", which reached the PP's own rank and file.

The revelation of a link with its Middle Eastern policy would have jeopardized the government's credentials because, like Tony Blair, Aznar had decided to follow the US lead despite overwhelming popular opposition. This anti-democratic turn and the government's propaganda through both private and state-run media had already damaged the prospects of Spaniards renewing their mandate. In the wake of the emotional shock caused by the attacks, Aznar did not really have alternatives other than trying to hide any links with his foreign policy choices. However, the bluff was called, and a public devastated by the tragic events decided to penalize the incumbent leaders further.[43] In the 18 March 2004 elections the PP was defeated beyond most expectations, gaining only 148 seats. José Luis Rodríguez Zapatero's PSOE won with 164 seats, just 12 short of a majority in the 350-seat Congress of Deputies. One of the victor's first moves was to announce that Spain would withdraw its 1,300 troops from Iraq, although there was no mention of the troops remaining in Afghanistan. The policy of "pre-emptive war" had now come full circle.

Zapatero could only reach a majority by obtaining help from regional nationalist parties for a total of 19 extra votes. After the attacks, "the Catalan and Basque press grew furiously dubious, then downright scornful, about ETA involvement".[44] The realignment with "old Europe", sealed by Zapatero's Paris and Berlin trips in late April, went a great way in the direction of a *rapprochement* with more pro-European Basque and Catalan nationalist parties. Yet the harm was done, and the hardest test for the new government has been to heal the rift and mend the legacy of Aznar's legitimacy deficit.

Police operations did contribute greatly to the weakening of ETA, although they could hardly defeat it. But, most of all, it was public pressure, with millions of people demonstrating against ETA's terrorist violence, which led to the latter's rapid delegitimation. By 2001 ETA's itinerary was approaching an inglorious end, and the termination of armed struggle was historically at hand. However, international events erupted to make the matter more complicated, in particular the Spanish government's collusion with American interests and the simultaneous attack on Basque civil liberties. In general, peripheral nationalists took advantage of the new crisis of government legitimacy by expanding their requests, with a spiralling trend towards secession.

In different degrees and for different reasons, both the central government under Aznar and ETA have touched low popularity levels. However, past experiences and comparisons with other nationalist movements show some distinctive patterns in similar situations. If the central government relies excessively on coercion to suppress a dissenting movement, be it violent or non-violent, it is generally the most radical fringes of both divides which stand to gain. In the end, no government is able to impose its rule and gain legitimacy if coercion is not accompanied by a search for democratic consensus. The banning of several non-violent Basque groups and media, including the closure of periodicals and the arrest of moderate activists who played no substantial role in any violent activity, led to widespread bitterness. In turn, this pushed towards new patterns of secrecy, distrust for the state, and radicalization among previously moderate sectors and individuals. The condemnation of terrorism has remained massive and without appeal. Yet calls for a return to armed struggle could have been anticipated if the situation had persisted under a renewed mandate for the neo-conservative government and if the restrictions of civil rights and freedom of expression had been extended further in time. In general, a climate of deepening radicalization characterized the last months of Aznar's rule. This sense of disaffection has subsequently expanded among moderate centrists as well.

In 2003 the moderate Basque Nationalist Party's leader and regional premier (*lehendakari*) Juan José Ibarretxe devised a plan to reform the Basque statute of autonomy and end violence. Ibarretxe's proposal for a "free associated state" would give the Basque country the right to determine its own sovereignty by referendum. The determination with which the Basque government and moderate nationalists have espoused Plan Ibarretxe would have been hardly conceivable before Aznar's own "mini-war on terror". However, the central government claimed that the plan was illegal and would lead to the country's break-up. Indeed, Plan Ibarretxe aimed at a form of sovereignty bordering on independence for the "greater" Basque country, incorporating Navarre and the three Basque provinces in France. Most mainstream Spanish parties, including the socialists (in power since March 2004), were strongly opposed to the Ibarretxe plan.

This clearly points to a polarization of the Spanish electorate. It is worth noting that the central government's inflexibility reflected the Bush administration's vehement antipathy for that very multilateralism which is at the core of both Spanish governance and European policy-making. The resurgence of domestic conflict in Spain tunes in well with the USA's neo-conservative mood, famously emphasized by Rumsfeld's calculated *gaffe* in January 2002 inaugurating a new dichotomy between "old Europe" and "new Europe".[45] Under Aznar, the new US-conceived division line could be said to cut across Spain, dividing a PP-dominated Madrid from the Basque country and Catalonia, nearer to "old Europe". With the post-11 March socialist victory, this potential fracture has been partially healed. Yet the victory of pro-independence parties or coalitions in two key regions, notably in Catalonia, clearly points to the long-term effects of the "war on terror" on Spanish stability. A cursory analysis of its effects on Spain's internal cleavages seems to lend credence to the view that the transatlantic neo-conservative *entente* has deeply destabilized the country.

A second element is that, by adopting a potentially bankrupting foreign policy, the Spanish state has aligned itself with American directives at a moment when the USA has reached unprecedented unpopularity levels throughout the world.[46] Like elsewhere, a sweeping critique of American politics has spread rapidly in Spain since the US attack on Afghanistan (October 2001), in contrast with the robust wave of pro-Americanism characterizing NATO's intervention in Kosovo (March 1999).[47]

Contrary to what was anticipated by Bush's advisers, the 11 March tragedy did not change this perception and may even have reinforced it. As a consequence, even Spanish nationalists, normally hostile to Basque separatism, looked with suspicion upon the uneven Aznar-Bush couple. In other words, since the beginning of the "war on terror" a creeping resistance to US policies has become a force uniting the entire political spectrum, from right to left, from Spanish unitarists to Basque separatists, both before and after the 11 March attacks. Spain's perceived loss of sovereignty, as a consequence of Aznar's unpopular support for US-led wars, has eroded government legitimacy in new and unpredictable ways. This trend has, of course, affected the neo-conservative rank and file, although party politics has required the rigorous muting of open internal dissent.

What have been the consequences of this policy? How did Aznar's government react to the first symptoms of this crisis? Largely because the neo-conservative government in Madrid was seen as a pawn of larger US corporate interests, a sense of disaffection had spread much beyond the hard-core nationalists of each region.

The Spanish government has therefore increased its appeal to Spanish patriotism. Flag-waving, nationalist rhetoric, public commemorations, military displays, and vitriolic attacks on peripheral nationalists as "traitors" of the homeland were an integral part of Aznar's own "war on terror". Individuals and groups who opposed the war on Afghanistan and Iraq were routinely accused of lacking loyalty to the *Patria*, while nationalist symbols began to become ubiquitous.

However, this had disastrous effects on Spain's long-term stability. In hitherto moderate Catalonia, nationalists have radicalized their posture in response: by the mid-November 2003 regional elections the pro-independence ERC (Esquerra Republicana de Catalunya) had nearly doubled its seats (from 12 to 23), holding the region's balance of power – a triumph dramatically confirmed in the 14 March 2004 general elections.[48] Its leader, Josep Luís Carod-Rovira, has been under the media spotlight after admitting to secret talks with two ETA leaders in Perpignan (capital of southern France's Catalan region).[49] Aznar even accused Carod-Rovira of assisting ETA in the selection of its targets.[50]

Yet the ERC became the principal force benefiting from the post-9/11 confrontational climate in Catalonia – reaping the grim harvest sown by Aznar's home-made "war on terror". The latter was indeed propitious to the rise of oppositional politics. But the "Americanization" of Spain's internal conflict had distressing consequences in a whole set of areas, both at the international and at the state level. While Spain's relationship with the Arab world, notably with Morocco, rapidly deteriorated, the relationship between Spain's central government and various regions was rapidly reaching a breaking point – at least in the case of a conservative victory at the March 2004 polls.

Post-9/11 politics led to a climate of increasing insecurity, implying that all regionalist parties had to radicalize their postures, increasing demands for full independence. Moreover, ahead of both regional and general elections, all the main Catalan parties had already tabled their own proposals for greater autonomy and self-determination. This radicalization was replicated in Galicia and the Basque country. The right-wing intransigence of the central government was the single major cause of this new political instability. Aznar's unwillingness to negotiate in matters of both internal and international security fed fissiparous tendencies and practices, particularly because this was accompanied by a new centralizing patriotism which inevitably provoked "spoiling" tendencies and practices.

A US-inspired "counterfeit" patriotism was used as a compensatory strategy to fill the legitimacy vacuum left by the "sell-out" of national foreign policy against Spain's own security interests. Although this was partially an internal development of Spanish politics, it was heterodirected and substantially inspired by the global foreign policy agenda taking shape in the wake of 9/11. In short, Bush's "war on terror" provided the catalyst factor and the inadvertent incentive for wider political changes within Spain itself.

Other external sources

No external actors had hitherto influenced the conflict in significant ways, because none had the political weight to do so. France had in the past provided a sanctuary for escapees and, generally, for activists prosecuted by Spanish police, but this role practically ceased with Spain's entry into the European Community (1986). What is more, the Spanish and French governments have continuously improved their coordination efforts in this matter. For instance, in July 1996 the Spanish Interior Minister, Jaime Mayor Oreja, and his French counterpart, Jean-Louis Debré, signed a bilateral treaty on police cooperation. These and other measures clearly pointed at the positive role of the EU (as opposed to the USA) and various inter-European initiatives in ending the conflict.

Before the French-backed military coup in Algeria (January 1992), the Algerian government had provided ideological support for Basque radicals and even hosted talks for negotiations (1987–1989).[51] The new "eradicationist junta" which replaced the formerly non-aligned government was no longer interested in promoting peace processes either at home or abroad. Therefore, Algeria no longer could play a role in the underground peace process.

Other governments, notably Libya and the Soviets via the KGB, have variously been blamed for hosting, supporting, and even financing Basque terrorism, but most accusations have proven to be largely unfounded. On the other hand, ETA has certainly cultivated links with various insurgent groups, such as the IRA, the Zapatistas EZLN (Mexico), the Tupamaros of Uruguay, the Colombian guerrillas FARC, and various paramilitary militias in Lebanon and Nicaragua, with which training was allegedly shared.

Financial aid for ETA often came from a variety of sources, but most were indigenous to the Basque country. Diaspora groups situated in the Americas played a less significant role than in other terrorist organizations of global reach, such as the Tamils and the Kosovars.[52]

Further policy implications have not been at the core of this chapter. More research is needed to speculate on how international institutions, such as the European Community and the United Nations, can influence the Basque peace process, and whether they will be able to play any viable mediating role in the future. The new "structure of opportunities" offered by the end of the neo-conservative regime and the beginning of the socialist government headed by Zapatero has provided a new ray of hope and novel avenues for demobilization. The unmitigated unpopularity of terrorism in Spain will make it much harder for the paramilitary to be welcomed, even amongst those very nationalist communities where, in Maoist slang, they were supposed to "swim like fishes in the water". In May 2004 Spain marked its first full year without any ETA killings – the first time in more than three decades, if one excludes the cease-fire.[53] The new scenario presents a truly unprecedented series of yet unexplored opportunities.

Conclusion

The question "why do peace processes collapse?" is answered here by adopting a "three-spoilers perspective". In other words, the emergence of potential spoilers should be identified at three interconnected levels:

at the local level, with the persistence of a "culture of violence" inherited from the late Francoist years; at the state level, with the central government officially adopting a non-negotiating, no-compromising posture; and, since 9/11, at the international level, with the intrusion of US foreign policy into strictly domestic matters.

The first part of this chapter analysed the internal dynamics of the Basque-Madrid conflict by identifying spoiling activities on both sides of the divide. It identified a hard-core *culture of violence*, creating and/or maintaining a boundary around Basque radical identity. From this culture of violence, grassroots spoilers tend naturally to emerge. Therefore, any attempt to reach some consensus by avoiding the emergence of spoilers needs to address this widespread culture of violence, especially among the youth. The final part explored this issue within the wider international situation, as defined by global actors who tend to act in their indirect spoiling capacity. The "three-spoilers" perspective identifies not only the central government and the paramilitary as key spoilers, but also crucial international players openly or covertly derailing peace initiatives.

This volume emphasizes that there is a capacity for spoiling in all actors at different phases of the process. Indeed, in the Basque case spoilers have emerged at different times on both sides of the divide. The persistence of conflict has hence become an issue of tactics, not actors. Different actors at different times may choose to opt out from, or rein in, the peace process. Whether their intent is to gain time, seize popular favour, or simply favour the *status quo*, both the government and ETA may opt for delaying and obstructionist tactics or intransigent postures. This chapter has argued that a dangerous turn has taken place with the intrusion of a possible third unexpected "spoiler", in the form of US pressures on Spanish internal politics. The Washington-Madrid axis introduced a new element of distortion in the fragile scenario of the already intricate interplay between the two main "veto holders", ETA and the central government.

Paradoxically, many terrorist groups and right-wing governments share a sort of extreme conservatism. ETA's "conservative" attitude – that is, its overriding idea that "nothing has changed" since the Transition – has been matched by the parallel conservative drift in Aznar's government, unwilling to attempt new routes to demobilization. In other words, both the terrorists and the neo-conservatives have tended to favour the *status quo* of "low-intensity conflict".[54] Their purposes may seem at odds with each other, but both of them endeavoured to exert persisting control over their constituencies through the intimidating mechanism of fear. For ETA and the radical *milieux*, "low-intensity" violence provided a continuous source of cohesion and capacity to mobilize.[55] This mobilizing capacity has persisted intact throughout the Transition. The 1998–1999 cease-fire briefly heralded an entirely new possibility of conceiving a mobilized Basque identity beyond, and independently from, political violence. By that time it was assumed that the central government was "conservatively" interested in maintaining a low level of violence for a series of reasons, mainly stemming from its unwillingness to initiate any sort of negotiation if ETA did not drop its maximalist programme. The incentives for the Spanish government to negotiate with ETA dramatically decreased, reaching their historical nadir once the PP government embarked on its US-inspired "war on terror".

Although all parties seek peace, incentives for the continuation, rather than cessation, of violent conflict are harder to identify. They may be non-rational as well as rational. The collapse of peace negotiations occurred at a time when Basque civil society was massively mobilized against terrorism. As a consequence, ETA can no longer claim to represent the Basque people as a whole. However, by backing Aznar's own personal crusade against home-grown terrorism in the framework of a global crusade against "evil", the US government has clumsily inserted itself into Spanish internal affairs. This has partially derailed a powerful, spontaneous, and hugely popular movement. It has damaged its inspiration and detracted from its rationale by calling into question its very spontaneity. It has also played into the hands of intransigents on both sides of the conflict. Despite police operations wrecking ETA's organizational structure, pro-independence nationalists may have gained an added stratum of legitimacy. But despite this, ETA's long trajectory of decline and waning popularity has not been reversed.

In January 2004 it seemed that mutual distrust between large sectors of Basque society and the central government would persist for years. If Aznar had stayed in power, pursing the same policy, it is likely that the ensuing confrontation would have been exploited by nationalist populists on all sides, jeopardizing the historic gains of the post-Franco years. The neo-conservative government may have "reinforced" its bargaining position in the short term, but its long-term legitimacy would have drained away. Under the aegis of the "war on terror", intransigent options have gained the upper hand in both camps, resulting in a process of deepening polarization. The latter has spread to hitherto moderate Catalonia and, further afield, to Galicia.

However, the popular awareness that the destiny of Spain is now mired in a global war no longer controlled by Spaniards themselves has once more recast the shape of Spanish politics. As a consequence, the new post-11 March scenario offers new windows of opportunities for solving the problem of political violence within the country.

Notes

1. See Coakley, John. 2002. "The challenge", in John Coakley (ed.) *The Territorial Management of Ethnic Conflicts*. London: Frank Cass.
2. Conversi, Daniele. 1997. *The Basques, the Catalans, and Spain: Alternative Routes to Nationalist Mobilization*. London: Hurst.
3. For a full historical account see *ibid*.
4. See Moreno, Luis. 2001. *The Federalization of Spain*. London: Frank Cass.
5. Percentages on participation and abstention rates in the four provinces can be found in Mees, Ludger. 2003. *Nationalism, Violence and Democracy: The Basque Clash of Identities*. London: Palgrave Macmillan, p. 42.
6. According to a 1982 survey, 38 per cent of the Basque population considered ETA activists to be idealists and patriots, while 31 per cent believed that they were criminals or insane. However, the same survey indicated that only 8 per cent of the Basques claimed to support ETA, while 77 per cent said that they were opposed to its activities. See Linz, Juan J. 1985. "From primordialism to nationalism", in Edward A. Tiryakian and Ronald Rogowski (eds) *New Nationalists of the Developed West*. Boston, MA: Allen & Unwin. There was hence a gap between "understanding" and outright support. This blend of justification and accusation may either derive from a persisting fear of expressing one's own view (memories of the dictatorship years) or from the fact that some people genuinely believed in the commitment of ETA's activists. However, successive surveys indicated a slow decline in ETA's popularity, which dipped sharply after 1987 as a result of indiscriminate killings and terrorist acts that seemed to diverge from its original tactics and methods. See also Mees, note 5 above, p. 99.
7. *El País*. 1987. "Herri Batasuna renovará a primeros de año a todos los componentes de su mesa nacional", *El País*, 24 December.
8. Mees, note 5 above, p. 43.
9. *El País*. 1987. "Javier Solana dice que los partidos integrados en HB dependen de ETA", *El País*, 24 December.
10. HB went from 19.97 per cent in 1979 to 28.11 per cent in 1987 (and 24 per cent in the 1989 legislative elections), while EE went from 12.62 per cent to 13.1 per cent. See *Anuario Estadístico Vasco 1985*. Bilbao: Gobierno Vasco/Eusko Jaurlaritza, 1986; *Anuario Estadístico Vasco 1988*. Bilbao: Gobierno Vasco/Eusko Jaurlaritza, 1989. For the data up to 1980, see SIADECO. 1981. *Análisis Descriptivo de la Comarca Rentería Pasages*. Donostia: Caja Laboral Popular, pp. 132–151.
11. Douglass, William. 2004. "Sabino's sin: Racism and the founding of Basque nationalism", in Daniele Conversi (ed.) *Ethnonationalism in the Contemporary World*. London and New York: Routledge.
12. Conversi, Daniele. 1999. "Nationalism, boundaries and violence", *Millennium*, Vol. 28, No. 3.
13. Conversi, Daniele. 2003. "Ethnoradicalism as a mirror image of state centralization: The Basque paradigm in Franco's Spain", in Farimah Daftary and Stefan Troebst (eds) *Radical Ethnic Movements in Contemporary Europe*. Oxford: Berghahn.
14. Preston, Paul (ed.). 1986. *The Triumph of Democracy in Spain*. New York: Methuen, p. 126.
15. In 1983 Francisco Letamendia (Ortzi) declared that the Basques in general, not only the nationalist left, were more persecuted than years before. *Egin*. 1983. "Lo vasco, en general, y no sólo la izquierda abertzale, está ahora más perseguido que hace algunos años", *Egin*, 16 July.
16. Some anthropologists identify a "culture of radical nationalism". See McClancy,

Jeremy. 1988. "The culture of radical Basque nationalism", *Anthropology Today*, Vol. 4, No. 5.
17. For a general theoretical view on the relationship between violence and ethnic boundaries see Conversi, note 13 above; Santiago García, José A. 2001. "Las fronteras (étnicas) de la nación y los tropos del nacionalismo", *Política y Sociedad*, No. 36; "Las Fronteras (Étnicas) de la Nación y los Tropos del Nacionalismo", Tribuna Libre, PURESOC, Departamento de Sociología, Universidad Pública de Navarra/Nafarroako Unibertsitate Publikoa, Pamplona, undated, available at www.unavarra.es/puresoc/pdfs/BP-Santiago.pdf.
18. See Mees, Ludger. 2000. "Basque country", in John Darby and Roger Mac Ginty (eds) *The Management of Peace Processes*. Basingstoke: Palgrave Macmillan; Darby, John and Roger Mac Ginty. 2000. "The management of peace", in John Darby and Roger Mac Ginty (eds) *The Management of Peace Processes*. Basingstoke: Palgrave Macmillan.
19. *El País-Domingo*. 1986. "Los 'históricos' de ETA dan paso a los jóvenes", *El País-Domingo*, 13 July.
20. *Garaia*. 1976. "Interview with Txillardegi", *Garaia*, Vol. I, No. 1.
21. *El País*. 1986. "Medios nacionalistas consideran 'un serio error' el alejamiento de 'Txomin'", *El País*, 12 July.
22. *El País-Domingo*, note 19 above.
23. *El País*. 1988. "ETA cometió en 1987, en Barcelona y Zaragoza, los atentados más sangrientos", *El País*, 29 January; *El País*. 1987. "Algo cambiará tras Hipercor", *El País*, 28 June.
24. From Elkarri's website, http://elkarri.org/en/textos/quienes.php.
25. Translation from www.euskadi.net/pakea/indicel_i.htm.
26. Tremlett, Giles. 2002. "ETA brings women fighters to the fore", *The Guardian*, 27 August; Daly, Emma. 2000. "ETA women emerge as top guns in terror war", *The Observer*, 24 September.
27. According to the organizers, a peak of 8 million demonstrators marched simultaneously in several Spanish cities in 1997: see Mees, note 5 above, pp. 91–100.
28. Irvin, Cynthia L. 1999. *Militant Nationalism: Between Movement and Party in Ireland and the Basque Country*. Minneapolis: University of Minnesota Press.
29. Alonso, Rogelio. 2004. "Pathways out of terrorism in Northern Ireland and the Basque country: The misrepresentation of the Irish model", *Terrorism and Political Violence*, Vol. 16, Winter; Conversi, Daniele. 1993. "Domino effect or internal developments? The influences of international events and political ideologies on Catalan and Basque nationalism", *West European Politics*, Vol. 16, No. 3.
30. Navarro, cited in Mees, Ludger. 2001. "Between votes and bullets. Conflicting ethnic identities in the Basque country", *Ethnic and Racial Studies*, Vol. 24, No. 5, p. 815; Mees, note 5 above, p. 164.
31. Amnesty International. 2003. "Spain: Closure of Basque newspaper must be investigated promptly", press release, EUR 41/002/2003 (Public), News Service No. 043, 25 February, available at http://web.amnesty.org/library/print/ENGEUR410022003.
32. *El Mundo*. 2003. "Las acusaciones de Rato contra Pasqual Maragall provocan incidentes en el Congreso", *El Mundo*, 6 March; *El Mundo*. 2003. "Caso Egunkaria. Caldera dice que el PSOE da 'crédito a las instituciones y no a las denuncias de torturas'", *El Mundo*, 5 March.
33. Stedman, Stephen J. 1997. "Spoiler problems in peace processes", *International Security*, Vol. 22, No. 2.
34. No "splinter group" from larger parties has emerged in recent years. However, during the early transition years one of the major splits in ETA's history occurred when ETA-pm decided to drop armed struggle altogether, forming Euskadiko Ezkerra.

35. Clark, Robert P. 1990. *Negotiating with ETA: Obstacles to Peace in the Basque Country, 1975–1988*. Reno: University of Nevada Press.
36. See Saideman, Stephen. 2002. "Overlooking the obvious: Bringing international politics back into ethnic conflict management", *International Studies Review*, Vol. 4, No. 3; Saideman, Stephen. 2001. *The Ties That Divide: Ethnic Politics, Foreign Policy and International Conflict*. New York: Columbia University Press. See also the chapters by Fred Halliday, Michael Cox, and Adrian Guelke in Michael Cox, Adrian Guelke, and Fiona Stephen (eds). 2000. *A Farewell to Arms? From "Long War" to Long Peace in Northern Ireland*. Manchester: Manchester University Press.
37. See Tremlett, Giles. 2003. "Supporters desert Aznar as Spaniards reject conflict", *The Guardian*, 18 February; Daly, Emma. 2003. "Aznar counts cost of war as voters rebel", *The Observer*, 6 April; Goodman, Al. 2003. "Polls: 90 per cent of Spaniards against war", *CNN News*, 29 March, available at www.cnn.com/2003/WORLD/europe/03/29/sprj.irq.spain/.
38. *El Mundo*. 2003. "Rajoy dice que Zapatero carece de patriotismo", *El Mundo*, 19 October.
39. There is increasing evidence that, well before 9/11, the Bush administration had already chosen terrorism as the strategic "calling point". For years US neo-conservative think-tanks and opinion-makers had highlighted it as the privileged and most powerful mobilizing tool in their agenda to reshape the world while tightening their grip on American society.
40. Joint press conference with President George W. Bush and President José Maria Aznar, Moncloa Palace, Madrid, 11 June 2001, available at www.whitehouse.gov/news/releases/2001/06/20010613-4.html.
41. See, for instance, Portillo, Michael. 2004. "Every country must learn the lesson of this new Guernica", *The Times*, 14 March.
42. Losowsky, Andrew. 2004. "A 21st-century protest", *The Guardian*, 25 March.
43. On the consequences of Aznar's policy of hiding the truth for reasons of electoral expediency, see Tremlett, Giles. 2004. "Aznar accused of cover-up as Spain mourns its dead", *The Observer*, 14 March.
44. Preston, Peter. 2004. "Why Spain's poll heroes turned to zeros", *The Observer*, 21 March.
45. Watson, Roland. 2003. "Rumsfeld seeks to isolate 'old Europe' opponents", *The Times*, 24 January; Ridgeway, James. 2003. "Rumsfeld's propaganda ministry. The Pentagon's ever-changing war stories", *The Village Voice*, 14 November.
46. For a brilliant interpretation of the roots of global anti-Americanism, see Sardar, Ziauddin and Merryl Wyn Davies. 2002. *Why Do People Hate America?* Cambridge: Icon.
47. For an analysis of Spanish (particularly Catalan) pro-interventionism following the Bosnian tragedy, see Conversi, Daniele. 2000. *La Desintegració de Iugoslàvia*. Barcelona, Catarroja: Editorial Afers-El Contemporani.
48. Davis, Andrew. 2004. "The November 2003 elections in Catalonia: The effects of the Partido Popular's absolute majority on the autonomous elections", paper presented at the Annual PSA Conference, Lincoln, UK, 6–8 April, Panel on Elections and Territorial Politics.
49. *The Guardian*. 2004. "ETA declares Catalonia ceasefire", *The Guardian*, 18 February.
50. *Ibid*.
51. The most important book describing this phase of the negotiations is Clark, note 35 above. See also Mees, note 5 above.
52. A 2003 communiqué from the US Council on Foreign Relations puts it this way: "Basque-Americans do not provide financial support, weapons, or political support for

ETA, experts say, although some Basques in the United States do support Basque self-determination." See www.terrorismanswers.com/groups/eta_print.html.
53. Tremlett, Giles. 2004. "Spain marks a year without ETA killings", *The Guardian*, 31 May.
54. See Kriesberg, Louis. 1998. *Constructive Conflicts: From Escalation to Resolution*. Lanham, MD: Rowman & Littlefield.
55. Conversi, note 2 above.

9

Peace on whose terms? War veterans' associations in Bosnia and Herzegovina

Vesna Bojicic-Dzelilovic

The 1992–1995 war in Bosnia and Herzegovina (BiH) was the most violent phase in the dissolution of the former Socialist Federal Republic of Yugoslavia (SFRY), of which, for almost 50 years, BiH was one of six constituent republics. In the course of the war BiH's three main ethic groups – Muslims, Bosnian Croats, and Bosnian Serbs, with the active involvement of neighbouring Croatia and Serbia – fought each other in pursuit of their own vision of BiH's political and territorial (re)organization. The causes and character of the war remain contentious, the main disagreement being over the issue of whether it was a war of aggression by BiH's neighbours or a civil war. Essentially it contained the elements of both, which determined the way the war was fought, the multiplicity of actors involved, and the complexity of agendas played out in the course of the conflict, its settlement, and the peacebuilding process. The fighting was brought to end by an intense international military and diplomatic campaign which pushed the warring parties into compromise, none of which considered this just. The task of implementing the complex terms of the peace agreement was put overwhelmingly in the hands of international actors, while local parties pursued a strategy of obstruction, trying to assert their own interpretation of the peace agreement that would accommodate some of their war aims.

This chapter focuses on war veterans' associations as one particular type of non-state actors engaged in undermining peace settlement in the specific context of the BiH war. For a number of reasons – in particular the associations' relationship with the political leadership negotiating the peace agreement – this case provides different insights into the issue of spoiling in contemporary conflicts characterized by a multiplicity of both actors and agendas, and complex strategies needed to pacify them. As former combatants opposed to the terms of the peace settlement, and formally not a party to the agreement, their capacity for spoiling is crucially defined by their links to the parties which are inside the peace process. Using violence and other means to hinder the implementation of the peace agreement, their intent is to create a context in which the political leadership can push for a renegotiation of the agreement that would accommodate some of their wartime aims.

The chapter starts with a brief analysis of the political and economic goals behind the 1992–1995 war, focusing on Bosnian Croat self-rule as a political project and goal of the spoiling pursued by Bosnian Croat war veterans' associations. It then reflects on the terms of the peace agreement, indicating some of the main areas in which its implementation was obstructed by this group. The analysis of the war veterans' associations deals with their origins and their position in the Bosnian Croat post-war power structures, the sources of their funding, and their official and hidden agendas. The probe into spoiling tactics focuses on three important aspects of the peace agreement: refugee return, war crimes prosecution, and institution-building. This is followed by a brief analysis of the impact of various strategies the international community, as a custodian of peace, has used to sustain its implementation.

The 1992–1995 war in Bosnia and Herzegovina: Why the war was fought

Political goals

The context in which the war was fought – the break-up of the common state and the creation of independent, majority nation-states, principally Croatia and Serbia – is essential to an understanding of the nature of political violence that raked BiH for more than three years, and also difficulties in consolidating peace. Before the war BiH was the most ethnically mixed of former Yugoslavia's republics. According to the 1991 Census, Muslims accounted for 43.7 per cent of the population, Bosnian Serbs 31.4 per cent, and Bosnian Croats 17.3 per cent; the remainder consisted of various other ethnic groups as well as those of mixed ethnic origin who declared themselves as "Yugoslavs". With the disappearance of the common framework of the Yugoslav state the very existence of BiH was brought into question, not least because of the ambitions of Serbia and Croatia to enlarge their territories by integrating parts of BiH where their respective ethnic group was a majority. To achieve congruence between the territory and a particular ethnic group's majority in BiH required massive population displacement,[1] which became the main political goal of the war. It was a devastating process, causing large-scale civilian casualties and physical destruction which in some aspects surpassed the carnage of the Second World War.

At the start of the war Bosnian Serbs and Bosnian Croats considered the creation of ethnically homogeneous territories as the first step towards secession from BiH. When in the course of the conflict international mediation made this option unfeasible,[2] the goals shifted towards securing the highest possible degree of independence for Bosnian Croats and Bosnian Serbs within the state of BiH. In contrast, Muslims pushed for a unified state of BiH, but one that would grant them, as the largest ethnic group, a privileged position. This tension in the political aspirations of the main protagonists of war would remain the key stumbling block in the implementation of the peace agreement.

Although the ultimate aims of the political leaderships of the three BiH peoples differed, they all strived to consolidate their hold over ethnically more or less homogeneous territories. The monopoly of power they enjoyed in these ethnic enclaves enabled them to control resources and secure a privileged position for their members and supporters. In the vicious fighting, in which numerous atrocities were committed, besides the three armies created by the political parties representing BiH's three main ethnic groups combatants included regular troops from Croatia and Serbia, local and foreign paramilitaries, and mercenaries. Diasporas, especially Croatian, played an important role in all phases of the conflict and its aftermath, providing not only money and military equipment but also recruiting some of the key political and military figures. Throughout all phases of the war and the post-war period there was and remains a large international civilian and military presence, which has in itself contributed importantly to the dynamics of the war, its termination, and progress in peace implementation.

Economic goals

During the war three largely independent socio-economic structures emerged, controlled by the three main nationalist parties: the Muslim Party of Democratic Action (SDA), the Serb Democratic Party (SDS), and the Croatian Democratic Union of Bosnia-Herzegovina (HDZ BiH). In effect these were three mini-party-states, run by ethno-political criminal structures, operated through close-knit networks of political, economic, and military élites engaged in the redistribution of assets accumulated in the public domain, and often connected to regional and international criminal networks. The development of BiH's criminal war economy was a response to a sharp decline in productive activity caused by the war and the disintegration of the former common Yugoslav market, which came on top of a prolonged and severe crisis that crippled the SFRY's economy, precipitating state collapse. War, sanctions, and large population movement within and across the borders of newly created Yugoslavia's successor states opened many opportunities for irregular activity, including organized crime with links to the highest political establishment. The combatants were provided with privileged access to resources, including looting and dispossession of other ethnic groups, and diversion of humanitarian assistance to compensate for irregular payments of salaries. The fact that this was condoned by the political leadership, and indeed sometimes openly encouraged, affected the combatants' perceptions of their position and expectations regarding their status (and the distribution of the spoils of peace) once the war was over. This type of profoundly irregular political economy survived the conflict to become one of the key obstacles to peace consolidation, as its operation could only be sustained in an ethnically divided and antagonized space. The preservation of ethnically homogeneous territory controlled by the HDZ BiH, the SDS, and the SDA provided many of the key protagonists of war and its criminal economy with impunity, which was another motive to obstruct reintegration of the country within the course of implementation of the peace agreement.

Evolution of Bosnian Croat self-rule project

Among the three mono-ethnic formations that emerged in the course of the BiH war, the most consistent and politically developed was that of the Bosnian Croats. As early as December 1991 the Croatian Community of Herzeg-Bosna (HZHB)[3] was established, as a community of all Croats living in BiH, with a professed aim to defend Croatian historic territory and Croatian people in BiH against the threat of aggression. Its jurisdiction extended over 30 municipalities across BiH, in most of which, but not all, Bosnian Croats were a majority. With the establishment of the Croatian Defence Council (HVO) in spring 1992 as the key executive and administrative body, which from July 1992 included its own armed force, the HZHB emerged as a para-state within BiH, of which the HVO was the *de facto* government. The armed force, which also bore the name HVO, operated as a military wing of the HDZ BiH and was controlled by it. Although formally part of BiH, the HZHB made the Croatian language and currency official within its jurisdiction, and closely aligned its armed forces with those of the Croatian army, receiving from

Croatia financial support as well as support in personnel, training, equipment etc. In economic matters such as customs the HZHB and Croatia functioned as one country. Croatia provided substantial financial support towards social care and the running of education and health system of the HZHB.

The mainstay of this creation was the HDZ party structure. Only HDZ BiH members were engaged in the governing structures of the HZHB, excluding from participation any other ethnic group living on its territory. Since the HDZ BiH was a part of Croatian HDZ, this link provided the umbilical cord through which the HZHB was related to the Croatian state.[4] The creation of the HZHB, in terms of its legal background, the intentions of its creators (among both the Bosnian Croat and Croatian political leadership), and in the minds of most Bosnian Croats, was a step towards integration into the Croatian state, despite a formal declaration that it was a temporary construct.

By late 1993 international engagement in the BiH conflict focused on finding territorial solutions based on the principle of ethnic demarcation within BiH, rejecting the secessionist option. Among several initiatives, the proposal by peace mediators David Owen and Thorvald Stoltenberg argued for the creation of three clearly demarcated entities, taking into account the results of military operations on the ground and population displacement. Bosnian Croats responded by the establishment of the Croatian Republic of Herzeg Bosna (HRHB) in December 1993, as the political entity of Bosnian Croats within BiH. This was a calculated step to exert pressure on the negotiators and pre-empt political solutions that would go against Bosnian Croats' aim of securing the highest possible degree of autonomy within the BiH state.[5] By this move, the parallel structures of government established within the framework of the HZHB were preserved, managing to survive long after the international community in February 1994 ordered the abolishment of the HRHB. Another attempt at creating a distinct Bosnian Croat entity was initiated in 2001 when the HDZ BiH tried to establish Bosnian Croat self-government, relying on the remaining parallel structures, which, although weakened, remained in place, particularly at the level of municipalities.

Peace settlement

The political solution to the conflict in BiH was achieved in two stages. Following intense fighting between Muslims and Bosnian Croats from May to November 1993, during which the non-Croat population (mainly Muslims and Serbs) were systematically driven out of the territories charted by the HZHB and large numbers of Bosnian Croats were expelled from central Bosnia and resettled in Herzegovina, mainly in and around Mostar,[6] an agreement establishing the Muslim-Bosnian Croat Federation – the Washington Agreement – was signed in March 1994. Following the principle of ethnic demarcation, the federation was organized into 10 cantons, of which only two were mixed; the remaining eight had a clear Muslim or Bosnian Croat majority. The solution was a result of intense international pressure on the local political leadership as well as on that of Croatia.

The establishment of the federation was ill received by a significant proportion of Bosnian Croats, particularly those in ethnically mixed cantons. Even though the highly decentralized structure of the federation assigned most powers to the cantons, there was resentment of the idea of giving up the prospect of a Bosnian Croat state and its close relationship with, if not outright annexation to, Croatia. After all, the HDZ BiH argued from the start of the BiH conflict that the full protection of Bosnian Croat interests was only possible in a sovereign Bosnian Croat political entity, the prospect of which was diminished by the establishment of the federation. The Croatian leadership, and in particular Gojko Susak,[7] the then defence minister who hailed from Herzegovina,[8] tried to dispel the resentment of many Bosnian Croats by arguing that the federation was necessity at that particular stage of the BiH conflict, and likely to be only a temporary solution. Continuing help from Croatia to Bosnian Croats was promised and the possibility of confederation with Croatia offered, thus rekindling the expectations of an all-Croat state – if not then and there, then at some point in the future.

Implementation of this imposed solution, against the reality of parallel Muslim and Bosnian Croat structures of government operating within the federation, was from the outset confronted by serious obstacles. This was best manifested in the example of the city of Mostar, divided in the course of the Muslim-Bosnian Croat fighting, which became the subject of a special agreement between the two sides reached in the aftermath of the Washington Agreement. The city, which was designated as the capital of the HRHB and which to this day has remained a stronghold of hard-line Bosnian Croat nationalists, was put under European Union administration over an interim period (1994–1996) to allow for the establishment of a multiethnic, unified city administration. Its reunification was considered of paramount importance for the reintegration of Bosnian Croats, particularly their separatist Herzegovinian faction, into BiH. In fact, sporadic violence and expulsions and intimidation of the non-Croat population continued in Mostar for a number of years after the Memorandum of Understanding on Mostar was signed in Geneva in 1994. The implementation of the Washington Agreement and the reunification of Mostar have been two closely interlinked processes, given the

HDZ BiH resistance to give up Bosnian Croat autonomy and the importance of Mostar in that project. Efforts at establishing joint local government structures in Mostar as the main goal set out by the memorandum were concertedly obstructed; it was only in 2004 that the inchoate unified city administration finally got off the ground.

The second stage of political settlement of the BiH conflict, involving Bosnian Serbs, was the signing of the Framework Agreement for Peace in BiH (the Dayton Agreement) in December 1995. According to the agreement, which included a new constitution, BiH was reorganized as a loose union of two entities – the Muslim-Bosnian Croat Federation, and Republika Srpska as the entity in which Bosnian Serbs are a majority. The promise of large and sustained international civilian and military presence was one of the key incentives accompanying negotiations of the Dayton Agreement. A unique framework of international assistance was designed for its implementation, which has garnered an unprecedented array of actors and provided resources at a scale considered in per capita terms to be the highest ever in the history of international aid.

Under the new political set-up, the central state was allocated minimal jurisdiction, with most powers resting with the entities. A complex system of power-sharing aimed at protecting ethnic interests[9] was put in place, providing the main mechanism to sustain the new government structure. Making this system operational, which rested on the local parties' readiness to engage in consensus-building, was essential for the implementation of the key aspects of the peace agreement. The responsibility for implementing the agreement thus rested with the same parties, and indeed by and large the same people, in the political establishment of the country which had waged the war, and which held the view that the agreement failed to provide satisfactory solutions to their demands. This in itself carried strong potential for spoiling.

A number of specific elements of the peace agreement are relevant in discussing the possible motives for obstructing its implementation in this case. Annex 7 of the peace agreement detailed refugees' return to their pre-war places of residence as one of the crucial aspects of peace consolidation and rebuilding BiH as a multiethnic state. To many displaced Bosnian Croats now living in other people's property and determined to stay in their new places of residence this was an ambivalent proposition. A large segment of this population is motivated by the feeling of security provided by living among their ethnic kin, understandable in the aftermath of a brutal war.[10] But equally important are economic calculations of some sections of the displaced population whose economic prospects had been improved by dislocation, and who usually managed to have a stronger voice than those who had suffered as a result of displacement and were more likely to exercise their right to return. Equally, younger generations had enrolled in education and grown attached to their new places of residence, and hence have been unwilling to move back to old homes to which they no longer have any attachment. On a political level, allowing refugees to return was a threat to the HDZ BiH goal of establishing a Bosnian-Croat-dominated entity in which its sovereign rule as the exclusive representative of Bosnian Croats would be secured.

The Dayton Agreement allowed for the preservation of the three ethnically based armies created during the war, thus reinforcing the semi-statehood status given to the entities. For Bosnian Croats, who were denied a separate entity, preserving their own army was seen as one of the channels through which to persevere with the political struggle to secure Bosnian Croat autonomy. Hence, the post of federation defence minister was allotted to individuals renowned for their allegiance to this project, namely Ante Jelavic and then his successor Miroslav Prce, both of whom were subsequently banned by the High Representative from holding public office. By preserving the HVO as the legitimate military force of Bosnian Croats, the military was given the same clout in Bosnian Croat politics as it had had during the war.

Among the peace agreement's many compromise solutions was one allowing for special relations between the BiH entities and their neighbours, i.e. the federation with Croatia, and Republika Srpska with Serbia. The presidents of Croatia and Serbia were signatories to the peace agreement, thus undertaking a commitment that their governments would participate in its implementation. The ambiguous stance of Slobodan Milosevic and Miroslav Tudjman's governments towards BiH sovereignty, and continuing support for their ethnic kin in BiH after the conflict was over, encouraged Bosnian Serbs and Bosnian Croats to continue pursuing separatist agendas, undermining the integrity of the BiH state. According to the Dayton Agreement, the structures of Herzeg Bosna were to be dissolved within 30 days of the passage of legislation necessary to establish federation institutions; the HDZ BiH had consistently opposed this ever since the Washington Agreement was signed.

Bosnian Croats perceived the Dayton Agreement as discriminating against them by depriving them of their own entity. They saw it as a threat of Muslim domination within the federation, where Bosnian Croats were a minority. Despite (reluctant) cooperation in building federation institutions, which has proceeded under concerted international pressure, they have never abandoned the goal of having the third "Bosnian Croat" entity.[11] The difference is that, unlike in early phases of the Bosnian conflict when this was a separatist project, it is now discussed as a matter of internal political reorganization of BiH, which, however, does not imply a reversal of the policies of "ethnic cleansing". The interests of the Bosnian Croat political leadership on the one hand, and large sections of the displaced population on the other, have remained focused on preserving an ethnically homogeneous territory while securing a disproportionate share for Bosnian Croats in the governing bodies at various levels of BiH government. The struggle for political autonomy has been additionally propelled by the fact that economically areas with a Bosnian Croat majority have been the most prosperous in BiH, having escaped wartime destruction and profiting from their links with Croatia.

War veterans' associations as spoilers of peace

Origins and profile

Following the signing of the Washington Agreement a number of war veterans' associations sprung up in the BiH Federation, especially among Bosnian Croats. There were several motives behind this. For the main actor – the military – the Washington Agreement and the later Dayton Agreement were perceived as unjust in terms of the political solutions they offered. Thus organizing itself in this way provided a channel through which to continue the struggle until a more acceptable political solution was achieved. This becomes a plausible motive given the close links between the military and civilian leadership of the Bosnian Croats, namely that the HVO was the *de facto* military arm of the HDZ BiH. While HDZ BiH representatives in the government were a party to the peace agreement, and rhetorically supportive of it, their genuine views and aspirations were different, and were expressed through the work of some of the veterans' associations. The existence and activity of Bosnian Croat war veterans' associations thus have to be understood in the context of the HDZ BiH post-war strategy to pursue its main wartime political goal. This explains the profoundly political impact most of the veteran associations' activities have strived to achieve. There were also genuine intentions of defending the interests and well-being of the veterans' population, who in their own eyes deserved a special status, having "defended" the interests of their own ethnic group. Setting up these associations was also a channel for redistributing funds provided by Croatia, to which the veterans believed they deserved a privileged access, having fought alongside the Croatian army both in Croatia and in BiH.

The two most prominent Bosnian Croat war veterans' associations are the Association of Croatian Military Invalids of the Homeland War (HVIDRA) and the Association of Volunteers and Veterans of the Homeland War (UDIVIDRA), both established in 1994. Of the two the former has been more active, positioning itself as the most extreme element within the Bosnian Croat post-war power structure. The key figure in establishing these two organizations is Mladen Naletilic-Tuta,[12] the commander of the "Convicts' Battalion", an HVO unit notorious for terrorizing the non-Croat population in and around the southern city of Mostar during the war, running trafficking routes and organized crime rings. He is an emigrant with close connections to the late Gojko Susak,[13] the then defence minister of Croatia, himself a former emigrant who returned to Croatia to support the HDZ in its project of establishing an independent Croatian state. Both Mladen Naletilic and Gojko Susak were made honorary presidents of the HVIDRA. Mladen Naletilic was highly positioned in the Bosnian Croat politico-military hierarchy during the war and was a member of an inner circle regularly received and consulted by the highest-ranking HDZ leaders, including the late Croatian president Franjo Tudjman.

The leadership of the HVIDRA has over the years included prominent wartime military figures and vocal proponents of ethnic separatism and establishment of a Bosnian Croat entity. The HVIDRA's headquarters were symbolically based in Mostar, with a network of organizations spreading throughout the territory included in the HZHB. The Mostar branch of the HVIDRA is estimated to have around 1,300 members, suggesting that an overall total could be in the region of 4,000–5,000 members for the whole of the HZHB. The organization of the HVIDRA is one of a well-functioning network controlled by the Mostar headquarters. It professes to be an association of war invalids – soldiers incapacitated in combat – which, given the ethnic sensitivities aroused by the war, has guaranteed its special status and importance. However, the HVIDRA's membership has included other members of the HVO, and at a later stage demobilized soldiers. Similarly, membership of the UDIVIDRA includes both active and demobilized soldiers as well as volunteers. Both associations have had in their ranks Bosnian Croat representatives in the BiH governing structures – a testimony to the amalgamation of political and military structures, which continued after the conflict was over. The highest-ranking Bosnian Croat government officials have regularly attended HVIDRA assemblies in a public display of their support to its activity and unquestioned unity behind the "Bosnian Croat" cause.

The official agenda, the hidden agenda, and the motives for spoiling

The declared goals of the HVIDRA, as formulated in its statute, are first and foremost the protection and advocacy of the interests of the veterans, killed and missing soldiers, and their families, and permanent, just, and systematic solutions to the socio-economic problems of the veterans' population. Other goals are concerned with the social and economic status of its members, and the HVIDRA pledges to preserve the continuity of comradeship, merits, and memories of its members. Thus its activity is driven as much by legitimate concerns over its members' well-being as it is by ideology, which is intricately linked to the promotion of exclusive nationalist politics under the guise of "the protection of Croat national interests". In reality, the HVIDRA has been one of the main levers used by the HDZ BiH to obstruct the implementation of the peace agreement. Effectively, the HVIDRA was established as a vehicle through which to secure continuing support for HDZ BiH rule, and could be said to represent its most radical political faction. In the course of the peace implementation HDZ BiH unity has been challenged by different factions' responses to the international pressure to solicit the cooperation of local parties. This at times has made consensus-building on the position of the HDZ BiH representatives in the BiH government structures difficult. A counteractive channel ensuring that the hard-line nationalist route is followed has been operated through the HVIDRA. Its capacity to incite nationalist fervour among the population by evoking fear of other ethnic groups has been deployed by the HDZ BiH to reassert itself as the sole protector of Bosnian Croat interests. Through the HVIDRA, whose membership has included Bosnian Croat representatives in the legislative and executive bodies of BiH government, it has been possible to pursue certain political goals more efficiently than through the HDZ BiH party structures.[14]

The ultimate goal of Bosnian Croat autonomy can only be to some extent justified by Bosnian Croats' genuine fear of marginalization as the smallest constitutive ethnic group in BiH. The elaborate power-sharing model in BiH essentially provides all the constitutional guarantees to prevent this from happening. Thus the true reasons for pursuing autonomy, as suggested before, are more likely to do with the ideology and aspirations of creating an all-Croat state, and equally so with the peculiar political economy of the BiH war, both of which were threatened by the implementation of the peace agreement.

War veterans have been in many ways a privileged segment of the BiH population, both during their active service and later. For many of them military uniform provided access to power and material wealth, be it in the form of looting, occupying or renting other people's property,[15] or after the war running perfectly legal businesses without paying electricity, water, or telephone bills,[16] not to mention taxes. Some of them opted to continue criminal businesses operated during the war, for which securing the protection of HDZ BiH rule was again essential, given that among the HDZ BiH government officials and top leadership involvement in these activities was not uncommon. This has bound them together in a struggle to preserve an order in which these activities will not be sanctioned. The existence of parallel structures of government along ethnic lines, and the better economic performance of areas with a Bosnian Croat majority, have provided HVO veterans with much higher compensation in the form of wages for regular soldiers and invalidity benefits for those incapacitated in the combat. The creation of unified federation structures such as a joint army and unified social security funds has directly threatened this privileged position compared to the soldiers who fought in the Muslim-dominated BiH army. Many of the war veterans, following demobilization, have found employment in the local police force, thus retaining formally the authority reserved for security forces in any society. This multiple identity[17] of the HVIDRA's (and the UDIVIDRA's) members and its actual and perceived power have made it one of the most feared organizations among the non-Croat population, but also among those Bosnian Croats opposed to its policy and methods.

The HVIDRA's tactics in obstructing the implementation of the peace agreement

Property law implementation

It was not until 1998 that the international community stepped up its efforts to implement Annex 7 of the peace agreement dealing with the return of refugees. The lack of strong international commitment to the enforcement of this particular aspect of the peace agreement, and slow progress in strengthening institutions of the BiH Federation, provided an opening in which the HVIDRA[18] could carry out activities directed against the return of the non-Croat population. Reports by the OSCE, the OHR, and the UN Mission to BiH point to the HVIDRA as the main obstacle to the implementation of property laws in the BiH Federation. During 1995–1996 the main strategy was to continue a low-intensity campaign of ethnic cleansing, in particular by forcing elderly residents out of their homes, and later on by attacking refugees returning to Croat-dominated areas. Bombing of houses of returning refugees and ethnically motivated violent attacks, including murders, were commonly pursued. The main goal was to create an atmosphere of fear and personal insecurity in order to discourage refugees from returning to their pre-war homes.[19] There were cases in which a refugee would succeed in returning to his home using informal channels, often bribing officials and paying the illegal occupants to vacate the property, only to be kicked out by an "unknown" group of persons who would carry out an attack. The most intense activity of this kind was in Mostar. For a long period of time a joint Muslim-Bosnian Croat police force in Mostar existed only on paper;

hence there was no recourse to the protection this force would normally have to provide to any citizen. Moreover, as pointed out earlier, many former HVO soldiers found employment in the local police force following demobilization, and were supportive of HVIDRA activity. Reports on various incidents involving refugees suggest that not only did the police offer no protection, but they were sometimes a party to violence.

Maintaining ethnically homogeneous Bosnian Croat territory has been the main aim and a necessary leverage if (and when) the time comes to set up a Bosnian Croat entity in BiH. In this the HDZ BiH relied heavily on the HVIDRA's tactics of terror and violence against the non-Croat population. Although this type of activity was particularly high profile and frequent in Mostar, it happened in other parts of BiH too, suggesting well-coordinated action. A parallel line of activity was directly related to particular developments in the course of implementation of the peace agreement. Most times, HVIDRA branches would organize various events simultaneously across the HZHB, creating tension and disrupting the functioning of formal institutions at all levels of government while trying to influence the final shape of a particular piece of legislation. The return of non-Croats to Bosnian-Croat-controlled west Mostar was systematically obstructed by physical attacks on returning refugees and organization of mass gatherings against returning refugees, riots, and appeals to Bosnian Croats from other parts of BiH settled in west Mostar not to return to their pre-war homes. There was evidence to suggest that in these early years the HVIDRA controlled the housing stock of the expelled non-Croat population in three Mostar municipalities under Bosnian Croat control. When the legislation setting out the terms for reclaiming property began to be implemented in 1999, stating that the illegal occupant should leave the property within 30 days of the issuance of a property certificate, the HVIDRA began preventing evictions of Bosnian Croats (often its own members).[20] The then HVIDRA president Zoran Prskalo issued a statement saying that the HVIDRA refused to accept the decisions of the international community asking illegal occupants to vacate property and hand in the keys to the relevant municipal office. Instead, the HVIDRA asked for the keys to be handed over to its headquarters. Protesting against the property law implementation, the HVIDRA issued an open letter in which it stated: "For the last time we are warning all relevant institutions, including courts, ministries and police stations, that we will use all means necessary to protect war invalids."[21] Often, the HVIDRA would organize large-scale gatherings at which popular Bosnian Croat or Croatian singers performed and HVIDRA and HDZ BiH functionaries addressed the audience. Wartime iconography was displayed prominently and demands for the protection of Bosnian

Croat interests, and in particular human rights of war veterans and invalids, were made. This particular method was aimed at rekindling Bosnian Croat feelings of ethnic homogenization and support for the HDZ BiH policy of obstructing the creation of joint BiH Federation institutions.

Prosecution of war crimes

Prosecution of crimes committed during the 1992–1995 war has been identified as one of the essential elements for long-term reconciliation of the three peoples of BiH, and has featured prominently at every stage of the peace agreement's implementation. Gradually, the handing over of suspects to the Hague War Crimes Tribunal has come to weigh heavily among the set of political conditions for economic assistance to BiH and progress in joining Euro-Atlantic associations, which are perceived as instrumental for peace consolidation.[22] Over the years a number of Bosnian Croats have been indicted on this account, including some prominent HVIDRA members, such as Mladen Naletilic and Vinko Martinovic, the two foremost Mostar warlords. Obstructing investigation by threatening and intimidating local officials and the population has been one of the methods the HVIDRA has used to obstruct the procedure, which it has claimed to be heavily biased against Bosnian Croats. Such a claim is perhaps based on the comparatively large number of Bosnian Croat indictees compared to Muslim ones, and the fact that they were, along with a number of Bosnian Serbs, among the first cohorts to be sent to the Hague.

The HVIDRA has used every single occasion when an indictment has been made public, extradition to the Hague completed, or the verdict on an indicted Bosnian Croat passed to wage a campaign against joint federation institutions and the international community, demanding the establishment of a third entity. For example, when the Hague tribunal sentenced Bosnian Croat former HVO general Tihomir Blaskic, the HVIDRA issued the following statement:

The sentence of General Blaskic and all innocently accused Croats should be reconsidered. The request of the ICTY for the extradition of the seriously ill Mladen Naletilic Tuta should be withdrawn. A protest meeting will be held at 13:00 in Mostar, on 08 March 2000. The veterans and volunteers request Bosnian Croat officials to immediately freeze their work in the joint institutions of the BiH Federation and BiH state, except for the Bosnian Croat member of the BiH Presidency. The veterans and volunteers ask the Government and Ministry of Justice of the Republic of Croatia not to fulfill the request of the Hague Tribunal for the extradition of Mladen Naletilic Tuta. We request from Bosnian Croat officials to organize a plebiscite on the future position and destiny of the Croat people in

BiH. The veterans and volunteers have anonymously decided not to take part in September parliamentary elections if their requirements are not fulfilled and they will call on their supporters to join them in their decision.[23]

The HDZ BiH control of the media and threats to media employees made it possible for the HVIDRA to have access to the media on terms it dictated regarding the content and timing of communication to the public. Mass gatherings and protests, including roadblocks, often accompanied tactics of inciting tensions among the population and putting pressure on the BiH political establishment over issues considered to be harmful to Bosnian Croat interests.

Institution-building

In addition to refugee return and prosecution of war crimes as two areas of most intense obstruction, the HVIDRA has been a prominent actor at every major step in the peace implementation directed at strengthening the federation. This is a structure which the hard-line faction of the Bosnian Croat political establishment has never condoned. When a change in the electoral rules in 2000 threatened HDZ BiH control over legal and political representation of Bosnian Croats, and improved prospects for strengthening joint state and federation institutions, the HVIDRA supported the HDZ BiH call for a referendum on Bosnian self-rule. The victory of the moderate alliance of political parties triggered another attempt to establish Bosnian Croat autonomy. When the self-rule project did get off the ground in spring 2001, the HVIDRA provided essential support by encouraging the HVO component of the federation army, in which many of its wartime comrades served, to leave the barracks of the joint federation army. The HVIDRA warned Bosnian Croat government representatives that there would be consequences if they gave in to international pressure.[24] The usual scenario of mass gatherings with speeches by political and religious figures, public announcements, and roadblocks was also deployed.

In April 2001, in an attempt to stamp out Bosnian Croat self-rule, the NATO-led stabilization force (SFOR) seized all branches of the Hercegovacka Bank[25] across Herzegovina. In response the HVIDRA was the key organizer and participant in mass protests around every single one of those premises. During the riots, 21 peacekeepers were injured in Mostar and SFOR troops were trapped in the bank branch in Grude, west Herzegovina. The attempt to establish Bosnian Croat self-rule was identified by the international community as the most serious violation of the Dayton Peace Agreement.

It is believed the HVIDRA has been involved in a number of violent attacks against Bosnian Croats who did not support the HDZ BiH hardline stance, as well as against international staff. In March 1999 a car bomb killed Jozo Leutar, BiH Federation deputy minister of interior, a Bosnian Croat from central Bosnia. The following day the HVIDRA issued a statement accusing Muslims of the killing and calling for protection of Bosnian Croats' rights. The HDZ BiH announced the Declaration on Bosnian Croats' Rights, which the HVIDRA supported by organizing mass gatherings across BiH. Leutar's killing was politically motivated and happened at a time when efforts at uniting the Federation Ministry of Interior had been stepped up. Also, shortly before the incident a final decision on the status of the city of Brcko[26] was announced, on which occasion the HVIDRA launched an action calling for the third entity. Although the case has not been resolved yet, it is believed that the murder was organized by HDZ BiH extremists, determined to obstruct federation institutions. Following the incident, a Bosnian Croat boycott caused a crisis in the federation government.

The trail of investigation led to the arrest of a Bosnian Croat in Mostar in September 2000; the HVIDRA reacted promptly by blocking the main bridge connecting west and east Mostar, demanding to know who exactly made the arrests and suggesting that these were Muslim police forces. The HVIDRA threatened that "hooded men", referring to the uniforms the special police force wore during the arrest, could soon appear on the east (Muslim-dominated) side of the city – only this time they would be Bosnian Croat hooded men. At the same time posters calling for a referendum on Bosnian Croat self-rule and for mobilization appeared throughout Bosnian-Croat-majority areas. In a series of actions following the murder of Leutar, the HVIDRA forced non-Croat staff of customs services in a number of offices in west Herzegovina to leave their posts and threatened federation financial police in the areas with a Bosnian Croat majority, thus directly challenging official institutions. Before this, in 1996, in Mostar an attempt was made to murder Josip Musa, a prominent local Bosnian Croat opposition politician, and the then head of the EU Administration, Hans Koschnik,[27] was attacked; in both cases involvement of the HVIDRA was suspected.

Conclusion: The HVIDRA's changing rhetoric and strategy

The context within which the HVIDRA's spoiling tactics have been pursued has been gradually changing over the years, causing a shift in both its focus and the way in which it pursues its agenda. There has not been a strategy of spoiler management specifically aimed at the HVIDRA; rather, the impact has come through undermining the position of the

HDZ BiH and altering the relationship between the two actors. The key role has been played by the international community, through applying concerted pressure on the HDZ BiH to cooperate in the implementation of the peace agreement. By using a range of strategies the international community has succeeded in weakening the HDZ BiH power base and forcing it increasingly to channel its grievances through the formal institutions. To this end the HDZ BiH officials obstructing the peace agreement have been removed from public office; the campaign against the war crimes indictees has continued unabated, culminating in the indictment of six prominent HZHB figures in the summer of 2004; and political conditionality accompanying economic assistance has been strictly applied. But the most effective of all have been strategies striking at the financial core of parallel HZHB institutions. These include the seizure of the Hercegovacka Bank and the curtailment of informal flows of funding from Croatia. Changes in Croatia's official policy towards Bosnian Croats and its increased susceptibility to international pressure in view of its desire to join the EU have not only dealt a financial blow to the sustainability of the Bosnian Croat political project, but have also decoupled it from Croatia's own political agenda. Croatia has given up pursuing the Dayton provision on special ties to the BiH Federation; instead it has redefined its relationship with the state of BiH. The outcome of an increasingly better-coordinated and targeted international effort has been incremental strengthening of federation and BiH state joint institutions and steady deconstruction of parallel structures of governance. In developing its multi-pronged strategy, despite all its shortcomings, the international community has applied its efforts to the particular context of BiH post-war rehabilitation, deploying the instruments available under its unique mandate. As an example of the latter, in addition to the above-mentioned strategies, in 2002–2003 the international community undertook an intense campaign to disclose the scale of corruption across BiH public institutions, which revealed the extent to which narrow groups in and around the HDZ BiH had misused the system. This highlighted the long-neglected reality of the uncertainty of the position of the Bosnian Croat war veterans outside the context of an "all-Croat" rule. In a way this provided a wake-up call for veterans' associations, which became increasingly critical of the work of some of the HDZ BiH high-ranking officials and accused them of guarding solely their own positions.

The best illustration of the change in the HVIDRA's position is its conduct in the course of the adoption of the federation law on war veterans and invalids, initiated under World-Bank-sponsored social sector reform. The adoption of the law was a condition for a World Bank loan, essential for the continuation of reforms. When the draft law was first proposed in 2003, the HVIDRA tried some of its old pressure tactics in an attempt to prevent the establishment of one social security fund and equalization of entitlements between HVO and BiH army veterans. In the prolonged procedure that followed the HVIDRA assumed a more moderate position, but refused to support the law and accused the HDZ BiH representatives in the government of "capitulation" for having accepted the main solutions suggested by the international community. However, the soothing factor for the HVIDRA's dissatisfaction was a proposition on continuing support, albeit on a much smaller scale, from Croatia. The HVIDRA announced that it had established a committee for drafting the law on additional veterans' rights – a sharp turn from its practice of violence, blackmail, and deals outside of official institutions. At this stage of the peace implementation process in BiH the chances of the HVIDRA resorting back to these tactics, which have in the past hindered efforts at peace consolidation, appear to have been significantly reduced. Its relationship with the HDZ BiH has been altered and so is the power of the latter; its determination to pursue Bosnian Croat autonomy will have to rely on formal political channels and instruments.

Notes

1. This practice was termed "ethnic cleansing".
2. In view of the region's complex political dynamics, to this day it is not possible to discard this option totally. It is certainly often evoked in the debates on the implications that the final Kosovo status could have for the political reconfiguration of the region.
3. For detailed analysis of the origins and evolution of the HZHB see Ribicic, Ciril. 2001. *Geneza neke zablude-Ustavnopravna analiza nastanka I djelovanja Hrvatske zajednice Herceg Bosne*. Zagreb: Jesenski I Turk.
4. The Croatian constitution allows for Bosnian Croats to vote (the "diaspora vote") in elections for the Croatian government; thus the HDZ BiH has an important role in sustaining HDZ power in Croatia.
5. The establishment of Herceg Bosna is one the main reasons behind the conflict between Bosnian Croats and Muslims, which started in spring 1993.
6. The exodus of Bosnian Croats from central Bosnia was partly due to BiH army (largely staffed by Bosnian Muslims) military activity and partly prompted by the HVO policy of relocating populations to create ethnically homogeneous territory. The latter involved resettlement of Bosnian Croats in Herzegovina.
7. Gojko Susak was the most prominent member of the Croatian diaspora supporting the HDZ rise to power. When the HDZ won the elections in Croatia, Susak left Canada to become Croatian defence minister and his wife became a highly positioned civil servant in the Croatian government.
8. The "Herzegovinian" faction in both the HDZ and the HDZ BiH has been the most radical one; the latter has favoured secession from BiH, in contrast to the Bosnian faction which is more supportive of the common BiH state.
9. This entailed the "vital national interest" clause at any government instance, where one ethnic group could be outvoted on a range of issues falling within the definition of "vital national interest".

10. Rekindling fear of ethnic others has been one of the main strategies used to obstruct the peace settlement.
11. Recently there have suggestions to scrap or renegotiate the Dayton Agreement from various corners of the policy-making and academic communities. The HDZ BiH leadership has remained adamant that any such move should consider the option of establishing the third entity.
12. Mladen Naletilic has been indicted by the War Crimes Tribunal in the Hague for war crimes committed during the 1992–1995 war. Croatia provided him with protection when he was first indicted by the tribunal, but had to extradite him under the threat of sanctions.
13. Gojko Susak, together with Ivic Pasalic, Tudjman's home affairs adviser, and Ljubo Cesic Rojs, a former general and deputy minister of defence, who all hail from west Herzegovina, were the key players in the creation of Croatian policy towards Bosnian Croats.
14. Within the HDZ BiH there have been two main factions: the separatist Herzegovinian one, and the generally more moderate Bosnian faction, more favourably disposed towards the BiH Federation.
15. There is evidence that the HVIDRA has controlled substantial property belonging to the non-Croat population, which it allocated to its members or rented out as a way of earning income for the individuals as well as funding the organization itself.
16. This has been made possible by the fact that the management of state-owned companies are HDZ BiH appointees who condoned this practice. See Electricity Board of HZHB Mostar. 2003. *The Report of the Special Auditor*, March, available at www.mans.cg.yu/ cijevna/Dokumenta/OSCE_RevizijaEPHZHBCro.pdf.
17. This is an important feature that underpins the alliance of actors taking part in actions aimed at obstruction of the peace agreement.
18. One of the HVIDRA's goals was to obstruct the building of federation institutions and undermine their work.
19. This included attacks on individuals crossing over to west Mostar from Muslim-controlled east Mostar, which for a long time hindered freedom of movement guaranteed by all relevant articles of the overall peace settlement, i.e. Washington, Dayton, and the agreement on Mostar.
20. By July 1998 of 6,507 claims for property return in three Bosnian-Croat-controlled municipalities in Mostar, only a handful had been processed and no eviction took place without the consent of the illegal occupant. ICG. 2002. *Reunifying Mostar: Opportunities for Progress*, ICG Balkans Report No. 90. Brussels: ICG.
21. *Vjesnik*, 9 February 1999.
22. Lack of progress in arresting war crimes suspects is the main reason for BiH's non-admission to NATO's Partnership for Peace programme.
23. Broadcast on Croat Radio Mostar, Croatian Radio Herceg Bosna, on 3 March 2000.
24. This message was issued immediately after Wolfgang Petritch, the then High Representative, announced that any individual or parallel structure engaged in anti-Dayton activities would be liable to sanctions, which included removal from public office. This indeed happened with the main protagonists of the Bosnian Croat self-rule project.
25. Financial aid from Croatia to Bosnian Croats was channelled through the Hercegovacka Bank.
26. The district of Brcko, the only unresolved territorial issue under the Dayton Agreement, was placed under the jurisdiction of the BiH state.
27. Soon after Koschnik resigned from his post, pointing at the local HDZ BiH structures as the main culprits for a lack of progress in the reunification of Mostar.

10
Spoilers in Colombia: Actors and strategies

Carlo Nasi

Colombia has experienced internal armed conflict since the late 1940s. In recent decades four different governments undertook peace negotiations with various rebel groups, seeking to find a peaceful settlement to the war. However, peace has remained an elusive goal. Spoilers threatened to derail every single peace process, even if only occasionally did they succeed. The identity of spoilers changed throughout the various peace negotiations. Depending on the peace process in question, spoiling activities were carried out by some rebel groups (or their splinter factions), the armed forces, the Colombian Congress, drug-traffickers, some entrepreneurs, right-wing paramilitary groups, and even the US government.

Stedman defined spoilers as "leaders and parties who believe that peace emerging from negotiations threatens their power, worldview, and interests, and use violence to undermine attempts to achieve it".[1] This definition will be slightly modified here by including non-violent means of sabotage. In other words, occasionally some individuals and groups attempt to undermine a peace process by resorting to devious (and partly illegal) tactics that stop short of violence: these leaders and parties should also be labelled as "spoilers".

This chapter begins with an introduction on the nature and evolution of the Colombian armed conflict in order to explain the context that has served as a background for different peace initiatives. Next it explores the peace negotiations of the governments of Belisario Betancur (1982–1986), Virgilio Barco (1986–1990), Cesar Gaviria (1990–1994), and

Andrés Pastrana (1998–2002), analysing the role, tactics, and relative success of spoilers in each case. It concludes with a short analysis of the impact of spoilers throughout the Colombian war.

The Colombian conflict

One can identify two different, albeit interrelated, cycles of armed conflict in Colombia. The first one, whose roots can be traced back to the mid-nineteenth century, is closely connected to the birth and consolidation of the two main Colombian political parties, the Liberals and the Conservatives. Although these two parties resembled one another in terms of social composition and ideology, they fiercely competed against one another to gain exclusive control over state resources and privileges. Between the mid-nineteenth and the mid-twentieth centuries, party élites often mobilized their mostly rural clientele against members of the other party during electoral contests, as well as in a series of violent clashes and civil wars.[2] Violence helped to forge partisan identities, in the sense that the memories of one's relatives killed by members of the other party resulted in deep hatred between Liberals and Conservatives.

The conflict between Liberals and Conservatives greatly escalated during the 1940s, a period of turmoil due to a series of urban strikes and also peasant mobilizations caused by the defective implementation of two agrarian reform laws.[3] In this context, the murder of populist politician and leader of the Liberal Party Jorge Eliecer Gaitán in 1948 triggered the most deadly cycle of bipartisan violence ever experienced in Colombia. Gaitán's assassination provoked the "Bogotazo", a massive urban insurrection of Liberals backed by the police that partly destroyed the capital city and spread out to other regions. Although violently suppressed by the army, the Bogotazo has been considered the only occasion on which Colombia has approached the brink of revolution.

Following Gaitán's murder, the bipartisan violence continued to escalate. In 1953, as the violence was spinning out of control, various Conservative and Liberal factions, the Catholic Church, the entrepreneurial sector, and the military forces backed a *coup d'état* by General Gustavo Rojas Pinilla, who installed a dictatorship. But in 1958 Colombia returned to a restricted form of democracy. By then, Liberal and Conservative politicians had crafted a power-sharing agreement known as the National Front[4] (NF) that helped to bring the bipartisan violence to an end. Between the mid-1940s and the early 1960s the bipartisan violence had left a death toll approximating 200,000.

Colombia was heading towards a second cycle of violence. Beginning in the mid-1960s, various (for the most part communist) revolutionary organizations were formed, seeking to overhaul Colombia's polity and socio-economic structure. This cycle has not ended yet, and its death toll exceeds 100,000 casualties. Different conditions account for the rise of insurgency in Colombia during the 1960s. The Cuban revolution, as well as the writings of Che Guevara and Regis Debray, helped to radicalize many university students and union members who joined revolutionary organizations. In addition, the country's vast territory, inaccessible mountains, thick forests, and a weak state presence in many rural areas facilitated the operation of rebel groups.[5]

During this second cycle of violence one observes a proliferation of rebel groups. In 1962 remnants of Liberal and Communist guerrillas of the previous cycle of violence established links with the Colombian Communist Party and formed the Revolutionary Armed Forces of Colombia (FARC). In the mid-1960s the break-up between the USSR and China led to the formation of a Maoist guerrilla organization, the Popular Liberation Army (EPL). In 1964 a group of students who were inspired by the Cuban revolution constituted the National Liberation Army (ELN). And after General Rojas Pinilla was defeated in seemingly fraudulent elections by Conservative candidate Misael Pastrana in the presidential contests of 1970, members his populist party Alianza Nacional Popular and a group of former FARC guerrillas created the Movimiento 19 de Abril (M-19). Founded in 1974, the M-19 became the first urban guerrilla organization of Colombia. These rebel organizations differed in terms of strategy, location, and the social origins of their members.[6]

In addition, at least three new (albeit minor) rebel organizations were formed during the 1980s: the Socialist Renovation Movement (CRS) and Workers' Revolutionary Party (PRT) that were splinter groups of the ELN,[7] and the indigenous MAQL (Armed Movement Quintín Lame) that resulted from conflicts over land rights.[8]

Whereas in their early years the rebel groups had little offensive capacity and were heavily repressed by the state,[9] since the mid-1980s they have undergone a tremendous expansion. Not even the partly successful peace process of the period 1990–1994 (that led to the demobilization of the M-19, EPL, CRS, PRT, and MAQL) helped to contain the overall growth of insurgency movements. In fact, while in 1978 the guerrilla organizations had only 17 fronts operating in remote rural areas, by 1991 their number had increased to 80 fronts in 358 municipalities, and by 1994 to 105 fronts operating in 569 municipalities.[10] In 2001 the rebel groups maintained 103 fronts operating throughout the country, and apparently only in 2004 did the number of guerrillas begin to decrease.[11]

Explaining the expansion of insurgency

Why did the Colombian insurgencies expand during this period? Some analysts put the blame on the political exclusions associated with the NF, a regime that was both rife with corruption and unresponsive to accumulating social demands. The NF prevented any political forces other than the Liberal and Conservative Parties from gaining access to the government, and reportedly various minorities were left with no choice but to join the revolutionary groups.[12] A significant anomaly of this approach is that the rebel groups gained strength precisely at the same time that Colombia experienced a political opening. Originally intended to endure 16 years (1958–1974), the NF was partly extended through informal inter-élite arrangements into the mid-1980s. However, from then on the NF was dismantled, and its final remnants were totally suppressed by the National Constituent Assembly of 1991. In other words, counterintuitively the expansion of insurgency coincided with a greater inclusion of hitherto marginalized political groups.

In any event, a nexus between political exclusions and insurgency exists. In spite of undergoing a democratizing trend, one could hardly characterize Colombia as a fully inclusive regime. Corruption, clientelism, and violence have often hindered the empowerment of political forces other than the traditional parties. Violence, in particular, has been used as a means of excluding some emerging political forces, especially those linked to the left.

Other analysts argue that the expansion of insurgency has been mainly due to economic exclusions. A flaw of this argument is that most economic trends were positive during the 1980s and 1990s, as they had been in the 1970s. Colombia's semi-orthodox economic policies averted radical adjustment measures or a debt crisis comparable to those that affected most other Latin American economies. Furthermore, between 1980 and 1992 the levels of poverty and inequality declined, while the real income of all social classes improved.[13] And contrary to what one would have expected, inequality did not increase substantially with the neo-liberal reforms of the early 1990s, according to the Theil index and Gini coefficients.[14] Only between 1995 and 1999 did Colombia experience a macroeconomic crisis leading to a dramatic increase in poverty rates.

Just as in the previous case, economic exclusions do help to explain the expansion of insurgency. In fact, Colombia's positive economic trends did not alter the country's ranking as one of the most unequal in Latin America (which is the region with the highest levels of inequality in the world). Furthermore, a study by the Economic Planning Department of the Colombian government revealed that the most unequal municipalities (as measured by the Gini index) also corresponded to the most violent ones, regardless of the fact that the rates of economic growth were positive.[15] Problems of land distribution have added fuel to the fire, as three major agrarian reform laws (the ones of 1936, 1944, and 1968) as well as more recent policy initiatives failed to change the structure of land rights in the countryside.[16]

The shortcomings of arguments related to both political and economic exclusions for explaining the expansion of insurgency have led other analysts to resort to the "greed thesis". Hence, authors such as Nieto,[17] Rangel,[18] and Chernick[19] have linked the growth of insurgency to the upsurge of the cocaine trade in Colombia. According to these authors, during the 1980s and 1990s the Colombian rebel groups acquired substantial wealth by taxing the drug-traffickers (or by directly engaging in drug-trafficking), which has allowed the guerrilla organizations to recruit many landless/unemployed peasants.

Overall, if any of these explanations is taken on its own while neglecting the others there is a risk of oversimplifying a rather complex case. The expansion of insurgency in Colombia has been due partly to political and economic exclusions, and partly to the availability of drug-trafficking money. On top of this, the Colombian state has lacked the capacity either to generate economic opportunities in the countryside or to repress effectively the revolutionary organizations, which has facilitated the growth of insurgency movements. With this background, one can now consider the different peace initiatives that have been undertaken since the 1980s and the corresponding role of spoilers.

Belisario Betancur's peace process

At a time when revolution had spread to Central America and violence was escalating in Colombia, President Belisario Betancur (1982–1986) made an initial attempt to find a bargained solution to the conflict. During his electoral campaign Betancur pledged to find a negotiated solution to an armed conflict that he conceived as a by-product of poverty, injustice, and a lack of opportunities for the underprivileged.[20]

Upon assuming office, Betancur formed various peace commissions that started negotiating with the rebel groups. By 1984 the government and the guerrilla organizations M-19, EPL, and FARC (but not the radicalized ELN) had already signed a truce. Subsequently, the government formed additional peace commissions that were put in charge of verifying the cease-fire as well as compliance with any peace accords.

However, within a short period of time the peace negotiations broke down due to both procedural mistakes and spoiling. In terms of procedural flaws, Betancur's facilitating commissions included spokespersons of various social sectors who could not assume any commitments on behalf of the government.[21] For their part, the commissions that were put in charge of verifying the cease-fire lacked the expertise, resources, and personnel that were needed to perform an adequate job.[22] The proliferation of peace commissions helped to confuse who was responsible for what, and the accords did not specify under what conditions the truce with the rebel groups would give way to a permanent peace. In addition, different spoilers sabotaged the negotiations.

The role of spoilers

Some authors mention that different entrepreneurs and politicians of the Liberal and Conservative Parties were opposed to Betancur's peace negotiations,[23] but this does not necessarily mean that they acted as spoilers. Whereas no documentation is available about spoiling activities carried out by these individuals, authors such as Chernick[24] argue that the army openly undermined Betancur's cease-fire orders and was partly responsible for the collapse of the truce with the rebel groups. This was due not only to the military's uncompromising stance *vis-à-vis* the guerrilla organizations, but also to the fact that Betancur generated hostility in the army by cutting down the military budget.[25]

Most of the rebel groups also acted as spoilers, thinking of the truce as an opportunity to create new fronts and expand both territorially and in terms of numbers of combatants. A former top leader of the M-19, for instance, openly admitted that during Betancur's tenure his group conceived the peace talks merely as "a [tactical] weapon of war".[26] In fact, after the Colombian army destroyed the guerrilla campground of Yarumales, the M-19 sought to regroup and revise its military strategy, and the peace talks represented an opportunity to do so. Not surprisingly, in July 1985 the M-19 was the first rebel group to abandon the truce.

The truce with the EPL also broke down following the assassination of the organization's spokesperson, Oscar William Calvo.[27] Even though one might question the EPL's commitment to Betancur's peace process, this rebel group seems to have been a victim of spoilers rather than a perpetrator of acts of sabotage against the peace process.

The FARC nominally maintained a truce, and even formed the political party Unión Patriótica (UP) that participated in the presidential elections of 1986 and the congressional and local elections of 1988. However, the FARC did not disarm and demobilize, but rather coexisted with the UP. UP spokespersons openly argued that the FARC would not relinquish any weapons because they constituted the best guarantee for the "revolutionary transformation" of Colombia.[28] As the FARC/UP sought power through elections or violence, right-wing sectors accused the UP of engaging in "armed proselitism" and waged a dirty war against this leftist party. As a result, between 1986 and 1995 right-wing paramilitary groups[29] killed over 2,000 members of the UP.[30]

Due to the high levels of impunity in Colombia, only a few individuals have been indicted for the crimes committed against UP members. Whereas some analysts consider the security agencies of the state as the main culprits for the systematic killing of UP militants,[31] military officers place blame on the drug-traffickers. According to a Colombian colonel, the Medellin cartel murdered scores of disarmed UP militants and whoever had connections with the FARC after the rebel organization stole money and took over some laboratories for processing cocaine that belonged to the drug kingpin Gonzalo Rodriguez Gacha.[32]

In conclusion, even though different spoilers did sabotage Betancur's peace process, other factors also help to explain the breakdown of the peace negotiations. Betancur's procedural mistakes as well as the existence of ambiguities with regards to the cease-fire accords greatly facilitated the role of spoilers during the peace talks. All these factors eventually led to a resumption of war.

Virgilio Barco and Cesar Gaviria's peace process

When Betancur's successor, Virgilio Barco, was elected president in 1986, the government was at war with all the rebel groups except for the FARC. Even the cease-fire with this guerrilla organization collapsed in 1987 in the midst of military clashes between the army and the rebels as well as the dirty war against the UP. But in 1988 Barco started a peace process that concluded during the tenure of his successor, President Cesar Gaviria, leading to the demobilization of 791 guerrillas of M-19, 2,149 of the EPL, 433 of the CRS, 205 of the PRT, and 148 of the MAQL.[33] Meanwhile the war went on (and later intensified) with the two strongest rebel groups, the FARC and the ELN, as well as a with a splinter faction of the EPL.

Various factors explain Barco's partial success. To begin with, his peace process coincided with the end of the Cold War, a period in which various guerrilla organizations started to question the validity of socialism. In addition, prior to the peace negotiations several rebel groups had incurred heavy military and political costs, which made them consider the option of a negotiated solution seriously.[34]

Barco also corrected procedural mistakes committed by Betancur. He redressed Betancur's error of appointing independent peace commissions, by making the government assume direct responsibility for both the peace negotiations and any verification tasks. To this end, the president created the Office of the Peace Counselor, which under his direct supervision was put in charge of negotiating with the rebel groups.[35] And prior to sitting at the bargaining table, Barco launched his Iniciativa Para la Paz (Initiative for the Peace: IP),[36] a road-map for the upcoming peace negotiations with the rebel organizations.

In 1988 only the M-19 agreed to negotiate following the guidelines of Barco's IP. In a short period of time the government and the M-19 agreed upon a series of reform proposals that Barco was expected to submit to Congress and transform into laws. However, some MPs torpedoed the peace process by including an addendum to the reform proposals which prohibited the extradition of drug-traffickers. In other words, had the Colombian Congress approved the reforms agreed upon with the M-19, it would have also granted impunity for the drug-traffickers. This occurred at the same time as Barco was waging a "war on drugs", so the president was left with no choice but prevent the approval of the reform laws.[37] Henceforth, the peace negotiations survived only because the M-19 decided not to condition its demobilization on any political reforms.[38]

Eventually the M-19 demobilized, formed a political party, and participated in the 1990 presidential elections, but its top leader and presidential candidate, Carlos Pizarro, was gunned down while campaigning.[39] After this unpromising start, the experience of the M-19 started to change in a positive sense. Following an internal debate in which the M-19 considered going back to war, the organization decided to compete at the polls with its second-in-command, Antonio Navarro. Navarro obtained over 12 per cent of the votes, by far the best electoral performance of the left in Colombia.

The M-19 obtained additional political gains down the road. In the aftermath of the presidential elections, a student movement successfully promoted the formation of a popularly elected National Constituent Assembly (NCA) to reform the Colombian polity. Shortly afterwards the Supreme Court of Justice increased the stakes for any organizations committed to changing the *status quo* by removing any limits to the constitutional areas that could be reformed. Due to its early demobilization, the M-19 (but not the other rebel groups) was able to campaign and eventually elected 19 out of the NCA's 72 delegates. The M-19 outperformed the Conservative Party, hitherto Colombia's second-ranked political force. This was an extraordinary outcome for the recently disarmed M-19, and a key stimulus for other rebel groups that became optimistic about the prospects of obtaining political benefits through electoral politics.

The new government of President Cesar Gaviria also presented the NCA as a unique opportunity for the revolutionary organizations to introduce structural transformations in Colombia, and pledged to appoint to the NCA spokespersons of those rebel organizations that demobilized in due time (which corresponds to the "departing train strategy" mentioned by Stedman). This facilitated the disarmament of the EPL, the PRT, and the MAQL. Eventually two delegates of the EPL (who enjoyed full voting rights) and one delegate from each of the rebel PRT and MAQL groups (who were only allowed to participate in debates) were appointed to the NCA.[40] In sum, Gaviria attained success by continuing Barco's policies.

The role of spoilers

There were a number of unsuccessful attempts to derail this peace process. As mentioned, the Colombian Congress was a spoiler in the sense that some MPs conditioned approval of the reform proposals the government had agreed upon with the M-19 on the non-extradition of drug-traffickers. Although this hindered the approval of the reforms, the peace process survived because the M-19 maintained its determination to abandon insurrection and embrace electoral politics.

Unlike what had occurred during Betancur's tenure, this time the security forces did not sabotage (at least overtly) the peace negotiations. This might partly be explained by the fact that the peace agreements did not entail any institutional transformations of the army (reforming the military was off limits, as the war with the FARC and the ELN went on). However, the government should also be credited for preventing spoiling actions. The first Peace Counselor appointed by Barco, Carlos Ossa Escobar, mended fences between the executive branch and military authorities. Later on the government asked some high-ranking military officers to cooperate with the Peace Counselor's Office in the design of the IP peace initiative.[41] Due to their early involvement in the crafting of the road-map for the peace process, the military forces had no incentives for sabotaging the negotiations at a later date. In addition, during the actual negotiations the Peace Counselors consulted on peace-related matters with the military forces on a regular basis,[42] which helped to secure the army's compliance.

For their part, the right-wing paramilitary groups sometimes carried out serious spoiling actions – occasionally in collusion with the armed forces. They were responsible for the murder of the M-19's chief commander, Carlos Pizarro, and for various other killings, including systematic attacks against members of the UP, but never admitted responsibility for these actions. As this peace process coincided with some clashes between the rebel groups and the drug cartels, it was easy for the government to blame the drug-traffickers for any assassinations of demobilized guerrillas.

The FARC also attempted to sabotage the peace process after accusing the rebel groups that had signed peace accords, especially the EPL and the M-19, of "treason of the revolution". For instance, the FARC unsuccessfully attempted to recruit demobilized M-19 guerrillas, so that they would merely switch from one rebel group to another.[43] The FARC was also responsible for murdering an important percentage of the approximately 400 demobilized EPL guerrillas who were killed in the region of Urabá. These killings were partly due to a decade-long deadly quarrel between both rebel groups that continued even in the aftermath of the EPL's demobilization.[44] The EPL resisted these provocations, probably because the government was not involved in the killings and even offered some protection to the demobilized EPL rebels. These were serious spoiling actions that threatened, but ultimately failed to derail, the peace process.

Andrés Pastrana's peace process

The latest attempt to find a negotiated solution to the Colombian armed conflict took place during the tenure of President Andrés Pastrana (1998–2002). President Gaviria (1990–1994) had attempted to arrive at peace agreements with the FARC and the ELN, but negotiation rounds held in Caracas (Venezuela) and Tlaxcala (Mexico) yielded no results. Then the rebel groups refused to negotiate with Gaviria's successor, President Ernesto Samper (1994–1998), after a scandal broke out revealing that the president had received funds from drug-traffickers of the Cali cartel. This was a practical rather than a moral issue for the guerrilla organizations: Samper faced such a deep legitimacy crisis that the rebel groups believed the government could not assume any credible peace-related commitments.

During these two governments the armed conflict continued to escalate, which helped to generate a sense of war fatigue in Colombia. This was evident in 1997, when citizens deposited over 10 million symbolic votes in favour of "finding a bargained solution to the Colombian armed conflict".[45] Shortly afterwards, Andrés Pastrana of the conservative Nueva Fuerza Democrática won the 1998 presidential elections, arguably because most citizens believed that he was the candidate most likely to reach a peaceful settlement with the FARC.

Pastrana started peace negotiations with the FARC, but soon encountered all sorts of obstacles. To begin with, Pastrana had to overcome strong opposition from the military forces in order to comply with a precondition demanded by the FARC, which consisted of the demilitarization of five municipalities where the negotiations would be carried out.

Eventually the peace process got started, but the parties made little progress during three-and-a-half years of negotiations. On three different occasions the FARC unilaterally suspended negotiations, thereby causing serious delays in the peace process. In mid-1999 the parties did reach an agreement on a complicated 47-point joint agenda,[46] but afterwards they did not discuss any of its issues – except for holding some preliminary talks on how to redress unemployment in Colombia. In fact, in 2000 the government and the FARC decided to conduct the so-called *audiencias públicas*, a mechanism that indefinitely postponed any negotiations on the issues of the agenda while allowing citizens to submit proposals for "building the peace in Colombia".[47]

From then on the negotiations between the government and the FARC revolved around the possibility of a cease-fire and a prisoner exchange, which were ultimately procedural issues about the conditions under which the parties would conduct peace talks. No agreement was ever reached on a cease-fire. From an early date the FARC stated that it would consider a cease-fire only after the government had implemented 80 per cent of any agreed-upon peace accords.[48] The government and the FARC did eventually reach a partial agreement on a one-off humanitarian prisoner exchange that took place in June 2001. But in February 2002 the peace process with the FARC broke down, due to a lack of progress at the bargaining table coupled with increasing levels of violence. The FARC's kidnapping of a commercial airplane turned out to be the last in a series of provocations by this rebel group which led Pastrana to bring an end to the peace talks.

Upon assuming office, Pastrana seemed to gamble it all on the peace process with the FARC while neglecting the militarily weaker ELN. Only after negotiations with the FARC deadlocked did the government pay greater attention to the ELN. However, the negotiations with the latter rebel organization also ended in failure.

Following the example that the FARC had set, in March 1999 the ELN demanded the demilitarization of four municipalities (an area considerably smaller than the one conceded to the FARC) in order to carry out a national convention and define a peace agenda. Towards the end of 1999, after Pastrana eventually agreed to demilitarize the municipalities requested by the ELN,[49] the government was unable to deliver its promise because right-wing paramilitary groups (since 1997 grouped under the umbrella organization Autodefensas Unidas de Colombia, AUC) prevented demilitarization both through violence and by sponsoring mass mobilizations and blockages of highways. When Pastrana's tenure ended, the negotiations with the ELN remained stalled.

Why did Pastrana's negotiations fail? They did so in part because of the government's mistakes. Pastrana should have thought more carefully about the risks of conceding a large demilitarized area to the FARC without establishing clear rules about its use. The enlargement of the bargaining agenda by the government and the postponement of any negotiations with the FARC due to the *audiencias públicas* were also careless actions.

On top of this, Pastrana repeated some of the mistakes made by Betancur. Pastrana appointed two novices as Peace Counselors, with little experience in negotiating with the rebel groups. Peace Counselor Victor G. Ricardo, in particular, mishandled relations with the military forces to the point that one minister of defence resigned and several top military officers refused to talk on the phone with him.[50] Ricardo's replacement, Camilo Gómez, improved the relations between the Peace Counselor's Office and the military, but tensions still remained high, which imperilled the peace process.

In addition, during the negotiations with the FARC the government appointed four subsequent bargaining commissions that were supposed to provide critical support to the Peace Counselor. However, the first three commissions included public figures who were only devoted part-time to the negotiations and could not assume any commitments on behalf of the government. Only the last bargaining commission, formed in June 2001, included state officials who were dedicated full-time to the negotiations, but by that point the peace process was doomed.

Apart from this, most of the parties acted as spoilers. The FARC acted as a spoiler, as did the right-wing paramilitary groups. The US government, in partnership with the Colombian government, also helped to escalate the war through Plan Colombia, a counter-drug/counterinsurgency initiative, while the military forces did not rein in the paramilitary groups. The following sections look more closely at the specific roles of the various spoilers.

The role of spoilers

The FARC

The FARC demanded as a precondition for sitting at the bargaining table the demilitarization of five municipalities, corresponding to 42,000 km². Even if this precondition was originally intended to provide a conflict-free zone in which to conduct negotiations, the demilitarized area (DA) gave a series of important military, political, and financial advantages to the FARC. The DA became a safe haven where the rebel leaders feared no attacks from the army, and from which FARC commandos planned and carried out attacks elsewhere, returning afterwards for protection.[51] The DA also made it easier for the FARC to trade drugs for weapons[52] and to recruit and train new members.[53] In the DA the FARC also held many kidnap victims prisoner and negotiated ransoms with their family members. The FARC was the undisputed authority in the DA, where the rebel group administered some rough form of justice and debated political issues with national and international guests.

While exploiting the various advantages of the DA, the FARC gave few (if any) indications of being truly interested in finding a peaceful settlement to the Colombian war. Realizing that it could extract concessions from a government that had gambled all its prestige on the peace process, the FARC assumed a defiant attitude from the very beginning. In January 1999 the top FARC leader, Manuel Marulanda Velez, failed to appear at the ceremony for the installation of the bargaining table because of the risks posed by an alleged assassination plot. Marulanda's excuse was difficult to believe because the ceremony took place in the DA, which was under full control of FARC guerrillas. Pastrana was left alone as keynote speaker, sitting beside an empty chair that was designated for Marulanda.[54]

From then on the FARC repeatedly tested the government's patience. In both 1999 and 2000 the FARC unilaterally suspended the peace negotiations, while demanding from the government tougher actions against the paramilitary groups. In 2001, for a third time in a row, the FARC unilaterally suspended negotiations after the government tightened security measures around the DA, following the detention of three IRA members who had spent time there, presumably training FARC guerillas in bomb-making techniques.[55]

During the second half of 1999, due to the slightly ambiguous wording of an agreement signed by Pastrana and Marulanda, the rebel group prevented the formation of an international verification commission that would have monitored both the activities of the FARC within the DA and compliance with any peace accords.[56] Later on the Colombian army obtained an internal document of a FARC summit held in March 2000, revealing that the rebels' aim to take power by military means had not changed, and that the peace talks merely facilitated advancing towards this strategic objective. This document also unveiled that the FARC was running short of middle-rank commanders, which helped to explain the FARC's strategy of kidnapping soldiers and policemen in order to force a prisoner exchange.[57]

Apart from this, the FARC's violence never abated throughout the negotiations. There were many expressions of international repudiation of the FARC's violent actions, and by 2000 domestic polls revealed that support for the peace negotiations had plummeted.[58] However, this rebel group did not change its behaviour. Perhaps the FARC deemed it unlikely that anyone would have preferred a full-fledged resumption of war to the *status quo*. Eventually the negotiations broke down due to the cumulative effect of the FARC's abuses and a bargaining table that yielded no results in over three years of negotiations.

Why did the FARC spoil the negotiations? One can think of several possible and not mutually exclusive interpretations. A first hypothesis is that the military capacity of the FARC had been improving through the years in terms of troops, weapons, and financial assets. Why would a rebel group negotiate precisely at a time when its military and organizational capacities were at their best? Perhaps Colombia was not fast approaching a revolutionary situation, but probably the FARC believed that it just had to wait for ripe conditions for taking power.

A second hypothesis is that the FARC spoiled the negotiations because of a historic legacy of mistrust. How could the rebel group forget the massacre of its political party, the UP? From the rebels' standpoint, perhaps Pastrana did not offer any credible security guarantees.

A third hypothesis is that the FARC had become a profitable drug-trafficking enterprise, with no political ideology whatsoever.[59] So why should the FARC sign peace agreements and thereby renounce such a profitable business? In regards to this hypothesis, even admitting that drug-trafficking is essential to the FARC's finances, the possibility exists that the drug trade might be just a means for the rebels to fight. Otherwise, why do most rebel leaders not utilize drug profits for retirement on some remote island? And why do the rebels keep carrying out other hostile actions that provoke heavy military retaliations instead of assuming a lower profile, as most drug-traffickers do?

Finally, the FARC might have acted as spoiler because the whole context of the peace negotiations made it very unlikely that a successful peace settlement could emerge. If there was no realistic chance of reaching a peaceful settlement, why should the FARC not take advantage of a peace process that offered the possibility of reaping short-term military benefits? If this were the case, one should analyse whether and how other actors such as the Colombian and US governments, the military, and the paramilitary groups also entered the negotiations only tactically, thereby acting as spoilers.

The Colombian/US governments

When Pastrana first approached the FARC he announced a vast fund-raising initiative aimed at financing peacebuilding: a sort of Marshall Plan for Colombia[60] favouring the underprivileged. However, Pastrana's initiative materialized in 1999 as Plan Colombia (PC), a US-led counter-drug policy that turned Colombia into the third-largest recipient of US military aid in the world and clearly targeted the FARC. From an early date the Clinton administration had manifested apprehension towards

Pastrana's peace initiative, fearing that the rebels would transform the DA into a gigantic "laboratory for processing and trafficking drugs".[61] In 1999 the US government suspended any contacts with the rebel organization after the FARC killed three American citizens, and after 11 September 2001 further hardened its position by labelling the FARC a terrorist organization.[62]

Although packaged as a mere counter-drug policy, for the most part PC was about counterinsurgency. In fact, PC did not target the Colombian drug cartels operating in various cities, nor the right-wing paramilitary groups that admitted receiving 70 per cent of their finances from drug-trafficking. PC clearly targeted the FARC's strongholds in the southern part of Colombia, spraying drug crops in the departments of Putumayo and Caquetá, which allegedly represented about 60 per cent of the rebels' income.[63]

According to American and Colombian officials, targeting the FARC's main source of revenues could actually push the peace negotiations forward, because only by forcefully reducing the FARC's finances would this rebel group seriously consider a bargained solution. But FARC spokespersons, European Union representatives,[64] and various NGOs and analysts criticized PC as a policy leading to military escalation. Retrospectively, PC did help to escalate the war.

Perhaps the peace negotiations were doomed from the start, in the sense that the FARC would not have relinquished drug-trafficking in the absence of PC, and anyhow the rebels had few (if any) incentives to turn in their weapons. But PC might have driven the FARC deeper into drug-trafficking. In fact, by providing an unprecedented boost to the Colombian military in terms of training, technology, logistics, and intelligence, PC might have started an arms race in which the FARC attempted to compete. Whether this was an intended or unintended spoiling action is debatable, but the point is that PC provided an important incentive to the Colombian government for waging war instead of finding a bargained solution to the conflict.

The paramilitary groups

Top paramilitary leader Carlos Castaño initially manifested a generic support for Pastrana's peace process with the FARC while assuming a far more radical stance in regards to any possible negotiations with the ELN. In mid-1998 Castaño declared that he would militarily defeat the ELN, a rebel group that he considered both weak and prone to engage in "terrorist behaviour".[65] In the end the AUC spoiled both peace processes, even if more so the one with the ELN than the one with the FARC.

The first act of sabotage of the peace process with the FARC occurred in January 1999, when the AUC went on a killing spree that caused over 137 deaths precisely at the same time that the government and the rebels were starting negotiations.[66] As a result the FARC unilaterally suspended the peace talks only 12 days after they had begun, while demanding that the government fight the paramilitary groups.[67] The negotiations remained stalled for a five-month period.

Later on, in October 2000 when the government and the FARC were forging an agreement on a prisoner exchange, the AUC kidnapped six MPs in an attempt to prevent Congress from approving a law aimed at liberating FARC guerrillas.[68] When Minister of the Interior Humberto de la Calle went to talk with Castaño in order to liberate the kidnapped politicians, the FARC unilaterally froze the peace negotiations again, "until the president and the government clarified before the country and the entire world their official position towards paramilitary terrorism, and developed policies to bring it to an end".[69] From the FARC's standpoint, the fact that the government actually met and talked with paramilitary leaders was tantamount to complicity. The negotiations between the government and the FARC were only resumed in February 2001. In sum, the paramilitaries were involved in two out of the three occasions on which the FARC suspended negotiations, thereby producing serious delays in the peace process.

The paramilitaries undertook greater efforts to derail the negotiations with the ELN, especially after the government agreed to demilitarize four municipalities for this rebel group.[70] In order to prevent demilitarization from occurring, between 2000 and 2001 the AUC carried out a string of massacres and selective killings in areas where the ELN was influential (the most gruesome massacres were those of El Salado and Ciénaga, and in Barrancabermeja the AUC killed 145 people during a six-week period[71]). In addition, the AUC along with regional associations of cattle-ranchers and other local entrepreneurs promoted mass mobilizations and blockages of highways aimed at preventing the demilitarization of any territories.[72]

In mid-2000 Castaño also attacked a provisional camp where the ELN had met a few days earlier with the Peace Counselor, as well as the rebels' headquarters of El Diamante, precisely at the same time when ELN spokespersons were holding peace talks with government officials and civil society representatives in Geneva.[73] These military actions ruined the Geneva talks, which had begun with optimistic prospects about peace. In 2001, after Pastrana persuaded some local communities to allow the demilitarization of four municipalities to proceed, Castaño undertook yet another offensive against the ELN in those same areas,[74] leaving Pastrana with no option but order the military forces to retake the zones.

In short, the AUC prevented any progress in the peace talks with the ELN. Apparently the AUC thought that it could militarily defeat the ELN before any peace negotiations started, which was unfortunate: the ELN was far weaker than the FARC, and its interest in the bargaining table was (prima facie) more credible. In the end the AUC did not defeat the ELN, but this rebel group was prevented from engaging in peace talks.

The Colombian armed forces

On a few occasions the Colombian military forces threatened to spoil the peace negotiations by engaging in open confrontations with Pastrana. However, after some arm-twisting, the army often complied with the orders of the president. For instance, it was difficult for Pastrana to deliver his promise to the FARC of fully demilitarizing five municipalities due to strong opposition from the military forces. Pastrana had to spend approximately four months persuading the military top brass to comply with demilitarization. Later on the Colombian military manifested opposition to a prisoner exchange with the FARC, fearing that this would give a belligerent status to the revolutionary organization and also encourage kidnappings whenever the FARC wanted to free its imprisoned commanders.[75] Once again Pastrana overcame opposition of the armed forces, and a one-time humanitarian prisoner exchange occurred in 2001.

Apart from this, the military-paramilitary nexus was far more problematic for the peace process and might have encouraged spoiling actions. Although the government did always claim to be fighting with the same intensity both the rebel groups and the right-wing paramilitaries, this was not the case. Figure 10.1, elaborated with data from the Colombian Ministry of Defence, shows how during Pastrana's tenure the government fought against the rebel groups far more intensely than against the paramilitary groups.

One should add that reportedly in some regions the security forces turned a blind eye to (and sometimes collaborated with) the activities of paramilitary groups.[76] Maintaining this double standard in the midst of peace negotiations generated a great deal of suspicion from the FARC and the ELN, because the government seemed to tolerate (or at worst condone) a dirty war against some sectors seeking to change the *status quo*. The government might have claimed lack of capacity to fight so many irregular groups simultaneously. But after Plan Colombia strengthened the security forces significantly, how could the military look the other way when the AUC carried out massacres and extra-judicial killings?

As the peace process stumbled, not only the rebel groups but also the United Nations, the European Union, several NGOs, and at one point even the US government[77] demanded that Pastrana should fight the

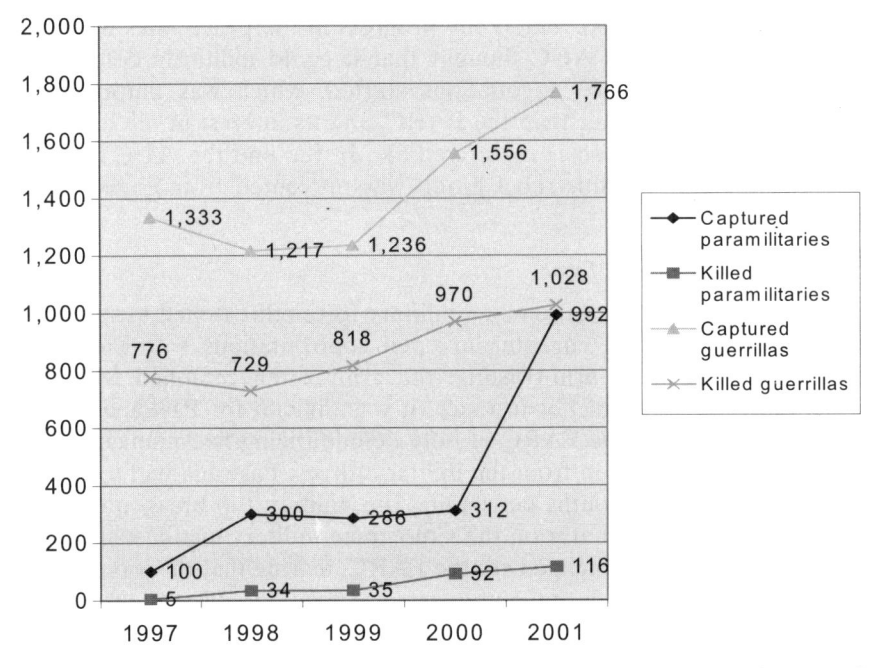

Figure 10.1 The war of the Colombian military forces against irregular armed groups, 1997–2001.
Source: Ministerio de Defensa Nacional de Colombia. 2002. Informe Annual de Derechos Humanos y DIH 2001. Ministerio de Defensa Nacional de Colombia, pp. 99–100.

paramilitaries more decisively. In this regard, the government took some action. Following the first suspension of the peace talks by the FARC, Pastrana pledged to reactivate the anti-paramilitary bloc of the security forces, and later on (due to pressures from the US State Department) dismissed two Colombian generals who had been accused of having links with the paramilitaries. After the AUC spoiled the peace process with the ELN, the president also fostered Operación Dignidad, a military offensive against the paramilitaries. However, none of these actions remotely sufficed to contain the paramilitary groups, which grew in numbers and remained defiant throughout Pastrana's tenure.

Concluding remarks

In Colombia a wide variety of actors have attempted to spoil the various peace negotiations in the past two decades, albeit with different degrees of success. Although the repertoire of spoiling actions has included mass mobilizations and other semi-legal actions, spoilers have increasingly resorted to violence in order to achieve their goals.

One could hardly place exclusive blame on spoilers for explaining why the peace processes of Presidents Betancur and Pastrana failed, or why the ones of Presidents Barco and Gaviria merely attained a partial success. In fact, no durable peace accord could have emerged from some ill-conducted peace negotiations. At the same time, though, spoilers contributed significantly to the failure of various peace negotiations.

It is no coincidence that the only partly successful peace negotiations in Colombia correspond to the ones in which the government resorted to spoiler management techniques. Perhaps Presidents Barco and Gaviria did not fully deter spoiling actions by the paramilitary groups and the FARC, but they did reduce the number of potential spoilers by preventing the military forces from sabotaging the peace process, and by lobbying rightist sectors (guerrilla leaders carried out additional lobbying efforts, which will not be elaborated on here). These two governments also offered some form of protection to demobilized guerrillas in order to contain the potential damage caused by spoilers. In the absence of such spoiler management initiatives, the peace negotiations would have fallen apart.

In any event, the war with the FARC and the ELN has continued. Should one consider the FARC and the ELN (and the AUC, which is presently undergoing a dubious demobilization process) as uncompromising "total spoilers" that cannot be either appeased or socialized? Is Colombia left with no options other than repressing or isolating these illegal organizations?

A problem with this prescription is that the government has resorted to coercive strategies for the past 40 years, but has been unable to defeat the irregular armed groups. The prospects of achieving victory remain dim, even after Colombia has received a great deal of US military aid through PC. The constant expansion of insurgency also suggests that isolation tactics have not worked that well. The rebel groups may be ideologically weak, and have been labelled by the Colombian government as "terrorist" or "criminal" organizations, but this has not reduced their power base in several depressed rural areas and urban shanty-towns.

Other things being equal, at some point the government and the guerrillas will have to return to the bargaining table. In this scenario it is important to address various aspects of the peace process other than spoilers, such as composition and role of the bargaining commissions, the agenda, the negotiation strategy, the security dilemma, the role of third parties, and so forth. Merely to focus on spoilers could make us forget that careless actions by different Colombian governments did contribute to failure in various negotiations.

In addition to this, spoiler management techniques will be essential for attaining success in any future peace negotiations. These techniques will be useful if most of the warring factions develop a genuine interest in finding a peaceful settlement to the war, and spoilers constitute relatively marginal groups. However, the obstacles to peacemaking and peace-building will be insurmountable if the major warring factions engage in peace negotiations while believing that they are better off with the war.

Notes

1. Stedman, Stephen J. 1997. "Spoiler problems in peace processes," *International Security*, Vol. 22, No. 2, p. 5.
2. Wilde, Alexander. 1982. *La quiebra de la democracia*. Bogotá: Tercer Mundo, pp. 39–41; Hartlyn, Jonathan. 1988. *The Politics of Coalition Rule in Colombia*. New York: Cambridge University Press, pp. 18–20.
3. Sanchez, Gonzalo. 1985. "La violencia y sus efectos en el sistema político colombiano", in *Once ensayos sobre la Violencia*. Bogotá: CEREC, Centro Gaitan Sánchez.
4. Dix, Robert H. 1987. *The Politics of Colombia*. California: Hoover Institute Press, p. 314.
5. Chernick, Marc. 1999. "Negotiating peace amid multiple forms of violence: The protracted search for a settlement to the armed conflicts in Colombia", in C. Arnson (ed.) *Comparative Peace Processes in Latin America*. Washington, DC and Stanford: Woodrow Wilson Center Press/Stanford University Press, p. 169; Bejarano, Jesus A. 1995. *Una agenda para la paz*. Santafé de Bogotá: Tercer Mundo, p. 85.
6. In terms of strategies, whereas the FARC was originally a self-defence organization, the ELN embraced Cuban-style *foquismo* and the EPL the Maoist "prolonged popular war" strategy. In terms of areas of operations, the FARC took root in the southern plains, the ELN in the north-eastern region, and the EPL in north-western coastal areas: Bejarano, *ibid.*, p. 85. As for the social composition of the rebel groups, the FARC was the only truly peasant guerrilla organization, while militants of the M-19, the ELN, and the EPL were for the most part students, dissidents of the Liberal Party, and urban middle-class professionals: Chernick, *ibid.*, p. 164.
7. Comisión de Superación de la Violencia. 1992. *Pacificar la paz*. Bogotá: IEPRI/CINEP/Comisión Andina de Juristas Seccional Colombia/CECOIN, pp. 112–115.
8. *Ibid.*, pp. 105–106; Peñaranda, Ricardo. 1999. "De rebeldes a ciudadanos: El caso del Movimiento Armado Quintín Lame", in J. G. Ricardo Peñaranda (ed.) *De las Armas a la Política*. Santafé de Bogotá: TM Editores/IEPRI.
9. Bejarano, note 5 above, p. 85.
10. Pecaut, Daniel. 1997. "Presente, pasado y futuro de la Violencia in Colombia", *Desarrollo Económico*, Vol. 36, No. 144, p. 896. Colombia has 1,071 municipalities.
11. UNDP. 2003. *El Conflicto, callejón con salida. Informe nacional de desarrollo humano Colombia – 2003*. Bogotá: UNDP, p. 83; UNDP. 2005. "El pié de fuerza de las FARC: Cifras vs. realidad", in *Boletín Hechos del Callejón No. 4*. Bogotá: UNDP; UNDP. 2005. "¿Cómo va el ELN?", in *Boletín Hechos del Callejón No. 5*. Bogota: UNDP.
12. Bejarano, note 5 above, pp. 85–86.
13. Altimir, Oscar. 1998. "Inequality, employment, and poverty in Latin America: An overview", in V. Tokman and G. O'Donnell (eds) *Poverty and Inequality in Latin America*. Notre Dame, IN: University of Notre Dame Press; Moorley, Samuel. 1995. *Poverty and*

Inequality in Latin America: The Impact of Adjustment and Recovery in the 1980s. Baltimore and London: Johns Hopkins University Press, pp. 28–38, 64.
14. Stallings, Barbara and Wilson Peres. 2000. *Growth, Employment, and Equity: The Impact of the Economic Reforms in Latin America and the Caribbean.* Washington, DC and Santiago: Brookings Institution Press/UN Economic Commission for Latin America and the Caribbean, pp. 120–123, 131.
15. Departamento Nacional de Planeación. 1998. *La paz: El desafío para el desarrollo.* Bogotá: Tercer Mundo/Departamento Nacional de Planeación, p. 41; Rangel Suárez, Alfredo. 1998. *Colombia, guerra en el fin de siglo.* Santafé de Bogotá: TM Editores/Universidad de los Andes Facultad de Ciencias Sociales, p. 36.
16. Reyes, Alejandro. 1996. "Una propuesta de paz que toma en cuenta el cruce de conflictos en Colombia", *Colombia Internacional*, No. 36, October–December, p. 29; Bejarano, Jesús A., Camilo Echandía, Rodolfo Escobedo, and Enrique León Queruz. 1997. *Colombia: Inseguridad, violencia y desempeño económico en la áreas rurales.* Santafé de Bogotá: Universidad Externado/FONADE, p. 252.
17. Nieto, Rafael. 2001. "Economía y violencia", in Jorge Londono de la Cuesta and Fernando Cubides (eds) *Colombia: Conflicto armado, perspectivas de paz y democracia.* Miami: Latin American and Caribbean Center, p. 106.
18. Rangel Suárez, note 15 above, pp. 4–5.
19. Chernick, note 5 above, pp. 166–167.
20. García, Mauricio. 1992. *De la Uribe a Tlaxcala: Procesos de Paz.* Bogotá: CINEP, pp. 48–49; Ramírez, William. 1990. "Las fértiles cenizas de la izquierda", *Análisis Político*, No. 10, p. 9.
21. Bejarano, note 5 above, p. 86.
22. *Ibid.*, p. 88.
23. García, note 20 above, p. 48.
24. Chernick, note 5 above, p. 176.
25. Interview with a Colombian former colonel, Bogotá, 2000.
26. Interview with a former top commander of the M-19, Bogotá, July 2000.
27. Comisión de Superación de la Violencia, note 7 above, p. 100.
28. *Ibid.*, p. 118.
29. In Colombia the term "paramilitary groups" is commonly used to identify a loosely connected network of private right-wing militias, and not entities like the police force. In the early 1980s some drug-traffickers, cattle-ranchers, and rural entrepreneurs formed these private militias in order to settle scores with the revolutionary groups. In earlier decades the Colombian armed forces had also promoted the formation of self-defence organizations in places where the guerrilla groups were strong. Even if presenting themselves as self-defence organizations, in the mid-1980s the paramilitary groups started murdering individuals who were perceived as having affinity with the rebel groups. See Romero, Mauricio. 2003. *Paramilitares y Autodefensas 1982–2003.* Bogotá: IEPRI.
30. Chernick, note 5 above, p. 177.
31. Comision de Superación de la Violencia, note 7 above, p. 118.
32. Interview with a Colombian colonel, Bogotá, July 2000.
33. Comisión de Superación de la Violencia, note 7 above, p. 266.
34. *Ibid.*, pp. 104, 108–109, 115.
35. García, note 20 above, pp. 50–51.
36. Presidencia República de Colombia. 1988. *Iniciativa Para la Paz.* Bogotá: Imprenta Nacional.
37. García, note 20 above, pp. 113–115.
38. The M-19 demobilized in exchange for a few particularistic benefits, though, such as subsidies for education and credits for reinserted guerrillas. Ramírez, William. 1991.

"Las nuevas ceremonias de la paz", *Analisis Politico*, No. 14, September–December; García, note 20 above.
39. Bejarano, note 23 above, p. 118.
40. Ramírez, note 38 above, pp. 12, 15, 30–31; Comisión de Superación de la Violencia, note 7 above, p. 100.
41. Interview with a former Peace Counselor, Bogotá, July 2000.
42. *Ibid.*
43. Interview with a former top leader of the M-19, Bogotá, July 2000.
44. For a review on this see Nasi, Carlo. 2006. "Colombia's peace processes 1982–2002: Conditions, strategies and outcomes", in Virginia M. Bouvier (ed.) *Colombia: Building Peace in a Time of War*. Washington, DC: US Institute of Peace.
45. Valencia, León. 2002. *Adiós a la política, bienvenida la guerra*. Bogotá: Intermedio.
46. This was a synthesis of a 12-point bargaining agenda that the FARC had set forth since 1998 and a 101-point agenda that the government submitted in 1999. Contrary to what one would have expected, the expansion of the agenda was proposed by the government's negotiators.
47. *Semana*. 1999. "El ajedréz del caguán", *Semana*, No. 895, 26 July.
48. *Semana*. 1999. "Tirofijo se destapa", *Semana*, No. 872, 15 February; see also *Semana*. 2000. "¿Cese al fuego?", *Semana*, No. 929, 19 February.
49. *Semana*. 2000. "Se instalan mesas de trabajo en el sur de Bolívar", *Semana*, No. 929, 19 February.
50. *Semana*. 1999. "¿De salida?", *Semana*, No. 871, 8 February; *Semana*. 1999. "Los otros damnificados", *Semana*, No. 875, 8 March; *Semana*. 1999. "Nuevo round Lloreda-Victor G.", *Semana*, No. 886, 24 May.
51. *Semana*. 2001. "Infamia", *Semana*, No. 975, 6 January.
52. *Semana*. 1999. "La paz amada", *Semana*, No. 873, 22 February; *Semana*. 1999. "Los negocios de las FARC", *Semana*, No. 879, 5 April.
53. *Semana*. 1999. "Del despeje al despojo", *Semana*, No. 885, 17 May; *Semana*. 2000. "La inocencia armada", *Semana*, No. 970, 2 December.
54. *Semana*. 1999. "Falla con excusa", *Semana*, No. 871, 8 February.
55. *Semana*. 2001. "La IRA y las FARC", *Semana*, No. 1007, 17 August.
56. *Semana*. 1999. "El diálogo que no fue", *Semana*, No. 900, 30 August.
57. Interview with a Colombian general, Bogotá, 12 August 2003.
58. *Semana*. 2001. "Gesto humanitario o táctica política?", *Semana*, No. 976, 13 January.
59. Estimates indicate that between 40 per cent and 80 per cent of the FARC's finances are derived from drug-trafficking. See *Semana*. 2001. "Golpe maestro", *Semana*, No. 984, 10 March; *Semana*. 2001. "La prueba reina", *Semana*, No. 987, 31 March. On the FARC's involvement in drug-trafficking see Ferro, Medina, Juan Guillermo, and Graciela Uribe Ramón. 2002. *El Orden de la Guerra, Las FARC-EP: Entre la Organización y la Política*. Bogotá: Centro Editorial Javeriano, pp. 96–103.
60. *Semana*. 1999. "Creo en la palabra de tirofijo", *Semana*, No. 869, 25 January.
61. In a 1998 meeting with FARC delegates in Costa Rica, functionaries of the State Department actually told the rebel group that drug interdiction efforts in Colombia were not negotiable. See *Semana*. 1999. "La lucha antinarcóticos no es negociable", *Semana*, No. 872, 15 February.
62. *Semana*. 2001. "La hora del garrote", *Semana*, No. 1011, 13 September.
63. *Semana*. 2000. "El cheque del tío Sam", *Semana*, No. 924, 15 January; *Semana*. 2000. "Guerra a la coca", *Semana*, No. 927, 4 February.
64. *Semana*. 2000. "El malestar europeo", *Semana*, No. 958, 9 September.
65. *Semana*. 1998. "Habla castaño", *Semana*, No. 850, 14 September.
66. *Semana*. 1999. "Ojo por ojo", *Semana*, No. 872, 15 February.

67. *Semana*. 1999. "Paras bajo fuego", *Semana*, No. 873, 22 February.
68. *Semana*. 2000. "El pulso," *Semana*, No. 965, 28 October; *Semana*. 2000. "Llegó la hora de negociar con las AUC", *Semana*, No. 966, 4 November.
69. *Semana*. 2000. "Y ahora qué?", *Semana*, No. 968, 18 November.
70. *Semana*. 2000. "El otro despeje", *Semana*, No. 923, 8 January.
71. *Semana*. 2000. "La caldera del diablo", *Semana*, No. 930, 26 February; *Semana*. 2000. "La barbarie", *Semana*, No. 971, 8 December; *Semana*. 2001. "A sangre y fuego", *Semana*, No. 982, 24 February.
72. *Semana*. 2000. "Bomba de tiempo", *Semana*, No. 947, 24 June; *Semana*. 2001. "La resistencia", *Semana*, No. 977, 20 January.
73. *Semana*. 2000. "La piedra en el camino", *Semana*, No. 953, 5 August.
74. *Semana*. 2001. "La batalla", *Semana*, No. 989, 11 April.
75. *Semana*. 1999. "El golazo del canje", *Semana*, No. 872, 15 February 1999; *Semana*. 2000. "El canje", *Semana*, No. 963, 14 October.
76. In 1999 the report E/CN.4/1999/8 on Colombia by the UN High Commissioner on Human Rights mentioned that "paramilitary groups do not act against the government and many of their actions are done in connection with military and civilian authorities". The report blamed the Colombian authorities for their "lack of will" to fight the paramilitaries efficiently. In 2000 the report E/CN.4/2000/11 on Colombia by the UN High Commissioner on Human Rights referred to the "direct participation of military personnel in the organization of new paramilitary blocs". It also denounced a collusion between the army and the paramilitary groups. In 2001 the report E/CN.4/2001/15 on Colombia by the UN High Commissioner on Human Rights mentioned the "possible direct participation" of members of the Colombian army in the massacres of Ovejas and El Salado that were carried out by paramilitary groups. In 2002 the report E/CN.4/2002/4 on Colombia by the UN High Commissioner on Human Rights again denounced the existence of links between members of the Colombian army and the paramilitary groups. The UNHCHR also accused the Colombian army of failing to protect the victims. These reports are available at www.hchr.org.co/documentoseinformes/publico.php3.
77. See the Colombia Project of the Center for International Policy, available at www.ciponline.org/colombia/timeline.htm.

11

The Israeli-Palestinian peace process: The strategic art of deception

Magnus Ranstorp

For decades the Israeli-Palestinian conflict has appeared to be intractable and irreconcilable. The breakthrough of the 1993 Oslo peace process represented, at the time, a major landmark in transforming once-implacable enemies into "partners of peace". Oslo was designed as an incremental confidence-building process that would build trust among the parties so they would eventually tackle the really tough issues, such as the future of Jerusalem, the Israeli settlements, and the most thorny final-status issue of all, the return of the Palestinian refugees. The euphoria did not last long, as the Israeli-Palestinian peace process frayed under the strain of violence by extremists and a growing mistrust about the intentions of the other side. Towards the end of the 1990s the "spirit of Oslo" had visibly dissipated and the Israeli-Palestinian peace process began to collapse, degenerating into violence with the second Palestinian *intifada* and the reimposition of Israeli control over some of the territories under the jurisdiction of the nascent Palestinian Authority. The Mitchell Report concluded that "despite their long history and close proximity some Israelis and Palestinians seem not to fully appreciate each other's problems and concerns", as the Israelis failed to comprehend Palestinian "humiliation and frustration" over the continuing occupation and the Palestinians did not comprehend the extent to which terrorism "created fear amongst Israelis and undermined belief in the possibility of co-existence".[1] Among the greatest dangers of all, according to Senator Mitchell, was that futility, despair, and a growing resort to violence had replaced the culture of peace nurtured for almost a decade.

The reasons and factors behind the failure of the Oslo process have been intensely debated in public, in the policy-making domain, and in academic circles. The complexities of the conflict and the interlocking issues have produced different analyses depending on a multitude of analytical frames, vantage points, and interests. These have also greatly differed according to context, time period, and whether the primary focus remained on the process itself or the behaviour, positions, and interests of the actors involved. Academics have focused on everything from "ripeness" and "readiness" to conflict management theory to explain the success and failure of the Oslo negotiation process, and the role of extremist violence in sabotaging the process as well as the influence of divergent identity politics, cultural perceptions, and social beliefs constituting the ethos of conflict.[2] Equally relevant contributions have been made by the negotiators of the Oslo process itself and the subsequent efforts to resuscitate it through interim agreements and the 2000 Camp David talks.[3]

A myriad of interrelated reasons for the failure of these processes has been advanced by practitioners and insiders: the absence of an authoritative third party; the asymmetry of power and institutional relationships; reluctance by Palestinians to refrain from violence and by Israel to forgo settlement activity during the process; lack of accountability to address violations; absence of grassroots initiatives and people-to-people contact; lack of political and psychological preparedness on both sides to go the final distance; and the lack of a clear endgame.[4] All these explanations underscore the underlying complex interplay between context and process in this intractable communal conflict that pursued gradualism as the negotiation model. However, as Joshua Weiss observed, the slow-moving gradualism made the Israeli-Palestinian peace process susceptible to manipulation and procrastination by the parties, and vulnerable to outside spoilers disrupting the process and destroying any trust between the parties. It also created discord amongst the populace between expectations and the actual benefits and costs that peace agreements would yield in a relatively short period of time.[5] Jan Egeland, one of the architects of the Oslo back channel, echoed these factors when identifying his own lessons from Middle East conflict facilitation. These lessons included keeping the process in secret; questioning the parties' intentions, because some would try to make an impression that they want a negotiated solution but in reality would have little interest in peace; disagreements within the parties intensify when the agreement is close to being concluded; power imbalance and the ability of a stronger party to "tilt an agreement" might cause the mediator to become perceived as biased in the eyes of another party; the parties want to be treated equally; and when the solution does not constitute a victory but is based on a compromise, public opinion about the leaders inside their countries might fall even if they gain international support.[6]

Egeland's second lesson merits further exploration as a major underlying factor as to why the Israeli-Palestinian peace process failed and ultimately degenerated into violence. The issue of using peace processes as a subterranean form of manipulation – as a palliative with no strategic intention of genuine peacemaking – has been advanced in Oliver Richmond's framework of "devious objectives" harboured by spoilers. According to this framework, the mediation process itself is harnessed not as a means of compromise or attaining peace but as a manipulative instrument for the adversaries, which may include "time to regroup and reorganise; internationalisation; the search for an ally; empowerment; legitimisation of their negotiation positions and current status; face-saving; and avoiding costly concessions by prolonging the process itself".[7] Alongside Stephen Stedman's typology of "spoilers" to peace processes – that is "leaders and parties who believe that peace emerging from negotiations threatens their power, worldview, and interests, and use violence to undermine attempts to achieve it" – and the three strategies to manage spoilers through inducement, socialization, and coercion,[8] Richmond's framework of "devious objectives" convincingly explains the great distance between the Israelis and Palestinians in the peace process and their spoiling behaviour.

An underlying rationale for using the "devious objective" framework is the school of thought advanced by Amr G. E. Sabet, who argues that failure to address the justice principle in the Israeli-Palestinian peace process has simply led to asymmetric issue transformation, focusing on "the effects of injustice rather than its causes".[9] According to Sabet, Israel has pursued a cleverly crafted tactic of bringing

the Arabs into, step-by-step, practical settlements and interim agreements as a gradual incremental process of "interlocking" the rivals into positive arrangements which may make it difficult for them to revert to open conflict and war. These tactics were consistent with the overall strategy of detaching Egypt from the Arab-Israeli conflict; isolating Syria; and on the Palestinian front, pursuing a policy of cantonization in Gaza and the West Bank.[10]

The structural asymmetric imbalance meant that Israel could unilaterally alter the rules of the game and redefine the norms of the process "from land for peace (as agreed in the 1991 Madrid conference), to peace for peace or security for peace".[11] As a result, the process becomes an end in itself rather than the means it was supposed to be.

This same theme has been explored further by Ian S. Lustick, who argues that two kinds of peace policies were adopted by successive Israeli governments which either used "gradualism, dissimulation, and fact-creation to avoid facing the real issues between the two sides" or pretended "to negotiate seriously while actually seeking to destroy any prospect for substantive success toward a two-state solution, by using the negotiations to camouflage massive and pre-emptive settlement of the West Bank and Gaza or to discredit the process itself".[12] Other scholars have argued the same rationale behind Arafat's behaviour, using the peace process to amass personal power, to balance different factional power centres, as a means to internationalize the Palestinian cause to accrue European financial aid, and to resist the conclusion of a final-status deal to ensure his place in the history of resistance. As forcefully argued by Malley and Agha, any unity between the Israeli and Palestinian leadership can be found in that "both are sure time is on their side. Both believe that they have more to lose by desperately seeking to end the chaos than by simply withstanding it. And both are convinced that the other feels absolutely and precisely the same way."[13]

Deciphering the contours and degree of "deviousness" in the negotiation process by both the Israelis and the Palestinians is compounded by the differing social orders and underlying values. As argued by Shaul Mishal and Nadav Morag, both sides entered the process and its functions with different political expectations and cultural perceptions that in turn reflect the logic of the strategies adopted by either party. Whereas Israel is influenced by a hierarchical "goal-oriented and process-oriented" political culture, the Palestinians are a networked society where the social order is "characterised by on-going conflicts, negotiations, and changing balances of power between various groups anxious to increase their influence, defend their honour and strengthen internal cohesion".[14] For a "high-context" society, the notions of rights and justice are primary driving forces underlying the Palestinian position.

Symptomatic of the mistrust and lack of understanding by each side of the other party's psychological and political needs is the societal ethos of conflict that provides the epistemic rationale for continuing violence. These societal beliefs have evolved in this intractable conflict and centre primarily on "the justness of the conflict, de-legitimization and victimization".[15] In many ways, the content of these labels and justifications are a mirror image of each other. These "narratives" are baseline positions, widely reflected across the respective societies. They also widely fuel the continuation of conflict and profoundly influence the strategies and spoiling behaviour adopted in the negotiations.

This chapter examines the role and influence of competing cultural and societal narratives within the context of the Israeli-Palestinian conflict that provide the strategic rationale for "devious objectives" and more tactical spoiling behaviour. It then proceeds to unpack the modalities of spoiling behaviour adopted by each side in respect to the process of negotiations.

Competing cultural narratives of the other

A number of challenges since 1967 in making peace between Israelis and Palestinians have meant navigating a course through a literal minefield of shared history, contested territory and sacred space, demographic reality, competing visions of nationalism, asymmetries in resources, and individual and shared collective memory. These competing influences have shaped the conflict environment to varying degrees and at various times. The sheer complexity of resolving the Arab-Israeli conflict lies in having so many interlocking positions and dimensions, coupled with layers of interests within each society and third-party intermediaries as well as perception and misperception. This is compounded by a shared historical narrative of victimization, dispossession, and suffering on both sides that feed into each other. Moving beyond a competing narrative rooted in fear and insecurity will require each side to recognize and "legitimize" the other side's fears as well as its own.[16] The asymmetric nature of the conflict with Israel, the militarily superior partner, has reduced the very essence of the conflict to control – over security, the economy, and the movement of people. For the Israelis peace essentially means security, while for the Palestinians it revolves around addressing the justice element and the restoration of legitimate rights. This asymmetry in capabilities and disjuncture in expectations between the parties has meant in practice that the conflict dynamic provides naturally for cascading domino effects and gives the spoilers on any side a rich opportunity to influence events and even drive the politics of peace and the levers of conflict, fear, and insecurity. In many ways the Israeli-Palestinian conflict is profoundly influenced by the empowerment of the extremes and the perceived sanctity of "resistance".

The modalities of the secret Oslo process itself were deliberately designed to minimize antagonism between adversaries, gradually breaking down existing barriers and deconstructing stereotypes while creating a minimal sense of trust and confidence before the commencement of actual talks and negotiations. This "spirit" of Oslo underpinned the peace process itself, but imploded from within as the peace process floundered successively over the years, exposing severe rifts within each camp and between the adversaries. The outbreak of the second *intifada* represented a major setback to the Palestinian-Israeli peace process, rupturing whatever fragile measure of confidence and trust had been built between the two parties since Oslo. In many ways the cycle of violent clashes between the Israelis and Palestinians dramatically re-exposed the underlying fear and suspicions about the true character of the enemy and their strategic "devious objectives". These interlocking and underlying cultural narratives about what these devious objectives entailed for the enemy seemed to be reinforced by the desire of both sides to create irreversible "facts on the ground", whether through the Israeli policy of expansion of settlements, carving up the West Bank with bypass roads, and unilateral separation through a security fence, or conversely the Palestinian strategy of using terrorism as a political tool while it sought to buy more time in an ultimate bid to use the demographic weapon to implode the Jewish state from within. The underlying cultural narratives or "myths" about the devious nature of the adversary were catapulted from the background to centre stage, and served to shape the politics of the moment and even strategically of the future – with or without the resumption of a peace process.

The Israeli perspective

Following the failure of the Camp David process in the summer of 2000 and the outbreak of the Al-Aqsa *intifada*, Israel lost all trust in the Palestinian leadership and in Arafat personally. For the Israelis, the breakdown of the Camp David talks was "an indictment of Arafat, the Israeli left and the entire Palestinian people",[17] as Barak had made unprecedented concessions, accepting a redivision of Jerusalem, shared power in the Old City, and Israeli withdrawal from more than 90 per cent of the occupied territories.[18] For Israelis, Arafat's obstinacy was seen as evidence that real, historic, ideological compromise was never really part of the Palestinian leadership's agenda.[19] This was compounded by the fact that Arafat had allegedly failed to make any counter-proposals, and moreover the Palestinians had reneged on their commitment against using violence. For Israelis, these events reinforced the perception that peace was unattainable as it lacked a viable and trustworthy partner with whom a negotiated resolution could be concluded. As a result, there was almost unanimous agreement within Israel that Arafat "cannot be a partner to peace talks and conflict resolution".[20] This perception was shaped by a number of interlocking myths about Arafat as a leader and the perceived strategy of the Palestinians.

From an Israeli perspective, a major problem revolved around the patriarchal nature of leadership within Palestinian society, epitomized by Yasser Arafat as essentially a "revolutionary" tribal leader pursuing an autocratic and constantly shifting policy of divide and rule among his cronies. Towards these ends he had allowed corruption and clientelism to flourish and managed to create overlapping bureaucracies and security agencies to prevent subordinates from challenging his power.[21] Endemic rivalry between the Preventative Security Forces heads in the West Bank and Gaza is indicative of the policy pursued by Arafat in omni-balancing various political centres of gravity among the most powerful PA officials. Israeli critics also argue that he turned a blind eye to terrorism during the Oslo peace process, and some charge that he was tacitly complicit in giving a "green light" to some terrorists to maintain his own political legitimacy among his people and avoid being seen as a security instrument of Israel. In this respect, Israeli critics have charged him with using terrorism instrumentally to sabotage advancement in peace negotiations or as a means to restart them at a different position.

A second perception held among Israeli leaders was of the true character of Arafat – the man himself. According to most Israeli leaders, Yasser Arafat perceived himself to be a "modern Saladin (the Kurdish Muslim general who defeated the Crusaders in the 12th century) [who] views a peace agreement with Israel as a modern version of a temporary truce of Hudaibiya that the prophet Mohammad concluded in 628–629, only to then violate".[22] This temporary truce or *hudna* has been employed by Hamas as a tactical tool to replenish its own strength before returning with increased levels of violence. In essence Barak argued that the cunning and wily nature of Arafat and the deceptiveness of "Arab culture" prevented an agreement at Camp David in the summer of 2000. "It is because of the character of the Arab discourse that their culture does not contain the concept of compromise. Compromise is apparently a Western concept of settling disputes."[23] As such, many Israelis believe that the only language Arafat and Arabs truly understand and respect is brutal force and deterrence. Any perceived weakness in the Israeli security posture would be exploited with further Palestinian campaigns of violence, as shown by the perceived correlation between Israel's withdrawal from south Lebanon in May 2000 and the subsequent outbreak of the Al-Aqsa *intifada*.

A third belief among Israelis is that "Palestinians are opposed to peaceful coexistence with Israel either because they are ideologically and religiously determined to destroy the Jewish state or because they are embedded in a culture of violence that makes peaceful coexistence impossible".[24] Polls within Israel in 2002 indicated that 68 per cent of the population surveyed believed that Arabs wanted to kill much of the Jewish population in Israel and thought their goal was to conquer Israel.[25] Israelis have pointed with concern to the strengthening of the Islamist movement Hamas within the grassroots of Palestinian civil society, whose charter advocates the annihilation of the Jewish state and the establishment of an Islamic Palestinian state stretching from the Mediterranean to the Jordan River. Other Israelis point to the continued anti-

Semitism and incitement in the Palestinian media and in Palestinian textbooks, which contain no map of Israel or demarcation of Israel's borders. In this Israeli strategic view "the Palestinians are still clinging to the 'phased theory' as a practical plan" – that is, the strategy of destroying Israel in stages.[26] This "phased theory" rests on the assumption that Palestinians are deceptively seeking to establish a Palestinian state without closing the door for further "legitimate" demands down the road. Accordingly, the "phased theory" seeks to turn Israel into a "state for all its citizens", with the Palestinians pushing for a binational state.[27] A combination of demography and attrition would eventually lead to a state with a Muslim majority and a Jewish minority, and would mean the destruction of Israel as a Jewish state. Towards these ends, Israelis believe that Arafat surreptitiously viewed the Palestinian refugees of 1948 and their descendants, numbering close to 4 million, as the main demographic and political tool for subverting the Jewish character of the state and its democratic nature.

A related fourth issue for Israelis is the acute threat of demography from within the occupied territories, as the Palestinians already comprise a majority among all inhabitants and many are under the age of 14. The relative youthfulness of Palestinian society lends itself naturally to a culture of revolution, violence, instability, and political activism. The burgeoning birthrate of Palestinians, with an average of 6.4 children per family, means that the population is expected to triple in the next 20 years. By 2025 it is estimated that there will be 4.4 million Palestinians in the West Bank and 2.9 million in Gaza.[28] Simultaneously, Israel is facing another threat on the demographic front from within, in the form of higher birthrates among Israeli Arabs and ultra-Orthodox Jews, the latter exempt from taxation and military service.[29] These ultra-Orthodox Jews are largely responsible for settlement in the lands they consider Eretz Israel, or Greater Israel. As Toft has argued, "over time this process of high reproduction and abstention from military service may threaten Israel's survival from within".[30] Given Palestinian birthrates, many Israelis feel that the Palestinians will never be acceptable as neighbours within a sovereign state and would constitute a threat to Israel's security over the long run. Some have advocated that Israel would eventually be forced either to engineer an apartheid system or force the mass migration of Palestinians to neighbouring Arab states under some security pretext.

These interlocking "myths" about Palestinian devious objectives and demographic realities have forced the Israelis to consider strategies incorporating various forms of unilateral disengagement from the Palestinians. These strategies centre on regrouping Israelis behind lines that would require the inclusion of a minimum number of Palestinians. This concept, making its entry into Israeli public discourse in the summer of 2001, is widely supported by over 60 per cent of Israelis in recent surveys.[31] The unilateral and rapid erection of the security fence is based on the underlying rationale that a controllable and near hermetically sealed frontier zone will curb Palestinian suicide attacks and bring greater security to Israel. However, as argued by Dani Rabinowitch, the "economic interdependence between Israeli employers and Palestinian labourers is likely to ensure that the border, however well-buttressed, will in the long run be as porous as it has been since 1967".[32] From a spoiler perspective, the motivations of Palestinians are unlikely to be influenced or deterred by a separation fence or barrier, and militants are likely to redirect their energy towards attacking the settlements and the routes leading to them. In the event of a resumption of final-status negotiations, the separation fence becomes inherently a potential negotiable asset for the future.

The Palestinian perspective

In this asymmetric conflict and power imbalance, the Palestinians hold on to their own "myths" and are distrustful about Israel's genuine commitment towards concluding a lasting and just peace. In principle, on the strategic level, the Palestinians fear that Israel is gradually seeking to destroy the Palestinian Authority and carve the occupied territories up into smaller non-aligned territories where they could strike deals with more pliable local leaders. For most Palestinians, whether Likud or Labour is in power, it is essentially two faces to the same coin in terms of their dealings with Israeli political leaders. In the eyes of most Israelis, until his death the next step had been to overthrow Arafat, the symbol of Palestinian unity and resistance. The result would be throwing Palestinian territory into civil war in the short term, but it would be easier to manipulate and impose a peace on terms more favourable to Israel through the cajoling of the next generation of leaders. In the end, Arafat's passing diffused this situation.

A second Palestinian preconception about Israel is that it uses the issues of terrorism and security as a convenient pretext to punish and subdue all elements of Palestinian society and bring them forcibly to their knees at the negotiation table. Under the pretext of being victims of terrorism, Israeli retaliation is carefully framed as part of Israel's right to defend its people and is designed to divert attention away from its daily occupation policies. As such, Israel manufactures multiple "crises" to provide a convenient pretext for not implementing agreements but also sometimes to restart negotiations.

A third Palestinian belief is that military attacks in combination with less dramatic policies (such as house demolitions, land expropriation, permanent closure and prolonged curfews, restrictions on freedom of movement, induced impoverishment, and economic warfare of various kinds alongside "bureaucratic" controls) are all designed as an overall Israeli strategic campaign to wear down Palestinian resistance over time. This campaign is also deliberately designed to weaken the fabric of Palestinian society and its ability to withstand military occupation. Towards these ends Israel maintains a complex web of bureaucracy to institutionalize the occupation, which it skilfully manipulates to create irreversible facts on the ground over time.

A fourth area of Palestinian concern is this perceived Israeli policy of systematically creating irreversible "facts" on the ground – extending a comprehensive security matrix over most of the occupied territories. Apart from 400,000 settlers living in some 200 settlements across the West Bank and (until recently) Gaza, the Israeli construction of 450 kilometres of highways and roads – so-called bypass roads – linking settlements on the West Bank creates a massive barrier for Palestinian movement and a *de facto* independent state. This security matrix involves the expansion of settlements in Israel's policy of the "Judaization" of Jerusalem (Old and New), discriminatory measures to control Palestinians' residency rights and house demolitions, and the encirclement of Jerusalem through settlements. This Greater Jerusalem concept, according to Palestinians, would isolate Arab east Jerusalem and divide the West Bank into half, stretching from Ramallah in the north to Hebron in the south and from Jericho in the east to Bet Shemesh in the west, covering almost 30 per cent of the West Bank. This of course excludes the control over the sacred space of the Dome of the Rock and the Al-Aqsa mosque, Islam's third-holiest place. Israel's past policies towards Gaza, with 6,100 settlers, were designed to maintain an instrument of security control in Palestinian affairs whilst settlements provided infinite cheap labour. The Israeli departure from Gaza diverted attention away from its continued consolidation of positions within the West Bank, attempting to deflate any future criticisms rather than reflecting further possibilities of similar moves in the West Bank.

A final Palestinian perception is that Israel will continue to resist and renounce the right of return of the 3.7 million Palestinian refugees in adjacent Arab territory. In effect the Palestinian leadership expect no fundamental shift on this issue, as they believe Israel will not allow significant numbers to return because that would shift its demographic balance. As eloquently summed up by Sam Husseini, "It appears the Palestinians have been offered a 'Jerusalem' that is not Jerusalem; the right of return for only a nominal number of the Palestinian refugees; a 'state' without control over water, borders or real sovereignty; 'territory' that is not contiguous; and symbols of nationhood that would become more signs of shame than of pride for an injured people."[33] The last point poignantly underscores the essence of making peace with "dignity", a critical ingredient within Arab society. It also highlights the legitimacy of making peace without justice.

These competing cultural narratives about the struggle and myths about the enemy from both Israeli and Palestinian perspectives interact on multiple levels and are part and parcel of daily societal discourse and used in shaping the "red lines" over policy on war and peace. In essence, they provide the strategic justification of spoiler behaviour at different places and times and to varying degrees. At the same time, it is critical to recognize the inherently different underlying concepts of time and space in this epic struggle spanning several generations. Partially this is due to the recurrent contested history and religious aspects that have served to define them over the last two millenniums. Partially it also revolves around the necessity to wait for "ripeness" over several generations, specifically in the Palestinian case in alleviating expectations over time of the prospects of a right of return of refugees. As such, Arafat predicted that "only '80 years' after 1948 will the Palestinians be historically ready for a compromise".[34] All these dimensions serve critically to define the strategic dimensions of spoiler behaviour.

Spoiling the process itself: The Oslo peace process and beyond

The asymmetric nature of the Israeli-Palestinian conflict and the structure of the peace process itself have made it ripe for spoiling behaviour. The incremental nature of the Oslo peace process, intending to build trust between the two parties through a step-by-step process of measures and by deferring the final-status issues, was exploited by both sides who "used their respective assets (territory, in the case of Israel, and the threat of violence, in the case of Palestinians)"[35] as the ultimate "bargaining chips to be deployed in the endgame".[36] The Oslo process itself had in place few effective enforcement mechanisms and yielded a succession of partial agreements to implement "previous unimplemented interim agreements".[37] As such, the Likud Prime Minister Binyamin Netanyahu began a reorientation programme in relation to the peace process, progressively altering "land for peace" to "peace with security", and decided to freeze the implementation of Israeli redeployment in West Bank territory until Arafat showed he was willing to rein in militant Palestinian terrorists. As forcefully argued by Lustick, most successive Israeli governments have pretended to negotiate seriously while they used the negotiations to "camouflage massive and pre-emptive settlement of the West Bank and Gaza or to discredit the process itself".[38]

Arafat, on the other hand, camouflaged his unwillingness to clamp down on militants through a "revolving-door" policy of arresting and releasing Hamas and Palestinian Islamic Jihad activists, both as a means to ensure his own legitimacy among his people and to use these militants in a subterranean fashion to activate and exert pressure on the Israelis. For Arafat, the interim agreements became a vehicle to bolster his own position in the negotiations rather than a road-map towards their implementation. In this sense Arafat used violence at select moments to reverse the Israeli-Palestinian negotiation balance and to improve his own future bargaining position. Apart from being designed to wear down the Israeli government and public by human casualties and economic costs, Arafat's "logic of violence" was designed to "internationalize" the conflict in an effort to produce sympathy and material support, and raise the possibility of an international presence on the ground as a means to squeeze Israel for major concessions.

A second structural problem with the Oslo process pertained to the presentation of the 1993 agreement as a *fait accompli* to the Israeli and Palestinian publics respectively. The very secretive nature of the negotiations initially bypassed political opponents, but once public the Oslo agreement exposed deep and sharp divisions within each society, leaving them susceptible to pressures and sabotage from extreme elements. The whole process of negotiations between élite leaders on both sides represented a failure of acknowledging the "ripeness" of the conflict situation and the need for a bottom-up transformation, as neither side prepared the ground for broad domestic approval within their respective publics of the necessary far-reaching concessions that would have to be made for a sustainable peace agreement.[39] This in turn fatally affected the legitimacy and viability of the policy of dismantling the terrorist infrastructure in return for dismantling the settlements. Simultaneously, suspicious prevailed on both sides as to the strategic intentions of the adversary and the prospects for a final peace settlement. It was compounded by publicly demonizing rhetoric across the divide by both leaderships and publics. In the words of Malley and Agha, "even assuming the best of intentions, concessions carry well-known costs and ill-defined gains".[40] This failure to prepare the ground extended to subsequent efforts to rescue the peace process. Even Yossi Beilin, one of the principal architects of Oslo, acknowledged that the 2000 Camp David talks collapsed not "because the two sides were far apart, but because they were too close together. That meant both sides realised that if an accord had been reached, they would have had to return to their constituents and admit that they had been promoting fiction."[41] From the Palestinian perspective, everyone knows deep down "that the right of return is deeply embedded in the Palestinian soul and can never be given up, that no leader can sign an agreement on their behalf which would settle it with a cheque instead".[42]

Another major obstacle to the success of the Oslo process was the asymmetry between the Israelis and the Palestinians in their obligations and the lack of mechanisms or even incentive for compliance or disincentive for any violations. In other words, a "major problem was a 'lack of accountability', with nowhere for the parties to turn if the other side violated the agreement".[43] Both sides committed frequent and numerous breaches to fortify their own bargaining positions without any perceived urgency or even need for accountability. Settlers, at times receiving tacit backing from the Israeli government and the Israeli Defence Forces (IDF), made every possible effort to undermine and spoil the Oslo process. At the same time, Israel insisted on the paramount nature of security above all else, and placed obstacles in the way of the implementation of agreements by avoiding further interim redeployments, opening safe passages between the territories, refusing to release prisoners, and imposing severe barriers for Palestinian development.[44]

Adding fuel to the fire through targeted assassinations, Israel imposed a semi-permanent policy of strict closures of Gaza and West Bank communities in place since the mid-1990s and imposed economic isolation on the Palestinian territories, either punitively in response to suicide bombings or as a means of attrition in wearing down collective will. This semi-permanent economic separation rather than integration imposed by Israeli closures hit the Palestinian community and economy hard both before and after the outbreak of the Al-Aqsa *intifada*.[45] These repeated closures led to a sharp rise in unemployment, combined with a fiscal crisis due to the withholding of taxes collected by Israel on behalf of the Palestinian Authority. The situation deteriorated sharply following the outbreak of the Al-Aqsa *intifada*: the World Bank reported that 60 per cent of the population lived below the poverty line and more than 50 per cent of the workforce faced unemployment.[46] Although some Israeli observers make the argument that the scale and intensity of Palestinian violence necessitated the closure policy as a response to suicide bombings, others argued that they "were instead employed as a psychological device aimed at the Israeli public, proof that 'something' was being done against the Palestinians".[47] It could also be argued that a secondary tactic behind the closures by Israel was its intention to promote Hamas as a counterweight to the influence of the Palestinian Authority, dividing the Palestinians against each other. In fact, each closure strengthened the social welfare role of Hamas, enhancing its stature and legitimacy as the effective provider among ordinary Palestinians while underscoring the corruption of Palestinian Authority officials. At the same time, Israeli officials demanded the total dismantling of Hamas and other terrorist group infrastructure as a precondition for any resumption of negotiations, placing Arafat between a rock and a hard place in terms of legitimacy among his own population whilst Israel moved to discredit him internationally and impose strict travel restrictions.

The Palestinian Authority, for its part, failed to collect small arms and light weapons of any militants as directed by Oslo. Instead, the intelligence services expanded in number, exceeding their stipulated size, while some of their members were found collaborating closely with Islamic militants and smuggling weapons in the same underground tunnels between Sinai and Rafiah in the Gaza Strip.[48] Similarly, Arafat and the Palestinian Authority failed to suppress the Islamist opposition seriously, preferring a deliberate policy of cooption rather than outright confrontation. This policy was indicative of the nebulous "grey area" of membership of militant factions cutting through cross-sections of Palestinian society both horizontally and vertically, even within the Palestinian Authority. Moreover, the policy of cooption over confrontation rested partially on the desire to integrate the militant Islamic movements into any political framework in order to control them and ultimately "lock" them into any commitment to any peace endeavours, and also on the overall utility of publicly divorcing dissident elements as a devious playing card in stalling peace negotiations. On the one hand, Hamas has represented a serious challenge to the authority of Arafat and the Palestinian Authority, as illustrated by the concerted pressure placed on the Hamas infrastructure. However, on the other hand Hamas has consistently argued that *fitna*, internal strife, between Hamas and the Palestinian Authority would only benefit Israel's strategic interest in dividing the factions within Palestinian society against each other. As a consequence, Hamas has frequently floated the proposition of a cease-fire as a tactical tool to engineer room for manoeuvre to replenish lost resources and personnel following Israeli arrests and targeted assassinations. These cease-fire proposals are also useful in providing the Palestinian Authority with an asset to use as a stalling tactic in peace negotiations and as a tool to place distance between itself and the extremist elements to test Israeli intentions. On another level, the Palestinian Authority has pressured Hamas to commit itself to a temporary, undeclared cease-fire in order to deny Israel any excuse for delaying the implementation of interim agreements. Sheikh Yassin, the spiritual leader of Hamas until his assassination, had apparently offered Israel a conditional cease-fire of 10 years subject to an Israeli withdrawal to the 1967 borders and various other "concessions".[49] Whether these reports were a deceitful veneer to buy time or contained genuine substance, Israel pursued a policy of targeted assassination of political leaders of Hamas in 2003, breaking previous "red lines" of engagement and effectively sabotaging efforts to resuscitate peace negotiations. Israeli officials have argued that this new targeting policy effectively prompted the movement to announce a temporary cease-fire.

Hamas has skilfully avoided what it regards as a negotiation "trap": it deliberately refrained from participating in the nascent Palestinian political structures since this would have *de facto* meant a contravention of its ideological principals through a tacit acknowledgement of the Oslo process and by extension recognition of Israel's right to exist. Instead Hamas's principal strength lies in the fact that confrontation is central to its activities in a mutually reinforcing way between its social, military, and political activities. As such, Hamas benefits in all its strands of activity from suicide bombings, as the Israeli military and security response bolsters its legitimacy as a resistance movement. Punitive closures reinforce its ability to fill the social vacuum and redress economic hardship, and it strengthens its political legitimacy in fulfilling the joint desire for revenge while remaining steadfast in not selling out the Palestinian cause. As such, Hamas skilfully benefits immensely from the violent cycles of "structural violence" and its ability to "confront".[50] Admittedly the driving force behind Hamas violence is dependent on a matrix of factors, including differing degrees of revenge, religious zeal, opportunity, and timing to maximize spoiling of the peace process and negotiations. As highlighted by Kydd and Walter, Hamas violence followed distinct patterns between 1993 and 2001, and the success of the spoiling efforts was dependent on "when mistrust was high, when the [Israeli] public and government are more hard line, and when the moderate opposition [Palestinian leadership] seems capable of preventing terrorist violence but fails to do so".[51]

Other academic experts have convincingly argued that Hamas is a limited spoiler, rather than a total spoiler as depicted by Israel, with pragmatic decision-making and a demonstrated willingness potentially to participate in the political structures. Employing Stedman's framework of spoilers, Jeroen Gunning convincingly argues that Hamas is a legitimate and multifaceted movement that may *ultimately* consider a compromise on the existence of Israel as its support derives primarily from its internal domestic reputation and not solely from its opposition against Israel.[52] He recognizes, though, that this contingency rests on a substantive change in Israel's policy on the issue of right of return for refugees, as well as an Israeli return to the 1967 borders and dismantling of settlements. Furthermore, the centrality of the refugee issue, as the single most contentious and critical issue for all Palestinians, is a critical ingredient in both Hamas's and Arafat's efforts to use violence as a pressure mechanism to sabotage rapid moves towards final-status agreement. As such, both Hamas and Arafat can be seen as cooperative spoilers within a unified strategic devious objective – to continue the sanctity of the resistance as a means of attrition against Israel to avoid locking them into a final agreement. Another decisive element in relation to the sacred issue of "right of return" is the Palestinian constituency on the outside, the refugee contingents themselves and the more radical Palestinian rejectionist factions, seeking sanctuary in Damascus and within Lebanon. This outside constellation of Palestinian militant groups have collectively rejected any accommodation with internal moderate Palestinian overtures towards Israel, focusing on forging a close-knit alliance and logistical relationship with Lebanese Hizballah in efforts to confront Israel violently from its northern border and from within. The outside refugees and their future play a decisive role in determining "red lines" as to how far the inside Palestinian leadership can sacrifice issues at the negotiation table with the Israelis.

Conversely, on the Israeli spectrum, the spoiling efforts by extreme Israeli right-wing elements have had seismic effects on the Oslo process, most notably with Yigal Amir's assassination of Prime Minister Yitzhak Rabin in November 1995, an incident motivated by both religious conviction and a desire to block any transfer of the West Bank to the Palestinians.[53] The assassination of the Israeli prime minister had been preceded by Dr Baruch Goldstein, a physician from the settlement of Kiryat Arba, outside Hebron, gunning down 29 Palestinians at morning prayer in the Cave of the Patriarchs on 25 February 1994.[54] This event catapulted Hamas into launching retaliatory suicide bombings against Israel. Although the Jewish extremists are relatively disorganized as a force within the ultra-Orthodox and settlement *milieux*, their violent actions have had a profound and critical impact on the Israeli-Palestinian peace process at select moments. Most Jewish extremist activities are usually confined to revenge attacks on Palestinian residents or individual assassinations that are primarily motivated by personal reasons rather than a grander desire to derail a peace process. These smaller pockets of Jewish extremism are embedded within the Israeli settlements and within ultra-Orthodox circles. It is worthwhile to note that despite their size these Jewish extremists have continuously inflamed Israeli-Palestinian relations for a long time, specifically beginning with the effort by a Jewish militant to burn down the Al-Aqsa mosque in 1969.[55] This was followed by a series of efforts to attack or blow up the Temple Mount, sparking an apocalyptic war between Israel and the entire Muslim nation; the most serious foiled attempt occurred in 1984.

Beyond the Goldstein and Amir attacks, the Jewish extremists have primarily focused on vocally protesting any Israeli withdrawal from the West Bank and Gaza while harassing Palestinians and at times killing them, usually in revenge.[56] Naturally, these Jewish extremists have the ability to mobilize wider support from the hundreds of thousands of settlers residing in the West Bank and Gaza in protesting against official Israeli efforts to dismantle settlements.[57] These Jewish extremist elements have a dangerous capability not only periodically seriously to derail the peace process but also to descend Israel into war with the Palestinians or its Arab neighbours in the event that a major attack on a Muslim holy site succeeds. Their militancy increases in proportion to efforts to dismantle settlements, as evidenced by security precautions taken to protect Israeli Prime Minister Ariel Sharon against assassination by Jewish extremists in relation to proposals to withdraw unilaterally from Gaza in 2004–2005.[58] Any signs or real moves towards official Israeli reconciliation with Palestinians in trading land for peace dramatically increase the spoiler effect by the Jewish extremists. As such the peace process is hostage to the empowerment of the extremes on both Israeli and Palestinian sides.

Conclusion

Most academic analysis trying to unpack the labyrinthine complexity of the Israeli-Palestinian peace process focuses understandably on modalities of why the negotiation process failed. This peace process is rich in analytical nuances, both theoretically and from an empirical perspective, extending to the analytical frames and perspectives of the negotiators themselves. These academic exercises are valuable *per se* but largely ignore the question of whether the disputants harbour so-called "devious objectives" for their individual reasons to engage in the peace process which may explain a range of spoiler behaviour more tactically. This chapter has provided an "alternative" road-map for viewing the enduring conflict between the Israelis and the Palestinians and the difficult, complex, and interlocking dimensions driving the behaviour of a spectrum of actors involved on the ground. It raises many interesting questions as to the uniqueness of the conflict itself and the prospects for achieving lasting and just peace in this enduring and protracted communal conflict.

From the preceding analysis it emerges clearly that the role of culture and competing narrative "myths" drive the underlying conflict dynamics between the parties. These mirror images of the other are widely reflected within respective communities across the divide, and fundamentally shape and drive the Machiavellian strategic behaviour of both the Israelis and the Palestinians. In this sense, understanding the cultural aspects and dynamics of conflict and negotiation becomes imperative and raises the question as to the viability of Western-imposed peace processes, especially as competing cultural traits are deeply embedded within social interactions on both sides. Moreover, it raises the issue of the effectiveness of third-party intervention that does not take into account these culturalist factors.

Many spoilers exist across the Israeli-Palestinian conflict spectrum with varying degrees of ability to shape, redirect, and sabotage the peace processes. The modalities of this spoiling behaviour can blind analysts as to the larger strategic canvas of conflict behaviour. The asymmetry of power is a driving force behind why the disputants adopt "devious objectives" in relation to how far to impose or resist the peace process itself. Both sides believe inherently in the justness of their cause and that the rhythm of time is on their side. In this respect, the Israeli-Palestinian peace process can be reduced to the ultimate strategic art of deception.

Notes

1. Sharm el-Sheikh Fact-Finding Committee. 2001. *Report (the Mitchell Report)*, 20 May. Washington, DC: US State Department.
2. For example, see Pruitt, Dean. 1997. "Ripeness theory and the Oslo talks", *International Negotiation*, Vol. 2, No. 2; Zartman, I. W. 1997. "Explaining Oslo", *International Negotiation*, Vol. 2, No. 2; Berkovitch, J. 1997. "Conflict management and the Oslo experience: Assessing the success of Israeli-Palestinian peacemaking", *International Negotiation*, Vol. 2, No. 2; Zartman, I. W. 2001. "The timing of peace initiatives: Hurting stalemates and ripe moments", *Global Review of Ethnopolitics*, Vol. 1, No. 1; Sabet, Amr G. E. 2000. "Peace negotiations and the dynamics of the Arab-Israeli conflict", *Peace and Conflict Studies*, Vol. 7, No. 1; Oren, Neta, Daniel Bar-Tal, and Ohad David. 2004. "Conflict, identity, and ethos: The Israeli-Palestinian case", in Y.-T. Lee, C. R. McCauley, F. M. Moghaddam, and S. Worchel (eds) *Psychology of Ethnic and Cultural Conflict*. Westport, CT: Greenwood; Kydd, Andrew and Barbara F. Walter. 2002. "Sabotaging the peace: The politics of extremist violence", *International Organization*, Vol. 56, No. 2; Mishal, Shaul and Navad Morag. 2002. "Political expectations and cultural perceptions in the Arab-Israeli peace negotiations", *Political Psychology*, Vol. 23, No. 2.
3. Savir, Uri. 1998. *The Process: 1,100 Days That Changed the Middle East*. New York: Random House; Peres, Shimon. 1995. *Battling for Peace*. New York: Random House; Aburish, Said K. 1999. *Arafat: From Defender to Dictator*. New York: St Martin's Press; Sayigh, Yezid. 1999. *Armed Struggle and the Search for a State: Palestinian National Movement, 1949–1993*. Oxford: Oxford University Press; Corbin, Jane. 1994. *Gaza First: Norway Channel to Peace Between Israel and PLO*. London: Bloomsbury; Ross, Dennis. 2004. *The Missing Peace*. New York: St Martin's Press; Morris, Benny. 2002. "Camp David and after: An interview with Ehud Barak", *New York Review of Books*, 13 June; Malley, Robert and Hussein Agha. 2001. "Camp David: The tragedy of errors", *New York Review of Books*, 9 August.
4. See Sommer, Alison Kaplan. 2001. "US ambassador: Oslo failed due to lack of US involvement", *Jerusalem Post*, 7 December.
5. Weiss, Joshua N. 2003. "Trajectories toward peace: Mediator sequencing strategies in intractable communal conflicts", *Negotiation Journal*, Vol. 19, No. 2.
6. *Negotiation Newsletter*. 1995. "Norway's back-channel success story," *Negotiation Newsletter*, Spring Summer.
7. Richmond, Oliver. 1998. "Devious objectives and the disputants' view of international mediation: A theoretical framework", *Journal of Peace Research*, Vol. 35, No. 6.

8. Stedman, Stephen. 1997. "Spoiler problems in peace processes", *International Security*, Vol. 22, No. 2.
9. Sabet, note 2 above.
10. *Ibid.*
11. *Ibid.*
12. Lustick, Ian. S. 2002. "Through blood and fire shall peace arise", *Tikkun*, May/June.
13. Malley, Robert and Hussein Agha. 2003. "A durable Middle East peace: Oslo didn't achieve it, nor has the Bush 'road map'. So what would satisfy both sides?", *American Prospect*, November.
14. Mishal and Morag, note 2 above.
15. Oren, Bar-Tal, and David, note 2 above.
16. West, Deborah. 2003. "Myth and narrative in the Israeli-Palestinian conflict", *WPF Reports*, No. 34.
17. Mufson, Steven. 2002. "Camp David: Whose story is it anyway?", *Washington Post*, 22 July.
18. *Ibid.*
19. Shoval, Zalman. 2003. "Separation and security: Can Israel's separation barrier help stop the violence", paper presented at the US Institute of Peace, 22 October.
20. Kam, Ephraim and Yiftah Shapir (eds). 2003. *The Middle East Strategic Balance 2002–2003*. Tel Aviv: Jaffee Center for Strategic Studies, p. 33.
21. Martin, Lenore. 2002. "Arafat's dueling dilemmas: Succession and the peace process", *Middle East Review of International Affairs*, Vol. 6, No. 1.
22. Carmel, Amos. 2003. "Arafat's remote control", *The New Leader*, July.
23. Slater, Jerome. 2001. "What went wrong? The collapse of the Israeli-Palestinian peace process", *Political Science Quarterly*, Vol. 116, No. 2.
24. Feldman, Shai. 2002. "Managing the conflict with the Palestinians: Israel's strategic options", *Strategic Assessment*, Vol. 5, No. 2.
25. Arian, Asher. 2002. *Israeli Public Opinion on National Security 2002*. Tel Aviv: Jaffee Center for Strategic Studies.
26. *Ha'aretz*, 2 February 2001.
27. *Ibid.*
28. Toft, Monica Duffy. 2002. "Differential demographic growth in multinational states: Israel's two-front war", *Journal of International Affairs*, Vol. 56, No. 1.
29. Soffer, Arnon. 2001. *Israel, Demography 2000–2020: Dangers and Opportunities*. Haifa: National Security Studies Center.
30. Toft, note 28 above.
31. Feldman, note 24 above.
32. Rabinowitch, Dani. 2001. "Borderline collective consciousness: Israeli identity, 'Arabness' and the Green Line", *Palestine-Israel Journal*, Vol. 8, No. 4.
33. Husseini, Sam. 2000. "No less than equal partners", *Washington Post*, 27 July.
34. Morris, Benny. 2002. "Inside story: Arafat didn't negotiate – He just kept saying no", *The Guardian*, 23 May.
35. Malley and Agha, note 13 above.
36. *Ibid.*
37. *Ibid.*
38. Lustick, note 12 above.
39. Soetendorp, Ben. 2002. "Choosing stalemate: The interaction between domestic politics and Israeli-Palestinian bargaining", paper presented at Forty-third Annual Meeting of the International Studies Association, New Orleans, 24–27 March.
40. Malley and Agha, note 3 above.
41. Mufson, note 17 above.

42. Grant, Linda. 2004. "A Tel Aviv tragedy", *The Guardian*, 8 April.
43. Sommer, note 4 above.
44. Pundak, Ron. 2001. "From Oslo to Taba: What went wrong", *Survival*, Vol. 43, No. 3.
45. Roy, Sara. 2002. "Ending the Palestinian economy", *Middle East Policy*, Vol. 9, No. 4.
46. World Bank. 2003. *Two Years of Intifada, Closures and Palestinian Economic Crisis – An Assessment*. Washington, DC: World Bank.
47. Pundak, note 44 above, p. 36.
48. *Jerusalem Report*. 2003. "Egypt trying, without much success, to thwart arms smuggling by tunnelling Palestinians", *Jerusalem Report*, 19 May.
49. Crooke, Alastair and Beverly Milton-Edwards. 2003. "Costly choice", *The World Today*, Vol. 59, No. 12, p. 16.
50. Moller, Bjorn. 2002. "A cooperative structure for Israeli-Palestinian relations", paper presented at "Mediterranean Crossroads: Culture, Religion and Conflict" seminar, September, Halki, Greece, pp. 7–8.
51. Kydd and Walter, note 2 above, p. 289.
52. Gunning, Jeroen. 2004. "Peace with Hamas? The transforming potential of political participation", *International Affairs*, Vol. 80, No. 2.
53. Friedman, Ina and Michael Karpin. 1998. *Murder in the Name of God: The Plot to Kill Yitzhak Rabin*. New York: Metropolitan Books.
54. Alianak, Sonia L. 2000. "The mentality of messianic assassins", *Orbis*, Vol. 44, No. 2; Sprinzak, Ehud. 1998. "Extremism and violence in Israel: The crisis of messianic politics", *Annals of the American Academy of Political and Social Science*, No. 555, January.
55. For a catalogue of these incidents see www.aqsa.org.uk/leafletsdetails.aspx?id=20.
56. Goldenberg, Suzanne. 2002. "Israel thwarts Jewish bomb attack on school", *Ha'aretz*, 13 May.
57. See Reuveny, R. 2003. "Fundamentalist colonialism: The geopolitics of the Israeli-Palestinian conflict", *Political Geography*, Vol. 22, No. 4.
58. Dudkevitch, Margot. 2005. "Shin Bet: Temple Mount attack more likely than attempt on PM's life", *Jerusalem Post*, 14 February.

12

Spoiling peace in Cyprus

Nathalie Tocci

Spoiling characterizes the very nature of the persisting conflict in Cyprus. In the Cyprus context, spoiling has taken the form of actions that have strengthened one party's position to the detriment of the basic needs of the other. Since the eruption of intercommunal fighting in 1963, and particularly since the 1974 partition of the island, the innumerable efforts of the United Nations to mediate the conflict have been victims of the spoiling activities of different actors at different points in time.

But what exactly has constituted spoiling in the context of Cyprus? Spoiling has not entailed actions inherently inimical to peace and peaceful reconciliation. Nor has it meant opting for violence and discarding negotiations. Due to the absence of a comprehensive agreement since 1963, spoiling has also not involved reneging on the obligations of a settlement, thus causing its failure. Spoiling has rather taken the form of actions undertaken by parties normally involved in the long-lasting peace process under the aegis of the United Nations. These actions have been aimed at bolstering specific (spoiling) bargaining positions. They have taken place both within the context of negotiations and outside it through unilateral measures. As such, distinguishing spoiling from legitimate political actions to bolster a party's bargaining strength has not been simple. Indeed, what has constituted spoiling to one party has represented legally and morally legitimate action to another. The distinction between spoiling and "normal politics" has thus been a question of degree, rather than one of clear-cut categories.[1]

If spoiling in Cyprus has not constituted actions inherently inimical to negotiations, but rather actions that have been inimical to a specific peace process and settlement, how can spoiling be pinpointed?[2] To do so, the starting point must be an appreciation of the contours of a peaceful settlement mutually agreed upon in the context of negotiations. Such an appreciation inevitably involves a degree of normative judgement. Spoiling would then constitute the actions of any internal or external party intended to attain other (devious) objectives.[3]

A peaceful compromise settlement in Cyprus is one which both respects norms of democracy, human rights, and good governance and also accounts for the basic needs of all principal parties.[4] In Cyprus these needs revolve around notions of self-determination, communal security, and the rectification of past injustices. The leaderships of the principal parties, supported by the governments of Greece and Turkey respectively, have sought these basic needs by presenting specific "satisfiers" (or bargaining positions) through which these needs could be attained.[5]

In Cyprus spoiling positions have constituted satisfiers revolving around ethno-nationalist ideologies and based on legalistic and modernist conceptions of sovereignty, statehood, and military power and balance. These positions have been spoiling because while aimed at fulfilling the basic needs of one party, they negate the basic needs of the other. Spoiling actions have been the activities intended to bolster the ethno-nationalist and modernist discourse. In some instances this has entailed abandoning peace talks and pursuing exclusively unilateral actions outside the context of negotiations. In other instances it has meant participating in negotiations as a means to gain time or legitimacy. The essence remained the unchanged spoiling positions. Circumstances dictated the precise form in which spoiling took place. Interesting in this respect was the participation of both the Greek Cypriot and the Turkish Cypriot leaderships in the 2002–2004 peace talks. As ensuing developments demonstrated, both leaders rejected the UN-mediated talks aimed at reaching an agreement on the UN-proposed Annan Plan. Yet both engaged in the process as a means to retain legitimacy and in response to internal and external pressures. When the process reached its concluding stages, both leaders revealed their preferences. As the costs of engagement rose, they withdrew their commitments by strongly and publicly rejecting the UN plan.

Spoiling has been grounded on both ideology and the perceived ability to attain maximalist objectives.[6] In other words, spoiling positions have been endorsed by actors who were both ideologically committed to a particular vision of a future Cyprus *and* believed that such a vision was attainable. Indeed, some of the more moderate actors did not necessarily espouse ideologies that were radically different from those underlying spoiling positions. Yet their different assessment of what could be realistically achieved led them to pursue compromise agreements. Noteworthy in this respect was the attitude of former Greek Cypriot President Glafcos Clerides in April 2004, who in supporting the Annan Plan argued that it reflected the only realistic outcome of a negotiated peace process. In contrast, the current President Tassos Papadopolous rejected the plan, arguing that the Greek Cypriots were sufficiently strong to secure a more favourable agreement in future.

While ideology and perceptions of power have lain at the heart of spoiling, vested interests in the persisting conflict have also played a role. Property, business interests, and undiluted control over a given territory certainly affected conflict continuation. However, ethno-nationalism and vested interests have been interconnected. For example, Greek Cypriot spoiling positions on property have been as much about property *per se* as about a narrative of the Turkish invasion and occupation. Likewise, the Turkish Cypriot reluctance to allow Greek Cypriot refugees to return to northern Cyprus has been due both to the ensuing dislocation of the Turks and Turkish Cypriots living in these properties and to the fear of intercommunal intermingling that could trigger renewed violence against them. Hence, interests have strengthened and reproduced the modernist discourse, while being embedded in it.

This close interrelationship is accentuated by the relatively low turnover of political élites within both communities. For example, in 2003 Presidents Rauf Denktaş and Glafcos Clerides negotiated peace in Cyprus, just as they had after the breakdown of the republic in 1963. Since 2003 southern Cyprus has been governed by Papadopolous, who back in the late 1950s was a member of the EOKA nationalist struggle against British colonial rule. In 1999–2002 Bülent Ecevit was the Turkish prime minister, just as he had been in 1974 when Turkey invaded the island following a Greek military coup. The absence of a comprehensive élite turnover has reduced the scope for constructive change by hindering a genuine transformation of élite interests, ideologies, and discourse in line with changing circumstances.

The needs of the principal parties and the spoiling positions of their leaderships

The existence and persistence of the Cyprus conflict are characterized by the fundamental reluctance of all principal parties to create, operate, or re-establish a unified independent Cyprus where Greek and Turkish Cypriots could peacefully coexist on the basis of a shared understanding of their political equality. This reluctance is driven by the parties' understanding of the ways in which they could attain their objectives of self-determination, individual rights, and communal security.

The conflict emerged in the 1930s–1950s when the Greek Cypriot community, supported by Greece, articulated its struggle for self-determination in terms of *enosis*, or union between Greece and Cyprus. Fearing Greek domination and spurred by the British, the Turkish Cypriot community and Turkey mounted a reactive counter-*enosis* campaign. By the late 1950s this countermobilization crystallized in the diametrically opposed position of *taksim*, or partition. In 1960, through heavy-handed pressure from Greece, Turkey, and the UK, a compromise was found. Cyprus would become an independent bi-communal republic. Yet the Greek Cypriot leadership remained implicitly devoted to *enosis*, and by 1963 the bi-communal republic had collapsed. With its breakdown, both community leaderships lost their already limited commitment to the 1959–1960 arrangements. Little international effort was exerted to prevent the 1974 Greek coup in Cyprus and the ensuing Turkish military intervention on the island.

The decades that followed the 1974 partition witnessed a series of failed negotiations and rejected proposals. Neither the Greek nor the Turkish Cypriot leaders were ready to abandon the *status quo* for the establishment of a genuine bi-zonal and bi-communal federal republic in which Cyprus would be reunified and sovereignty would be shared between its two communities. The Greek Cypriot leadership was relatively content with the legal, political, and economic supremacy of its republic. It was unwilling to relinquish this status for genuine power-sharing with the smaller Turkish Cypriot community. The Turkish Cypriot leadership also was unwilling to renounce its *de facto* independence in favour of power-sharing within a nominally reunified state. Both parties articulated their claims in the mutually exclusive language of absolute statehood and sovereignty.

The sections below review the basic needs of the principal parties and the "spoiling" positions and actions intended to satisfy those basic needs.

The Greek Cypriot community and Greece

The Greek Cypriot community seeks the reunification of Cyprus and the prevention of secession or annexation to Turkey of the northern part of the island. It aims to restore to the greatest possible extent the *status quo ante*, i.e. that pertaining prior to the 1974 Turkish military intervention, which led to its loss of control of over 37 per cent of the island's territory and the displacement of 140,000–160,000 Greek Cypriots. Within a reunified island, the Greek Cypriots call for a fair and fully functioning arrangement in terms of territorial distribution and government structures. This implies that the larger Greek Cypriot community would benefit from a larger share of territory and political representation. The Greek Cypriots insist on the liberalization of the "three freedoms" of movement, settlement, and property, and on respect for human rights, including the right of refugee return. They call for security guarantees against Turkish aggression. The perceived threat of Turkey is due to Turkey's proximity, size, military capability, and, most critically, its history of relations with Cyprus from the days of the Ottoman Empire to the 1974 intervention.

Since 1974 Greece has supported the Greek Cypriot cause of reunification. This is because of the ethnic, linguistic, cultural, and historical ties between Greeks and Greek Cypriots. It is also because of Greece's integral role in the evolution of the conflict, from its role in the *enosis* campaign in the 1930s–1950s to its guarantor status in the 1960 accords and the Greek military coup in 1974 that triggered the Turkish invasion. Since 1974 all Greek governments, while pursuing the Cyprus dossier with differing intensities and through different means, have always supported reunification. While backing strong ties with Cyprus, they have never advocated their pre-1974 aim of *enosis*.

Nationalism within the Greek Cypriot community, and subsequently positions on the conflict, historically took two different forms: Hellenocentrism or Greek Cypriot nationalism, and Cyprocentrism or Cypriot nationalism.[7] Greek Cypriot nationalists emphasized notions of Greekness in the Cypriot identity, and up until the 1974 partition they gathered around the banner of *enosis*. Since 1974, while no longer advocating *enosis*, they have emphasized the Greekness of Cyprus in the context of an independent republic that would be organically linked to Greece. Variants of this political ideology were espoused by the moderate centre-right (DISY), the more hard-line centre-right (DIKO), and the extreme right (New Horizons), as well as by the nationalist socialists (EDEK/KISOS) and the Greek Orthodox Church.

On the other side of the political spectrum, Cypriot nationalists emphasized the *sui generis* nature of the Cypriot identity, shared by both Greek and Turkish Cypriots, as well as the civic elements of identity based on common economic, social, and political interests. Their political ideology emerged after 1974. They imagined a shared history of intercommunal coexistence and amity. Turks, and not Turkish Cypriots, were viewed as "the enemy". Cypriot nationalists strongly supported the reunification of Cyprus and its independence from external interference. This also included independence from Greece, whose irredentism and ethnonationalism were seen as partly responsible for the events of 1974. Since 1974 variants of Cyprocentrism have been espoused by the leftist AKEL (whose positions, however, had hardened by the turn of the century) as well as by the moderate liberal EDI.

In their rhetoric most Greek Cypriot political parties have accepted that their basic needs could be achieved within the confines of a bi-communal and bi-zonal federal settlement in the post-1974 period. Yet a bi-zonal and bi-communal federation has meant different things to different people. Spoiling positions on all of the major elements on the conflict settlement agenda have come from various actors at various points in time, depending on their ideologies and their perceived capabilities. These positions have been advocated predominantly by ethno-nationalist actors who also genuinely believed that their views were achievable. However, on issues such as refugee rights, the "three freedoms", and the role of Turkey, Cypriot nationalists have also taken hard-line positions, especially in recent years. This has been due to their insistence on the immediate intermingling between the communities and the non-interference of external actors.

Concerning the constitutional structure of a future Cyprus, spoiling positions have departed from the rhetorical commitment to a genuine federation. These positions have insisted on a tightly integrated state with single and undivided sovereignty, international personality, and citizenship. Within this state most competences would be dealt with by the central level of government. Federated entities would be subordinated to the centre and would not enjoy sovereign competences as such. They would deal with limited issues in the areas of culture, education, and religion. Within the centre, representation would reflect to the greatest possible extent the demographic balance on the island. As such the centre would be controlled by the larger Greek Cypriot community. Legislative and executive decisions would be taken on the basis of majority vote. The federation would unambiguously represent the continuation of the existing Republic of Cyprus, into which the Turkish Cypriots would be reintegrated. Any ambiguity on the question of state succession would entail the recognition of the self-declared Turkish Republic of Northern Cyprus (TRNC).

Despite the rhetorical commitment to bi-zonality, Greek Cypriot spoiling positions have insisted both on a significant redistribution of territory to the Greek Cypriot zone and on an uncontested implementation of the right of return for all Greek Cypriot refugees. In addition, they have called for the full liberalization of the freedoms of movement, settlement, and property. Due to the numbers of Greek Cypriot refugees and the size and economic strength of the Greek Cypriot community, the full implementation of these rights and freedoms would erode bi-zonality in practice.

Spoiling positions have also been categorical about the non-interference of Turkey in Cyprus's security system. They have called for the full withdrawal of Turkish troops from the island and have rejected the continuation of the 1959 Treaty of Guarantee, giving guarantors Britain, Greece, and Turkey unilateral rights of intervention in Cyprus. On the contrary, they have sought international guarantees to prevent Turkey's interference. Spoiling positions have insisted also on the full withdrawal of all Turkish immigrants who settled in Cyprus after 1974.

The Turkish Cypriot community and Turkey

The Turkish Cypriot community, supported by Turkey, seeks political equality with the larger Greek Cypriot community. Its greatest fear is the return to the *status quo ante* (1963–1974), when following the Greek Cypriot unilateral alteration of the bi-communal 1960 constitution and the ensuing intercommunal violence, Turkish Cypriot officials left all public institutions and most Turkish Cypriots were relegated to small enclaves. In light of the 1963–1974 events, the Turkish Cypriots feel that due to their smaller size, their political equality warrants the highest degree of self-rule and physical separation from the Greek Cypriots. They also call for Turkish security guarantees, given their mistrust of other foreign involvement, which failed to prevent the injustices committed against them in the past.

Turkey has specific security concerns which go beyond the welfare of the Turkish Cypriots. Due to the vicinity of Cyprus, Turkey aims to prevent Greek domination of Cyprus. Lying behind these views is the "Sèvres syndrome", still prevalent in Turkey's political and security culture. The large majority of the Turkish élite and public view with suspicion European intentions, fearing that in the legacy of the Sèvres Treaty after the First World War European powers are inclined to dismember Turkey by collaborating with hostile neighbours, such as Greece. Hence, preventing Cyprus from falling into Greek hands, and thus becoming the "dagger" pointing at the Turkish mainland, is considered an utmost priority. Turkey has thus supported the political equality of the Turkish Cypriots, has called for a balance between the roles of Greece and Turkey in the eastern Mediterranean, and has demanded a role in Cyprus's security arrangements.

Beyond the consensus on these general aims and needs, the Turkish Cypriots have been divided between the nationalist camp, which up until 2004 had been consistently in power under the leadership of Rauf Denktaş, and the centre-left and liberal camp. In Turkey divisions have also existed between those who shared the views of Turkish Cypriot nationalists and those who argued that while Turkish and Turkish Cypriot interests should be protected, Turkey should loosen its grip on Cyprus and allow the island's reunification.

The nationalist camp has emphasized the ethnic differences between Greeks and Turks and the impossibility of the two communities living together. It has stressed the commonality between Turkish Cypriots and Turks, and the organic links between the Turkish Cypriot community and "motherland" Turkey. The history of 1963-1974, i.e. when the 1960 constitutional arrangements collapsed and ethnic violence re-erupted, has been flagged both as evidence of the endemic incompatibility between Greeks and Turks and as the justification for rejecting an integrated federal solution. The 1974 Turkish intervention is considered as irrefutable proof that the Turkish Cypriots need and only need Turkish guarantees for their security. In northern Cyprus there have been two major parties in the nationalist camp: the UBP and the DP, which have together consistently won the lion's share of the vote since 1976. Up until 2005 Rauf Denktaş was the leader of the Turkish Cypriot community and of the *de facto* state in the north.

The Turkish Cypriot nationalist establishment, and Rauf Denktaş in particular, enjoyed close ties with the nationalist establishment in Ankara. The Turkish Cypriot government would not take any key decisions without Ankara's consent. Particularly in view of the non-recognized status of the TRNC, the latter could not survive without Turkey's support. This is not to say that Denktaş was a puppet in Ankara's hands. The Turkish Cypriot leader, having retained power longer than any Turkish politician, enjoyed considerable support and respect in Turkey, particularly amongst the military, the foreign ministry, and nationalist right- and left-wing circles. Furthermore, to the extent that Denktaş shared similar views with Turkish nationalists, the key question was not so much one of the relative strengths of Denktaş and Ankara, but the relative strengths of the conservatives/nationalists and the progressive forces in Turkey and north Cyprus combined. In this respect, Denktaş added considerable weight to the strength of the former against the latter.

The centre-left camp instead, while recognizing the important differences between Greek and Turkish Cypriots, has emphasized equally the differences between Turks and Turkish Cypriots. As such, it has opposed the immigration of mainland Turks to the north, arguing that the different political, cultural, and economic background of the immigrants "diluted" the Turkish Cypriot identity. The centre-left, while sharing the leadership's understanding of Turkish Cypriot basic aims, has been traditionally more flexible about future solutions. It has argued that Turkish Cypriot aims could be achieved within the confines of a federal settlement. A federation would guarantee maximum Turkish Cypriot self-government and minimum interference of both Greek Cypriots and Turkey in Turkish Cypriot affairs. The two main parties on the centre-left have been the CTP and the TKP..Since the late 1990s the centre-left has included also the liberal business community, embodied by the Turkish Cypriot Chamber of Commerce. With the 2005 presidential elections, power has shifted to the centre-left camp through the election of Mehmet Ali Talat, leader of the CTP.

Beginning with the constitution, Turkish Cypriot spoiling positions have generally come from the nationalist camp. These positions have insisted on unambiguously divided sovereignty as a means to ensure Turkish Cypriot political equality. Objecting to the legitimacy of the Republic of Cyprus, they have argued that a solution should be based on the prior recognition of two existing sovereign states. Most Turkish Cypriots have called for a loose common state, in which most competences would be dealt with separately by the two constituent states. However, spoiling positions have insisted rigidly that the centre's competences should "emanate" from the divided sovereignties of the two previously independent sovereign states. At the centre, political equality should be institutionalized through the greatest possible numerical equality, rotation, and unanimity in decision-making between the communities.

Turning to territory, spoiling positions have rejected extensive territorial readjustments, despite the disproportionate Turkish Cypriot control of territory (37 per cent). Perhaps most importantly, spoiling positions have refused to discuss territorial concessions before an agreement on constitutional questions, despite the clear interlinkage of these items on the conflict settlement agenda. Extensive territorial concessions (that would allow many Greek Cypriots to return to their properties under Greek Cypriot rule) have not only been rejected, but also the return to and settlement of Greek Cypriots in northern Cyprus have been categorically turned down. The difference between spoiling and non-spoiling positions in this respect has been one of degree. No Turkish Cypriot is willing to see an immediate huge influx of Greek Cypriots to northern Cyprus. However, spoiling positions have been more rigid on the overall numbers of Greek Cypriots allowed to return and settle in the north, as well as on the time-frames in which these movements could take place. They have insisted that reciprocal property claims should be solved almost exclusively through compensation and property exchange between the communities.

Spoiling and politics

Before proceeding, it is important to specify how and why the positions discussed above have been "spoiling" rather than normal and legitimate political positions. The spoiling nature of these positions is given by the fact that they deny the mutual fulfilment of the principal parties' basic needs. Greek Cypriot calls for a tightly integrated federal state with single and undivided sovereignty contradict Turkish Cypriot needs for political equality given the relative size and strength of the two communities. Turkish Cypriot calls for divided sovereignty and quasi-statehood negate Greek Cypriot needs to reunify the island and prevent secession. Spoiling on the question of state succession invalidates the other community's reading of history. A clear-cut continuation of the Republic of Cyprus entails a dismissal of the injustices of 1963–1974 and recognition of the republic's legitimacy as the sole representative of the Cypriots and the basis for Greek Cypriot control. Yet recognition of the Turkish Republic of Northern Cyprus entails legitimizing the 1974 intervention and partition, and thus the ultimate victory of the historical Turkish cause of partition. It also creates the basis for future Turkish Cypriot secession. Finally, the full implementation of the right of return and of individual freedoms refutes Turkish Cypriot calls for bi-zonality based on their understanding of communal security. Yet an absolute rejection of any Greek Cypriot presence in the north denies Greek Cypriot individual rights and fails to rectify perceived historical injustices.

A final note on spoilers and spoiling positions is temporal change. Spoiling positions have not been advocated consistently by the same domestic actors; hence the inappropriate use of the term "spoiler", indicating a permanent characteristic of a particular political actor. Spoiling positions have not been fixed over time. Actors have changed and positions have evolved. In some instances a surge in nationalist discourse within one principal party was the result of a domestic political change. From 1974 to 1981, following the restoration of democracy in Greece, Prime Minister Constantine Karamanlis (New Democracy) took a low profile on Cyprus, embracing the doctrine of "Cyprus decides, Greece supports".[8] Yet with the election of Andreas Papandreou's socialist PASOK in November 1981 this logic was reversed. In 1981 PASOK represented an extreme form of a populist catch-all party thriving on a nationalist rhetoric.

The rhetorical positions of the same actors have also evolved over time. It was the same Clerides who in 1993 campaigned against the 1992 UN "Set of Ideas", and who a decade later declared himself willing to negotiate a solution on the basis of the UN Annan Plan, which provided for a more decentralized federation. It was the same Rauf Denktaş who in 1974 adamantly called for a bi-communal and bi-zonal federation, and who in 1998 discarded a federal solution in favour of a confederal one. In Turkey the stance of the military has also changed. While historically considered a monolithic actor firmly based within the nationalist camp, in 2004 the Turkish military acquiesced to the moderate stance of the Turkish government in its support for the Annan Plan.

Whether these temporal changes went beyond the level of rhetoric remains an open question. At times changes have been genuine. At other times they have been rhetorical shifts to bolster unchanged positions of substance. Actors may have felt that engagement in negotiations was beneficial to the attainment of their unchanged objectives. As such they may have modified their rhetoric to trigger a relaunch of peace talks. Yet the same actors could then walk out of negotiations, believing that engagement would weaken their positions. For example, in December 2001 Denktaş relaunched the peace process and modified his rhetoric, abandoning the clear-cut references to the establishment of a confederation. Yet this did not entail a genuine change in his objectives, as ensuing developments revealed.

Equally difficult to disentangle are the reasons determining changing positions. Do positions alter as a result of changing ideologies and a process of socialization into different modes of operation? Or does change occur as a pragmatic and calculated response to different perceived opportunities and capabilities? At this point, suffice it to say that whether rhetorical or real, whether ideological or pragmatic, a change of context has frequently altered spoiling positions in Cyprus.

Spoiling tactics and actions: Strengthening spoiling positions

Spoiling may change over time as the result of interrelated domestic, regional, and international changes, and most critically as a result of actor responses to these contextual changes. The sections below examine the discursive tactics and actions used to bolster spoiling positions and garner domestic and international support.

The domestic legitimization of spoiling positions

All actors within the conflicting parties have attempted to legitimize their positions to garner domestic support. Following the logic of two-level games, they have done so also to bolster their bargaining strength *vis-à-vis* each other.[9] In Cyprus, technical legalistic language has been used to mask and legitimize uncompromising nationalist positions. These positions have been grounded on a notion of absolute and monolithic sovereignty that has been inherently inimical to flexibility. Spoiling positions have also been based on the discourse of moral rights, political and historical imperatives, and security needs.

Since 1974 the Greek Cypriot public has been persuaded by its governments, civil society, and media of the moral and legal superiority of the Greek Cypriot cause. Refugee return and the liberalization of the three freedoms have been portrayed as undisputed human rights. Relative

Greek Cypriot control of central institutions has been described as an absolute necessity emanating from the imperatives of majoritarian democracy. The political class has never invested in arguing the need for, let alone the desirability of, true compromise with the Turkish Cypriots. In turn, the logic driving spoiling positions has never been seriously questioned. So when leaders have appeared more willing to reach out to the Turkish Cypriots they have often been punished by the people. The electoral defeat of moderate George Vassiliou in 1993 by the (then) more hard-line Glafcos Clerides and the 2003 defeat of Clerides by the tougher Tassos Papadopoulos are both cases in point. The Greek Cypriot public's overwhelming rejection of the Annan Plan in the referendum of April 2004 (by 76 per cent) can be explained also by the community's conviction that a better plan existed and was realistically achievable.

While endorsing a similar rhetoric, spoiling tactics in Greece have rested on the additional argument of historical responsibility. Due to the 1974 Greek military coup in Cyprus that ousted Archbishop Makarios and triggered the Turkish invasion, Greece has acknowledged its share of responsibility in causing partition. As such, Greek governments have legitimized morally any policy instrument devoted to strengthening the Greek Cypriot cause. While these instruments have generally excluded the use of force, they have included defence initiatives such as the 1993 Joint Defence Doctrine promoted by Andreas Papandreou's government in Athens. Any attempt by Greek governments to exert any pressure on the Greek Cypriot leadership has been attacked internally as a betrayal of the Greek Cypriot cause and a default of Greece's historical responsibilities. This line of argument was used to motivate the government's noncommittal stance towards the Annan Plan in the referendum campaign in April 2004. The government in Athens simply stated that it would support any decision taken by the Greek Cypriot community.

Turkish Cypriot spoiling tactics have instrumentalized fears of renewed domination to bolster the quest for independent statehood. The return of Greek Cypriot refugees and the liberalization of the "three freedoms" have been equated with Greek Cypriot domination and violence against the smaller and weaker Turkish Cypriot community. The Turkish Cypriots have been induced to believe that intercommunal contact would entail a return to 1963. Older generations remembered the atrocities of the past; younger generations were constantly reminded of them by the media and the education system. Until April 2003 they had little way of testing this narrative through personal experience due to the blockaded green line. It was indeed interesting to observe how, following Denktaş's decision to open the border in April 2003, nationalists on the Turkish and Turkish Cypriot side were quick to warn that the honeymoon would soon be over and intercommunal contact could spark violent intercommunal clashes. When these clashes did not materialize, the same actors argued that they would occur once the Greek Cypriots reclaimed their properties in the context of a federal settlement.

Turkish Cypriot spoiling tactics have fed into fears of displacement. As far as the displacement of Anatolian settlers was concerned, evidence was often manipulated. Despite Greek Cypriot demands, federal proposals have normally provided for the retention of most settlers in Cyprus. The Annan Plan allowed most of the settlers to remain on the island. A large proportion would be naturalized as Turkish Cypriot citizens, and most of the rest could remain through residence permits. Yet Turkish and Turkish Cypriot nationalists claimed that the plan would inhumanely force the displacement of these people. A problem in countering this argument has been the deficient communication between the moderate parties in northern Cyprus and the Turkish settlers.

A more compelling argument concerned the displacement of persons as a result of territorial readjustments. Territorial readjustments are an inevitable element of a package deal. Yet spoiling positions have resisted significant readjustments. To bolster such positions, actors have emphasized the considerable human suffering that would result from the displacement of thousands of Turkish Cypriots living in the territories to be handed over to Greek Cypriot rule. In 1992 Denktaş rejected the map presented by UN Secretary-General Boutros Boutros-Ghali, arguing that it would lead to extensive Turkish Cypriot displacement. Likewise, in 2002–2004 Denktaş rejected the map presented in the Annan Plan, again referring to the displacement of persons that it entailed.

Turkish spoiling tactics have also manipulated the "Sèvres syndrome" still prevalent in the country. Cyprus could not be compromised upon because it is key to Turkish national security, protecting Turkey against hostile Greek designs.[10] No Turkish politician could afford to accept a solution in Cyprus with the slightest element of perceived treachery in it. As such, nationalists in Turkey have depicted their positions as the bastions of Turkish security and have accused moderates of bending to foreign pressure and compromising vital security interests. Indeed, when in 2004 the AKP government in Turkey declared its support for the Annan Plan, critics from the opposition CHP, from the presidency, and from the nationalist right- and left-wing circles argued that the government was dangerously compromising on Turkish security and Turkish Cypriot rights.

Using and responding to the international environment

Spoiling has not been justified only by presenting particular narratives of the past. Domestic actors have also actively used and responded to external factors as a means to strengthen their positions. Since 1974 the parties have responded to EU and UN actions in particular. They have also triggered European and international decisions to bolster their positions, often beyond the awareness of these international actors themselves. Spoiling actions have used the resources bestowed by third parties to strengthen, legitimize, and attain their spoiling or devious objectives.[11]

Particularly since the late 1980s, the Greek Cypriot side has backed its positions through a strategy of internationalization.[12] This strategy has been supported by Greece since the election of Andreas Papandreou in 1981. But how have international forums been used to strengthen Greek Cypriot positions, and how have these strategies fed into Greek Cypriot spoiling aims and positions? The Greek Cypriot side has taken advantage of its internationally recognized status as the only legitimate authority on the island. It has used this status to lobby for UN resolutions condemning Turkey and the Turkish Cypriots and reinstating the RoC's status as the sole legitimate authority on the island. These resolutions were then flagged as evidence backing rigid positions on statehood and sovereignty. When for example the Greek Cypriot leadership reacted against the UN Secretary-General's statements in September 2000 calling for political equality, it argued that the statements ran contrary to the parameters of a solution "as determined by UN principles, decisions and resolutions".[13]

Particularly since the 1990s the Greek Cypriot authorities have also concentrated on European legal forums to ensure condemnation of Turkey. Perhaps the most critical case has been that of Titina Loizidou, a Greek Cypriot who in March 1989 attempted to cross the green line in order to reach her property in Kyrenia, and thereafter filed a complaint to the European Court of Human Rights (ECHR). The principal aim of the case was that of setting the parameters of a future solution along Greek Cypriot lines.[14] Not only did international law confer unreserved support for the Greek Cypriot position on the right of return, but the Loizidou precedent also made the acceptance of Turkish Cypriot proposals less feasible. Even if the two communities were to agree on a restricted implementation of the right of return, could the issue be considered settled if any individual could challenge the agreement by appealing to the ECHR? Since the Loizidou case there have been an unending number of Greek Cypriot cases filed against Turkey in the ECHR.[15] The Loizidou case had a spoiling effect on the peace process not necessarily because of the actual ruling of the court. Its spoiling effect was due to its attempt to settle a key issue of the conflict through arbitration rather than negotiation, in a manner that would fulfil the maximalist aims of one party without accounting for the fears of the other.

Finally, the Greek Cypriot side, aided by Greece, applied for and pursued EU membership. The fundamental reasoning behind this was to bolster the Greek Cypriot bargaining strength in the conflict. Cyprus's accession process and ultimate membership would strengthen the RoC's status as the only legitimate government on the island, would discredit further the TRNC, and would provide the RoC with an additional forum in which to present its case. Cyprus's accession would increase Greek Cypriot leverage on Turkey both because of an expected rise in EU pressure on Turkey and because of Turkey's own aspirations to join the EU. EU membership would also yield key security gains to the Greek Cypriots, alleviating perceived Turkish threats.

Perhaps most critically, EU membership would create a framework for the liberalization of the "three freedoms" with the implementation of the EU *acquis communautaire* that provides for the liberalization of the "four freedoms" of movement of goods, services, capital, and people in the EU. The way in which Greek Cypriot spoiling arguments have manipulated the issue of the *acquis* to legitimize their discourse has been particularly interesting. Whereas in the past uncompromising positions were couched in the language of human rights and majoritarian democracy, the accession process allowed the far more specific and binding language of the *acquis* to justify inflexibility. EU obligations were used to criticize the United Nations and reject UN positions. This was particularly evident in the leadership's criticism of key provisions of the Annan Plan. Since then, and with the EU accession of the divided Cyprus, the Greek Cypriot leadership has incessantly called for a "European" solution which would entail the full liberalization of the three freedoms.

Turkish Cypriot spoiling tactics and actions have mirrored those of the Greek Cypriots. The more the international community supported the legitimacy of the Republic of Cyprus, the more Turkish Cypriot nationalists argued that political equality could only be secured through a prior recognition of their sovereignty. For example, the 1983 unilateral declaration of independence (UDI) was made after the RoC brought its case to the UN General Assembly, securing a resolution in favour of the immediate withdrawal of Turkish forces. Frustrated by the Greek Cypriot advantages of recognized statehood, the Turkish Cypriot leadership persuaded Ankara to support the UDI.[16] Nationalists also portrayed Greek Cypriot legal cases harming Turkish Cypriot interests as further justification for their calls to separate statehood. A 1994 European Court of Justice case banning Turkish Cypriot certificated exports was flagged as evidence that the TRNC needed international recognition for its economic and political survival. It was no coincidence that soon after the ruling, the Turkish Cypriot Assembly withdrew its commitment to a federal settlement and supported the recognition of Turkish Cypriot sovereignty instead.

The Greek Cypriot application for and pursuit of EU membership have also been used and abused by Turkish Cypriot nationalists to bolster their case. In the 1990s the perceived zero-sum nature of Greek Cypriot gains from membership automatically made many Turkish Cypriots view EU accession as a threat. These perceived threats were nurtured by Turkish Cypriot spoiling tactics, which consistently argued that EU accession meant an enhancement of the RoC's status, increased leverage on Turkey, the erosion of bi-zonality on the island, and the end of Turkey's protection of Turkish Cypriot security. Denktaş repeatedly accused the EU of wanting to reduce the Turkish Cypriots to a minority deprived of any collective rights. So, the argument went, reunification within the EU had to be avoided at least until Turkey's own (uncertain) accession. In fact, the separate membership of Greek Cyprus could foster a permanent partition on the island. This was viewed as a more desirable outcome by Turkish and Turkish Cypriot nationalists.

On the Turkish and Turkish Cypriot sides, spoiling tactics have also been linked to Turkey's own EU membership aspirations. Due to the obstacles that a divided Cyprus posed to Turkey's own European path, a basic overlap emerged between hard-liners on the Cyprus conflict and nationalist and Eurosceptic forces in Turkey. Officially the Turkish establishment rejected any link between a Cyprus settlement and its EU membership ambitions. It feared that such a link entailed that a settlement would become a precondition for Turkey's accession. Yet spoiling arguments implicitly linked these questions in two ways. On the one hand, they affirmed that Cyprus was a national issue which could not be compromised for the sake of the EU. Furthermore, given the perception of the EU's bias against Turkey and its reluctance to include Turkey in the EU club, a settlement would entail unacceptable compromises for Turkey. EU decisions that were viewed as inimical to Turkey consolidated this feeling. This was particularly evident in the aftermath of the 1997 Luxembourg European Council, in which Turkey was denied EU candidacy. On the other hand, Turkish Eurosceptics felt that spoiling peace in Cyprus would add another welcome obstacle in Turkey's EU path. This would dampen the momentum in favour of what conservatives viewed as threatening domestic reforms. In other words, to Eurosceptics a non-solution in Cyprus became an externally given opportunity to cool down Turkey-EU relations rather than a threat to Turkey's foreign policy goals.[17]

International responses to spoiling in Cyprus

By way of conclusion, the following paragraphs turn to the role played by the international community in managing spoiling in Cyprus. In particular, in view of the failure of the 2002–2004 peace process, in which respects did the international community fail?

The UN's role over the course of 2002–2004 was an important positive influence over negotiations, particularly in view of the publication of the Annan Plan. The plan provided for the simultaneous reunification and EU accession of the island. In doing so, it invalidated spoiling arguments by demonstrating concretely to many Turkish Cypriots that EU membership would not threaten their security, and that their needs could be fulfilled within the confines of a common state, member of the EU.

Yet, other than presenting a comprehensive proposal, the UN's potential to manage spoiling was limited. The United Nations did not have the necessary instruments to generate incentives for a settlement, either by moderating spoiling positions or by discrediting them altogether.[18] At most the United Nations could have coordinated better, or rather sooner, with the EU (close coordination between the UN team and the European Commission existed, but not until late 2001, almost a decade after the launch of Cyprus's accession process).

A separate question is whether the Annan Plan could have countered more effectively Greek Cypriot resistance if its provisions had conformed more squarely with the parameters of international law. In other words, could Greek Cypriot spoiling have been managed if it had been measured against a different solution? Arguably not. Most of the details of the plan came from the bargaining positions of either the Greek Cypriot or the Turkish Cypriot negotiators. The UN mediators largely attempted to manage and balance the parties' conflicting requests (with some input of their own). Hence, the leadership's rejection of the plan on the basis that it was an externally imposed initiative was simply an excuse to relieve itself of the responsibility of a failure. It could still be argued that a different balance in the plan could have been possible. But a sufficiently different balance, necessary to shift the strongly opposed Greek Cypriot community, would probably not have been acceptable any more to the Turkish Cypriot public.

The EU potentially did have the necessary instruments to generate incentives towards reunification.[19] However, the role of the EU as an actor was far more problematic.[20] Rather than fostering a new consensus within all principal parties on the desirability of shared sovereignty, multiple identities, porous borders, and collective security, many EU policies and decisions paradoxically heightened the perceived importance of recognized statehood and sovereignty, thereby bolstering spoiling tactics and arguments.

This was not done intentionally. It was the unintended effect of successful spoiling policies which domestic actors in Cyprus articulated and legitimized by using and abusing the EU discourse. Spoiling by using the

EU discourse succeeded because EU actors paid insufficient attention to the reasons behind the strong Greek Cypriot commitment to join the EU. Political and security interests, specifically related to the conflict, led the Greek Cypriot side to engage in the accession process. These gains were not related to an expectation that the EU would foster the emergence of a post-nationalist Cyprus in which ethnic rivalries would subsume. The attraction was rather that of strengthening the Greek Cypriot national cause against its local enemies. As the receipt of EU-related benefits became freed from progress in the peace process, the accession process reduced the incentives to seek an early agreement of those Greek Cypriot nationalists who sought considerable changes in UN guidelines. This continues to be the case in the post-accession period. The Greek Cypriot government, represented within EU institutions, has used its comparative advantage to strengthen its bargaining position and prevent EU initiatives to improve the lot of the Turkish Cypriots by easing their international isolation.

Lifting the condition of a settlement on Cyprus's EU accession moderated the positions of the previous leadership in south Cyprus. Clerides's presidency over the entire decade of EU accession may have had a socialization (or Europeanization) effect on the leadership, inducing its moderation.[21] Yet with the rise to power of Tassos Papadopolous, Greek Cypriot nationalist discourse resurfaced. In such a context, Cyprus's assured accession to the EU failed to deter Greek Cypriot spoiling positions.[22] The views of the new leadership were shared by the wider public, as shown by the referendum results in southern Cyprus in April 2004. There appeared to be a two-way relationship between the spoiling positions of the leadership and the views of the community. Whereas the popular resistance to the Annan Plan aided the president in upholding spoiling positions *vis-à-vis* the international community, the president's strong rejection of the plan influenced the people's scepticism about the plan.

Throughout the 1990s the EU also unintentionally failed to deter Turkish Cypriot spoiling. The fact that full membership of a divided Cyprus could consolidate partition was viewed as a desirable outcome by the most nationalist forces in northern Cyprus and Turkey. Their views were strengthened over the 1990s because EU actors insufficiently highlighted the attractive gains of membership and unintentionally generated (or failed to deter) Turkish Cypriot fears. In addition, the general climate of mistrust amongst the Turkish Cypriots of Greek Cypriot and EU intentions fuelled the siege mentality in northern Cyprus in the 1990s, bolstering the legitimacy of the spoiling discourse. Hence, implicit EU conditionality on the Turkish Cypriot side both hardened and legitimized Turkish Cypriot spoiling during the 1990s.

By 2002–2003 the Turkish Cypriot leadership had come under increasing pressure from the people, who were increasingly persuaded of the desirability of a settlement within the EU. In the referendum of April 2004 65 per cent of Turkish Cypriots indeed voted in favour of the Annan Plan and EU accession. The growing appreciation of the gains from membership and of the inevitability of Cyprus's accession (in Stedman's terms, the strategy of the "departing train") ultimately succeeded in marginalizing Turkish Cypriot spoiling and altering the internal balance in north Cyprus in favour of moderate views. EU conditionality alone would not have triggered these key changes. Yet as it interacted with other domestic, regional, and international changes, it became a powerful external determinant of constructive domestic change.

Finally, and particularly until the turn of the century, perhaps the most serious flaw in EU policy was the absence of a strategy towards Turkey. As a result, EU default incentives were insufficiently strong to trigger a change in Turkey's Cyprus policy. Following the Turkish elections in November 2002, the domestic dynamics in the country were seriously altered. A more credible EU accession process together with the rise to power of a government that has been seriously committed to the goal of membership transformed the internal dynamics in Turkey, bringing about a change in state policies towards Cyprus.

The principal lesson drawn from the failure of EU policies in Cyprus is thus the failure to account for the diverse make-up of the parties in the conflict. With the exception of attitudes towards the Turkish Cypriot side (where the objective was manifestly that of marginalizing Denktaş), EU policies failed to appreciate the complex make-up of views within the principal parties. Their policies were not directed at discrediting spoiling positions and arguments. On the contrary, EU actors failed to appreciate how their very decisions were often manipulated and used as excuses to justify and legitimize spoiling positions. Needless to say, gaining that level of awareness and acting upon it would have necessitated a common and consistent EU foreign policy towards the conflict, which alas never materialized.

Notes

1. Zahar, Marie-Joëlle. 2003. "Reframing the spoiler debate in peace processes", in John Darby and Roger Mac Ginty (eds) *Contemporary Peacemaking: Conflict, Violence and Peace Processes*. Basingstoke: Palgrave Macmillan.
2. Stedman, Stephen. 1997. "Spoiler problems in peace processes", *International Security*, Vol. 22, No. 2, p. 7.
3. Richmond, Oliver. 1998. "Devious objectives and disputants' view of international mediation: A theoretical framework", *Journal of Peace Research*, Vol. 35, No. 6, p. 709.

4. Burton, John (ed.). 1990. *Conflict: Human Needs Theory*. London: Macmillan.
5. *Ibid*.
6. Zahar, note 1 above.
7. Mavratsas, C. 1997. "The ideological contest between Greek Cypriot nationalism and Cypriotism 1974–1995", *Ethnic and Racial Studies,* Vol. 20, No. 4; Papadakis, Y. 1998. "Greek Cypriot narratives of history and collective identity: Nationalism as a contested process", *American Ethnologist*, Vol. 25, No. 2; Stavrinides, Z. 2001. *Greek Cypriot Perceptions on the Cyprus Problem*, available at http://website.lineone.net/~acgta/Stavrinides.htm.
8. Tsardanidis, C. and Y. Nicolau. 1999. "Cyprus foreign and security policy: Options and challenges", in S. Stavridis, T. Couloumbis, T. Veremis, and N. Waites (eds) *The Foreign Policies of the EU's Mediterranean States and Applicant Countries in the 1990s*. London: Macmillan.
9. Putnam, R. 1988. "Diplomacy and domestic politics: The logic of two-level games", *International Organization*, Vol. 42, No. 3.
10. Interviews with Turkish officials and politicians, Ankara and Istanbul, February and May 2002.
11. Richmond, note 3 above, p. 712.
12. Stavrinides, Z. 1999. "Greek Cypriot perceptions", in Clement Dodd (ed.) *Cyprus: The Need for New Perspectives*. Huntingdon: Eothen, p. 56.
13. Republic of Cyprus. 2000. *House of Representatives Resolution 11/10/00*. Nicosia: RoC, available at www.pio.gov.cy/news/special_issues/special_issue034.htm.
14. Interview with UN officials, Brussels, November 2001.
15. Commission of the European Communities. 2002. *Regular Report on Cyprus Progress Towards Accession,* available at www.europa.eu.int, p. 28.
16. Interview with a former Turkish foreign minister, Istanbul, March 2002.
17. Brewin, C. 2000. *The European Union and Cyprus*. Huntingdon: Eothen, p. 192.
18. Joseph, J. 2000. "Can the EU succeed where the UN failed? The continuing search for a settlement on Cyprus", paper presented at the International Studies Association Forty-first Annual Convention, Los Angeles, CA, 14–18 March.
19. Emerson, M. and N. Tocci. 2002. *Cyprus as Lighthouse of the Eastern Mediterranean*. Brussels: CEPS.
20. Tocci, N. 2004. *EU Accession Dynamics and Conflict Resolution: Catalysing Peace or Consolidating Partition in Cyprus*. Aldershot: Ashgate.
21. Stedman, note 2 above, p. 12; Borzel, T. and T. Risse. 2000. "When Europe hits home: Europeanisation and domestic change", *European Integration Online Papers*, Vol. 4, No. 15, available at http://eiop.or.at/eiop/texte/2000-015.htm.
22. On this see Annan, Kofi. 2004. *Report of the Secretary-General on His Mission of Good Offices in Cyprus*. New York: United Nations, para. 65.

13
The Abkhazia and South Ossetia cases: Spoilers in a nearly collapsed peace process

George Khutsishvili

The fall of the Soviet Union and subsequent liberation of the 15 Soviet republics, which became newly independent states (NISs) in 1991, was marked by upheaval and insurgencies. In a number of cases this was a defining dynamic, particularly in those parts of the former "empire" that contained ethnically defined autonomous constituencies. These included Abkhazia and South Ossetia in Georgia, Nagorny-Karabakh in Azerbaijan, Transdniestria in Moldova, and Chechnya in Russia. Security and self-identification problems in this rapidly changing environment concerned not only the NISs but also former autonomous entities that were exploited by pro-Soviet forces in order to hinder the NISs' course to independent statchood. Most of the disputes between the union of republics-turned-states and their autonomous entities ended with violent clashes and the emergence of secessionist quasi states seeking independence from their former "patrons". They remained unrecognized by the international community, however.

In Abkhazia and South Ossetia the conflict has passed a high-intensity phase with armed hostilities (1992–1993 in Abkhazia and 1991–1992 in South Ossetia) and large-scale humanitarian crisis (almost 300,000 internally displaced persons and refugees, the absolute majority of which in the Abkhazian case were ethnic Georgians). These states have now entered a protracted, frozen situation of "no peace, no war". Yet the corresponding peacebuilding process has never moved beyond an inadequate and undeveloped stage. In order to understand the key dynamics of the peace process and the spoiling phenomenon in the Abkhazian and South Ossetian cases, we need to examine the major stages of the dispute.

The Abkhazia conflict[1] is deeply rooted in the imperialist geopolitics of the Russian empire and the Soviet Union, and from the dawn of communist rule alienation between the Abkhaz and Georgians grew.[2] A significant part of Abkhazia is a subtropical Black Sea recreational area, which attracted support for the Abkhaz secessionists from the Russian military and its political establishment at the first signs of Soviet decline and the rise of a Georgian national liberation movement. The alienation of the Abkhaz from the Georgians grew as the view prevailed in Georgian historiography that Abkhazia was historically an alias for Western Georgia, while Abkhaz insisted on their distinct historical and ethnic origin. Significantly, Abkhazian sources blamed not Russian or Soviet imperialist policy but Georgian nationalism – very weak and undeveloped until the late 1980s – for systematic assimilative measures against the Abkhaz. Eventually, as Georgian-Abkhaz relations were aggravated by the new Georgian leaders' ethno-nationalism, the whole dispute was manipulated by the advocates of an imperial revival to create maximum alienation between Georgians and Abkhaz.

The nature of the Georgian-Osset dispute was significantly different. Georgian-Osset relations developed in a peaceful and tolerant manner: Ossets were among the best-integrated ethnic groups in the highly diverse Georgian society. The first signs of Georgian-Osset tension were visible as early as the 1920s, after the establishment of Soviet rule, but never led to a secessionist platform until the awkward nationalist policies of the first post-Soviet Georgian leader, Zviad Gamsakhurdia, triggered the emerging conflict in late 1990.[3] Inevitably, the struggle of a smaller community for higher autonomy and broader sovereignty in a transitional period turned into ethnic intolerance towards Georgians and a growing pro-Russian mood. In view of the growing Georgian-Osset tension, President Gamsakhurdia later made efforts to avoid conflict escalation in Abkhazia by offering the Abkhaz privileges to secure their support, but it was too late.

Actors and parties involved in the conflict's development and in mediation

As in most other cases, conflicts in Georgia involved multiple parties, both inside and outside the country, which had varying degrees of influence. The parties to the Abkhazian and South Ossetian conflicts at their

high-intensity stages (respectively, 1992–1993 and 1991–1992) were as follows.
- The secessionist ethnocratic élite of the Abkhazian Autonomous Republic (led by the Supreme Council chaired by Vladislav Ardzinba, elected while the Soviet Union still existed), which was primarily responsible for the escalation of anti-Georgian sentiment in Abkhaz society.
- After the armed conflict began, a group of anti-secessionist ethnic Georgian deputies of the Supreme Council of Abkhazia, led by deputy chairman Tamaz Nadareishvili, formed the so-called "legitimate government of Abkhazia in exile" based in Tbilisi.
- The secessionist ethnocratic élite of the South Ossetia Autonomous Oblast (led by the Soviet-elected Supreme Council chaired by Torez Kulumbegov). They had not been resolutely against the idea of living in a common state with Georgians. However, the nationalist slogans of the first president of independent Georgia, Zviad Gamsakhurdia, triggered the confrontation with South Ossets and enhanced their nationalist agenda.
- Georgia's State Council (Eduard Shevardnadze, Tengiz Sigua, and Jaba Ioseliani) and the interim government. The State Council was led by the former Soviet Foreign Minister Eduard Shevardnadze, who replaced the ousted President Zviad Gamsakhurdia after March 1992 and was responsible for the military inspection that led to the escalation of hostilities in Abkhazia in August 1992, and engaged later in the unsuccessful post-conflict negotiation process.
- The Confederation of the Mountainous Peoples of the Caucasus. This was a Moscow-influenced paramilitary and political association in the North Caucasus, with Chechen and Cossack regiments most active during the Georgian-Abkhaz war, which provided the main offensive force to achieve the military success of the Abkhaz over the Georgians in September 1993. Pro-Soviet forces in Russia applied "divide-and-rule" policies to weaken the NISs and attempted to facilitate the recreation of the Moscow-dominated union.
- Supporters of the ousted President Gamsakhurdia (or so-called Zviadists). They had a double-standard approach: on the one hand they stressed their patriotic and nationalist agenda, and therefore rejected the Abkhaz and Osset secessionism; on the other they did everything possible to weaken Shevardnadze's administration, which they declared illegitimate and dubbed as a "junta", and called for instability and even public upheaval in the country. As a result, a temporary alliance with the Abkhaz "rebels" emerged.

Participants in peace negotiations in the "frozen" stage (since 1993 in the Osset case and 1994 in the Abkhaz case) are defined as the parties immediately and necessarily present at the negotiation table, the absence of one of which made any meeting invalid.[4] In the Georgian-Abkhaz dispute those were the official representatives of the Georgian state authorities and the Abkhazia *de facto* government, the Russian mediation group (sponsored by the Group of Friends of the UN Secretary-General on Georgia and composed by the Russian Ministry of Foreign Affairs), and the UN Observer Mission in Georgia (UNOMIG).[5] In the Georgian-Osset dispute the representatives were the Georgian state authorities, the South Ossetia *de facto* government, official representatives of the North Ossetia–Alania Republic (part of the Russian Federation adjacent to South Ossetia), and representatives of the federal Russian authorities, including the representative of the CIS peacekeeping forces.

Custodians of the peace process, based on agreement between the so-called "Friends of the UN Secretary-General", in resolution of the conflicts in Georgia have been as follows.
- The OSCE in the South Ossetia case (the OSCE Mission in Georgia has mostly concentrated on South Ossetia).
- The United Nations in the Abkhazia case (UNOMIG, led by the special representative of the UN Secretary-General).
- The Russian Federation in both cases and throughout the process. The Kremlin has insisted on leading all the peace negotiations in Georgia and exerted pressure on the UN Security Council on decisions relating to Georgia. Russia has set up the peacekeeping forces (officially called the CIS forces) stationed along the Inguri River demarcation line in Abkhazia and at the entrances to the South Osset territory (the Roki tunnel in the north and Ergneti, near Tskhinali, in the south-east).

Normally the Russian Federation should act on the mandate and in accordance with the Group of Friends of the UN Secretary-General (five countries – the USA, the UK, France, Germany, and Russia – cooperating in supervision of the peace process in Georgia). In reality that group has delegated its power to Russia, confirming the geopolitical status of Georgia as part of Russia's sphere of influence.

Russian diplomats have often stressed that Georgia is not a sphere of Russia's special interest, and being involved in disputes over minor territories such as Abkhazia and South Ossetia is merely a headache for them. However, the reality proves to be different: the State Duma has repeatedly encouraged Abkhazia and South Ossetia to apply for associated membership in the Russian Federation, whilst most Abkhaz and South Ossets have already obtained Russian passports and citizenship. Russians have also purchased real estate in Abhazia, and otherwise developed ties with the seceded territories. There have been frequent alerts from the Georgian side that the conflict is really political, not ethnic, and that Russia is really a party to the conflict and therefore cannot act as a mediator.

The Russian State Duma, the Ministries of Foreign Affairs and Defence, and the Federal Security Service (FSB) expressed support for secessionists; whilst that would normally be a sufficient indication of Russia's deep partiality in another country's internal affairs, it did not prevent the international community from supporting Russia's role as main broker to negotiate peace agreements.

Spoilers in the South Caucasus conflict resolution process

The impact of various kinds of spoiling in peace processes has been studied from different angles. Stedman defines spoilers as "actors who aim to undermine the peace process";[6] that is, a peace process needs to be ongoing for the spoilers to enter the scene. In the unresolved South Caucasus conflicts – Nagorny-Karabakh, Abkhazia, and South Ossetia – a peace agreement has never been signed, negotiations are stalled, and the positions of the parties have been "frozen" for years. Nevertheless, the peace process is often considered not only as ongoing, but also as having something to its credit in all these cases. Rather than a collapsed peace agreement (such as cases where signed peace agreements were broken and civil wars renewed), it would be more accurate to speak about a failed or collapsed peace process, especially if agreement has not been achieved in over a decade of negotiations. Yet the mandate of custodians is defined so as to escape such an assessment. As the assessment "no result" is unacceptable, it is always replaced by "the process is ongoing with serious difficulties" – caused, of course, by spoiling behaviour, partly because a custodian of the peace process appears to be a spoiler itself.

The legal basis of any negotiation between the parties to conflict should be international agreements and documents such as UN Security Council resolutions; in this case these documents have acknowledged the territorial integrity of Georgia (an OSCE statement of 1998 acknowledged the fact of ethnic cleansing of Georgians in Abkhazia), but also called for the parties to adhere to peaceful and non-violent ways to negotiate an agreement. The only document so far that realistically assessed the situation and offered a mutually acceptable solution was the so-called Boden's document (2001), which the Abkhaz side refused even to receive for consideration and which has never been published.[7] Boden's document offers, as the only realistic solution to the dispute, the incorporation of the Abkhazian state into the federal Georgian state with limited sovereignty but with broad responsibilities delegated by the federal constitution.

Result of the peace process according to the parties' positions

Conflict can be considered as a kind of relationship that involves an incompatibility of goals. The incompatibility of the national projects of Abkhazians and Georgians became the main obstacle on the way to reconciliation. The Abkhaz are agreed in seeking independent statehood of the Republic of Abkhazia, or at least a limited statehood associated with the Russian Federation. Georgians are committed to the return of refugees to Abkhazia and to reincorporating the Abkhazia Republic in the redefined federal Georgian state. The world views of the parties are defined according to this perceived dilemma. International organizations and intellectual think-tanks involved in dispute resolution have been trying to figure out a combination of conditions that would overcome this dilemma and allow the sides to reconcile their positions. But the Abkhazian and Georgian positions, complicated as they may be, are marked with consistency, while the Russian position involves double standards.

The declared and actual Abkhazian position

The sides should commit themselves to non-violent negotiation towards the elaboration of the *separation* agreement, according to which Georgia agrees to the status of the independent Republic of Abkhazia, adopted by the Abkhazian parliament and based on results of the referendum held in 1999 among the current population of Abkhazia. Georgia must also agree to the terms for return of refugees and internally displaced persons (IDPs) decided by the Abkhaz authorities.

The declared and actual Georgian position

The sides should commit themselves to non-violent negotiation towards an elaboration of the *integration* agreement, according to which the *de facto* Abkhaz and the state Georgian authorities agree on a certain schedule involving the safe return and settlement of all refugees/IDPs to Abkhazia in a limited period of time, and the status of autonomy or limited sovereignty of the Abkhazia Republic within the Georgian federal state.

The declared Russian position

Russia respects the internationally recognized territorial integrity of Georgia, and negotiates the parties' agreement towards a mutually acceptable model of reintegration in a common state, or towards any other status acceptable for the parties to conflict and the custodians.

The actual Russian position

Russia supports the inspiration of the Abkhaz to achieve an independent statehood if it is combined with a pro-Russian orientation of Abkhazia. There were several statements of the Russian State Duma on Abkhazia, supporting secessionism and raising the possibility of accepting Abkhazia as an associated member of the Russian Federation. Russia is ready to consider the incorporation of the self-proclaimed Republic of Abkhazia in the Russian Federation if a serious external threat is posed to Russian citizens in Abkhazia, who now represent the majority of Abkhazia's population due to a policy of mass passport provision.

Obviously, there is incompatibility between the positions of the immediate parties to the conflict. Remarkably, there is also incompatibility between the declared and actual positions of the Russian Federation – a custodian to the peace process and a chief broker/mediator – with regard to the Georgian-Abkhaz dispute.

Post-conflict development as perceived by sides in the Georgian-Abkhaz dispute

It is clear that the main sides in the peacebuilding process are the Georgian and Abkhaz societies collectively, whose positions are represented by their respective élite groups. There is high-level social involvement and identification with the conflict cause on both sides. Apart from these main groups, other actors influence the process are parts of Russia's political, military, and economic élite (the most invariant groups throughout the dispute), the USA, the EU, the United Nations, and the OSCE, as well as the IDP community, North Caucasus communities kin to the Abkhaz, and ethnic/demographic groups within Georgian society.[8] In the existing distribution of forces, any peace agreement would have as signatories representatives of the Georgian state authorities and the Abkhazia *de facto* leadership. Most probably a Russian official representative would also be a signatory to the agreement.

One cannot envisage to a credible extent the future impact of spoiling unless one considers possible scenarios of (post-)conflict development involving the most important factors. In the following analysis, positive and negative scenarios of development in the Abkhazia conflict (eight in total) will be divided into "ideal" and "rational", and these, respectively, divided into "positive ideal" and "negative ideal", "positive rational" and "negative rational", for each of the parties to conflict.

Remarkably, an ideal scenario for Georgians does not mean that it exists for all Georgians. It exists for quantitative (numerous) and qualitative (publicly influential) groups of Georgians, mutually incompatible in a number of attitudes. Some would be satisfied only if they ideally get even with their opponents, while others would be happy only if they ideally reconcile. It certainly implies that the perception and identification of the Abkhazia problem is not uniform for Georgians, and that it represents a difficulty for Georgians themselves to identify this problem. The style chosen in the description of scenarios reflects the discourse of the relevant party to the conflict (e.g. persons who left Abkhazia as a result of war are called "refugees" in Abkhaz scenarios and "IDPs" in Georgian).

Positive ideal scenario from the Georgian perspective

Abkhaz actors realize that politically and culturally they have never been essentially different from Georgians, have never constituted a state independent from Georgia, and cannot seek independence from the nation that sheltered them from external domination and supported them during Soviet rule. They admit their struggle cannot be qualified as a national liberation movement, but only a rebellion inspired by separatist groups in Abkhaz society and their Russian and North Caucasian supporters. The ruling Abkhazian political élite group must change their position or abandon political life. Russia weakens/disintegrates so much that it is unable to support separatist regimes (Russia changing its attitude is unimaginable in this scenario). The Abkhaz publicly and officially express their regret for the rebellion, and offer an apology for the mass ethnic cleansing of ethnic Georgians they and their allies executed in 1992–1993 and in following incidents. Unambiguous acknowledgement follows that Abkhazia will never be in a position to create an independent state, supported by a mass demonstrations of affection for Georgia and willingness to collaborate in restoring Georgian rule over the whole territory of Abkhazia and rapid repatriation of all IDPs to their homes. Abkhazia will not even insist on receiving autonomous republic status if Georgia prefers a unitary state structure to a federalist one, and accepts rights of cultural autonomy.

Negative ideal scenario from the Georgian perspective

The Abkhaz unambiguously state they will pursue independence or incorporation into the Russian Federation at all costs, continue publicly to express their intolerance towards Georgians, and strengthen their links with Russian nationalists and military. Russia ensures sustainability of the internationally still-unrecognized Abkhazian state. The Abkhazian authorities form sustainable alliances with the ethnically related North

Caucasus nations, which express their solidarity with and provide armed support for the Abkhazian cause. Ignoring the UN/OSCE etc. decisions and resolutions, the Abkhaz expatriate all remaining or returned ethnic Georgians from Abkhazia, and close and land-mine the border with the help of Russian "peacekeeping" forces. Abkhazia remains an uncontrolled territory active in trafficking, illegal trade, and smuggling of weapons and drugs. Maintaining trade links with Russia and Turkey[9] and developing ties with international terrorist groups allow them to prolong indefinitely their *de facto* independence, unless their supporters in the Russian State Duma succeed in incorporating Abkhazia in the Russian Federation. Abkhazia supports South Ossetia and Nagorno-Karabagh in maintaining their *de facto* independence, and supports nationalist anti-Georgian movements in ethnic minority settlements in Georgia. Georgian state power degencrates, and the international community – despite official warnings and statements – reacts passively, allowing the separation to be legitimized in the long run.

Positive rational scenario from the Georgian perspective

The Abkhaz (political leadership on behalf of the nation, or comparably considerable/influential groups) declare they want to restore friendly relations with Georgian society, and willingly accept their entry in the Georgian federal state. They realize that in their best national interest they should oppose Russian political domination, and never more be a tool of Russian or any other great-power politics. Being ethnically different from Georgians, they agree they have historically and culturally been related to the Georgian nation, that they respect centuries-long common traditions and ties with Georgians, and are committed to restoration together with Georgians of what was ruined by the conflict and war. Being committed to maintaining their autonomy on federalist principles within the Georgian state, the Abkhaz nevertheless sign an agreement according to which they will not seek full independence unless provoked by aggressive nationalist policies of Georgian authorities, in which case the Abkhaz will appeal to international law for protection. The international community achieves the replacement of Russia as an intermediary to settle the Georgian-Abkhaz dispute with appropriate international structures.

Negative rational scenario from the Georgian perspective

The Abkhaz negotiate with, yet decline all proposed solutions from, Georgians, insist on their *de facto* achieved and self-proclaimed independence, and become more sustainable by strengthening ties with Russian communists/nationalists, pro-Abkhaz North Caucasian nations, and their diasporas in Turkey and other countries. Finding a solution for the IDP repatriation problem and the Abkhazia conflict is postponed indefinitely. The Georgian repatriate-populated Gali region of Abkhazia, the only area where joint supervision (in a stronger case, *de facto* jurisdiction) of Georgian authorities might be accepted, turns into a high-risk zone. Finally, the Georgian authorities have to sign the only version of a negotiable agreement acceptable to the Abkhaz, whereby Abkhazia and Georgia, as two equal subjects of international law, sign a treaty by which they form a confederative state on a symmetrical basis which delegates certain prerogatives (like foreign diplomatic relations, foreign trade, border control, communications, etc.) to the federal structures and authorities. Abkhaz maintain their right of secession and formation of an independent state.

Positive ideal scenario from the Abkhazian perspective

Georgians realize they should not even attempt to offer any status for Abkhazia, but should accept whatever kind of statehood the Abkhaz people choose to build for themselves, and whoever they would want to affiliate with politically. Georgians acknowledge they have acted as aggressors towards Abkhazia and have executed forceful assimilation policies against the Abkhaz nation in the past, as a result of which the Abkhaz became a minority in their homeland. Georgians express their acceptance of whatever decision is arrived at by the Abkhaz, and, if the Abkhaz decision is to develop a common confederate state with Georgians, will negotiate (soft bargaining only) the principles of peaceful coexistence. If the Abkhaz refuse to have any political relationship with Georgia, the two parties willingly sign an agreement of neutrality and non-interference in each other's affairs. Georgia undertakes an obligation not to use military force, or third parties' or international influence, to press Abkhazia into a political or economic alliance, and not to raise the issue of repatriation of the refugees of the 1992–1993 Georgian-Abkhaz war to Abkhazia.

Negative ideal scenario from the Abkhazian perspective

Georgia manages, either by military force or by Western-aided economic and political pressure, to crush the Abkhazian statehood, restore Georgian jurisdiction over the whole Abkhazia territory, and forcibly settle masses of refugees (or would-be refugees) in Abkhazia, giving them a free hand in occupying Abkhaz homes whenever claimed by the repatriates and allowing acts of vengeance. Abkhazia is overwhelmed by criminal activities and the whole subregion plunges into turmoil. Abkhazia is declared (and acknowledged by UN and other international structures as) another province of Georgia and is again subject to forcible assimilation, extending to the full extermination or dissolution of the Abkhaz nation.

Positive rational scenario from the Abkhazian perspective

Despite the political and economic pressure, Abkhazia manages to achieve internal stability and sustainability, develop trade and barter exchange with neighbouring countries like Turkey or Russia (especially North Caucasus autonomies), and strengthen its position in negotiations on the future status of Abkhazia. Seeing that Abkhazia is able to sustain itself at least for another decade, Georgia agrees to sign the federative union treaty with the Abkhazia Republic, based on which they form a confederation or an asymmetrical federation wherein the Abkhaz preserve all the rights that ensure their sovereignty, security, and autonomous development. Abkhazia succeeds in including a secession right in the treaty. Georgian authorities keep to the prerogatives delegated to them by the union treaty. Limited groups of Georgian refugees return to places prescribed by the Abkhaz authorities where they cannot destabilize the local situation.

Negative rational scenario from the Abkhazian perspective

Georgia manages to activate the CIS governments and the international community to exercise political pressure and strengthen the blockade of Abkhazia, escalates guerilla war, and succeeds in aggravating economic, social, and political conditions in Abkhazia to the extent that the internal situation is seriously destabilized. Crime and corruption further undermine Abkhaz society. Negotiations with the Georgian leadership are at a stalemate because Georgia does not want to negotiate an equal partnership agreement on forming a confederal/federal state, and insists on refugee return to the entire territory of Abkhazia. In this case Abkhazia is forced to seek incorporation in the Russian Federation or pursue *de facto* independence through an alliance with North-Caucasian-friendly and ethnically related nations (e.g. in the proposed United North Caucasus republic).

Realistic outcomes

Needless to say, the rational scenarios have a considerably higher probability of materializing, although it is hard to make a decisive choice between them at the moment. The "magic formula" for both avoiding and overcoming inter-ethnic disputes, especially of a titular ethnic group with minorities, is making life in the country attractive, if not for economic prosperity, than for safety, tolerance, and openness, thus creating stimuli for minorities to stay rather than to secede. Georgia is gradually turning into a stable country. In spite of a severe energy and production crisis caused by the collapse of the Soviet internal market, the country has managed not only to survive but to build up its capacity to play a significant role in regional and international relations.

The perception of spoiling and spoilers amongst the parties to conflict

The perception of spoiling in this case is formed according to the ideas of a *just* approach to the issue and its *just* solution. Spoiling is seen wherever one side acts contrary to the other side's *perceived* goal of the peace process.

The Abkhaz

The spoilers are Georgian state authorities, as they act contrary to their expressed commitments and signed agreements; they undermine and violate bilateral and multilateral agreements, sponsor guerillas, and impose sanctions and blockades. Loyalty is expressed by the Abkhaz party both to the Russian mediation and to IOs, INGOs, and IGOs. Cautious tolerance is expressed to the selected Georgian NGOs/CSOs involved in a very limited dialogue process (approved by the *de facto* Abkhaz authorities).

The Georgians

The spoilers are Russian mediators and the official structures involved in the negotiation process: they act contrary to their expressed commitments and signed agreements, and are siding with the Abkhaz and prevent rapprochement. The Abkhaz *de facto* authorities are not spoilers: they just adhere to what they strive for. Tolerant scepticism is expressed towards IOs and INGOs, although loyalty is expressed towards Western GOs and IGOs.

The Russians

The spoilers are Georgian state authorities, as they act contrary to their expressed commitments and signed agreements; they undermine and violate bilateral and multilateral agreements, sponsor guerillas, and impose sanctions and blockades. Spoilers are also Western IGOs which support the Georgian side.

Discussion

The interest represented by the Abkhazia case lies in that it differs from most studied cases of conflict and post-conflict situations. In the first place, there are no spoilers unambiguously recognized by both sides, but there are actors unilaterally identified as spoilers by one party to conflict, or by a third party. In Rwanda, Cambodia, Sri Lanka, Mozambique, Angola, South Africa, Bosnia, and many other cases the dynamics of the process involved a change of role/interest/resourcefulness of the actors immediately engaged in peace negotiations and a fulfilment of the agreement. Efforts of the international community led to signing peace agreements in all these countries after a period of intensive post-civil-war negotiations, followed in some cases by a renewal of civil war or genocide perpetrated by the former parties to the peace process or even signatories of the peace agreement. In the South Caucasus cases it has never come to the stage of elaborating or signing a peace agreement, but only to provisional and interim agreements on a cease-fire, and the creation of commissions of joint control on a cease-fire.

Azerbaijan and Georgia have been careful about taking any decisions that might lead to or be interpreted as a legitimization of the *de facto* authorities of the seceded territories; at the same time, it became clear that boycotting and the "no negotiation" strategy was not a managing tool. Georgia's approach in Abkhazia has been less rigid than Azerbaijan's in Nagorny-Karabakh, but it did not bring the parties' positions closer.

The insufficient impact of the efforts of international organizations has been obvious to all (proven by the non-existence of substantial stimuli for the parties involved to hurry after "the departing train"[10]). Yet there has been little analysis specifically on the causes of this inefficiency, as this might reveal the degree of rigidity in international peacekeeping operations and an awkward circumstance that freezing the conflict may comply with the bureaucratic needs of huge intergovernmental structures. It was much easier to blame the situation on the marginalities of post-Soviet space and the inability of the parties to negotiate.

A view has emerged in the outside world about seceded formations that may be described as the "Tom and Jerry effect":[11] the smaller are perceived as weaker and needing protection from their larger adversaries, sympathies are rearranged accordingly, and efforts to defreeze[12] the conflict are therefore rejected and even condemned as jeopardizing stability in conflict zones. As a result, the secessionists and their supporters manage to mobilize resources that balance the powers, which, in turn, prolongs the *status quo* but at the same time leads to manipulation of on-site situations and eventually to "sterilization" of the peace process.[13] The secessionists therefore grow in their own vision as victorious small nations successfully establishing themselves against larger "imperial" powers.

All the UN Security Council resolutions and positions of member states unambiguously adhere to the territorial integrity of Georgia and Azerbaijan, meaning that no legitimization may be accepted for the self-proclaimed republics of Abkhazia, Nagorny-Karabakh, and South Ossetia without prior consent of the respective South Caucasus states. Most cases of ethnic separatism have remarkably ended in the international community finally legitimizing the secession and sponsoring the creation of new independent states.

The "fog of the peace process" in the Abkhazia case may be illustrated by the Russian Federation's acceptance (rather than assignation) by the international community as the broker of the peace agreement in a conflict zone where it does not act as a neutral party. An internationally sponsored mediator and custodian of the peace process has appeared to be acting as a spoiler. In their turn, Georgia and Azerbaijan have looked at international mediation as a tool to exert pressure on the secessionists, while the radical groups in their societies have pressured their governments not to negotiate at all, as this, in their view, in itself already means legitimization of secessionist authorities. An ideal process according to such groups would take place if the international organizations "mediated" the imposition of ultimata on secessionists while host governments consistently kept a non-negotiating stance. The Abkhazia case also shows another peculiarity. The radical group of Georgian IDP leaders from the "Abkhazia government-in-exile" – which was obviously in opposition to the peacebuilding process in the 1990s – were never openly criticized by the international custodians of the peace process, although informally the reaction to this group has been extremely negative. UN and OSCE missions in Georgia have always stressed that their policy is to cooperate with that group, as it had been supported and backed by the Georgian state authorities.[14]

The peace process in the Abkhazia case may succeed only if "the fog is cleared": clear definitions lead to the abandonment of the double standards and ambiguous policies of some of the "peace custodians", the parties to conflict and subjects of peace process are clearly defined, and international mediation is done via "outsider-neutral"[15] parties and is combined with a substantial effort to exert pressure on the parties violating the internationally recognized rules and norms of the peace process.

Defreezing as spoiling? The case of South Ossetia intervention

The first serious attempt in the whole post-war period to change the balance of forces in a conflict zone was made in summer 2004 by the Georgian authorities. 'After the "rose revolution" (November 2003), President Mikheil Saakashvili at his inauguration in January 2004 publicly promised the Georgian people "Georgia will be whole again".' That meant he would restore the territorial integrity of the country within the period of his presidency – of course by non-violent means. After the second successful milestone of the Georgian revolution – ousting a Moscow-backed rebellious Ajara provincial leader, Aslan Abashidze, in early May 2004 – the Georgian government started to prepare the third stage: they developed a strategy for defreezing the Abkhazia and South Ossetia post-conflict process. Efforts were first made with regard to South Ossetia, combining "carrots" (humanitarian assistance, free medical aid to Osset and Georgian villagers, putting the former on the Georgian state payroll for pensions, etc.) and "sticks" (dissolution of the Ergneti market at the entrance to the South Osset capital Tskhinvali, where ethnic Georgian and Ossets traded together, illegal goods were smuggled, and criminal money was laundered; increasing of the number of Georgian armed block-posts, especially in the Georgian-populated villages, etc.). Georgian intervention was a risky experiment intended to bring the "frozen" system out of equilibrium to make it more manageable. It seems that the Georgian government expected understanding of, if not full support for, these actions from the Russian authorities, especially in view of the visible thaw in Georgian-Russian relations earlier in spring 2004. But the result was exactly the opposite: the Russian mass media and State Duma denounced Saakashvili's policy as spoiling and attempted to launch a new stage of the "rose revolution" in South Ossetia. The Western reaction has been spectacularly different.

The Russian view of this process has focused on concrete cases of violation of the agreements, as well as unilateral action on the Georgian side, which they assessed as risky and irresponsible. The Georgian view of the same process focused on the generally biased attitude of the Russian peacekeepers in the conflict zone and the State Duma's expressed statements of support for the secessionists.

In the Russian perspective, no actions of the Georgian authorities in the conflict zone were legitimate unless approved in advance by the four-sided commission (dominated at that time by the Russian-appointed commander of peacekeeping forces who never hid his anti-Georgian approach[16]). According to the Russian authorities' view, the Georgians attempted in summer 2004 to establish their military control in the conflict zone and *de facto* Georgian jurisdiction in South Ossetia by treating both Osset and Georgian populations according to Georgian law (even by paying pensions), while the entire population of South Ossetia is in fact subordinate to the constitution and legislature of the South Ossetia Republic (Russian official documents avoid calling it "self-proclaimed", or otherwise stressing the lack of legitimacy of that entity). An interim solution to the aggravated situation in the conflict zone, in the Russian view, may be achieved only through the full submission of the Georgian authorities to the *de facto* distribution of powers in place for the entire post-war period.

According to the Georgian perspective, the Russian approach has been illegitimately imposing on the Georgian side the attitude that the South Ossetia Republic is a separate state, and was contrary to Russia's international obligations and official declarations of the Russian leadership. If it is internationally acknowledged that South Ossetia is part of Georgia, then why should Georgian humanitarian initiatives and actions require special permission for implementation in the conflict zone? The Georgian perspective presupposed also the right of movement for Georgian law enforcement agencies in South Ossetia, which had never been requested in previous years. For many years the Georgians had not interfered in the practically unlimited domain of the peacekeeping operation zone for the sake of maintaining the fragile stability. In return, Georgian villagers in South Ossetia were kept by the local *de facto* authorities in relatively safe conditions. The Osset secessionist government led by then President Ludwig Chibirov collaborated with the Georgian authorities on practical matters in a balanced manner, and movement between the conflict zone and mainland Georgia had been simplified. The election of Eduard Kokoity as president of South Ossetia in 2002 indicated a more intrusive approach by Russia to the seceded regions of Georgia: Russian passports were openly distributed among the population of Abkhazia and South Ossetia, control of local mass media and NGOs hardened, and movement to/from Tbilisi was complicated. Kokoity's government repeatedly tried to push towards the incorporation of South Ossetia in the Russian Federation – an initiative unacceptable in international law but always positively reacted to and encouraged by the Russian State Duma, which had repeatedly threatened to impose sanctions on Georgia for the protection of Russian citizens[17] in South Ossetia and Abkhazia. According to Georgia's view, it is legitimate to defend the rights (at least) of the Georgian population of South Ossetia, who have never acknowledged themselves as citizens of another country.

According to the Western perspective represented by European and US media sources, academic writings, and analytical papers (official documents are much more reserved), Russia is not a neutral party, as it has been siding with one – and remarkably, a secessionist – party in all post-Soviet conflicts and cannot play the role of impartial mediator in the internal conflicts of Georgia. If it is true that defreezing contains certain threats to stability and peace (a cease-fire in this case), then freezing is no more credible and praiseworthy than defreezing, and freezing the conflicts is what the "custodians to peace" have been contributing to in all the post-war years of the so-called peace process in Georgia. Russia's role has been spectacular in this regard, although it did not ideologically contradict the roles and mandates of the international structures on site.

Conclusions

Logically speaking, "spoiling" is a term applicable to actual, not virtual or simulated, peace processes; spoiling can take place where there is something to spoil, i.e. a valid peace process. The peace process in Georgia has balanced for years on the brink of disappearing. Therefore one needs a certain amount of caution and clarity when speaking of the role of spoiling in Georgia. The parties' mutual perception includes a specific vision and understanding of spoiling. The specificity of the peace process in the Abkhazia and South Ossetia conflicts corresponds to the specificity of spoilers and spoiling in these cases. In order to identify a spoiling party and the nature of spoiling in a given case, it is important to be as far removed as possible from the impact of subjectivity present in the parties' vision of the roots, causes, and resolution of the conflict. Specifically, in the Georgian conflicts one can observe the influence of an external spoiler.

In the Abkhazia and South Ossetia cases Russia has displayed partiality and double standards: officially declaring neutrality and adherence to internationally recognized principles, and actually siding with a secessionist party. Russian mediation has contributed to the frozen state of negotiations and deepened the gap between the parties to conflict, which is incompatible with the role of a custodian of the peace process. A custodian of the peace process acting as insider-partial is actually a party to conflict, and loses legitimacy as an objective mediator.

A lack of communication between the conflicting parties, persisting negative stereotypes, and deadlocked negotiations diminish the chances of a negotiated peace agreement and increase the probability of renewal of armed clashes. Therefore attempts at humanitarian intervention and other non-violent forms of "defrosting" cannot be rejected as such. The general attitude of the European interparliamentary, interstate, and human rights structures prior to and after the Georgia developments in summer 2004 has been limited to appeals to stay within the confines of bilateral actions and refrain from any attempts at "defrosting". A complicated conflict scene and casualties in South Ossetia were later referred to as evidence of the futility and danger of any attempt to interfere in the distribution of forces in a conflict zone and the structure of frozen conflict. This should not mean, however, that "freezing" is a better situation than "defreezing", especially if international mediation efforts have been unsuccessful for over a decade and at least one custodian to the peace process has really done nothing towards the reconciliation of the parties.

Notes

1. Prior to the conflict, ethnic Abkhaz people (80,000–90,000) represented 18 per cent of the population of the Abkhazian Autonomous Republic in Soviet Georgia and 2 per cent of the entire population of Georgia, according to the 1989 Census. The 1993 ethnic cleansing of the ethnic Georgian population (around 260,000) allowed the Abkhaz people to obtain demographic control in Abkhazia. UN-supervised return of internally displaced persons has been managed so far only in the border territory of the Gali district of Abkhazia. The Abkhaz people barely form a majority even in the present depopulated seceded territory, along with Russians, Armenians, Greeks, and other local minority groups.
2. The South Caucasus territories were incorporated into Tsarist Russia during the nineteenth century. The First World War and the subsequent revolutionary process in Russia allowed Georgia, Armenia, and Azerbaijan briefly to restore their independent statehood in 1918, aborted by Red Army intervention and the following seven decades of Soviet rule. The first tension in Abkhazia dates back to the late nineteenth century (the Samurzakhano crisis of the Mukhajirs).
3. On 18 November 1990, in the still existing but fatally weakened Soviet Union, the newly elected Georgian parliament abolished the South Ossetia Autonomous Oblast as "an artificial entity implanted by the Bolsheviks to facilitate their imperialist national policy of divide and rule".
4. The quadrilateral "Chuburhinji" Commission for Abkhazia and quadrilateral "JCC" (Joint Control Commission) for South Ossetia were created. In South Ossetia the permanent participants in negotiations are Georgian, South Osset, North Osset, and Russian official delegations, whose chiefs make a Council of Co-Chairpersons of the Commission.
5. In the Nagorny-Karabakh conflict a special OSCE-sponsored interstate Minsk group was created to monitor and mediate a negotiated solution, but no such permanent group was ever created for the Abkhazia and South Ossetia cases. Rather, an understanding was expressed of Russia's special role and right to mediate and broker negotiations in the Georgian internal conflicts.
6. Stedman, Stephen J. 1997. "Spoiler problems in peace processes", *International Security*, Vol. 22, No. 2.
7. Dieter Boden was in the mid-1990s the OSCE head of mission to Georgia, and in the early 2000s chief of UNOMIG.
8. ICCN. 2002. *The Abkhazia Problem Reflected by Public Opinion (Findings of Sociological Surveys)*. Tbilisi: ICCN.
9. Turkey has adhered to the territorial integrity of Georgia, yet private Turkish companies have been actively involved in barter trade with Abkhazia via the Black Sea ports.

10. Stedman, note 6 above.
11. Khutsishvili, George. 2004. "The 'Tom and Jerry effect' in the picture of ethno-political conflict", *24 Hours*, 21 July.
12. Cf. Khutsishvili, George. nd. "What freezes and what unfreezes conflicts?", available at http://sef-bonn.org/events/2000/kaukasus/khutsishvili.html.
13. Khutsishvili, note 11 above.
14. The Abkhazia government-in-exile was created after the civil war in Abkhazia and its secession from Georgia, as an alternative to and in the same format as the Soviet-style Abkhazia Supreme Council that had led the seceded autonomy, accompanied by all the ministries and departments which existed prior to the armed conflict. Contrary to the constitution, 10 seats were guaranteed for this group in the Georgian parliament until November 2003. Georgian revolution has put an end to this practice. It would be fair to mention that the government-in-exile has become more constructive after its chairman, Tamaz Nadareishvili, was voted down in February 2004.
15. Lederach, John Paul. 1995. *Preparing for Peace. Conflict Transformation Across Cultures*. New York: Syracuse University Press; Lederach, John Paul. 1997. *Building Peace: Sustainable Reconciliation in Divided Societies*. Washington, DC: US Institute for Peace Press.
16. Georgian TV channels, especially the leading Rustavi 2, gave in summer 2004 much evidence of this, in the form of live broadcasts and interviews with the head of the Russian peacekeepers, General Nabdzorov, on his biased attitudes towards Georgians.
17. Russia has double citizenship. Any other country's citizen may obtain Russian ID and will be considered in such a case to be a Russian citizen. Multiplying citizens in other countries is another tool to exert pressure on those countries.

14

Spoilers and devious objectives in Kashmir

Jaideep Saikia

If there were to be a single pronouncement about peace in Kashmir, the simplest response could be that there might never be peace. Indeed, this would seem to be true if the predicament of Kashmir – and the dynamics that have governed the problem since its inception – is considered in its entirety. The impasse, as it were, has become too complicated and variegated for a holistic solution to present itself. The *dramatis personae*, too, have expanded, and newer players are joining in with even newer agendas, with serious consequences for a viable solution to be even considered. Therefore, while there have been plenty of peace "initiatives", a serious reconciliation course has eluded the valley. Kashmir is the oldest conflict to be recorded under the aegis of UN resolutions, and few other conflicts in the post-Second World War period have proven to be so complicated. This is precisely why an appraisal of the "spoiling" experience in Kashmir is vital. Initiatives – were these carefully managed – that could have taken the shape of peace processes were all thwarted because of the unwillingness of the players to give up the stations from which they perceive the problem. The "spoiling" phenomenon in the case of Kashmir presents itself in a number of ways, the most important of which stems from the insincerity of the parties involved and the reluctance to make sacrifices. Moreover, there exist groups that are inherently (and publicly) opposed to any form of peaceful settlement – but even such groups are in reality hidden surrogates of the real players, the latter entering a "peace process" only in order to gain legitimacy and assuage external sentiment.

Background

Kashmir was the sole Muslim-majority "princely state" (ruled by a Hindu maharajah) to accede to India in 1947, following a massive Pakistan-sponsored incursion. The lapse of paramountcy (when the British were leaving) had offered the princely states in India the option of acceding either to India or to Pakistan. Whereas certain princely states, such as Junagadh, came under the ambit of India by dint of the majority population being Hindu (despite the fact, in Junagadh's case, that the ruler – a Muslim – had already acceded to Pakistan), the aberration in Kashmir is the root cause of the Kashmiri insurrection, and continues to be the core of the dispute.

The two most important protagonists continue to be India and Pakistan. This is so despite the fact that the stage has broadened to accommodate a new group of actors whose script proclaims a programme that has hijacked the initial libretto of *azadi* (freedom). Kashmir today bears the countenance of yet another battleground in the global *jihadi* progression that was started on 9/11. The *salafi* strain of Islam and its extreme militant manifestations have more or less usurped the cloak of insurrection from the local actors, and the present rebellion is by and large controlled and executed by guest separatists[1] and their minders from across the borders.[2] Indeed, the *modus operandi* of the guest separatists approximates warlordism, where leaders of armed bands hold territory, act financially and politically without interference, confront national governments, exterminate uncooperative populations, and derail peace processes.[3] Although it would not be entirely accurate to state that the uprising is devoid of local participation (as the Indian authorities are claiming),[4] the fact of the matter is that the past few years have seen a visible dwindling in local involvement. Independent estimates, however, hold that were a head count of separatists done, the indigenous Kashmiris would continue to be in a majority. These inconsistencies notwithstanding, it is quite clear that the rebellion in Kashmir is being carried out on a range of fronts – an issue that is not inconsiderable when the question of dialogue is raised.

The disingenuous approaches to Kashmir by both India and Pakistan have, moreover, allowed the situation to worsen, without an endgame in sight. The two countries continue to cling to the stubborn positions that informed the opening days of the crisis. This obstinacy has begotten only a debilitating stalemate. Therefore, as Stephen Cohen writes:

For the Pakistanis, Kashmir remains the "unfinished business" of the 1947 partition. Pakistan, the self-professed homeland for an oppressed and threatened Muslim minority in the Subcontinent, finds it difficult to leave a Muslim-majority region to a Hindu-majority state. Indians, however, argue that Pakistan, a state defined and driven by its religion, is given to irredentist aspirations in Kashmir because it is unwilling to accept the fact of a secular India. India, a nominally secular state, finds it difficult to turn over a Muslim-majority region to a Muslim neighbour *just because* it is Muslim.[5]

India also fears that abandoning its claim to Kashmir would trigger off a domino effect, and other insurrectionary movements inside the country would demand secession from India as well. As for Pakistan, the severance of East Pakistan in 1971 continues to unsettle it and it has yet to come to terms with its undermined eminence in the region. According to an avid Kashmir watcher, "the two states had come to accept the Westphalian and Weberian concepts of statehood, which, among other matters, prohibit states from willingly ceding territory that they deem to be their own".[6]

In this mêlée of contradictions it is the Kashmiri who suffers. Both India and Pakistan prevaricate on the issue without seriously taking into account the aspirations of the indigenous people. The two countries differ about the mechanism for determining Kashmiri sentiment and also about which of the two countries should control it, but both India and Pakistan seem united in their opposition to Kashmir acquiring sovereign status.

The only political, pro-independence conglomerate in Indian-administered Kashmir that purportedly has a representative authority is the All-Parties Hurriyat Conference. The Hurriyat (Liberation) is a conglomerate of 26 parties, variously dedicated to either independence or a merger with Pakistan. Indeed, until the Hurriyat split of September 2003,[7] which brought to the fore the pro- and anti-talk factions (which continue to be the heart of the split), the amalgam had been consistently sponsored by Pakistan in the latter's pursuit of instituting legitimacy to its claims over Kashmir.

In the peace initiative of late 2003, New Delhi began a dialogue with both Pakistan and the pro-talk Hurriyat faction, indicating that a degree of charity and an intentioned initiative had begun. Hurriyat pro-talkers welcomed the offer of talks and held meetings with representatives of New Delhi. However, the prospect of talks got mired in controversy because the split in the Hurriyat – exposing the moderate and hard-line positions[8] – is leading to the bifurcation of the Kashmiri polity they represent. The leader of the pro-Pakistan and anti-talk Hurriyat group, Syed Ali Shah Geelani, rejected the Indian offer to hold talks by stating "unless New Delhi calls for a tripartite dialogue, pursues invocation of the UN resolution or allows mediation by a neutral country, the talks are bound to fail".[9] Moreover, the obduracy with which Geelani greeted the offer of talks seems to have an agenda which calls into question Pakistan's role in the Hurriyat split, despite the fact that later attempts (however futile) were made by Pakistan to unify the two factions – observers are of the opinion that a united Hurriyat can be more useful for creating the impression anew that the entire Kashmir Valley would like to be part of Pakistan.[10] Whereas on the face of it, it is ego that seems to be coming in the way of Hurriyat unification, the fact of the matter is that Pakistan was responsible in the first place for egging on the differences between the moderates and the hard-liners in the Hurriyat and for attempting systematically to neutralize all opposition within the conglomerate – a former leader, Abdul Ghani Lone, was assassinated as a result of his participation in a "deal with India".

But it would be incorrect to blame only Pakistan for the Hurriyat split. India, too, is suspected to have a hand in it, and it is a possibility that the Indian establishment forced Geelani's hand and engineered the split in order to open a course of dialogue with the moderates. The Indian strategy seems to be clearly one by which Geelani was sought to be alienated, as the continuance of a united Hurriyat – with Geelani's sustained intransigence – was perceived as a stumbling block to an intentioned initiative. But why was New Delhi eager to talk to "representatives" of the Kashmiri people? Was the change in the Indian perception occasioned by the general elections that were held in April–May 2004 (and the need to rein in the Muslim votes, and also to project a centrist magnanimity to the Indian electorate)? Is it also possible that the USA pressured Pakistan to allow India a window by which a process of dialogue can be carried out, accomplishing thereby not only India's "electoral commitments" but also forcing a process which once begun could actually trigger off an important initiative, as indeed to a certain degree it has? Writing about the politicking that reportedly characterized the theory, an observer opines:

Several explanations have been offered for this sudden turn-around. Some observers believe there was intense US pressure to give their Afghan war ally, General Pervez Musharraf, some legitimacy, some legitimacy-inducing concession on J&K. This school of thought points to a dramatic reduction in fatalities in J&K in October [2003], which fell to a record low compared to the same month in 2001 and 2002 – and, indeed, to a level not seen since March this year [2003]. This can be interpreted to be a partial fulfilment by Musharraf of India's "no-terrorism" precondition.[11]

A successful third-party "behind-the-scenes" chaperoning – if the above is to be believed – precariously hinges on the USA's ability not merely to pressure Musharraf to rein in the separatists, but to ascertain that he is *actually* able to do so. However, notwithstanding Musharraf's ambitious 12 January 2002 speech (when the Pakistani president spoke of reining in the Islamists in his country and stopping sponsorship of terrorism in Kashmir), the fact of the matter is very little has been done in this direction, and even the decrease in infiltration into Indian-administered Kashmir by separatists is primarily due to the fence which has been erected on the Indian side of the line-of-control (LoC) and better vigilance. Therefore, the question which the USA should ask is not whether Musharraf is well-intentioned but whether he has adequate sway within his own realm to implement his objectives. This is particularly relevant when seen in the context of reported "concessions on Kashmir" by Musharraf and the reaction (including assassination attempts on the Pakistani leader) within Pakistan by hard-liners. Therefore, while a "third-party behind-the-scenes mediation" by the USA has been able to absorb, as it were, the immediate shocks of spoiling attempts, it has actually encouraged spoiling of a different kind. Indeed, it must be understood that the stubbornness of some of the parties involved in Kashmir will ensure that novel spoiling tactics continue to be engineered in order to counter the myriad attempts at peace.

At any rate, what is clear is that a modicum of peace has been achieved. Whereas India has been able to open a dialogue with the moderate faction of the Hurriyat and hold a reasonably peaceful election in Indian-administered Kashmir, the armies of both India and Pakistan stationed in the LoC[12] have received some respite as a result of the cease-fire. The lessening of troop strength by India in Indian-administered Kashmir has also aided the process, and has credibly contributed to a "space for democracy to flourish".[13] The Kashmiris, too, are beginning to benefit from the situation, despite the fact that there has been little let-up in the separatist violence in the valley: the peace dividend is goading India, the Hurriyat, and Pakistan to prolong the peace, and even welcome an Indian initiative to begin a bus service between Srinagar and Muzaffarabad and, later, a Pakistani initiative (in the aftermath of the devastating earthquake of 8 October 2005 when thousands of Kashmiri lives were lost) to open up five points in the LoC so that relief workers can cross the line and ferry relief and reconstruction material for the earthquake victims. Indeed, the peace dividend has allowed India and Pakistan to use the space to "iron out" other peripheral aspects as well, such as exchange of prisoners who have been languishing in each other's jails, and decrease the level of normal Indo-Pak rhetoric.[14] While it is difficult to predict whether such a peace can be sustained, a unique phenomenon that is being experienced in Kashmir is that the three major parties are "disunitedly" coming together not only to increase the "spoiler threshold", but also actually to alienate spoiling.

Spoilers in Kashmir

The spoiling phenomenon in Kashmir is motivated by an array of drivers. The tactics, funding, and impact of the spoilers, too, are unique. Indeed, all conflicts are locale-specific and have their peculiarities; spoiling reflects this. The spoiler phenomenon, moreover, germinates well in a scenario where a full-blown peace process is visible. But a viable peace process is yet to take shape in Kashmir, a consequence of the rigidity with which India and Pakistan hold on to their respective positions, despite exhibition of acts of concession. Indeed, devious objectives and spoiling have come to the fore whenever constituents of either or both the countries have sought to take bold initiatives at peacemaking. The Kargil crisis erupted shortly after the signing of the Lahore Declaration on 21 February 1999. Writing about the matter, one analyst has suggested:

Despite the positive and cooperative sentiments expressed in Lahore and in the weeks thereafter, the Pakistani military with the acquiescence of Nawaz Sharif, planned a military operation in Kashmir designed to revive the Kashmir issue on the international agenda and possibly jump-start the flagging insurgency.[15]

Spoilers have, therefore, been working overtime in the region in order to ensure that peace initiatives do not even get off the ground. As has been seen in the case of the Lahore-Kargil imbroglio,[16] the Pakistani army resorted to a low-intensity war to prevent a peace process from emerging.

The initiative and the subsequent events (particularly by way of the encouraging Hurriyat response and the cease-fire in Kashmir) of 2003–2004 present a situation which allows not only an opportunity for a serious engineering of a robust peace process, but also a chance to monitor closely the mechanism by which spoiling attempts may present themselves.[17] But the spoiler effort has to be read with care; even the current Indian peace initiative is confronted by hard-liners not just within the Hurriyat and Pakistan, but within the Indian establishment as well. The chapter has already observed the significance of elections in India and the US pressure. Alternatively, it is also a possibility that an opportunity presented itself the moment the Hurriyat split occurred. And India, sensing a gambit, took the plunge. Is it that India (whether it had a hand in the Hurriyat split or not), having appeased the moderates and neutralized the political opposition, wished to make short work of the hard-liners and the gun-wielding separatists militarily? The strategy could have been to catch Pakistan on the wrong foot and render it irrelevant. After all, whatever else the moderates in the Hurriyat have demanded, they have not demanded the immediate involvement of Pakistan, as Geelani has repeatedly sought to do. It is otherwise difficult to understand the Indian call to the pro-talk Hurriyat, and, of course, the faction's rather charitable response to New Delhi. But the moderates have been careful not to be seen to be too close to India. Indeed, not only did they make their stand clear on the release of political prisoners and on the question of human rights, but also asked the Kashmiris "not to be a part of" the Indian electoral process, the latter a clear departure from what would earlier have been an all-out boycott. Jargon and temperance – whether or not motivated by New Delhi – make for better initiative ingredients.

But would a peace initiative that is forced and/or motivated by such considerations as the above qualify as a peace initiative? Will a premeditated division in the space in Kashmir, the Hurriyat, or for that matter keeping out Pakistan, bring about durable peace? Or would it, as has been the case with other insurrectionary theatres in India, usher in a peace that is impermanent? New Delhi has been known – in order to resolve knotty questions – not only to engineer splits in political or strategic opposition, but also to adopt devious objectives by which opposing forces are lured to the table with the intention of "wearing them out". Analysts who follow the Naga peace process, for instance, seem to be of the opinion that New Delhi has adopted just such a strategy in the case of the 57-year-old north-eastern Indian uprising.

At any rate, engineering of splits, incarcerations of political opponents, and the invocation of the president's rule in "truant" provinces by New Delhi are not recent phenomena. The incarceration of Sheikh Abdullah by India when he sought to raise the question of self-determination for the Kashmiri people, and the stage-managed coup that unseated the former chief minister of Kashmir, Farooq Abdullah, and made his brother-in-law, G. M. Shah, the chief minister on 2 July 1984 are some of the ways in which past regimes in India have sought to silence opposition.

However, the issues that egg on India and Pakistan to maintain their intransigent positions in Kashmir are the inheritances and preambles of 1947.[18] But if the irregularity in manner and circumstance in which Kashmir acceded to India bore the genesis of the problem, the policies of the succeeding years have only furthered that flaw.

Spoilers: Indian

Kashmir provides certain institutions in India with an opportunity for leverage in governance. Whereas the vastness of the Indian geographical entity has given rise to many a fissure,[19] the Kashmir imbroglio continues to be a *prima donna*. The reason for this is quite simple. Kashmir and energy are the two most important aspects that propel Indian strategic policy. Therefore, even as other insurrectionary movements in India have occupied the Indian security apparatus, Kashmir allows the Indian security machinery the opportunity to brandish not only its primary role on which its *raison d'être* rests,[20] but also an opportunity to partake of aspects of statecraft which would not have normally come its way. Internal strife in India, for instance, has occasioned phenomenal budgets not only for an armed response but also for psychological operations against such movements, and for the rehabilitation of surrendered separatists as well. Although it is the Indian Ministry of Home Affairs that allocates such funds, the end-users are the police and the army. Such controls have, in the past, brought forth allegations of misappropriation. Whereas such cases have been few and far between in respect of the Indian army, fingers that have been pointed at the police and the paramilitary forces have not been insignificant. Reports have also alleged that certain members of the Indian Border Security Force, which mans separatist infiltration routes into Indian-administered Kashmir, receive money for allowing separatists to cross over unchallenged; other reports talk about the spiriting away of monies unearthed during counter-separatist operations for personal consumption. While such irregularities are reportedly non-organizational in nature, the fact of the matter is that the continuance of the Kashmir problem has been illegitimately beneficial for some Indian security personnel. This manner of spoiling, which characterizes sundry, non-institutionalized Indian attempts to keep the problem alive, can be said to be the handiwork of peripheral beneficiaries. Indeed, spoiling the peace process may not be their actual intention – but attempts to maintain *status quo* indirectly obstruct the peace process.

Indian intelligence

The involvement of the Indian intelligence agencies in the present Hurriyat split cannot be ruled out. But while it is true that certain members of the Indian intelligence establishment held several rounds of talks with the Hurriyat leaders, and perhaps even clandestinely aided Geelani's estrangement with the moderates by resorting to a variety of subterfuges, the charge that they were responsible for the split is yet to be proven. However, the fact that New Delhi has stolen a march as a result of the split is not in question: the charge of splitting the Hurriyat (so that New Delhi can talk to the more moderate of the two sides) is not tantamount to spoiling in the classic sense, although the fact that a division of space has disallowed the hammering out of a composite dialogue cannot be disregarded. Indeed, it is "spoiling" by another name, especially as it would prevent a long-term solution.

Other accusations have also come the Indian intelligence agencies' way in Indian-administered Kashmir. In the year 2000, on the eve of the former US President Bill Clinton's visit to India, suspected separatists gunned down 35 members of the Sikh community in Chhatisingphora. Separatist leaders, including Geelani,[21] condemned the incident and termed it the handiwork of Indian intelligence agencies. While the response of the Indian agencies in the aftermath of the massacre, when five "separatists" in Pathribal were shot amidst claims that they were the ones responsible for the massacre, was an absolute hoax,[22] a lesser-known fact (and one which accidentally came this writer's way during his study tour of Indian-administered Kashmir in 2000) was the information about an interception of a Lashkar-e-Toiba[23] relay to Muridke (Lahore) in the days preceding Clinton's India visit. The separatist group's local commander queried his minders in Pakistan by radio: "Clinton ko kitni ki salaami deni he?" (How many gun salutes must Clinton be accorded?) A few days later, at Chhatisingphora, the desired number of guns dealt out their death salutes.

But the Indian intelligence agencies' ability to resort to a variety of subterfuges in order to score over "rivals" (which could even include the Indian-administered Kashmir provincial government, especially if it is not affiliated or allied to the ruling party in New Delhi) cannot be ignored.

Indian army

Kashmir also allows the security apparatus a ringside view in the decision-making. Thus, while the deployment of the Indian army in Indian-administered Kashmir is considerable, the dynamics that occupy the Indian intelligence community and the paramilitary forces are also significant. However, the Indian army is not politicized, and unlike in Pakistan it has kept away from the corridors of power. But the Indian army has been turned into what Cohen terms a "paramilitary force",[24] and "more than one half of the army is engaged in internal security activities".[25] It feels that it deserves not only a budget[26] but also recognition for its heightened sense of alert. Consequently, even as the Kargil conflict heralded a media war, bringing into living rooms the sacrifices of the Indian army in the icy heights, the Indian army man began to perceive himself as a symbol of the nation's honour. In Cohen's words, "the Indian army saw itself as a sword which held India together".[27]

But symbolism and jingoism have not affected the Indian army's general belief in the continuance of democratic institutions in India. While it is perhaps true that certain sections of the Indian army see a prolongation of the Kashmir conflict as a means to attain some leverage and legitimacy[28] in a civilian-dominated structure, the spoiling phenomenon presents itself only as an aside.[29] It is not as if a deliberate effort is made to spoil a peace initiative.

Indian bureaucracy

The bureaucracy in India is yet another institution that would not actively seek a solution to Kashmir which would undermine its position. Although this "doctrinaire" stems from the belief that any solution in Kashmir would mean a measure of "giving up",[30] the fact of the matter is that the agencies which comprise the bureaucracy in India are against a political compromise with Pakistan or the Kashmiri representatives that would "give away" an advantage. The politicians, too, have been wary of bold initiatives in Kashmir:[31] the reasons which analysts proffer have included a tame "let the next generation tackle the situation, we are quite content with the *status quo*". Moreover, the Indian people, too, will never accept the giving away of Kashmir, particularly to Pakistan. Although the reasons would be largely nationalistic, it would not be inappropriate to say that the Indian establishment mirrors the Indian populace to a significant extent. Thus, if a show of hands was made in the Indian establishment there would be spoilers aplenty who would rather a peace initiative is destroyed than give in to the demands of Pakistan and/or the Kashmiri people. There is also evidence that there is an interest in keeping the problem *just alive*, in order to be able periodically to benefit from it. The spoiling range on the Indian side, therefore, extends from being able to benefit from the continuance of conflict to purely nationalistic reasons that prevent the giving up of territory. However, the impact this range of spoiling has on a peace process is considerable, the most important influence being the pressure applied to a party that has begun a peace process. Indeed, were it not for the personal initiative of the former Indian Prime Minister Atal Behari Vajpayee (which the present incumbent, Manmohan Singh, has been seen to have endorsed), the present initiative would not have even got off the ground. However, even Indian political leaders cannot wish to be seen as too soft – especially if the electorate does not want it.

Spoilers: Pakistani

Pakistan, on the other hand, cannot be so easily acquitted. Notwithstanding the cease-fire along the LoC (which was incidentally an offer made by Pakistan), the reality is that Indian "intimidation" is crucial for Pakistan in order to maintain its unity. As Cohen writes:

Distrust of India and the Kashmir conflict do serve as a national rallying cry for Pakistanis, and thus as a device for smoothing over differences between Pakistan's dominant province, Punjab, and the smaller provinces of Baluchistan, Sind, and the Northwest Frontier. India-as-an-enemy is also useful to distract the Pakistani public from other concerns, such as social inequality, sectarian (Sunni-

Shi'ia) conflict, and the distinct absence of social progress in many sectors of Pakistani society.[32]

Pakistani army

Even as Pakistan prepares to wage, as Benazir Bhutto once commented, "a thousand-year war" with India in order to uphold its reason for existence, the Pakistani army has endowed itself with a "special right to power", with those in "the infantry feeling that they understand Pakistan better".[33] It is the army – whether in or out of power – which calls the shots in Pakistan. It is concerned that if India were not tied down in Kashmir, its conventional military advantage would overwhelm Pakistan.

If the analysis of Cohen's latest book – *The Idea of Pakistan and the Fate of a Troubled State* – is any indication, the Pakistan army "would continue to rule the nation in a never-ending cycle".[34] When the Pakistani newspaper *Dawn* commented that "Kashmir is not a core issue but a corps commander issue",[35] it was not merely semantics but a statement of fact. Kashmir is the Pakistan army's obsession, a fixation that has been compounded after the defeat of 1971. Indeed, no Pakistani ruler can afford to be soft on Kashmir. Nawaz Sharif was ousted because of the humiliation of Kargil, and records state that even civilian leaders have sometimes used the Kashmir issue to browbeat the military.[36] The statement by Musharraf that Pakistani army officers were involved in the two attacks against him in December 2003 (at the time of the Islamabad summit when an Indo-Pak rapprochement was being built) is significant in the matter.[37]

But a general distrust of India in the Pakistan army, which sometimes manifests itself in obsessive behaviour, cannot necessarily be said to be the outpourings of an "Islamist army". Indeed, the armies of both countries continue to be run on the lines of the British system, and the typical Pakistani army officer is more or less secular in his outlook and enjoys "drinking whisky to the tune of bagpipes at regimental dinners".[38] Zia did, however, seek to bring Islam into almost every aspect of Pakistani life, including that of the army. Recruitments and indoctrination during his regime gave rise to a select "élite" within the army – almost on the lines of the Schutzstafel (SS) in the Second World War German army. Cohen writes that "Zia's stress on Islam, in an already conservative society, encouraged the Islamic zealots in the army".[39]

Although a significant number of such officers of the "Zia generation" survive despite a concerted "purge" by Musharraf, the Pakistan army is more interested in the geopolitical importance of Pakistan than Islam. Islam is only being utilized as a tool to foment trouble in Kashmir, as was the case in Afghanistan when the Pakistan army (along with the Inter

Services Intelligence of Pakistan) created, armed, and aided the Taliban. A popular belief that continues to make its round is about how the Taliban (after its creation) was presented with Afghanistan in order to keep it out of Pakistan. With Operation Enduring Freedom and the de-Talibanization of Afghanistan, the accepted theory is that the minders of the Taliban have given them Kashmir. Therefore, as Cohen elucidates, the Pakistan army's strategic core might continue to be one that speaks of an avoidance of a full-fledged war with India, but its agenda to support Kashmiri separatists will continue.[40] The cease-fire and soft-LoC offer by Pakistan, in the opinion of this author, is a manifestation of this operational code. This is so despite the fact that Islamabad has decided to crack down on separatist organizations such as Lashkar-e-Toiba and Jaish-e-Mohammad. Indeed, former Indian Deputy Prime Minister L. K. Advani stated that "there is no evidence of Pakistan having abandoned terrorism. It continues unabated."[41] Kashmir cannot be abandoned, not only because of the imperatives of the founding principles of Pakistan, the unity (and distraction) it provides to the Pakistani *milieux*, and the humiliation of 1971, but also because of the practical considerations, *à la* the *jihadi*.

Pakistani intelligence and the jihadi

The Inter Services Intelligence (ISI) of Pakistan is the organization that is entrusted with the task of creating disorder in Kashmir.[42] It plans, trains, funds, and controls the anti-India *tanzeems* (separatist groups). Endowed with huge sums of money for carrying out covert operations in Kashmir, the ISI reportedly spends as much as IRs 2.4 crore every month in Indian-administered Kashmir. Operation Tupac is, reportedly, the name of the plan to liberate Kashmir, initiated by Zia in 1988 after the failure of Operation Gibraltar. Another plan of action has been made operational by way of Operation K-2. Although all separatist groups reportedly receive arms and training from Pakistan, the pro-Pakistani groups are reported to be favoured by the ISI. At least six major militant organizations, and several smaller ones, are operating in Kashmir. Their strengths are variously estimated at between 5,000 and 10,000. They are roughly divided between those who seek *azadi* and those who support accession to Pakistan. The oldest militant organization, the Jammu and Kashmir Liberation Front (JKLF), had spearheaded the movement for an independent Kashmir. Latest reports, however, suggest that the JKLF has fallen from the ISI's grace because of its neutrality. The powerful pro-Pakistani group Hizbul-Mujaheedin has replaced it, as have the Lashkar-e-Toiba, the Jaish-e-Mohammad, and new groups such as Inquilab, which are beginning to operate directly under Al-Qaeda direction. According to media reports, several hundred fighters from Afghanistan

and other Muslim countries have also joined some of the militant groups or have formed their own *tanzeems*. Indeed, with the closure of the Afghan bureau of the ISI, the intelligence agency's entire concentration is focused on Kashmir and other parts of India. A compendium of the ISI's *modus operandi* in Kashmir may not be possible at this juncture. However, by way of an enumeration, the principals would include the following.
- Recruiting separatists from Indian-administered Kashmir and the Muslim world and training them in anti-India activities.
- Funding of the *tanzeems*, including certain leaders of the Hurriyat. The funding takes place through the *hawala* method and direct payments are made in places such as the Middle East and Nepal, and, as has been unearthed, through legitimate businessmen in other parts of India. At least one report has suggested that funds to the tune of IRs 4–5 billion come by way of expatriate Kashmiris who have lucrative businesses in the Gulf. Even Muslims from other countries are contributing to the separatist coffer. The UN Drugs Control Programme has alleged that about US$2.5 billion accrues annually to the ISI,[43] and recent press reports have said that narcotics smuggling may be funding the activities of the Jaish-e-Mohammad.[44] It is also of interest that the ISI-chaperoned Jihad Council's printing press in Pakistan-administered Kashmir's Muzaffarabad allegedly prints fake Indian currency notes. In the year 2000 a racket was unearthed in Srinagar in which IRs 6.5 million was discovered by the security forces. Interestingly, compensation to families of local separatists who were killed by the Indian security forces was made using the counterfeit notes.
- Planning and aiding infiltration/exfiltration of separatist groups into and from Indian-administered Kashmir.
- Assassination of moderate Kashmiri leaders like Abdul Ghani Lone who wanted to open a dialogue with India. In this context, it is of interest to mention that the present crop of moderate Hurriyat leaders such as Ansari and Bhat are under threat, which is why leaders like Ansari showed some initial hesitation about talking to New Delhi.
- Planning and executing sabotage activities in Indian-administered Kashmir and elsewhere in India, the notables being the attack on the Indian parliament and the Akshardham temple in Gujarat. The ISI is also entrusted with the task of setting up explosions in places such as Mumbai.
- Aiding the Taliban and Al-Qaeda to enter Indian-administered Kashmir to give the present insurrection a novel direction.
- Pumping in money for the setting up of Deobandi-style *madrassas* in Indian-administered Kashmir and other parts of India with an eye to creating a Taliban-like militia in Kashmir.

- Planning and executing the killings of minorities inside Indian-administered Kashmir.
- Waging a propaganda war against India in Indian-administered Kashmir.
- Stoking Islamist fundamentalism and fanning communal disharmony in Indian-administered Kashmir and the rest of India.

The ISI has the ability to spoil the infant peace initiative in any of the above ways. Indeed, these methods have already been demonstrated in its Kashmir operations. Whether it has the ability to cross the spoiler threshold or not (in the present scenario) is a matter that will have to await the passage of time. A serious clamping down on its Kashmir operations would be tantamount to downsizing it by grave degrees.

The ISI, the *jihadi*, and the Pakistan army thus comprise the troika that seek the continuance of the Kashmir problem the most, and the spoiling of which they are capable can be perceived in the 57 years of subterfuge they have been engineering. Moreover, the impact this spoiling has had on myriad peace processes has testified that their sole intention has been to destroy any sort of negotiated settlement with India. Indeed, the pan-Islamic resurgence that is manifesting itself in different parts of the world has only emboldened the resolve to liberate Indian-administered Kashmir from Indian hands. The Islamists – despite whatever President Musharraf is purportedly doing to curb their activities – have their own agenda, which is moored to ideology. Hafiz Mohammed Saeed, the head of the Lashkar-e-Toiba, recently stated to his supporters, "Let me make it clear to you that a solution to the [Kashmir] issue is not at the negotiating table. It is not even in the Security Council, but in *jihad*."[45] It is therefore not clear whether the Pakistani president has complete control over the *tanzeems* and the ISI. The global *salafi* movement, of which the non-local separatists in Kashmir see themselves as a part, characterizes the *jihadi* zeal to "liberate" Kashmir. A tacit understanding exists between the Pakistani establishment and the *jihadi*: Pakistan (which comprises various entities beside Musharraf) will exhibit attempts to rein in the *jihadi* at home, and express its helplessness about the ones waging war in Indian-administered Kashmir. It will be these *jihadi* elements acting as "freedom fighters" that will play spoiler. The spoiler phenomenon will take on a new dimension, with proxies doing the bidding of hidden spoilers. Violence has not lessened in Indian-administered Kashmir – even in the aftermath of the terrible earthquake of 8 October 2005, when observers opined that the untold destruction on both sides would momentarily halt the *jihadi* campaign in Kashmir. Days after the earthquake, suspected Lashkar-e-Toiba members gunned down Dr Ghulam Nabi Lone, a minister in Indian-administered Kashmir, allegedly to disrupt relief and rehabilitation work in the quake-hit valley. Indeed, throwing all humanitarian sentiment to the winds, the *jihadi* are utilizing the opportunity to cross over to the valley unhindered and perpetrate terror on the victims of the earthquake.

Conclusion

Spoilers in Kashmir wear many faces. While the primary perpetrators are important appendages of the Pakistani establishment and their surrogates inside Indian-administered Kashmir, those in India too take an interest and a role. The reasons are quite different. For Pakistan a solution to Kashmir cannot be anything but its appropriation by Islamabad. Considerations that have "quieted" Pakistan momentarily include US pressure, a desire not to be left out from the India-Hurriyat parleys, and, of course, the need for some space in which it can redraw its plan in Kashmir. Indeed, it is even a possibility that the current "peace dividend" has presented itself as a strategy by which the Kashmir problem can be allowed to simmer, ensuring that a long-term solution is avoided. A peace process thus seems to be more important than a settlement – as neither of the sides can perceive a settlement that would satisfy them or the parishes they represent.

In his testimony to the US Senate Committee on Foreign Relations, Cohen stated:

India-Pakistan relations have moved from crisis to détente and back again for many decades ... crises have alternated with periods of normalisation and even cordiality, marked by several summit meetings ... Negotiations take place at a moment when the two countries are in political and strategic balance; they find themselves momentarily agreeing that talks are worthwhile, but sooner or later one or the other side concludes that the risks of moving ahead are greater than the costs of breaking off discussions.[46]

But the current peace initiative has withstood the peripheral attempts at sabotage with fortitude and has successfully absorbed spoiling attempts, manifested by intransigence, violence marking the positive Hurriyat response, the cease-fire and post-earthquake mutual charity, hawks within the Indo-Pak establishments, and assassination attempts on Musharraf and the Kashmiri leadership. However, deliberate spoiling attempts, which could be successful, could take a variety of shapes at this juncture. These could include:
- unprovoked firing across the LoC, triggering both retaliation from India and an abandonment of the cease-fire
- assassination of moderate Hurriyat leaders
- activation of the *tanzeems* inside Indian-administered Kashmir –

Pakistan will, however, say that such *tanzeems* are not in their control, and the ones that are fomenting trouble inside Indian-administered Kashmir are local elements
- activation of a movement inside Indian-administered Kashmir by political hard-liners like Geelani
- statements and/or conditions by Musharraf or other Pakistani leaders which insult India
- assassination of Musharraf and/or his replacement by a hard-liner.

Certain members of the establishment in India, on the other hand, are goaded by a need to pursue not only a nationalistic agenda, but one which is personally beneficial to them. After all, it is conflict such as Kashmir which generates medals, money, and manoeuvrability within the corridors of power. Polemics apart, one aspect which comes through this time around is that a difference is being perceived. As an editorial opined, all efforts must be made to "ensure that a positive approach is adopted, that nothing is allowed to trip up talks with the Hurriyat – and that the Kadam Taal[47] is broken at least one step at a time".[48] The US pressure has aided the process to an extent, including in the Hurriyat.[49] Although India has been categorical about non-mediation, behind-the-scenes diplomacy has helped, particularly in the case of Pakistan's offer for a cease-fire. But there are many who blame the USA for militarizing Pakistan – the surpluses of the anti-Soviet uprising made their way into the Kashmir Valley, with disastrous results. Unfortunately, UN efforts have come to naught, with the bilateral agreements like Simla and Lahore supplanting them. Moreover, India has never been very comfortable about either third-party mediation or a UN role – the latter because of the "plebiscite" clause. The fact that Pakistan would continue to promote the clause may also play spoiler. This would be particularly true were such questions to be raised when a bilateral dialogue is progressing.

The need of the hour is to tread slowly and with patience, and build on the new sentiment that has accompanied the new thaw. For the present initiative to be successful, India and Pakistan (as also the Kashmiris) must share a vision and carve out a common resolve to rise above history and press on in the face of devious objectives. "Peace processes are always frustrating, often agonizing, and occasionally seem hopeless," Tony Blair told the US Congress on 18 July 2003. "But for all that," he went on to say, "having a peace process is better than not having one."

Notes

1. Guest separatists come to the valley from countries such as Afghanistan, Algeria, Bangladesh, Saudi Arabia, and Sudan. Recent reports, however, seem to indicate that mercenaries are coming to Kashmir only from Pakistan.

2. The insurrection is confined to Indian-administered Kashmir across the line of control from Pakistan-administered Kashmir. As many as 123 separatist camps are located inside Pakistan.
3. Mackinlay, John. 2000. "Defining warlords", in *Building Stability in Africa: Challenges for the New Millennium*, Monograph 46, February. London: Centre for Defence Studies.
4. The Hijb-ul-Mujahideen, the separatist group that is spearheading the movement, is an indigenous group.
5. Cohen, Stephen P. 2001. "India, Pakistan and Kashmir", revised version of paper presented to Conference on India, University of Texas, Austin, December, p. 17.
6. Ganguly, Sumit. 2001. *Conflict Unending: India-Pakistan Tension since 1947*. New York: Columbia University Press, p. 6.
7. Thirteen Hurriyat members owing allegiance to Geelani had "ousted" the Hurriyat chairman, Abbas Ali Ansari, on 7 September 2003 and declared the hard-liner Syed Ali Shah Geelani the interim chairman.
8. Islah, Mufti. 2003. "Geelani frowns, moderate smile", *Indian Express*, 23 October.
9. *Ibid*.
10. Mishra, Bisheswar. 2004. "Pak's unified Hurriyat hopes hit ego hurdle", *Times of India*, 26 November.
11. Swami, Praveen. 2003. "A prime minister in wonderland: The peace process and its perils", *South Asia Intelligence Review*, Vol. 2, No. 17.
12. Responding to a Pakistani call, India agreed to a cease-fire along the international boundary, the LoC, and the Siachen Glacier in Jammu and Kashmir with effect from 26 November 2003. This is the first ever cease-fire between the two armies since separatism erupted in Kashmir. See Baruah, Amit and Sandeep Dikshit. 2003. "India, Pak. cease-fire comes into being", *The Hindu*, 26 November.
13. Barman, Abheek. 2004. "Does the pull-out of troops from Kashmir make sense?", *Times of India*, 28 November.
14. The serial bomb blasts of 29 October 2005 in Delhi by suspected Islamist militants would normally have raised the anti-Pakistan rhetoric in India. But this did not happen, and while Pakistan condemned the acts, Indian authorities made it clear that the blasts will not affect the ongoing dialogue with Pakistan. Indeed, responding to a Pakistani proposal, India – a day after the explosions – agreed to open five points in the LoC for better passage and facilitation of earthquake relief.
15. Ganguly, note 7 above, p. 115.
16. Similarly, the prospect of recovering some lost ground in Agra (July 2001) was thwarted when Musharraf – during the course of a press conference – took a particularly hard line on Kashmir and also "made some intemperate remarks about ongoing violence in Kashmir". Hope finally disappeared when bureaucrats of the two countries reportedly failed to agree on the language for a joint communiqué, and when the Indian authorities turned down Musharraf's request for another press conference.
17. An interesting reading of the spoiler phenomenon could also be the statements of politicians out of power when they call upon one of the parties involved in the negotiations not to respond to the overtures of their opposition who are in power. The reasons could be quite valid. However, such statements gain significance when seen in the light of the larger context and compared to similar situations when such politicians were themselves in power. See for instance *Indian Express*. "Don't talk with govt: Omar tells Hurriyat", *Indian Express*, 14 February.
18. When both India and Pakistan achieved independence.
19. Including the north-east of India where separatist movements continue to rage.
20. Most Indian army formations, for instance, have their primary role detailed as against either China or Pakistan. An unwritten assumption pervades the Indian army that its role in Kashmir is tantamount to engaging Pakistan.

21. In an exclusive interview with this writer in Srinagar on 25 April 2000, Geelani said: "The Indian state is responsible for the massacre. This has become amply clear now that the five people [who were killed in the aftermath of the massacre] have been found to be innocent civilians. Tell me, would the freedom fighters dare do such a thing – and risk being outlawed – when the US President was visiting? Even Clinton has made a statement saying that in ten years not a single Sikh has been touched."
22. Three years after the Chhatisingphora controversy the bodies of the innocent civilians branded as separatists were exhumed and handed over to their families. Sharma, Arun. 2003. "Bodies exhumed, army changes tack", *Indian Express*, 10 November.
23. One of the primary separatist groups in Kashmir.
24. Cohen, Stephen P. 1990. *The Indian Army: Its Contributions to the Development of a Nation*, 2001 edn. New Delhi: Oxford University Press, p. xiv.
25. *Ibid.*, p. xiii.
26. India reportedly spends a little over 3 per cent of its annual GDP or about IR 50,000 crore on defence. Estimates have also suggested that nearly 60 per cent of the annual administrative expenses of the state of Jammu and Kashmir are now devoted to security-related activities. See Ganguly, Sumit. 1997. *The Crisis in Kashmir: Portents of War, Hope of Peace*. Washington, DC: Woodrow Wilson Center Press, p. 2.
27. Cohen, note 25 above, p. 124.
28. An Indian army officer told this writer that "most general officers in the Indian army are pulling strings to get postings in the valley as that is where the medals are".
29. If certain journalists are to be believed it sometimes takes the form of hoax "high-profile counterterrorist operations" such as Operation Sarp Vinash. Writing about such a reported hoax, Praveen Swami states "Operation Sarp Vinash is a hoax that is unprecedented in the annals of the Indian army. It is a hoax that has brought its perpetrators one step closer to medals and promotions, but has undermined India's claims on cross-border terrorism, dishonoured the sacrifices made by the military and police personnel fighting in Jammu and Kashmir ..." Swami, Praveen. 2003. "The hype and the folly", *Frontline*, 4 July. But understandably (and if such reports are true), this is as far as the Indian army would go.
30. It is of interest to note that India would be quite happy to convert the LoC into an international boundary.
31. India has been cautious of Musharraf's proposal to "demilitarize" Kashmir (in the aftermath of the earthquake) because it would mean "giving away an advantage".
32. Cohen, Stephen P. 2001. *India: Emerging Power*. New Delhi: Oxford University Press, pp. 204–205.
33. Cohen, quoted in *Indian Express*. 2003. "Pak is paranoid: Cohen", *Indian Express*, 6 November.
34. *Ibid.*; Cohen, Stephen P. 2005. *The Idea of Pakistan*. New Delhi: Oxford University Press.
35. Quoted in Bhat, Anil. 2003. "A desire as big as a subcontinent: When it comes to Indo-Pak peace, it's people versus the establishment", *Indian Express*, 18 November.
36. Zulfiqar Ali Bhutto had attacked General Zia-ul-Haq for being soft on India. See Bhutto, Zulfiqar Ali. 1979. *If I Am Assassinated*. New Delhi: Vikas, pp. 130, 218, 220.
37. *Times of India*. 2004. "Officers tried to kill me: Pervez", *Times of India*, 28 May.
38. Ali, Tariq. 2000. *On the Abyss: Pakistan after the Coup*. New Delhi: HarperCollins, p. 6.
39. Cohen, Stephen P. 1998. *The Pakistan Army*. Karachi: Oxford University Press, p. 169.
40. *Ibid.*, p. 173.
41. *Indian Express*. 2003. "Ceasefire on, so is infiltration", *Indian Express*, 27 November.
42. See Federation of American Scientists, Intelligence Resource Program, available at www.fas.org/irp/world/pakistan/isi/index.html.

43. Bhosle, Varsha. 1999. "Logistics of Pakistan's proxy war", *Rediff News*, 22 November.
44. *The Hindu*. 2003. "Narcotics may be funding Jaish activities", *The Hindu*, 18 September.
45. *Times of India*. 2005. "Hafiz: Man behind the Lashkar *jihad*", *Times of India*, 2 November.
46. 28 January 2004.
47. The parade-ground art of marching on one spot without actually moving forward. Earlier efforts to bring about a negotiated settlement in Kashmir had resembled what soldiers term *Kadam Taal*.
48. *The Hindu*. 2003. "Breaking the *Kadam Taal* in Kashmir", *The Hindu*, 24 November.
49. Mirwaiz Umer Farooq and Shabir Shah are considered to be close to the USA.

Index

Abkhazia and South Ossetia, 282–300
  Abkhazia conflict, 283
  actors and parties, 283–286
    custodians of peace process, 285
    participants in peace negotiations, 285
    parties to high-intensity stages of conflict, 284
    Russian Federation, position of, 285–286
  application of term "spoiling", 298
  fall of Soviet Union, 282
  Georgian-Osset dispute, 283
  lack of communication between conflicting parties, 298–299
  "no peace, no war", 282–283
  perception of spoiling and spoilers in, 293–295
    Abkhaz, 293
    "fog of the peace process", 295
    Georgians, 293
    identification of spoilers, 294
    insufficient impact of international organizations, 294
    Russians, 293–294
    "Tom and Jerry effect", 294–295
  post-conflict development, 288–293
    negative ideal scenario from Abkhazian perspective, 291–292
    negative ideal scenario from Georgian perspective, 289–290
    negative rational scenario from Abkhazian perspective, 292
    negative rational scenario from Georgian perspective, 290–291
    positive ideal scenario from Abkhazian perspective, 291
    positive ideal scenario from Georgian perspective, 289
    positive rational scenario from Abkhazian perspective, 292
    positive rational scenario from Georgian perspective, 290
    realistic developments, 292–293
  result of peace process according to parties' positions, 287–288
    Abkhazian position, 287
    Georgian position, 287
    Russian position, 287–288
  South Ossetia intervention, 296–298
    "carrots" and "sticks", 296
    defreezing strategy, 296
    Georgian perspective, 297
    Russian perspective, 296–297
    violation of agreements, 296
    Western perspective, 297–298
  spoilers in, 286
    spoiler, definition, 286

Absolutism
  makes for poor peace, 170–171
Angola
  "new wars" and spoiling, 142–143
Armed humanitarianism, 54
Azar, Edward
  intractable conflict, on, 24–25

Basque conflict, 173–199
  9/11, and, 187–192
    2004 general election, 189
    Catalonian nationalists radicalization, 191–192
    climate of increasing insecurity, 192
    creeping resistance to US policies, 191
    low popularity levels of government and ETA, 189–190
    Madrid atrocities, 188
    neo-conservative authoritarian turn, and, 187–192
    unpopularity of US, 191
    US government as spoiler, 187
    USA sponsorship of Aznar's "war on terror", 187
  cease-fire, end of, 182–183
    2000 general elections, 182
    military crackdown on ETA, 183
    targets of violence, 183
  culture of violence, 194
  ETA's "conservative" attitude, 194–195
  etiologies, 174–175
    socio-cultural factors, 175
    two distinct sets of, 174
  external actors, 192–193
    Algerian government, 193
    financial aid, 193
    France, 192–193
    insurgent groups, 193
  factors in cease-fire, 183–185
    anti-terrorist legislation, and, 185
    criminalization of entire Basque movement, 184–185
    government as spoiler, 184
    international model versus domestic pressures, 183–185
  "free associated state", plan for, 190
  from autonomy statute to cease-fire, 180–182
    gap between "Spanish" forces and nationalist forces, 181
    Lizarra Declaration, 181
    mobilization of civil society, 181
    Pact of Ajuria Enea, 180–181
  historical sources of violence, 175–178
    consitution 1978, 176
    ETA, foundation of, 175–176
    Herri Batasuna, formation of, 177
    KAS, 177–178
    Statute of Guernica, 176
    the Transition, 176
    violence, 176–177
  polarization of Spanish electorate, 190
  secret negotiations, 185–187
    initiation of peace process, 186
    lack of identifiable spoilers, 186
    Yoyes, assassination of, 186
  static images of enemy, 178–179
    advocates of violence, 178–179
    culture of radical violence, and, 178–179
    rhetoric and language of armed factions, 178
    role of culture of violence, 179
  three types of spoiler in, 173–174
  vocational spoilers, production of, 179–180
    marginalization, 179–180
    radicalization, 179–180
Bosnia
  "new wars" and spoiling, 143–145
Bosnia and Herzegovina, 200–218
  Bosnian Croat self-rule project, evaluation, 203–204
    Croatian Community of Herzeg-Bosna (HZHB), 203
    Croatian Defence Council (HVO), 203
    HDZ party structure, 204
  causes of 1992–1995 war 200, 201–203
    aims of political leadership, 202
    criminal war economy, 203
    economic goals, 202–203
    political aspirations of protagonists, 202
    political goals, 201–202
    population statistics, 201
    socio-economic structures, 202
  HVIDRA's tactics in obstructing implementation of peace agreement, 211–215
    federation law on war veterans and invalids, 216–217

Bosnia and Herzegovina (cont.)
  HVIDRA's changing rhetoric and strategy, 215–217
  institution building, 214–215
  international community, role of, 216
  property law implementation, 211–213
  prosecution of war crimes, 213–214
  peace settlement in, 204–208
    Dayton Agreement, 206
    establishment of federation, 205
    implementation of solution, 205
    motives for obstruction of peace agreement, 206–207
    perceived discrimination of Bosnian Croats, 207–208
    preservation of ethnically based armies, 207
    special relations with neighbouring states, 207
    two stage solution, 204
  war in, 200
    implementation of peace agreement, 200
  war veterans' associations as spoilers, 208–211
    hidden agenda, 209–211
    motives for spoiling, 209–211
    official agenda, 209–211
    origins, 208–209
    profile, 208–209
Burton, John
  intractable conflict, on, 24–25

Coaxing
  limits of, 45–46
Coercive implementation
  dangers of, 53–54
Colombia, 219–241
  Andres Pastrana's peace process, 228–236
    Colombian armed forces as spoilers, 235–236
    Colombian government as spoiler, 232–233
    FARC as spoilers, 230–232
    negotiations with ELN, 229
    paramilitary groups as spoiler, 233–235
    peace negotiations with FARC, 228–229
    procedural issues, 229
    reasons for failure, 229–230
    spoilers, role of, 230–236
    US government as spoiler, 232–233
    War of Colombian Military Against Irregular Armed Groups 1997–2001, table, 236
  Belisario Betancur's peace process, 223–225
    "armed proselitism", 225
    breakdown of EPL truce, 224
    formation of peace commissions, 223
    procedural flaws, 223–224
    rebel groups as spoilers, 224
    spoilers, role of, 224–225
  conflict in, 220–221
    1953 coup d'etat, 220
    escalation during 1940s, 220
    expansion of rebel groups, 221
    new rebel organizations from 1980s, 221
    proliferation of rebel groups, 221
    revolutionary organizations, 221
    two cycles of armed conflict, 220
  expansion of insurgency, 222–223
    economic exclusions, 222–223
    "greed thesis", 223
    political exclusions, 222
    reasons for, 222–223
  FARC and ELN as "total spoilers", 237
  importance of spoiler management techniques, 238
  spoilers in, 219–241
  Virgilio Barco and Cesar Gaviria's peace process, 225–228
    correction of procedural mistakes, 225–226
    demobilization of guerillas, 225
    end of Cold War, and, 225
    FARC attempted spoiling, 228
    government prevention of spoiling, 227
    M–19 political gains, 226
    NCA, formation of, 226–227
    reform proposals, 226
    spoilers, role of, 227–228
Conflict
  four types of, 108
  joint problem, as, 29
Conflict management
  notable failures, 2
  notions of success, 1–2
Credibility
  potential spoiling and. *see* Spoiling
  problem of, 32

INDEX 323

Custodian monitoring, 33–34
Custodians
  role of, 41–42, 51–54
    armed humanitarianism, 54
    choice of methods, 53
    dangers of coercive implementation, 53–54
    insistence on exit strategies, 52
    politics of peace implementation, 51–52
    potential for blackmail, 54
    power-sharing arrangements, 53
    pressures of "early exit", 52–54
    privileging compliance and process over peacebuilding, 52–53
Cyprus, 262–281
  Greek Cypriot community, 265–268
    aims, 265–266
    constitutional structure of future Cyprus, 267
    Cypriot nationalists, 266–267
    Greek support for, 266
    insistence on redistribution of territory, 267
    nationalism within, 266
    spoiling positions, 267–268
  international responses to spoiling in, 277–280
    Annan Plan, 278
    EU, role of, 278–280
    UN, role of, 278
  nature of peaceful settlement in, 263
  principal parties, needs of, 264–272
    failure of negotiations, 265
    reluctance to establish unified Cyprus, 264–265
    start of conflict, 265
  spoiling in, 262–281
    ability to attain maximalist objectives, 263–264
    ideology, 263–264
    low turnover of political elites, 264
    nature of, 262
    satisfiers, 263
    vested interests in persisting conflict, 264
  spoiling and politics, 270–272
    rhetorical positions, 271
    spoiling nature of political positions, 270–271
    temporal change, 271
  spoiling tactics and actions, 272–280
    1983 unilateral declaration of independence, 276
    basis of, 272
    displacement as result of territorial readjustments, 274
    displacement, Turkish fears of, 274
    domestic legitimization of spoiling positions, 272–274
    Greek Cypriot application for EU membership, 275–276
    Greek Cypriot dominance of central institutions, 272–273
    Greek use of European legal forums, 275
    historical responsibility, 273
    internationalization strategy of Greek Cypriots, 275
    justifications of spoiling, 274–275
    "Sevres syndrome", 274
    Turkey's EU membership ambitions, and, 277
    Turkish Cypriot spoiling tactics, 276–277
    Turkish fears of renewed domination, 273–274
    using and responding to international environment, 274–277
  Turkish Cypriot community, 268–270
    centre-left aims, 269–270
    division within, 268
    fears, 268
    nationalist aims, 269
    rejection of territorial readjustments, 270
    spoiling positions, 270
    ties with Ankara, 269
    Turkey's security concerns, 268

Dayton Agreement, 206
Democratic Republic of Congo
  "new wars" and spoiling, 145–146
Democratization
  terrorism, and, 99–100
Devious objectives 2, 4, 59–77
  linking spoiling and, 71–74
    compromise entails concessions in practice, 73
    disputant's objectives regarding third parties, 72–73
    identifying perceptions and misperceptions, 72

Devious objectives (cont.)
    peace process must "do no harm", 73
    value of peace process, 71
  peace processes and, 61–64
    compromise solutions, 61
    disrupting or terminating negotiations, 61
    forcing further concessions, 61
    need to be seen to be cooperating, 62
    objectives unrelated to finding compromise, 62
    perception and misperception, 62–63
    symmetry and asymmetry, 63–64
  reasons for emergence of, 66–71
    acceptance of peace process, 66
    access to resources, 70
    benefits of third party assistance, 70
    depth third party is involved in dispute, 68–69
    disputants' resources and status, 66
    divisions among disputants, 68
    "enticing opportunity model", 66
    "entrapment model", 66
    imposed peace process, 71
    mediator as part of conflict, 69
    peace process as means to an end, 67
    previous attempts at mediation, 68
    progress depends on balance of power, 69–70
    recognition and legitimacy, 68
    stalemates, 69
    threat of further violence, 67
  spoiling behaviour and, 59–77
    outside-in view of peace process, 60
  third party, and, 64–66
    change in perception, 65
    conflict environment, 65
    mediator, role of, 64
    pre-negotiation objectives, 64
    relationships between negotiator and mediator, 65–66
Diasporas
  catalysts, as, 107
  complicating analytical category in IR theory, as, 108–109
  determinants of capacity to influence conflict/peace, 118–122
    attitudes to receiving "outsiders", 121
    character of host states, 118–119
    level of global security, 122
    level of integration into host societies, 119–120
    organizational strength of diasporic institutions, 118
    prevailing trends in global political economy, 118, 121
    situation in kin-state, 120
    spoiler, ability to act as, 118
    symbolic resources, 120–121
    Tamil diaspora in Norway, 119
  diaspora-conflict link, 125–127
    diaspora suport sustains struggles, 126
    diasporas as catalysts in peace processes, 127
    higher risk of renewed conflict with large diaspora, 125–126
    presence of large diaspora increases risk of conflict, 125
  dynamic interaction between homeland constituencies and, 128
  identity issues, 128–129
  meaning, 108
  means used by to influence conflict/peace, 122–125
    justifying causes and actions, 124
    lobbying foreign governments, 124
    poor bilateral relations between home and host, 124
    propaganda and communications, 123
    securing financial support, 124
    "shedding blood for the homeland", 122–123
  motivations of diasporic involvement in conflict, 109–118
    ability to finance conflict, 110
    alliance with foreign victors, 109
    Armenian case, 115–117
    Armenian Secret Army for Liberation of Armenia (ASALA), 112–113
    diasporic segment's right to oppose homeland's government, 113
    economic interests in homeland, 117–118
    end of conflict reduces diasporic interest, 114–115
    ethnic affinity, 109–110
    homeland government pursues reconciliation with historic enemy, 113
    homelands regard themselves as defenders of their "people", 111

inviolability of homeland's territory, 110–111
issues of identity, 110–111
maintenance of memory of catastrophic events, 112
organizational or bureaucratic interests, 114–117
who speaks for the people, 111–114
outside the state but inside the people, 128
role in peace processes, 105–133
spoilers, as, 107
"triangular relationship", 118
  society of origin, 118
  society of settlement, 118

Enforcement mechanisms
  absence of in peace agreements, 33
Ethnic homogeneity
  claim to power on basis of, 25
Exit strategies, 52
External spoiling, 32–35
  custodian monitoring, 33–34
  effects on negotiation process, 32–35
  elitist and exclusive, peace process as, 34–35
  leadership, and, 33
  meaning, 32
  negotiating signals weakness, 34
  popular support of spoilers, 34
  power and implications of, 33–34

Globalization
  new wars, and, 137

Insiders
  custodians, role and responsibilities of. see Custodians
  loyalty in peace processes, 47–51
  peace processes, in, 41–42
    custodians, role of, 41–42
    meaning, 41
    "technical aid", 42
    use of violence in post-agreement phase, 41
  violence of, 40–58
    sustainability of peace agreements, and, 40
Intractable conflict, 24
  Burton and Azar on, 24–25
  collapsing or weak states, within, 25–26

ethnic homogeneity
  claim to power on basis of, 25
  examples, 24
  identity-based, 25
  increasing number of, 25
  intervention of third parties, 30–31
  meaning, 24
  non-negotiable nature of, 27
Israeli-Palestinian peace process, 242–261
  competing cultural narratives of the other, 246–252
    complexity of resolving conflict, 246
    modalities of Oslo process, 246–247
    shaping of conflict environment, 246
  differing social orders, 245
  societal ethos of conflict, 245
  intractable and irreconcilable nature of, 242
  Israeli perspective, 247–250
    character of Yasser Arafat, 248
    loss of trust in Palestinian leadership, 247
    "Palestinians opposed to peaceful coexistence", 248–249
    patriarchal nature of Palestinian leadership, 247–248
    threat of demography, 249
    unilateral disengagement, 249–250
  Oslo process, 252–258
    asymmetry in obligations, 253–254
    closures of Gaza and West Bank communities, 254
    "devious objective" framework, 244
    failure of Palestinian Authority to collect weapons, 255
    Hamas, 255–256
    Hamas as limited spoiler, 256
    modalities of failure of negotiation process, 258
    potential for spoiling, 252
    presentation as *fait accompli*, 253
    protests at Israeli withdrawals, 257–258
    reasons for failure of, 243
    "revolving-door" arrest policy, 252–253
    right-wing Israeli spoilers, 257
    using peace processes as form of manipulation, 244
  Palestinian perspective, 250–252
    creation of irreversible "facts", 251

deliberate campaign to wear down resistance, 250–251
fear of destruction of Palestinian Authority, 250
"red lines" over policy, 252
refugees' right to return, 251
security as pretext to punishment, 250
second intifada, 242
structural asymmetric imbalance, 244
underlying orders, 245

Justice
issue of in negotiation process, 26–27

Kashmir, 301–319
deliberate spoiling attempts, 315–316
history, 302–305
1947 accession to India, 302
2003 peace initiative, 303–304
All-Parties Hurriyat Conference, 303
disingenuous approaches to, 302–303
modicum of peace achieved, 305
protagonists, 302
third party chaperoning, 304–305
impasse in, 301
spoilers in, 306–315
Indian, 307–310
Indian army, 309
Indian bureaucracy, 310
Indian intelligence, 308–309
jihadi, 312–315
monitoring of, 306
motivations for, 306
Pakistani, 310–315
Pakistani army, 311–312
Pakistani intelligence, 312–315

Leadership
implementation of peace agreements, and, 33
Loyalty
conflict termination, and. *see* Peace processes

Negotiating
effect of external spoiling on. *see* External spoiling
good faith, in
implementation of agreements, 28
meaning, 28
ripeness theory, 28

obstacles to, 29
commitment, notion of, 29
competitive negotiation strategy, 29
intervention by third parties, 30–31
negotiating for side-effects, 30
publicity forum, negotiation process as, 30
used for reasons other than achieving agreement, 30
New wars, 134–150
changing nature of conflict, 135–136
motives, 135
protagonists, 135
spatial context, 135
characteristics, 136
dealing with spoiling in, 147
decline in interstate wars relative to civil wars, 136
departure from "earlier" forms of conflict, 135
economic motives to continue violence, 138
exploiting political economy for material gain, 134
forms of warfare, 139–140
globalization, and, 137–138
effect, 137
incentives for continuation of, 135
motives of protagonists, 138–139
lack of political objectives, 139
refugee movements as central objective of, 140
"resource curse", 138
social and economic context, 137
social, material and human impact of, 139
civilian casualties, statistics, 139
victimization and displacement, 139
spoilers, and, 134–150
spoiling, and, 140–146
Angola, 142–143
Bosnia, 143–145
Democratic Republic of Congo, 145–146
"new war economy", 140–141
Sierra Leone, 141–142
undermining of state, 136
violence by private groups, 136
"war economy", 134
"warlords", 137
Northern Ireland, 153–172
accidental spoiling, 153–172

interpretation of spoiling, 153
"peaceful spoiling", 153–154
conflict and peace process, 154–158
  broadening appeal of peace process, 156
  culture of ambivalence to violence, 155
  economic dimension, 158
  main protagonists, 154
  origins of peace process, 155
  political contest between nationalist projects, as, 154
  political violence, 154–155
  religion, and, 154
  society, 154
  three-cornered low-intensity conflict, 155
Good Friday Agreement, 156–157
  constitutional position within UK, 156
  power-sharing Assembly, 156
  referendum on, 156–157
narrow and broad interpretations of spoiling, 158–159
peace process
  cease-fires, 156
  failure of previous, 153
  Good Friday Agreement, 156
  identification of spoilers, 157–158
  inclusion of militant organisations, 156
  inclusion of veto holders, 153
  lack of support for spoilers, 157
spoilers in, 159–167
  actors who undermined peace process as by-product of their actions, 164
  broad view, 164–167
  CIRA and RIRA military campaigns, 161–162
  collapse of power-sharing Assembly, 163
  Continuity IRA as, 161
  Democratic Unionist Party, 164
  feuding between UDA and UVF, 166–167
  identifying loyalist spoilers, 163
  inadvertent spoiling, 166
  inhibiting others' participation in peace process, 165
  IRA as, 160
  IRA use of violence tactically, 160–161
  lack of political platforms, 162–163
  limited impact of, 167
  loyalist militant organizations inclusion in peace process, 159
  Loyalist Volunteer Force (LVF), 163
  militant organisations fissured into gangs, 166
  narrow view, 159–164
  non-political crime, 167
  Omagh bombing, 162
  parties blocking peace process, 165
  peaceful spoilers, 164
  Real IRA as, 161
  rejection of, 162
  RIRA cease-fire, 162
  Sinn Fein consultations with core constituency, 160

Pacta sunt servanda, 33
Palestine
  peace process. *see* Israeli-Palestinian peace process
Peace agreements
  sustainability of
    violence of insiders. *see* Insiders
Peace implementation
  compliance, as, 45–46
    coaxing, limits of, 45–46
    need for incentives, 45–46
    vulnerability to insider spoiling, 45
  funding, 51
  meaning of, 44
  peacebuilding, as, 47
    societal transformation, 47
  politics of, 51–52
  process, as, 46–47
    exit, problem of, 46–47
    functioning of institutions, 46
    post-war Lebanon, in, 46–47
    power-sharing, 46
  three understandings of, 44–47
Peace processes
  "a road to peace", as, 79
  actors invited into. *see* Insiders
  cost of failed, 1
  criteria for, 27
  deconstruction of term, 79
  devious objectives, and, 2, 4. *see also* Devious objectives
  extended, 59–60
  external factors causing failure, 81
  failure of, statistics, 79
  failure to address critical issues, 79–80

Peace processes (cont.)
  four types of, 108
  ideal, 28
  implications of spoiling for, 3–4
  incentives for continuation of violence, 6
  initial failure of, 1
  insiders use of violence. *see* Insiders
  internal armed conflicts resolved by, statistics, 78–79
  loyalty, and, 42–44
    exogenous factor, loyalty as, 43
    instrumental loyalty, 44
    inverse relationship between exit and voice, 43
    process-based loyalty, 43
    value-based loyalty, 43
    voice-exit framework, 44
  negotiations qualify as, whether, 79
  obstacles to, 1–19
  "outside-in" view, 60
  role of diasporas. *see* Diasporas
  role of violence in, 81–83
    cease-fires, 81–82
    effects of violence, 82
    increase following key turning points, 82
    modified forms of, 82–83
    peace process can continue despite violence, 83
  spoiler-centred approach to failure of, 80–81
  spoiling, vulnerable to, 108
  starting propositions, 4–6
  terrorism as tactic of spoilers in. *see* Terrorism
  third-party mediation, 8
  trade-off between disputants, 60
Property law
  implementation of
    Bosnia and Herzegovina, in, 211–213

September 11th
  effect on Basque conflict. *see* Basque conflict
Sierra Leone
  "new wars" and spoiling, 141–142
South Ossetia. *see* Abkhazia and South Ossetia
Spain
  Basque conflict. *see* Basque conflict

Spoilers
  categorising, 90
  classification of, 81
  definition, 219, 286
  diaspora as. *see* Diaspora
  four types of, 106–107
  funding, 7
  identification of, 81
  meaning, 106
  motivations, 7
  "new wars", and. *see* New wars
  popular support of, 34
  tactics, 7
  terrorism as tactic of. *see* Terrorism
  three types of, 106, 107
  vocational, production of, 179–180
  war veterans' associations as. *see* Bosnia and Herzegovina
Spoiling
  accidental 32. *see also* Northern Ireland
  action based on situational rationality, as, 35
  actors, 3
  credibiility and potential spoiling, 27–32
    mutually advantageous alternatives, 28–29
    negotiating in good faith, 27–32. *see also* Negotiating
    "problem of credibility", 32
    turning warriors into peacemakers, 31–32
  devious objectives, and. *see* Devious objectives
  dynamic nature of, 36
  external. *see* External spoiling
  favourable conditions for, 24–27
    features of intractable conflict, 25–26
    justice, issue of, 26–27
    mutually hurting stalemate, 26
    negotiation, problem of, 24–27
    "new" intractable conflict, 24–27
    recognition and legitimacy, 27
  "inside-out" perspective, 5–6
  intentional and unintentional, 169
  internal and external dynamics of, 23–39
  predictable nature of, 23
  issue of tactics, as, 5
  narrow and broad interpretations of, 158–159
  "new war", tactic of, 8
  new wars, and. *see* New wars

normative implications of term, 4
peace processes vulnerable to, 108
phenomenon of, 3–4
  implications, 3–4
rejection of peace process, as, 59
subjective and broad concept, as, 6
understanding, 1–19
value-laden concept, 36
varying potential, 169
violent and non-violent, 168

Terrorism, 78–104
  confidence-building measures, 98
  definition, 83
  democratization, and, 99–100
  functions during and after conflict, 83–89
    asymmetric conditions most favourable for terrorism, 88
    asymmetrical nature of terrorism, 85–86
    conflict-related terrorism, 84
    crime distinguished, 84–85
    during peace process, 89
    employed by non-state actors, 86
    humanitarian law, and, 85
    means of escalation of violence, 88
    mode of operation, 88–89
    operational purposes, 89
    politically motivated violence distinguished, 85
    state support to terrorism, 87
    status asymmetry, 86
    tactic, used as, 84
    target of violence, 85
    use in confrontation between actors of different status, 87
  link between peacemaking and anti-terrorism, 96
  major parties, countering terrorist activities by, 90–94
    capability and determination to employ terrorist means, 91
    categorising spoilers, 90
    destabilizing implications for political system, 93
    formalizing informal links with spoiler organizations, 92
    indoctrination, 91–92
    isolation and exclusion strategy, 94
    organizational competence of terrorist groups, 91
    political transformation of militant actors, 92–93, 93–94
    spoilers' capabilities, 90
    strategic dilemma posed by peace process, 93
  measures of constraint, 98
  measures of transparency, 98
  monitoring compliance, 98
  non-military confidence-building tools, 99
  role of violence in peace processes. see Peace processes
  separating anti-terrorism from negotiations, 96
    problems caused by linking, 96–97
  splinter groups, countering terrorist activities by, 94–96
    capabilities, 95
    characteristics of, 94–95
    classification of spoilers, 95
    nature and management of peace process, 95–96
    operational level, at, 95
  tactic of spoilers, as, 78–104
    heightened expectations of peace process, 78
Third parties
  devious objectives, and. see Devious objectives
  intervention in intractable conflicts, 30–31

Voice-exit framework, 44

War crimes
  prosecution of
    Bosnia and Herzegovina, in, 213–214
War veterans' associations
  Bosnia and Herzegovina, in. see Bosnia and Herzegovina
Warlords, 137